CANTERBURY ARCHAEOLOGICAL TRUST OCCASIONAL PAPER NO 9

PREHISTORIC AND ANGLO-SAXON DISCOVERIES ON THE EAST KENT CHALKLANDS

INVESTIGATIONS ALONG THE WHITFIELD–EASTRY BY-PASS 1991–1996

by
Paul Bennett, Keith Parfitt and Jon Rady

and
Tim Allen, Ian Anderson, Trevor Anderson†, Robin Bendrey, Gill Campbell, Tim Champion,
Peter Couldrey, Richard Cross, Mark Davey, Alex Gibson, Joanne Gray, John Hammond, David Holman,
Nigel Macpherson-Grant, Ian Riddler, Mark Robinson, Isobel Thompson and Tania Wilson

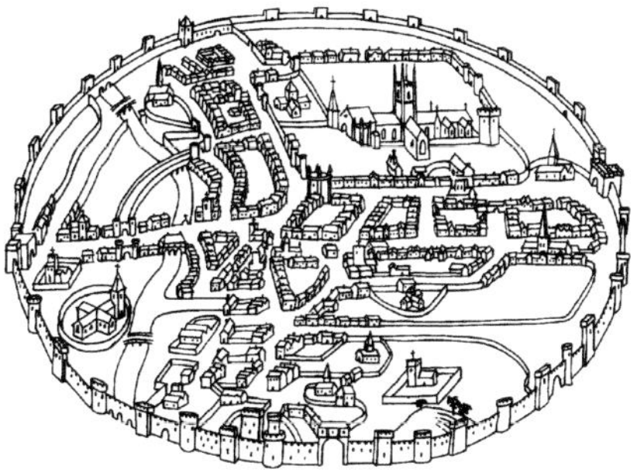

2014 Produced by Canterbury Archaeological Trust Ltd
Printed in UK by Parkers Design and Print

This publication was funded by Kent County Council Highways and the Friends of Canterbury Archaeological Trust

ISBN 978-1-870545-26-6
British Library Cataloguing-in-Publication Data
A catalogue record for this book is available from the British Library

Contents

List of figures

List of plates

List of tables

Summary

Between 1991 and 1995 a programme of investigation was undertaken by the Canterbury Archaeological Trust on behalf of Kent County Council, ahead of the construction of the new A256 Whitfield–Eastry by-pass.

Initial survey and fieldwalking identified a number of archaeological sites on the chalk downland crossed by the new route. Some 250 evaluation trenches were then cut along the line of the road and consequent excavation took place at a number of locations.

Two sites were examined in detail. Close to Eastling Wood a complex prehistoric barrow was excavated with evidence for burial and ritual use extending from the late Neolithic into the late Iron Age. A Roman period ditch was also excavated at the site. At Church Whitfield crossroads late Neolithic and early Bronze Age flintwork indicated activity predating two successive Iron Age farmsteads. Some six centuries later an Anglo-Saxon hamlet, with at least two hall-houses and four sunken-featured buildings was located on the site, all possibly deliberately located at the crossing point of two downland trackways, a crossroads that was to survive until the new road was pushed through in 1995.

Acknowledgements

Thanks are due to many people who have been involved with the project in a variety of ways, both in the field and during post-excavation and report preparation.

First and foremost, our sincere thanks are extended to the officers of Kent County Council who oversaw the entire project, initially through the good offices of Dr John Williams and Sally Howard of the Heritage Conservation Section, and latterly by John's successor, Lis Dyson. Fieldwork, post-excavation and publication was funded by Kent County Council Highways Department and thanks are extended to John Farmer, Major Projects Manager. Preparation of drawings for inclusion in the report on the Eastling Down excavation was funded by a generous grant from the Friends of the Canterbury Archaeological Trust.

At Canterbury Archaeological Trust, Jon Rady acted as overall manager of fieldwork with Richard Cross co-ordinating the preliminary survey work. Tim Allen supervised the excavations at the Eastling Down barrow. Keith Parfitt directed all the work on the Church Whitfield settlement site. The hard work of field teams, without whom little could have been achieved, must be fully acknowledged. A number of local volunteers also assisted, including members of the Dover Archaeological Group. At Church Whitfield, members of the White Cliffs Metal Detecting Club carefully searched the spoilheaps and were subsequently able to conduct a more general survey of fields adjacent to the newly built road.

Louise Harrison, Tania Wilson and Pan Garrard processed, recorded and administered the finds, whilst Enid Allison oversaw the palaeoenvironmental sampling. Gill Campbell examined the charred plant remains and Mark Robinson studied the land snails. Tania Wilson reported on the prehistoric flint assemblages; Tim Champion, Ian Riddler and Joanne Gray prepared the small finds reports and David Holman and Ian Anderson reported on the coin discoveries. Alex Gibson, Nigel Macpherson-Grant, Isobel Thompson, Peter Couldrey and Mark Davey made detailed studies of the various pottery assemblages. The late Trevor Anderson studied the human remains with his usual skill and Robin Bendrey undertook a careful examination of the large animal bone assemblages. Much of this work was undertaken soon after fieldwork was complete, some as part of the assessment process, and it has not been possible in all cases to take account of new discoveries. John Hammond's contribution, attempting to describe the Eastling Down barrow in its prehistoric context, brings together some more recent studies.

Barry Corke, Peter Atkinson and Mark Duncan prepared the field drawings for publication. Dominique Bacon, Mark Duncan, Beverley Leader, Nigel Macpherson-Grant and Will Foster drew the finds. Paul Bennett and Peter Clark provided support, encouragement and advice throughout the course of both the excavation and post-excavation study. The volume was prepared for print by Jane Elder and Mark Duncan.

1
Introduction

Richard Cross, Keith Parfitt and Jon Rady

This report presents the results of archaeological survey and excavation work carried out by the Canterbury Archaeological Trust between 1991 and 1996 prior to and during the construction of the Whitfield–Eastry by-pass, built across the east Kent chalklands north of Dover.

Detailed plans for improvements to ease traffic flow along the A256 Dover–Sandwich road between Whitfield and Eastry were first drawn up by Kent County Council in 1991. Two alternative by-pass routes were initially proposed, the Red (outer eastern) route and the Blue (inner eastern) route. As part of the assessment of the environmental impact that a new road might have on the historic landscape, the Trust was commissioned to undertake archaeological surveys of both of the proposed lines. The main objectives were to give an initial understanding of the landscape history and to provide an inventory and evaluation of the archaeological remains present.

Running northwards from Dover for some 8.5km across the undulating chalk downland of the North Downs dip-slope, the new by-pass was to form a direct replacement of the existing Dover–Sandwich road, which had been constructed at the start of the nineteenth century as a turnpike. Both the Red and Blue routes had a common starting point on Dover's eastern by-pass (A2) about 1.5km east of Whitfield. From there they diverged but took roughly parallel courses across the downs, the Blue route passing to the south-west of Church Whitfield and the Red to the north-east of that hamlet. North of Whitfield, the two alternative routes merged and followed a common line, immediately adjacent to the existing A256, until their meeting with the southern end of the existing Eastry by-pass. In the event, the Red route was chosen as the preferred line for the new road (Fig 2) and construction work on this began in the summer of 1996.

It was clear from the outset that the new route corridor passed through an area of considerable archaeological potential. Indeed, the road lines provided a transect across the heart of the 'Sutton chalklands', identified by the former Royal Commission for Historic Monuments as a block of downland remarkably rich in cropmark sites extending for some 13km between Aylesham and the outskirts of Deal (RCHME 1989, 9.2; Perkins 2010, there termed 'the Sutton Wedge'; now also see satellite imagery provided by *Google Earth*). Overall, the project offered an unparalleled opportunity to examine a north–south section across this key archaeological landscape, which had previously seen only limited fieldwork. Beginning in the summer of 1991, fieldwalking along the entire route corridor was followed by the excavation of a series of machine-cut evaluation trenches on the centre-line of the chosen Red route.

The work undertaken along the line of the new by-pass followed a series of several archaeological investigations conducted during earlier road schemes in the region. Excavations had been carried out on the Sandwich by-pass by Canterbury Archaeological Trust and Dover Archaeological Group in 1978 and 1979 (Parfitt 1979), whilst the Kent Archaeological Rescue Unit worked on the adjoining Eastry by-pass during 1989 (Willson 1990). Significant discoveries were made on both these routes, including a small Roman villa near Sandwich (Bennett 1978; Parfitt 1980) and part of an Anglo-Saxon cemetery and a Bronze Age enclosure at Eastry (Willson 1990; Willson 1993; Philp and Keller 2002). During the 1970s, a series of Bronze Age burial monuments had been investigated ahead of roadworks at the northern end of the A256, at the Lord of Manor on the Isle of Thanet (Macpherson-Grant and Perkins 1980; *see* pp 79–81) and to the south, Lower Palaeolithic finds were made during the construction of Dover's eastern by-pass around Whitfield and Guston (Gaunt *et al* 1977).

The study area

Richard Cross, Keith Parfitt and Jon Rady

Topography and landscape

The new road corridor passed through the modern downland parishes of Whitfield, Sutton, Tilmanstone and Eastry, with the former medieval parish and settlement of Waldershare now defunct, having been replaced during the early eighteenth century by Sir Henry Furnese's great mansion and its associated estate (Waldershare Park). Of the original medieval parishes, all but Sutton are recorded in Domesday Book, with Eastry also mentioned in an eighth-century land charter. Eastry itself was apparently the site of an early Anglo-Saxon *villa regalis* (Dickinson *et al* 2011). A series

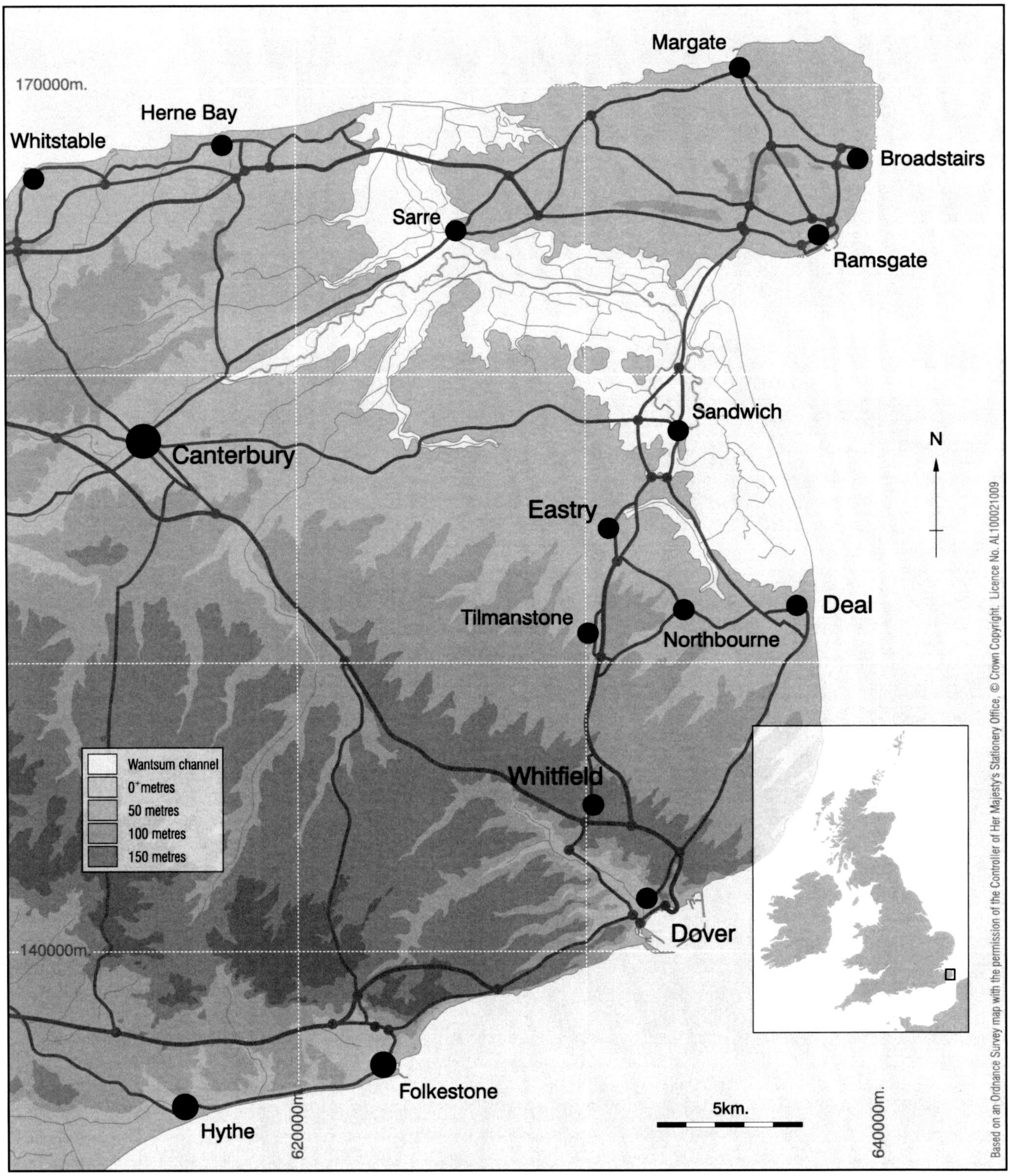

Fig 1. Whitfield-Eastry by-pass: location and topography.

of isolated farms and hamlets lying close to the route of the new road (Pineham, Minacre, Malmains, Barville and Betteshanger; Fig 2), are all named in various medieval documents, demonstrating that these are long-established sites.

The line of the new road generally ran across open, arable land, with some pasture at the southern end near Pineham and tracts of woodland in the area of Waldershare and Tilmanstone. The underlying solid geology of the region consists entirely of Upper Chalk. At the south, the route began on the high plateau above Dover, which stands at an elevation of about 125m above OD. This plateau is capped by deposits of Clay-with-Flint, which around Whitfield are heavy and ill-drained. From the plateau, the land falls away gently to the north-east, dissected by a series of dry valleys that increase in size and depth as they run north-eastwards, down the dip-slope towards Deal and Sandwich. The bottoms of these valleys are occupied by extensive deposits of Head, Head Brickearth, dry-valley and Nailbourne deposits (Shephard-Thorn 1988, 33–6) and in some, layers of colluvium occur (see Table 1), but none now contain running water.

Study of the general size and shape of the existing fields along the new road corridor suggested that the contemporary landscape essentially reflected an enclosure pattern of post-medieval date. Many of the field boundaries were delineated by modern fences and they presumably represent quite recent

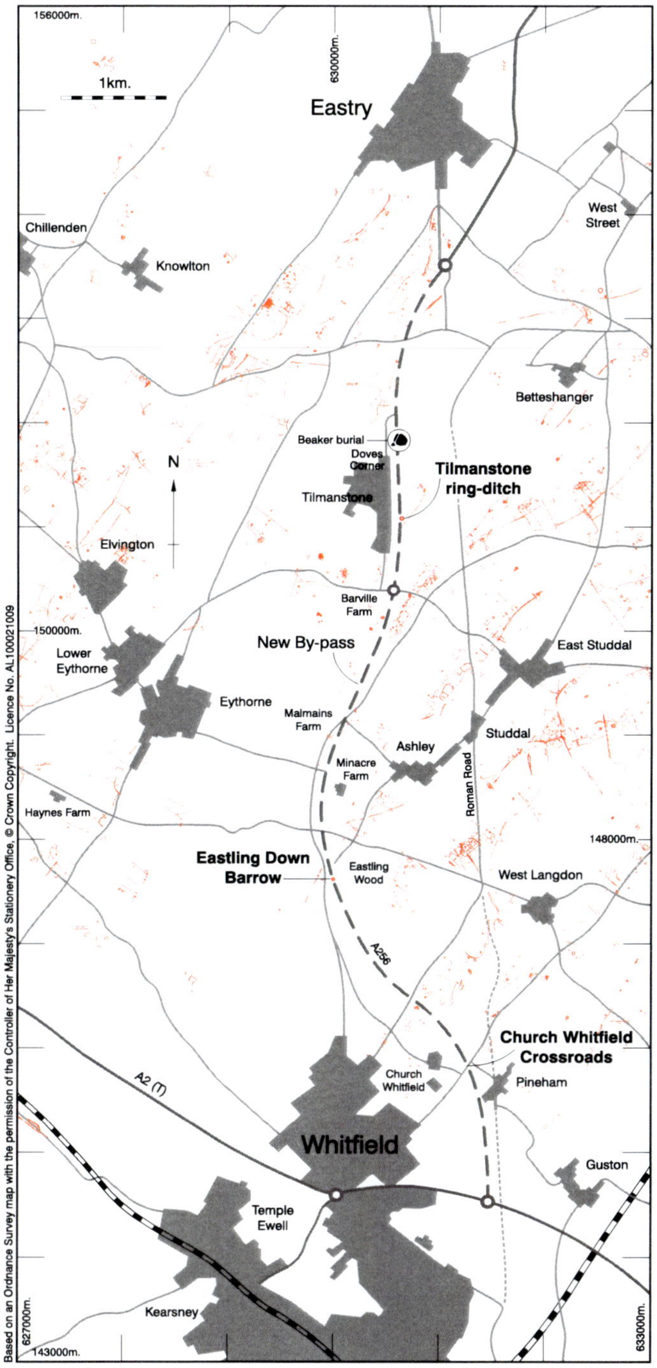

Fig 2. Whitfield-Eastry by-pass: cropmarks in the locality and the main sites.

field enclosures. Where hedge lines were present these were often of single species, without associated ditches or banks, a common feature of enclosure on open downland. Field banks were observed at a number of locations. In some cases these were related to the recent removal of late post-medieval boundaries and hedge lines to create larger fields. Other lynchets and banks representing defunct field boundaries were also observed in a few places, and though undated, may be the relict traces of later medieval field systems. No large fields of obviously medieval layout were observed. Edward Hasted, writing at the end of the eighteenth century, noted the bulk of the land in this region was then 'open and uninclosed', with a significant proportion being arable (Hasted 1800, vols IX and X).

Significant tracts of woodland were extant along the line of the route near Waldershare and Tilmanstone. Near Waldershare, an expanse of deciduous woodland named variously Eastling (formerly Haddling), Friends, Church and Poutty Woods, together with nearby Northbourne Carvett, all located on the edges of the parishes of Tilmanstone and Sutton, may preserve something of the medieval silvicultural history of the area. Eastling, Friends and Poutty Woods are classified as Ancient Woodland, dating from before AD 1600. Late post-medieval and modern conifer plantations are situated on both sides of the road north of Tilmanstone. Here, Lower Longlands, Longlands, and Sangrado's Wood form parts of the Betteshanger estate.

Situated well to the west of the line of the Richborough–Dover Roman road, probably first laid out during the late first or early second century AD, the route of the new by-pass cut across a number of metalled lanes and by-roads, together with several unmetalled trackways. Most of these are aligned either south-west to north-east, following the dip-slope, or run north-west to south-east across the downs. A number of them are sunken by up to 2m, indicating that they are of some antiquity and most are likely to be of medieval origin. The excavations at Church Whitfield suggested that the crossroads there perhaps originated in Anglo-Saxon times (*see* p 180), whilst the lane leading to Ashley near the Eastling Wood barrow site is likely to be at least as early (*see* p 6). The main Dover–Sandwich road, built in 1801 as one of the last turnpikes in the county (Keith-Lucas 1984, 368), clearly cut across the line of many of these minor roads and has subsequently been partially incorporated into the route of the new by-pass.

Archaeological survey and fieldwalking

Initial survey and fieldwalking of both the Red and Blue routes was undertaken during the summer and autumn of 1991 (Cross 1991). For ease of reference each field affected by the proposed new road was given an identifying reference number (Field Nos 1 to 43) independent of the Ordnance Survey parcel numbering system and these field reference numbers are referred to in the present report (Table 1).

The modern downland landscape between Whitfield and Eastry appears essentially as a product of the medieval and post-medieval periods, seemingly little influenced or affected

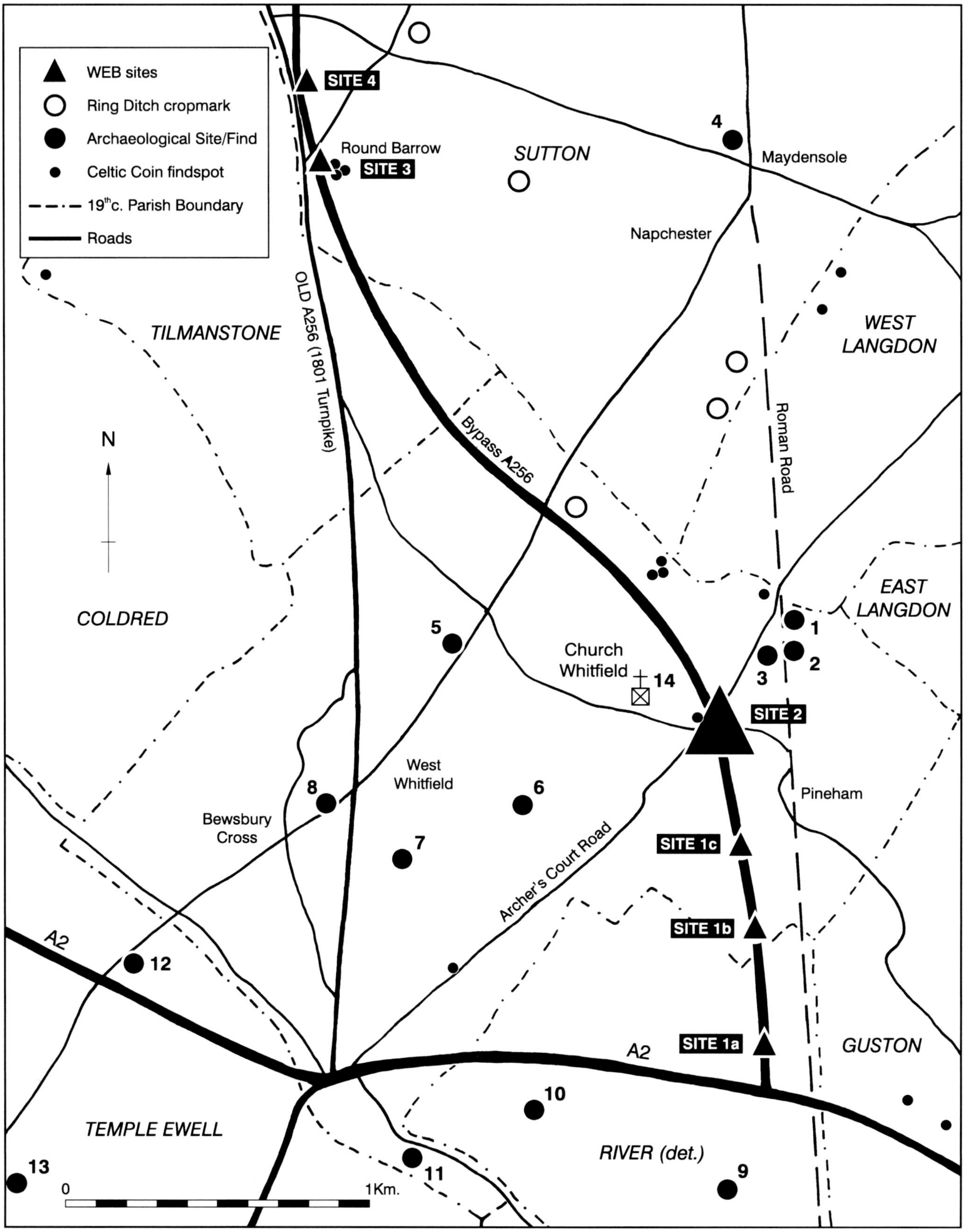

Fig 3. Whitfield-Eastry by-pass: the southern end of the route showing nineteenth-century parish boundaries, local road system and significant archaeological finds and sites. 1 Iron Age scatter; 2 Roman burial; 3 enclosure cropmarks; 4 late Iron Age-Roman settement (Maydensole); 5 enclosure cropmark; 6 enclosure cropmark; 7 Iron Age ditches (Recreation Ground); 8 probably Roman inhumation burial; 9 Roman settlement and burials (Honeywood Parkway); 10 early Bronze Age pit; 11 Roman settlement and burials (Old Park); 12 late Iron Age settlement (Green Lane); 13 Anglo-Saxon cemetery (Lousyberry Wood); 14 Anglo-Saxon church (Whitfield).

by the activities of earlier times. However, the numerous complex cropmark sites shown on local air photographs make it clear that there is a very extensive series of much earlier remains concealed below this relatively recent landscape (Fig 2). The subsequent discovery during fieldwalking and evaluation trenching of scatters of prehistoric flintwork, together with smaller amounts of Iron Age and Roman pottery further reinforced this view.

No upstanding buildings were directly affected by the construction of the new road but a number of above-ground earthworks and negative landscape features were observed during the field surveys. Many of these were preserved within the woodlands. The woods to the north of Tilmanstone were extensively occupied by troops during the Second World War, leaving a significant number of dug-outs and other earthworks. Earthen banks were recorded in both Church Wood and Northbourne Carvett at Waldershare. These are presumably medieval or early post-medieval tenurial divisions marking out tenanted parcels of coppice woodland. Before road construction began the buried remains of a Mark V Spitfire that crashed in 1945 were recovered from the eastern part of Friends Wood by aviation historians (David Brocklehurst, pers comm).

Oval and circular depressions or pits were observed close to the edges of a number of field boundaries and roads. Most of these features are likely to represent the sites of now disused post-medieval chalk quarries or marling pits, opened and exploited for agricultural rather than commercial purposes. A trial trench subsequently cut across one of these to the south of Pineham (Field 4), however, yielded a small amount of Iron Age and early Roman pottery suggesting that this could be much earlier (Table 1).

Fieldwalking along the route corridor produced some useful information but unsuitable conditions for the collection of surface material limited the quantities of artefacts recovered. Nevertheless, it was abundantly clear that extensive scatters of prehistoric lithic material occurred along most of the proposed routes, with finds including implements of Mesolithic, Neolithic and late Neolithic–Bronze Age types (*see* Table 1). A greater concentration of flint artefacts, including types more diagnostically Neolithic in tradition, was noted to the north-west of Church Whitfield, and east and north of Eastling Down Farm. Taken together, the evidence of these lithic scatters indicated widespread, if only casual, prehistoric activity along most of the route corridor.

Significant surface scatters of pottery were limited (see Table 1) but at Betteshanger, on the southern edge of Lower Longlands Wood (TR 30750 51070), some sixty sherds of prehistoric pottery were recovered from the base of a fallen tree located immediately to the east of the new road line. These were of two quite distinct periods, dating to the late Bronze Age–early Iron Age transition, *c* 800/700 to 600 BC, and the late Iron Age *c* 150 to 100/50 BC. Further smaller amounts of Iron Age and Roman pottery were recovered from several other locations (see Table 1).

Occasional sherds of medieval and late medieval pottery, ranging in date from the twelfth to mid sixteenth centuries, were also recovered from various sections of the route, with a slight concentration to the east and south-east of Tilmanstone. These finds, together with the widespread distribution of post-medieval material, in the form of pottery, slate, bottle glass, and fragmentary peg-tile, which occurred in greater or lesser concentrations in most of the arable fields surveyed, are most likely to be attributable to field manuring.

Trenching, excavation and watching brief

Following the fieldwalking, some 250 machine-cut evaluation trenches were dug along the line of the Red route between 1992 and 1994. These trenches were excavated to lengths of either 20 or 25m and were generally spaced at 20m intervals, thus ensuring thorough coverage of the complete road line (Cross 1994; Houliston 1994; Parfitt 1995b; Parfitt 1995e). The trenches yielded small quantities of archaeological finds and also revealed a number of cut features (summarised in Table 1). Several localities containing potentially more significant remains were identified. These were earmarked for more detailed investigation and were allocated Area/Site numbers (Sites 1–7). The trenching confirmed the importance of sites previously identified at Church Whitfield crossroads (designated Site 2) and adjacent to Eastling Wood (Site 3), discoveries at which are detailed in the following chapters. Investigations at the other sites identified more limited remains, which often were not closely dated.

As a follow-up to the main fieldwork, a detailed watching brief was maintained throughout the construction phase of the new road in 1995 and 1996. This resulted in several additional finds being made. Further remains were excavated and recorded at the Church Whitfield site and several new prehistoric discoveries were made near Tilmanstone. These included part of a substantial ring-ditch, a probable Beaker burial and a pit producing Deverel-Rimbury ware, details of which are set out in Chapter 3.

A short distance to the south of the Eastling site a scatter of shallow features was located cutting into the Clay-with-Flints subsoil. Their fillings contained burnt clay and charcoal, together with a small number of potsherds probably of Bronze Age or Iron Age date. These remains are suggestive of habitation in this area and may well be connected with the later prehistoric activity noted at the barrow site (*see* p 37).

Despite the undoubtedly high archaeological potential of the region, the actual number of major sites located during the investigations associated with the Whitfield–Eastry by-pass was remarkably few. The regular occurrence of prehistoric flintwork, sherds of Iron Age and early Roman pottery and a scatter of excavated pits, ditches and gullies located along the entire route, taken with the impressive array of cropmark sites recorded on the adjoining downs, fully affirm that there was extensive ancient habitation across the area. Nevertheless, the line of the new road itself, perhaps largely by chance, seems to have missed most of the principal habitation sites and other localities where ancient activity had been focussed. Many of the excavated features seem best interpreted as boundary ditches associated with enclosed fields set at some distance from their associated settlements. One factor of possible significance in this may be the details of the local topography, with a sizeable length of the route running along north and north-west facing slopes, generally less favoured amongst settlers in the past. Nevertheless, such discoveries collectively provide further clear evidence for ancient activity across the region and perhaps highlight general locations where further work might be profitably undertaken in the future.

Details of all significant discoveries made along the new road corridor are set out in Table 1.

Summary and overview of the main excavated sites

Paul Bennett and Keith Parfitt

Two sites on the Red route were considered to be of sufficient importance to require full excavation and preservation by record (Fig 3). The earlier of these sites lay adjacent to Eastling Wood, near Waldershare, where a complex Bronze Age burial monument was examined. At the Church Whitfield crossroads, some 2.5km further south, an extensive multi-period settlement, mainly of Iron Age and Anglo-Saxon date, was examined.

Eastling Down barrow

This prehistoric barrow site was situated 6km north of Dover, just within the western boundary of the historic parish of Sutton, about 650m to the north of Eastling Down Farm (Fig 2), and immediately west of Eastling Wood. The monument fell entirely within the boundaries of the new carriageway and after full archaeological excavation it was completely removed. Prior to excavation, the site occupied a ploughed field (CAT Field 19) defined by Eastling Wood along the east and south-east sides, the existing A256 on the west and a minor road leading to Ashley along the north-west side. Eastling Wood itself was formerly known as Haddling Wood and is designated as an area of Ancient Woodland.

The excavated site[1] stood on a piece of relatively level ground on the top of a broad downland ridge at an elevation of about 95m above OD at TR 29998 47622. The geology here is Upper Chalk without any overlying drift deposits. Aerial photography and independent ground survey first located this monument during the 1970s. After ploughing in 1977, the site appeared as a low chalky mound about 0.20m high, surrounded by dark soil assumed to be a ditch (field observation by Keith Parfitt). In 1980 it appeared as a cropmark in a field of oats and in 1989 the re-occurring cropmark was plotted for inclusion in a gazetteer of Kentish barrows (Grinsell 1992, Sutton 2).

Having again been observed as a clear soil mark during fieldwalking in November 1991, the site was evaluated by trial trenching in April 1995 and then fully excavated between June and September of the same year (Pl 5). Machine removal of agricultural topsoil to the level of the plough-truncated natural chalk was followed by hand excavation of all exposed features. No trace of any surviving mound material was found. The ploughsoil directly overlay the natural chalk which stood slightly proud of a surrounding, more heavily plough-truncated landscape, preserving both the footprint of a former barrow and the 'false' low mound as previously observed (see above). The natural chalk was scored by furrows within and outside the barrow indicating a long and destructive agricultural history with only deeply cut features surviving the plough.

The excavation proved the remains to represent a complex prehistoric barrow of multi-phase construction, with evidence for burial and ritual use extending from the late Neolithic into the late Iron Age. Although the centre of the barrow had been badly disturbed by burrowing animals and truncated by ploughing, the fragmentary remains of perhaps two children (possible primary burials) were recovered from disturbed soils. In addition, and unusually, the site yielded evidence for at least one crouched inhumation (a child) of late Neolithic or early Bronze Age date, three crouched burials (two infants and one adult) and an 'urned' cremation (adult) of early Bronze Age date, three crouched inhumations (infants) of the middle Bronze Age, a series of at least five contemporary 'placed' deposits containing human bone and in three cases cremated bone with pyre debris, and a later pit cremation (adult) of late Bronze or early Iron Age date. A large flat-bottomed pit or sunken structure, cut through a late ditch on the south side of the mound in the later Iron Age, contained a possible votive deposit of horse bones.

The only other significant feature located within the excavated area was a Roman period ditch, perhaps for an estate boundary, found cutting the north-eastern edge of the barrow. Significantly, the south-west–north-east orientation of this boundary ditch was exactly the same as the adjacent modern lane leading to Ashley. This would seem to imply that the two had been laid out in relation to each other and suggests that the existing road is of considerable antiquity. The course of the modern lane intersects with the Richborough to Dover Roman road 1.95km north-east of the excavated site but its line is not straight, with a distinct kink at Ashley (Fig 2), so that the full route need not be Roman.

The chalk downlands around Sutton are exceptionally rich in cropmarks, including many ring-ditch sites, most of which presumably represent the remains of ploughed-out round barrows (Perkins 2010, 286; Figs 2 and 3). More than twenty such monuments are known within Sutton

1 This is referred to in the original field records as 'Site 3', but has erroneously been described in interim reports as 'White Caps' barrow. For convenience here and in the absence of any helpful alternative, it has been designated 'Eastling Down' barrow, to reflect the name of the nearby farm. There is no sound historical basis for this name; until the early twentieth century Eastling Down Farm was known as Heasledown Farm and no named 'Eastling Down' appears on Ordnance Survey maps.

parish alone. A group of four on Sutton Hill, two double ditched, are scheduled as an Ancient Monument (No 1004204). Taking in parts of the neighbouring parishes of Tilmanstone, Shepherdswell and Whitfield, there are at least ten such ring-ditch sites within a 1.6km radius of that excavated at Eastling Down. Some of these are single monuments but a group of four with two outliers occurs near Malmains Farm (see below). Seldom do any of these local sites preserve evidence of a mound.

A previously unknown upstanding mound was discovered within Eastling Wood, about 250m east of the excavated site, during the fieldwork in 1995. This had a diameter of approximately 21m and survived to a height of about 0.40m. It potentially represents another round barrow, although this cannot be certain. On the same ridge about 500m to the north-east of the excavated site is the cropmark of a ring-ditch about 20m in diameter, with no trace of any associated mound remaining. About 1.5km to the west of the Eastling Wood site, in the grounds of Waldershare Park, the remains of an eroded mound surviving up to 0.30m high lie on the ridge-top west of the mansion (field observation by Keith Parfitt, 1997). Satellite imagery indicates that it has an encircling ring-ditch of about 32m diameter. A cluster of four ring-ditches is known from aerial photographs at Malmains Farm, about 1.3km to the north of Eastling Wood. Here the largest monument is around 30m in diameter and double ditched.

Of these various local ring-ditch sites only two others have seen any previous excavation. About 1.6km to the south-east of the excavated Eastling Wood monument, a single 19m diameter ring-ditch located just north of Cane Wood at West Langdon, was evaluated in the 1990s. A single trench established that no mound survived and there was no trace of any central burial (Richard Cross, pers comm). Three kilometres to the north-west of Eastling Wood, trenching at a site near Haynes Farm, Eythorne in 1982 identified a triple ring-ditch associated with the base of a surviving mound (Parfitt 2004; *see* p 81). The upper filling of the middle ditch produced an unaccompanied crouched inhumation dated by radiocarbon to 1900–1650 cal BC (2 sigma; Beta 129270). At the end of the eighteenth century this monument still survived as a substantial *tumulus* (Hasted 1800, vol X, 64).

In addition, work during the watching-brief phase of the present road scheme allowed the partial examination of another ring-ditch site at Tilmanstone, 3.5km north-north-east of Eastling Wood. Details of this are given below (*see* pp 83–4). Also worthy of mention is an upstanding round barrow that was excavated ahead of its destruction by an extension to Tilmanstone Colliery in 1911. This lay about 3.5km north-north-west of the Eastling Wood monument and seems to have been about 10m in diameter, surrounded by a ditch, with an inhumation burial placed near the centre of the enclosed area. The most important find recovered, unfortunately without a recorded context, was a small slotted incense cup of early Bronze Age date (Ashbee and Dunning 1960, 50, 57; Needham 2006, 66). Further consideration of the significance of the present site within its east Kent context is provided in Chapter 2 (pp 73–82).

Settlement at the Church Whitfield crossroads

The multi-period settlement site excavated at the Church Whitfield crossroads (designated as Site 2 in the field records) was situated some 4.5km north of Dover, on the eastern side of the parish of Whitfield. At this point the line of the by-pass cut diagonally through a long-established crossroads, requiring a deep cutting to accommodate a new flyover bridge, and the realignment of existing roads. The extensive earthmoving proposed facilitated archaeological examination of a substantial area, revealing some significant evidence for early settlement.

Archaeological remains had first been observed in this area by Keith Parfitt in October 1982, when a narrow pipe-trench cut in the field east of the existing crossroads (CAT Field 8), allowed the recording of six separate features, some containing late Iron Age pottery (Dover Museum Accession No DOVRM 26). Evaluation trenching in 1994 located further features here and confirmed the presence of a significant site (Cross 1994, 9). Accordingly, large scale excavations (Pl 19) were undertaken between June and September 1995. These excavations and the subsequent watching brief provided important evidence for Iron Age and Anglo-Saxon occupation.

The excavated site (TR 31313 45797 centred; Fig 2) was located on the summit of a broad chalk ridge defined by dry valleys to the south-east and north-west. Shallowly buried features, some heavily plough-damaged, extended across three separate fields (CAT Field Nos 6, 8 & 9) situated on either side of Archer's Court Road at its junction with the lane running between Pineham and Church Whitfield. Whitfield's Anglo-Saxon parish church lies about 250m to the west, whilst the line of the Richborough to Dover Roman road (Margary 1967, Route 100) now maintained as a public bridleway, passes around 200m to the east (Figs 2, 3 and 4). The site stood at an elevation of about 102m above Ordnance Datum, with slightly higher ground to the south-west, but with clear views north-eastward across lower downland to the Channel coast between Deal and Ramsgate, some 12km distant.

Although intermittent, occupation on the site had occurred over a long period of time. Struck flints and a pit dated by radiocarbon testing suggested limited activity in the area during late Neolithic–early Bronze Age times (Period 1), but the first clear evidence for settlement was provided by a boundary ditch, pits and a four-post structure, associated with early Iron Age pottery of the fifth to mid fourth century BC (Period 2). After a significant break, re-occupation during the late Iron Age was represented by a small rectangular ditched farmstead enclosure (Period 3). The enclosure ditch produced an important assemblage of pre-Conquest pottery, dated to *c* 150–50 BC, together with a quantity of animal bone and other artefacts.

The farmstead was abandoned well before the Roman conquest and there was no definite evidence for any Romano-British settlement on the site, although the Roman road, which was probably built during the late first

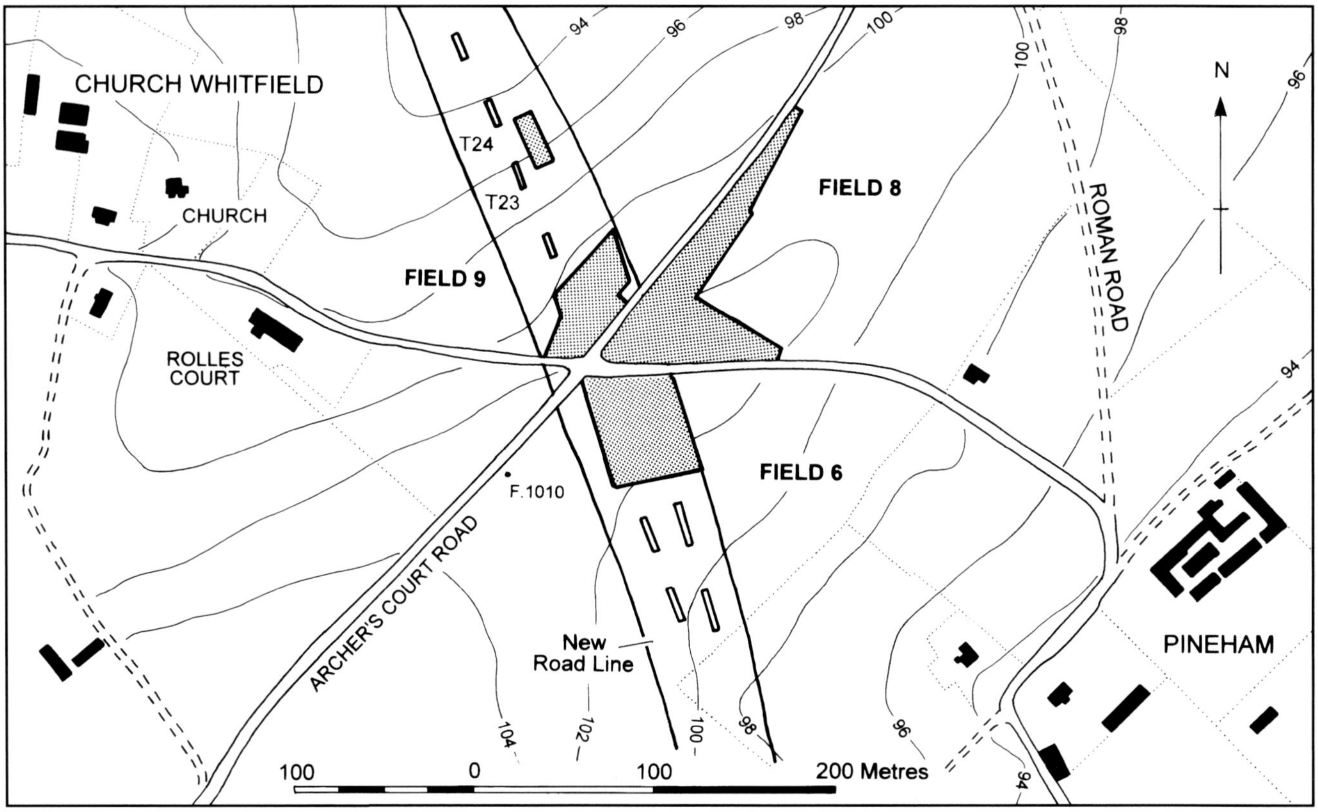

Fig 4. Whitfield-Eastry by-pass: evaluation trenches and excavations between Church Whitfield and Pineham and local topography.

or early second century AD, passes close by and a small amount of Roman material has been found in the general area (Hawkes 1940; Table 1). During the late sixth to seventh century AD an Anglo-Saxon farmstead or hamlet was established across the site of the abandoned Iron Age settlements, which by this time are likely to have been largely invisible on the surface. This new, somewhat dispersed settlement apparently contained at least two hall-houses and four sunken-floored buildings (Period 4). It was perhaps deliberately sited here because of the local road system, positioned at the intersection of two downland trackways that were to survive and eventually form the modern crossroads.

The small assemblage of pottery and other artefacts associated with the Anglo-Saxon settlement make precise dating difficult, but the site was perhaps given up around AD 700. Sometime during the late eighth or ninth century AD, however, a small flint-built church was constructed a short distance to the north-west (Loftus Brock 1895; Livett 1928; Taylor and Taylor 1980, 655; Parfitt 2000b). This church is traditionally regarded as being the original focus for the medieval settlement of Beauxfield, the name by which Whitfield was known before the seventeenth century (Molyneux 1986). Beauxfield is recorded in Domesday Book, under the possessions of St Augustine's, Canterbury; Odilard held one *sulung* here. The place-name is thought to incorporate the Anglo-Saxon personal name *Beaw*, hence the original meaning appears to be '*Beaw's field*' (Kelly 1995, 59). This same personal name is also preserved within the local Hundred name of Bewsborough. The traditional meeting place of the Hundred lay at a crossroads near West Whitfield–Bewsborough Cross (Hasted 1800, vol IX, 374). Today, the parish church and a small group of adjacent modern farms and houses constitute the hamlet of Church Whitfield, now quite detached from the expanding modern village centre at West Whitfield.

The valley to the south-east of the crossroads site contains the historic hamlet of Pineham which stands astride the Roman road and is also recorded in Domesday Book (*pinn ham*, perhaps meaning an enclosed settlement (Glover 1982, 148), but probably enclosed by hills rather than a fence or earthwork). It seems possible that the hamlets at Church Whitfield and/or Pineham represent direct successors to the excavated Anglo-Saxon settlement.

With the abandonment of the Anglo-Saxon settlement at the crossroads, the area became farmland, eventually with the field boundaries being formally defined by small ditches (Period 5). These fixed the position and width of the local roads to the lines still in use at the beginning of the new road building programme.

Area	Parish	Field No	Trench No	Project or Site Ref No	Topography and NGR	Brief description, dating evidence and notes
Dover Eastern By-pass (A2) (N of)	Whitfield	1	10	-	Summit of ridge/ plateau, 116m OD TR 31630 44545	Seven fresh **potsherds** recovered from the ploughsoil. Early to mid Iron Age flint-tempered ware, rusticated type, *c* 600/500–400/350 BC (Cross 1994, 9).
Dover Eastern By-pass (A2) (N of)	Whitfield	2	14	1a	Gentle NW facing slope of dry valley, 112m OD TR 31481 44687	Isolated field boundary **ditch** running diagonally across the slope; aligned roughly north–south and traced for about 10m. Width, 1.20m; depth, 0.54m. The upper filling produced a single piece of flint-tempered Iron Age ware, perhaps suggesting the date of the ditch but several sherds of early Roman pottery recovered on the surface nearby during fieldwalking could indicate that it is slightly later (Fig 3).
Pineham (S of)	Whitfield	4	151	1b	Summit of ridge (Light Hill), 110m OD TR 31451 45028	Shallow **ditch**, aligned roughly north-east by south-west; associated with a slight surface terrace. Probably an old field or hedge boundary. Width of ditch, 0.92m; depth, 0.35m. No datable finds but probably medieval or early post-medieval (Parfitt 1995b; Fig 3).
Pineham (S of)	Whitfield	4	152	1b	Summit of ridge (Light Hill), 110m OD TR 31454 45087 (centred)	Large, **bowl-shaped depression** visible on surface, 55m (NE–SW) by 42m (NW–SE) and up to 1m deep. Trench 152 cut near its centre showed it to be a large chalk-cut pit 0.87m in depth with a roughly level base. Well consolidated fills produced a few sherds of Iron Age and early Roman pottery, including fragments from a Dr 27 samian cup. Probably a chalk quarry and perhaps of Roman date. Located 150m west of the Richborough–Dover Roman road and possibly related (Parfitt 1995b; Fig 3).
Great Pineham Farm (SW of)	Whitfield	5	157, 158 & 159	1c	Bottom of shallow dry valley, 98m OD TR 31422 45349 (centred)	In Trenches 157 to 159, across the floor of a dry valley, substantial **deposits of colluvium** between 0.70m and 1.40m thick were revealed. These rested on natural brickearth and clay and contained quantities of prehistoric struck flint, calcined flint and twenty potsherds. Most of the sherds were of prehistoric flint-tempered wares, probably of late Bronze Age to early Iron Age date, *c* 900–600 BC, with five pieces of later Iron Age 'Belgic' grog-tempered ware. Cultivation and erosion of the adjacent slopes between the late Bronze Age and the end of the Iron Age period is implied (Parfitt 1995b). A pit located in Trench 160 (see below) provides further evidence for prehistoric activity in the area (Fig 3).
Great Pineham Farm (SW of)	Whitfield	5	160	1c	Lower SE facing slope of dry valley, 99m OD TR 31399 45454	Half a circular or oval **pit** 1.64m across and 0.29m deep, cut into the natural brickearth. Steep sides and a dished base. The filling produced a quantity of struck flints, calcined flints and five small fragments of late Bronze Age–early Iron Age pottery, *c* 900–600 BC (Parfitt 1995b; Fig 3).
Church Whitfield crossroads	Whitfield	6, 8 and 9	Detailed excavation	2	Summit of broad ridge, 102m OD TR 31313 45797, centred	**Iron Age farmsteads and Anglo-Saxon settlement** see Chapter 4.
Church Whitfield	Whitfield	9	23	2a	Gentle NW facing slope of dry valley, 97m OD TR 31265 45887	Terminal of a curving **ditch** aligned east–west. About 1.00m wide and 0.60m deep, with sloping sides and a flat base. The lower filling contained early – mid Iron Age flint-tempered pottery, broadly dated *c* 700 to 400 BC (Cross 1994, 12–13).
Church Whitfield	Whitfield	9	24	2a	Gentle NW facing slope of dry valley, 95m OD TR 31250 45920	Shallow **ditch** or **gully**, undated, but possibly prehistoric (Cross 1994, 13). Subsequent clearance of a large area adjacent to 9/23 and 24 failed to reveal any further archaeological features (Fig 4).
Eastling Wood (S of)	Sutton	Watching brief discovery		Features 3100S, 3105S and 3210S	Summit of broad ridge, 107m OD TR 3015 4720 – TR 3012 4731	Three **probable pits** located during road construction around 350m south of the excavated barrow in Field 16; not examined in any detail. Two produced a few sherds of prehistoric pottery (Rady 1997, 8).
Eastling Wood	Sutton	16	66	-	Summit of broad ridge, 100m OD TR 30027 47538	Seven **potsherds** recovered from the base of the ploughsoil. Five Iron Age, *c* 600–100 BC; two probably 'Belgic'/early Roman (Cross 1994, 18).
Eastling Wood (W of)	Sutton	16	67	-	Summit of broad ridge, 97m OD TR 30010 47580	Two potsherds from the base of the ploughsoil. Fragments of the same vessel; fairly fresh flint-tempered, rusticated type, early to mid Iron Age, *c* 600 to 400/350 BC (Cross 1994, 19).
Eastling Wood (W of)	Sutton	16	Detailed excavation	3	Summit of a broad ridge, 95m OD TR 29998 47622	**Multi-phase Bronze Age round barrow** see Chapter 2.
Friends Wood (SE of)	Sutton	18	175 and 176	4	Lower NW facing slope of dry valley, 83m OD TR 2994 4787	Substantial L-shaped **ditch**, perhaps forming the northern corner of a rectangular enclosure, situated on a north-west facing slope. Ditch about 2.20m wide and 1m deep. Possibly contained within the enclosed area, part of a pit at least 1.40m wide and 0.27m deep; no finds. Just outside the enclosure, part of another large feature, also probably a pit, at least 3.40m across and 0.40m deep; again, no datable finds (Houliston 1994, 1; Fig 3).

Area	Parish	Field No	Trench No	Project or Site Ref No	Topography and NGR	Brief description, dating evidence and notes
Malmains Farm (E of)	Sutton	26	78	-	NW facing slope of dry valley, 75m OD TR 30092 49085	Flat-bottomed **ditch**, aligned roughly north-east by south-west. Originally about 2.00m wide and 0.70m deep. No datable finds (Houliston 1994, 3).
Malmains Farm (NE of)	Tilmanstone	Watching brief discovery		Feature 5600S	West facing slope of dry valley, 66m OD TR 3027 4961	Oval **pit** measuring *c* 1.50 by 1.00m exposed during roadworks. Partially investigated but no datable finds were recovered (Rady 1997, 8).
Barville Farm (NE of)	Tilmanstone	32	226	5	West facing slope of dry valley, 50m OD TR 30417 50403	Undated **ditch**, aligned almost east–west, running across the trench. Width, 2.20m; depth, 0.60m. No datable finds.
Barville Farm (NE of)	Tilmanstone	32	229; subsequent detailed excavation & watching brief	5	West facing slope of dry valley, 50–54m OD TR 30445 5050 – TR 30508 50400	Broad, re-cut field boundary **ditch** aligned WNW–ESE. A large area cleared around it revealed no other features adjacent. Length of ditch exposed in excavation, 18m; width, 2.60m; maximum depth, 0.88m. The fills produced a quantity of prehistoric flintwork and a few indeterminate prehistoric sherds. During the watching brief the continuation of this ditch was observed running in a straight line eastwards towards the Barville crossroads. At a point 5m from the crossroads, the ditch turned a near right-angle to the north and was observed for another 10m, aligned almost parallel with the existing A256 (Rady 1997, 8–9).
Barville Farm (NE of)	Tilmanstone	32	232	5	West facing slope of dry valley, 50m OD TR 30444 50386	Substantial **ditch**, aligned south-east by north-west, running across the trench. Width, 2.10m; depth, 1.08m. Not closely dated but perhaps contemporary with the ditches discovered in Trenches 226 and 229 (see above).
Doves Corner (S of)	Tilmanstone	35	104	-	West facing slope of dry valley, 47m OD TR 30600 51240	Five **potsherds** from the base of the ploughsoil. Two Iron Age sherds, *c* 600–400/350 BC; three medieval, *c* AD 1150–1250/75 (Cross 1994, 27).
Court Hill Road (S of)	Tilmanstone	Watching brief discovery		Feature 420N	West facing slope of dry valley, 53m OD TR 3060 5080	Small **pit** about 0.50m deep, exposed during roadworks. Vertical sides with a flat base. The filling consisted of a mid brown clay loam with a darker carbon rich band at the base (Rady 1997, 9). Finds recovered included a quern fragment and a few Bronze Age potsherds of Deverel-Rimbury ware. The type of vessel and decoration represented is rare in Kent, the closest regional parallel known being a biconical jar from Broadstairs, Thanet.
Plough and Harrow PH (SE of)	Tilmanstone	Watching brief discovery		Feature 498N	West facing slope of dry valley, 50m OD TR 3060 5088	Probable **pit** exposed during roadworks. Bowl-shaped in profile, 2.50m wide and 0.60m deep. The filling consisted of a fairly loose brown loam with much angular flint and charcoal fragments, especially at the base. Inclusions of amorphous burnt clay present but no datable artefacts were recovered. Possibly prehistoric (Rady 1997, 9).
Plough and Harrow PH (SE of)	Tilmanstone	Watching brief discovery		Feature 510N	West facing slope of dry valley, 50m OD TR 3060 5089	Probable **ditch** aligned roughly east–west, only very briefly observed during roadworks. No datable finds were recovered but it was probably a fairly recent field boundary ditch, since it was approximately parallel to present-day field boundaries north and south (Rady 1997, 9).
Plough and Harrow PH (NE of)	Tilmanstone	Watching brief discovery		Feature 680/700N	West facing slope of dry valley, 48m OD TR 30629 51069	Portion of prehistoric **ring-ditch** excavated during roadworks (see Chapter 3).
Doves Corner (S of)	Tilmanstone	Watching brief discovery		Feature 1033N	West facing slope of dry valley, 50m OD TR 3061 5143	Remains of a probable **Beaker burial** revealed during excavations for new road cutting (see Chapter 3). Cropmarks of three ring-ditches (one double) lie about 200m upslope to ESE.
Doves Corner (S of)	Tilmanstone	Watching brief discovery		Feature 976N	West facing slope of dry valley, 49m OD TR 3062 5138	Probable **pit** located on the eastern side of new road cutting. About 1m across and 0.50m deep, with steep sides and a flat base. The filling yielded two indeterminate potsherds of Roman or medieval date, which could be residual (Rady 1997, 10).
Doves Corner (N of)	Tilmanstone	Watching brief discovery		Feature 1392N	West facing slope of dry valley, 52m OD TR 3060 5175	Curving **ditch** revealed during roadworks, apparently following the fall of the contours, ie deepening to the east. About 1.50m wide and 0.80m deep, with steep sides and a flat base. The filling contained occasional small daub fragments and some burnt flint. Very limited excavation yielded no datable finds. Probably a medieval field boundary ditch (Rady 1997, 11).
North Court Plantation (E of)	Tilmanstone	Watching brief discovery		Feature 1773N	West facing slope of dry valley, 50m OD TR 3060 5215 (approx)	Boundary **ditch** running east–west across the line of the new road. Width, *c* 2.20m; depth, 1.50m; profile was not clear. A few prehistoric flint flakes were recovered from the filling but no pottery (Rady 1997, 11).

Area	Parish	Field No	Trench No	Project or Site Ref No	Topography and NGR	Brief description, dating evidence and notes
North Court Plantation (N of)	Tilmanstone	36	256	6	West facing slope of dry valley, 49m OD TR 30604 52332	**Ditch** aligned roughly north-west by south-east but slightly curved; traced for about 6m. Width, 1.43m; depth, 0.73m. The filling produced struck flints and two prehistoric flint-tempered potsherds, probably datable to the late Bronze Age. The ploughsoil over the ditch produced a single sherd of Iron Age flint-tempered ware, together with a significant number of struck flints including the probable butt-end of a chipped axe (Parfitt 1995e). The ditch investigated is shown on air photographs where it appears to form the curving western side of a circular or oval enclosure at least 70m across, mostly situated under the old A256 and Lower Longlands Wood to the east. Cropmarks of several ring-ditches and a probable Neolithic causewayed enclosure are known immediately to the west.
Sangrado's Wood (SW of)	Eastry	40	121–126; subsequent excavation & watching brief	7	Gentle north facing slope of dry valley, 30–35m OD TR 30793 53095 – TR 30917 53318	Surface scatter of burnt flints and a few late post-medieval sherds. Initial trenching revealed a light scatter of Iron Age pottery in the base of the ploughsoil (Cross 1994, 30–2). Three larger, deeper trenches subsequently cut in the area showed that the ploughsoil rested on colluvium containing significant quantities of prehistoric struck flint and calcined flint, together with several flint-tempered Iron Age sherds and a few pieces of late Iron Age–early Roman grog-tempered ware. Sealed under the colluvium were two **pits** and two **ditches** cutting the natural brickearth. Limited dating evidence suggests these were probably of early Iron Age date, but the general lack of finds from their fills suggests that they did not lie at a settlement focus. The ditches could relate to a field system.

Table 1. Summary of archaeological sites and finds made on the Whitfield–Eastry by-pass, 1991–1996.

2
Eastling Down Barrow

Paul Bennett

The excavated evidence

Evaluation by targeted trial trenching (p 5) established that the barrow at Eastling Down lay entirely within the carriageway of the new road and as a consequence it was decided to strip a sufficiently large section of the proposed road to expose the entire feature. The area was excavated in two phases.

An initial trench measuring 74 x 11m was opened approximately along the proposed centre line of the road, aligned roughly north–south. The western half of the barrow fell within the trench and a second phase strip measuring 46 x 13m exposed the remainder with the eastern edge of the barrow lying adjacent to the proposed eastern edge of the proposed carriageway.

Pl 1. Eastling Down: air photograph during excavations, looking south.

A 0.25m thick deposit of agricultural loam was removed to the level of Upper Chalk. On completion of stripping, the barrow and associated features were clearly visible cutting the white chalk (Pl 1). These exposed features were mapped and an investigation strategy predicated upon total excavation was devised.

The intercutting soil stains indicated that the barrow was of more than one phase of construction (Fig 5) and that a substantial linear feature formed part of the evolutionary development of the monument. In addition, a complex of soil stains contained by the intercutting ring-ditches indicated the presence of features (including animal burrows) beneath or cut through the former barrow mound. A small number of additional features were also identified south and west of the monument.

The curvilinear soil stains, measuring at their greatest extent 27.30m by 21.10m, described an oval with long axis aligned approximately north–south (Pl 2). For the excavation, the footprint of the multi-period barrow was subdivided into eight approximately equal segments or sectors (numbered 1–8), separated by 0.50–1.0m wide baulks (Fig 6). The baulks were left standing throughout the excavation process and were sampled for environmental evidence and drawn before they too were excavated. A length of the linear earthwork was examined, together with all features within the barrow footprint. Most of the features within the barrow footprint were associated with or contaminated by animal burrows.

The excavated sequence (Fig 5) is described in six phases.

Phase 1: the primary mound and ditch

Although Mesolithic and early Neolithic flintwork and pottery was present in the recovered corpus of excavated material from early (and later) features, particularly the ring-ditches, most of the assemblage associated with the barrow ditches was of a later Neolithic or early Bronze Age tradition.

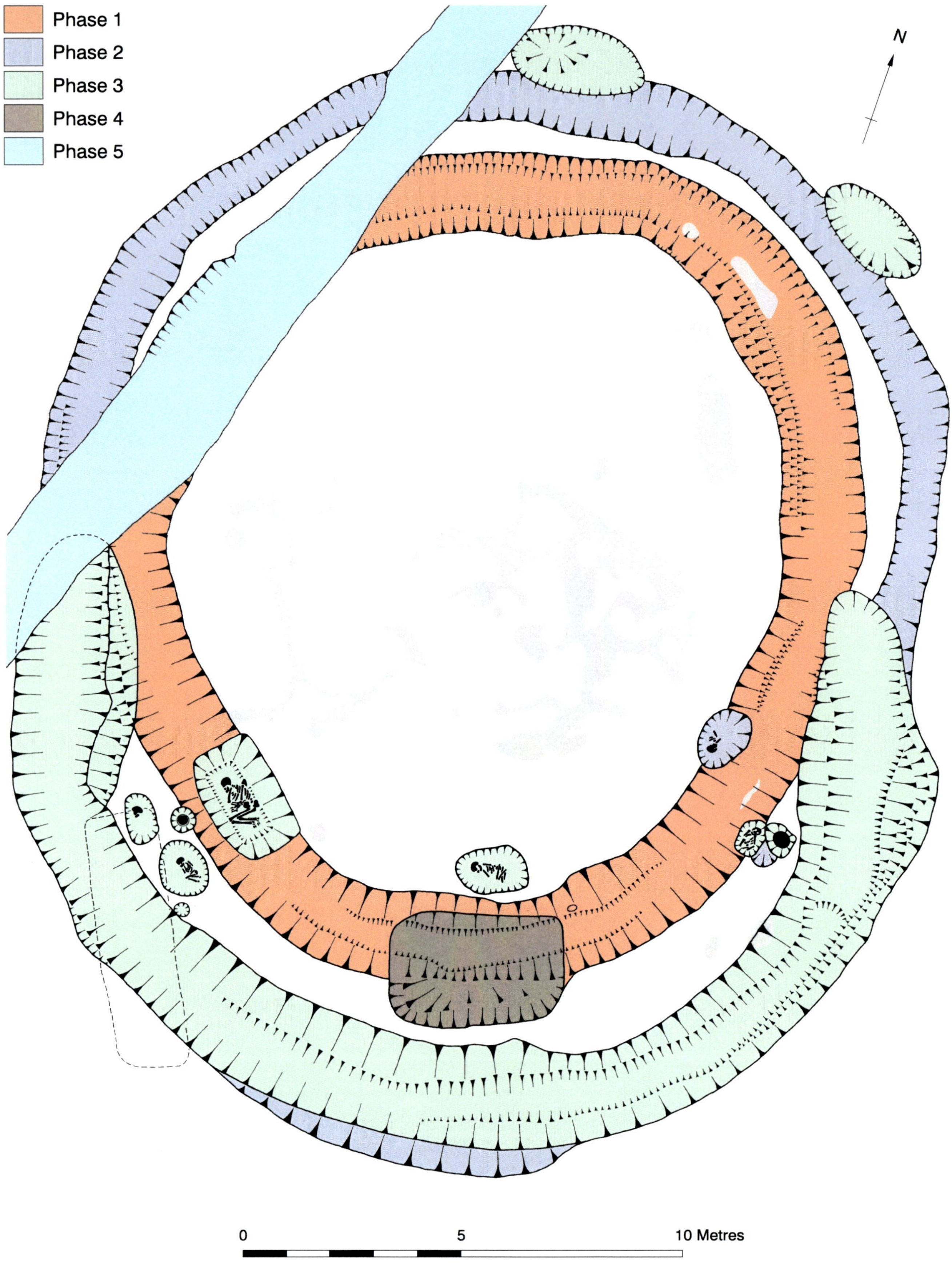

Fig 5. Eastling Down: phasing. Scale 1:125.

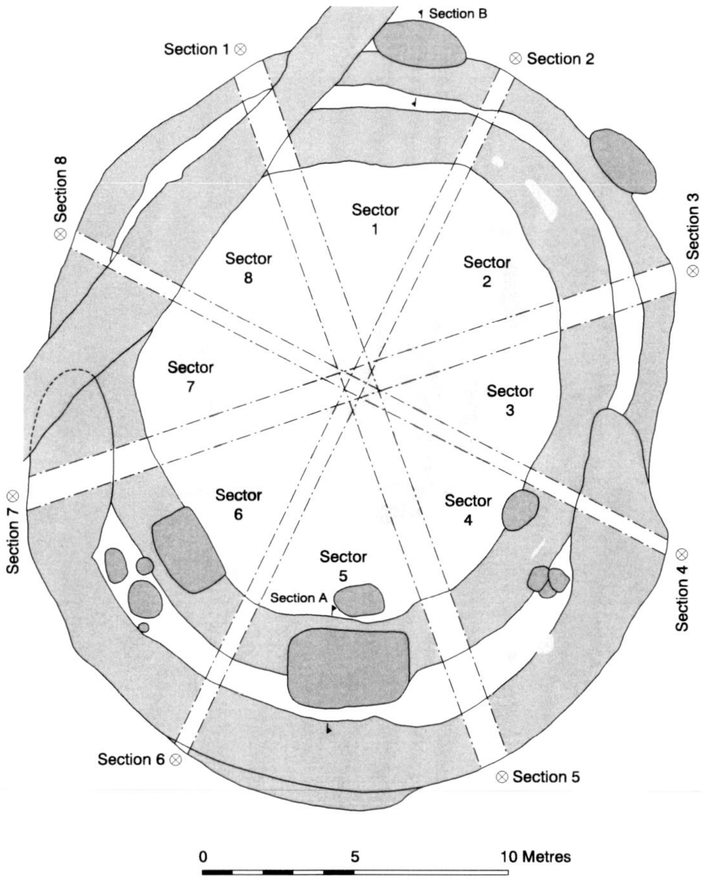

Fig 6. Eastling Down: excavation sectors, baulks and section locations. Scale 1:250.

No primary burial associated with the first mound was found but fragments of human bone recovered from soils associated with a rabbit warren and badger sett occupying the centre of the enclosure formed by the ring-ditches, may derive from a disturbed primary burial or burials. The presence of neonate pig in the assemblage may further suggest disturbed primary 'placed', 'votive' or 'feasting' deposits. Radiocarbon dates were not obtained for the disturbed deposits but dated burials associated with the later barrow and pottery and worked flint recovered from early ditch fills, places construction of the primary ring-ditch and burial mound in the later Neolithic period.

Deposits capping laminated 'rapid silt' at the base of the ring-ditch were generally sealed by eroded chalk from an accompanying mound. Later fills of chalk and loam also derived from an eroding mound and represent a long history of mound slumping resulting in the complete infilling of the ditch and perhaps the 'migration' of the mound to the south, beyond the limits of the ring-ditch.

The upper ditch fills contained significant quantities of worked and burnt flint and potsherds of earlier Neolithic to early Bronze Age date. This material was thought to have been largely residual, deriving perhaps from nearby habitation and incorporated into the barrow mound accidentally or deliberately as a ritual act at the time of barrow construction. Modest quantities of similar dated debris were recovered from the fills of later ditches.

Phase 2: the rebuilt mound and the earliest intact burial

The infilled primary ring-ditch was surrounded by a new earthwork, cut to encircle the remains of the original tumulus as part of the process of forming an enlarged new mound. The new earthwork was oval-shaped, measuring externally some 20.10m east–west by up to 27.50m north–south. The second-phase ditch was best preserved to the north, east and west, where it closely followed the line of the primary ditch. To the south the new ditch had been largely re-cut. Surviving elements however suggest that it was cut to follow a more southerly arc, either to contain a mound that had 'migrated' through time to the south or to form a southern ditched annexe to an enhanced mound that occupied the same footprint as the primary earthwork. The ditch fill contained residual worked flints and a small number of late Neolithic or early Bronze Age potsherds.

A crouched inhumation of a child found cutting the upper fill of the primary ring-ditch in sector 4 of the mound dated by radiocarbon to the early Bronze Age (2265–1910 cal BC; lab no 141269: Table 2) may relate to this phase of mound rebuilding. Remaining burials have been dated somewhat later in the early and middle Bronze Age. An undated 'placed' deposit of cremated human bone and possible pyre debris was recovered from a small pit cutting the infilled primary ditch. Other 'placed' deposits were directly associated a later, third-phase ditch.

Laboratory number	Sample code	Skeleton number	Grave/ context	Conventional radiocarbon age	Calibrated date (2 sigma)	Notes
141269	95/08/00	SK 639	533	3690 ± 60BP	2265-2260 BC 2220-1910 BC	Earliest dated burial
UB18136	95/432	Crem 432	433	3542 ± 34BP	1964-1756 BC	Cremation in Collared Urn
141268	95/07/00	SK 566	439	3490 ± 60BP	1955-1670 BC	Double burial, upper
141270	95/09/00	SK 730	729	3460 ± 60BP	1920-1625 BC	Adult coffined inhumation
UBA20691	95/3/552	SK 552	537	3431 ± 37BP	1878-1636 BC	South-west group of burials
UBA20689	95/3/691	SK 692	687	3351 ± 33BP	1737-1531 BC	South-west group of burials
130971	95/53/05	SK 623	439	3140 ± 60BP	1520-1280 BC	Double burial, lower
130970	95/53/02	SK 558	479	3090 ± 80BP	1515-1120 BC	Centred south burial
141271	95/10/00	Crem 600	495	2690 ± 50BP	920-795 BC	Latest dated burial, cremation or placed deposit
UBA16780	95/3	horse bone	pit fill 698	2206 ± 23 BP	364-201 BC	Horse bones

Table 2. Radiocarbon dates from Eastling Down.

Pl 2. Eastling Down: general view, pre-excavation, looking north-west. The backfilled evaluation trench is visible bottom left.

Phase 3: the southern annexe, later burials and 'placed' deposits

Later in the early Bronze Age, as part of a remodelling of the barrow mound, or to re-form a south-facing annexe to the mound, the southern arc of the Phase 2 ring-ditch was re-cut. Possible terminals for a new horseshoe-shaped ditch were found to cut the earlier ring-ditches at a mid-way point east and west of the mound. Perhaps associated with the cutting and subsequent re-cutting of the ditch were six crouched inhumations (including two burials in one grave) and two cremation burials. The burials were contained in the southern third of the monument footprint (sectors 4–6), within the arc of the third phase ditch. Although the interments could have been inserted into a pre-existing mound contained by the Phase 3 ditch, an alternative possibility is that the terminals of the ditch marked the edges of the mound at that time, with the southern edge of the ditch falling well outside the footprint of the mound. If this was the case then the area to the south of the mound may have formed a relatively flat cemetery annexe, bounded by a ditch, within which all the recovered burials were interred.

The third phase ditch was wider, deeper and more irregular than its predecessor. The irregular sides of the ditch suggested that it may have been re-cut or cleaned a number of times, perhaps as a preliminary to the interment of new burials.

Four crouched inhumation burials and a cremation in a Collared Urn were found cutting the primary ring-ditch fills in sector 6; excluding the early burial nearby, a single crouched inhumation was found cutting the primary ring-ditch in sector 4 and a single crouched burial was located close to the inner edge of the primary ditch mid-way between the two groups in sector 5. One grave in the south-west group contained two children. Radiocarbon dates suggest that centuries may separate the two burials, with the earlier of the two burials being in the upper fill of the grave. A single post-hole located near each of the grave groups was taken to represent a possible marker for the group or for one particular grave in each of the groups.

Of the six inhumations and two cremations contained within the southern annexe, three inhumations and the cremation in a Collared Urn have been dated to the early Bronze Age with dates ranging from 1964–1636 cal BC, and three inhumations to the middle Bronze Age with dates ranging from 1737–1120 cal BC (*see* Table 2).

In addition, 'placed' deposits of cremated human bone and perhaps pyre debris were located in the lowest fills of each of the Phase 3 ditch terminals. Two small pits were cut into the northern external edge of the Phase 2 ring-ditch in sectors 1 and 2 at this time. Both pits contained fragments of human bone in their lowest fill. It was not possible to carbon date the human bone in these pits or any of the 'placed deposits'.

The latest burial, found in a pit in sector 4, was a cremation or perhaps a 'placed' deposit of cremated human bone and pyre debris, dating to the late Bronze or early Iron Age (920–795 cal BC; lab no 141271, Table 2).

Phase 4: the late Iron Age feature

In the late Iron Age, perhaps 500 years after the final burial had taken place a large, rectangular, shallow, flat-bottomed feature was cut within the annexe against the inner edge of the Phase 3 ditch, on the north–south centre-line of the barrow in sector 5. The feature, possibly a large pit or a small 'sunken' building, contained a cache of horse bones laid on the base of and at the centre of the feature. Only parts of the horse were represented, but their positioning suggested that the feature and the bones may have been located and deposited for a ritual purpose. The bones were dated 364–201 cal BC (lab no UBA16780, Table 2).

A small number of possible post-holes were located south of the monument. One post-hole provided a single sherd of prehistoric pottery, but all the post-holes remain undated and of undetermined significance.

Phase 5: the Roman ditch and later activity

A final phase of activity unrelated to use of the monument as a place of burial was represented by a wide and deep north-north-east to south-south-west aligned ditch, found cutting the north-west side of the monument. The ditch containing material of the late first to third centuries AD is likely to have been for a major boundary, perhaps defining a Roman agricultural estate or field system, with the barrow acting as a landmark within those contexts. If this is correct the implication must be that an upstanding mound then still survived as a prominent feature in the local landscape.

Middle Anglo-Saxon and early medieval pottery recovered from the uppermost fill of the Phase 3 ring-ditch and from the latest fills of the boundary ditch, suggest that the mound, ditch and linear boundary may have been visible in the landscape until at least the thirteenth century.

Phase 6: the animal disturbances and later features

The burial mound was badly damaged by a badger sett and rabbit warren with the burrows, runs and chambers mostly concentrated in the eastern half of the mound (Pl 3). A small number of features was recorded outside the barrow together with discrete but amorphous patches of disturbed chalk thought to represent natural 'tree throws'. The site had also been truncated by the plough to the extent that no trace of mound material survived and the surface of the natural chalk was scored by furrows. The site was evident as a cropmark and a low chalky rise from at least 1977.

Phase 1: the primary mound and ditch (Fig 7)

Pre-mound activity

Early occupation at the site was suggested by worked flints of early, middle and later Neolithic tradition recovered from the fills of the barrow ditches and the Roman ditch and a dominant early to middle Neolithic element in pottery recovered from the same features. Although most of the assemblage may be considered residual, a small but significant proportion of the retouched flint material and the pottery may be tentatively dated to the later Neolithic, the postulated period of primary mound construction.

Pl 3. Eastling Down: animal burrows under excavation, looking south.

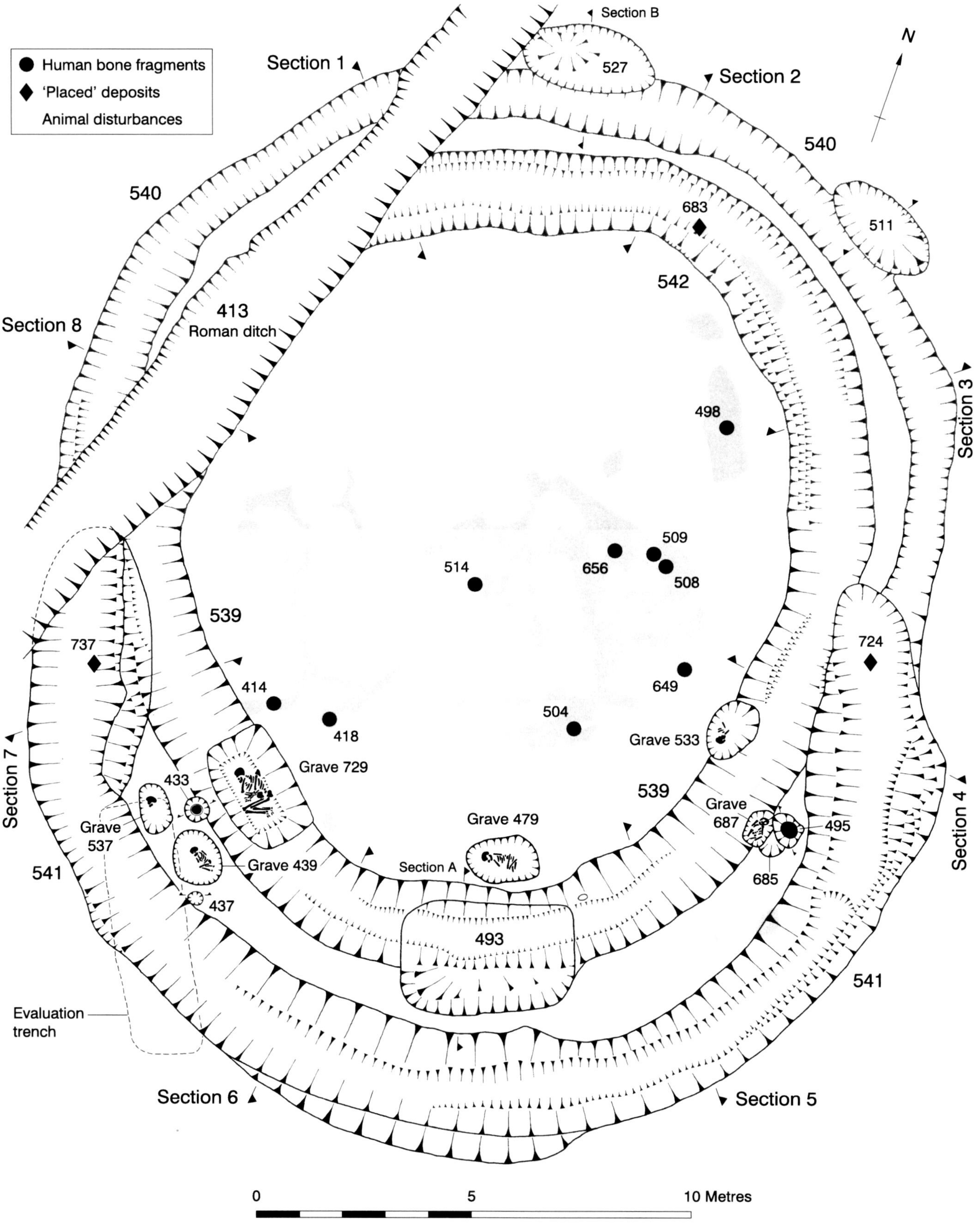

Fig 7. Eastling Down: location of human bone fragments in animal disturbances, graves and 'placed' deposits in ditches. Scale: 1:125.

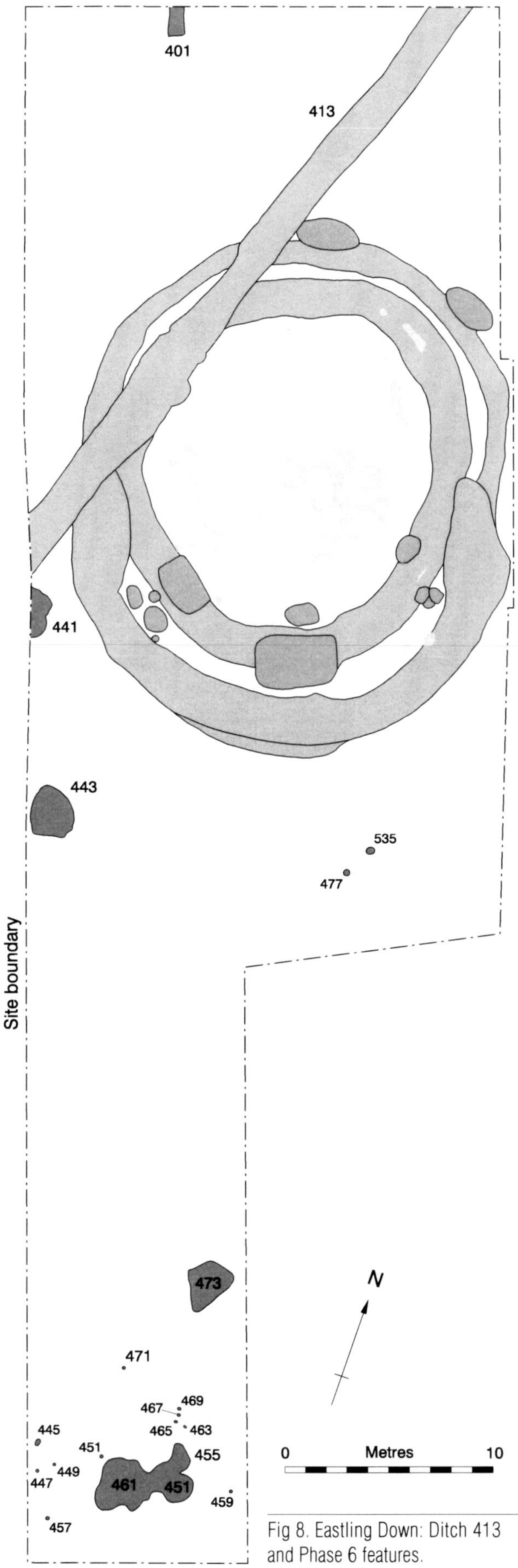

Fig 8. Eastling Down: Ditch 413 and Phase 6 features.

The early flintwork

The excavation provided a collection of some 1,735 flints, of which 1,450 pieces were classified as debitage (mainly flakes and blades), forty-three as cores and the remainder as burnt flint. There were 112 retouched pieces defined as implements (*see* p 46), including forty blades (only one with silica 'glossing' from cereal harvesting), sixty scrapers, three transverse arrowheads, one laurel leaf arrowhead, one knife, four chisel-like tools, three waisted core or notched tools, twelve points and a reworked polished flint axe.

Although Mesolithic and earlier Neolithic flintworking traditions may be represented in the assemblage, the arrowheads, waisted core tools and the polished axe suggest a mid to late Neolithic date with the significant number of blades, blade-like flakes and end-on-blade scrapers perhaps further suggesting a later Neolithic element.

Most of the flintwork was recovered from the fill of the barrow ditches (50 per cent) and the Roman ditch (20 per cent), with the remainder evenly distributed throughout other features. Only one burial (729), found cutting the fills of the primary ring-ditch, provided a significant collection of fifty-two flakes, four blades, an end scraper and thirty-five calcined flints. The flints, randomly distributed in the backfill of the large rectangular grave (493) were almost certainly residual. The grave contained the burial of an adult male dated by radiocarbon to the middle Bronze Age (*see* p 34).

Pottery and associated finds

Other than complete pots recovered from a later grave and a cremation (439 and 433 respectively), it is unlikely that much of the cultural material recovered from the ditches was laid down during 'ritual' use of the monument (eg as a by-product of feasting or as votive offerings), either during the process of mound reconstruction, the interment of individual burials, or in seasonal commemoration of the dead. Rather, the highly abnormal quantity of material recovered from the ditches and features may be a result of the inclusion of residual material garnered from nearby during construction of the primary mound. In addition to worked flint, including implements and burnt flint (from cooking fires, perhaps) there were lumps of burnt clay (including fragments of daub from burnt structures, *see* p 43) animal bones (697 bones were present of which 42 per cent were recovered from the barrow ditches) and pottery, including Peterborough Ware and Grooved Ware.

The possibility remains that the site of the barrow may have been significant and had perhaps been used for a ritual purpose over an extended period before any barrow mound was built. The irregularity of the primary ring-ditch could perhaps reflect longer use, defining both an earlier 'open' or 'flat' enclosure and a later mound. To counter this, no early features were found within the footprint of the barrow or in the near vicinity save for two undated, but possibly prehistoric post-holes south of the mound (477 and 535, *see* p 37 and Fig 8), nor was there evidence to suggest that

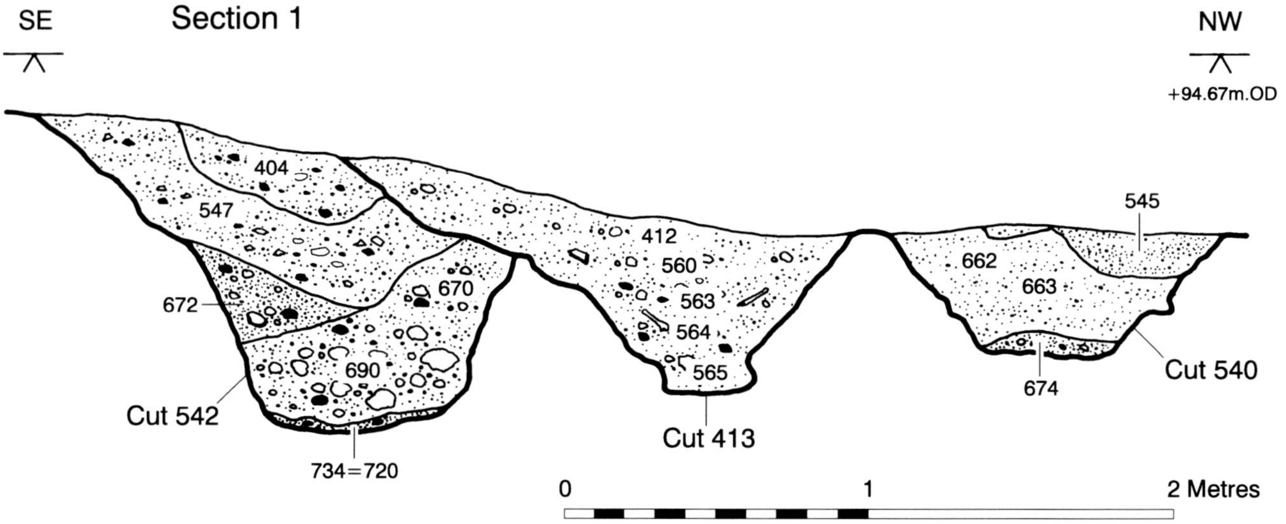

Fig 9. Eastling Down: Section 1. Scale 1:25.

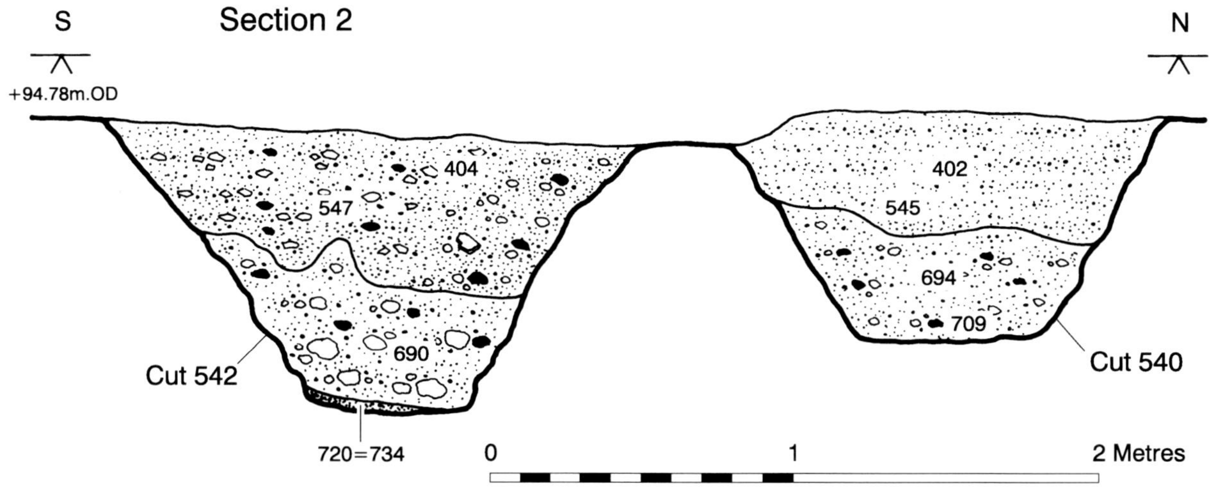

Fig 10. Eastling Down: Section 2. Scale 1:25.

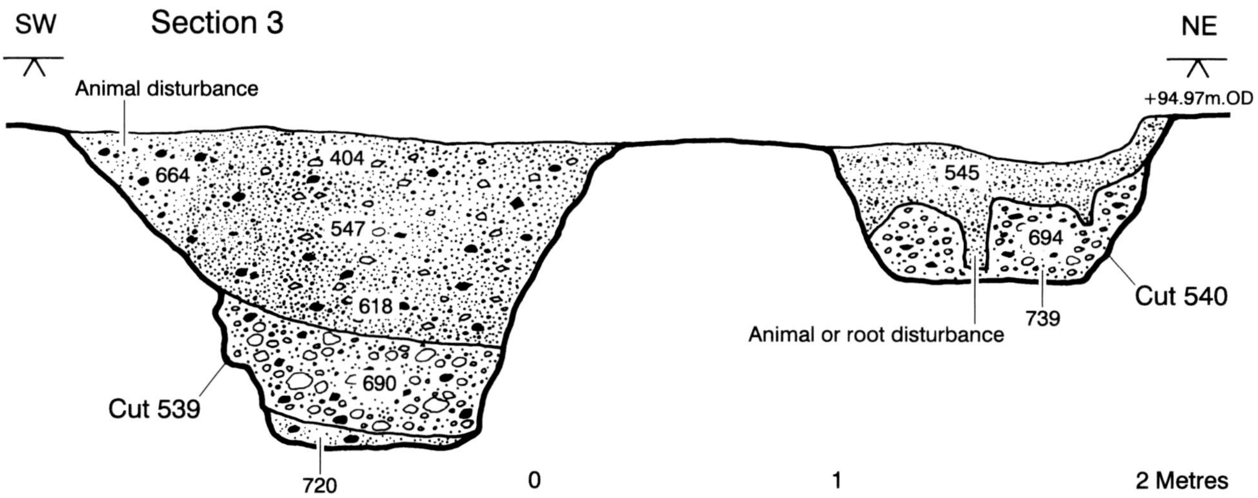

Fig 11. Eastling Down: Section 3. Scale 1:25.

the primary ditch defined a different kind of monument. There was no indication of a causeway for example, nor was there a suggestion of an outer bank. Indeed, the fills of the primary ring-ditch appeared to derive entirely from within the enclosure, presumably from an eroding mound.

How did the cultural material come to be incorporated into such a mound? Topsoil in the area will have been thin and there may have been a need to supplement chalk from the cutting of the primary ditch with other imported materials to create a mound of reasonable size. If this was the case then soils and even 'middens' from the surrounding area may have been excavated and transported to the site to form the mound and it is perhaps this material that found its way into the early and later ring-ditches.

There remains the possibility that the residual cultural material may have been transported to the site from some distance away and deliberately included in the mound as part of mound-building ritual.

The early ring-ditch (Figs 9–16)

The early ring-ditch formed an irregular, oval enclosure with a flat, almost straight and approximately east–west aligned northern side. The ring-ditch measured internally some 15.50m north–south by 14m east–west. The ditch (539, 542), cut with a flat base into the natural chalk, was 0.90m deep to the north, increasing to a depth of 1.42m in the south. Excavated to an average width of 2m, with even, sloping sides, descending to a base on average 0.70m wide, the ring-ditch may have been formed of five or more linking trenches, suggested by the variable depth of the ditch and the wasting of the ditch width at several locations. The slight differences in ditch width and depth and the irregularity in overall shape of the ring, perhaps suggests that the primary earthwork may have been formed by more than one team working simultaneously.

Capping the base of the ditch were thin 0.03–0.05m thick deposits of dirty chalk, taken to represent a construction trample and rain-washed and weathered chalk 0.05–0.10m thick (contexts 659, 720 and 734). The latter deposit probably accumulated as 'rapid' silt soon after the monument was completed. These fills present in most parts of the ring-ditch yielded a single degraded undated potsherd, nine struck flint flakes, one animal bone and two limpet shells.

The ring-ditch interior

No trace of an intact burial or burials was found within the footprint of the primary ring-ditch and no early features were identified. The interior of the monument was badly disturbed by intercutting burrows, runs and chambers associated with a rabbit warren and perhaps badger sett (Fig 7; Pl 5). In places disturbance was so considerable, that only isolated islands of intact chalk survived. Post Second World War ploughing and more recent subsoiling had further truncated the natural chalk, leaving a criss-cross patterning of plough furrows in the natural chalk bedrock and in animal disturbed ground.

As well as a wide variety of animal, bird and amphibian bones recovered from soils infilling the burrows (*see* p 67), nine fragments of human bone were recovered from contexts 414, 418, 498, 504, 508, 509, 514, 649 and 656 including skull fragments from contexts 509, 649 and 656 (Fig 7) that may derive from two children (*see* p 61). Where identifiable, other bone fragments were also probably from children. There were in addition some thirty-seven fragments of neonate or very young pig bones, seven neonatal sheep bones and two foetal cattle bones that may originally have formed part of a ritual offering, or a by-product of ritual feasting (below, p 82). Although the evidence is tentative in the extreme, these few fragments may indicate that primary burials possibly included at least two children accompanied perhaps by a ritual offering of neonate animals. The fragments of human and animal bone were not submitted for radiocarbon dating.

The ring-ditch fills

Capping the primary fills of the ring-ditch was a banded deposit of loose textured weathered chalk and loam, taken to represent erosion products from a mound. The layer, approximately 0.40m thick (contexts 657, 670, 671, 672, 679, 690, 698, 699, 700, 706, 712, 713, 714, 716) was a ubiquitous deposit which appeared to be present in all sectors of the ditch. The deposit of compact dirty chalk nodules mixed with pale brown chalk provided a single undated potsherd (context 679), together with animal bones including neonate pig and sheep and a fragment of deer antler (Table 9). Amongst the struck flints were a number of cores, three scrapers including FN479, from context 672 (Fig 27) and two points (Fig 28, FN 1277, context 712; FN 513, context 706, not illustrated).

The upper fill of the ditch was of compact pale brown chalk loam with fewer chalk lumps than the underlying deposit. Although banding of the fill was observed, the layer, in places 0.50m thick, had the appearance and compactness of a soil that had developed through natural weathering. The deposit (contexts 404, 538, 547, 618, 620, 621, 622, 626, 634, 636, 654, 655, 664, 673, 677, 696 and 697) provided twenty-six potsherds including Peterborough Ware, Beaker and Urn (*see* p 53). A number of struck flints including a complete hammerstone (Fig 26, FN 1219), an extensively worked point (Fig 28, FN 597), an elongated point (Fig 28, FN 334) and a possible plane (Fig 29, FN 596g) were recovered from context 538 and from context 547 came an unfinished laurel leaf arrowhead (Fig 29, FN 367) and a possible rod (Fig 28, FN 371). Another scraper (Fig 27, FN 1252a), a possible knife fragment (Fig 29, FN 417a) and a waisted core tool (Fig 29, FN 416j) were recovered from context 620. Contexts 538, 547 and 654 also provided a fragment of human femur and two other fragments of human bone (*see* p 61). The fragments suggest the presence of at least one satellite interment predating the earliest burial (Grave 533) and the rebuilding of the monument in Phase 3, but post-dating construction of the primary mound. The same context also provided a small

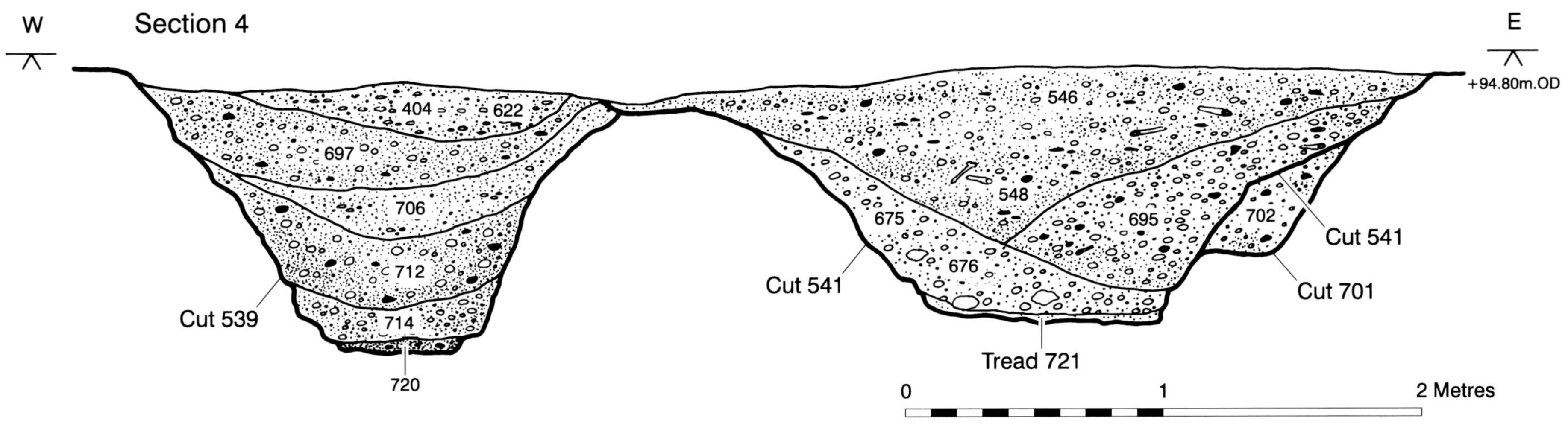

Fig 12. Eastling Down: Section 4. Scale 1:25.

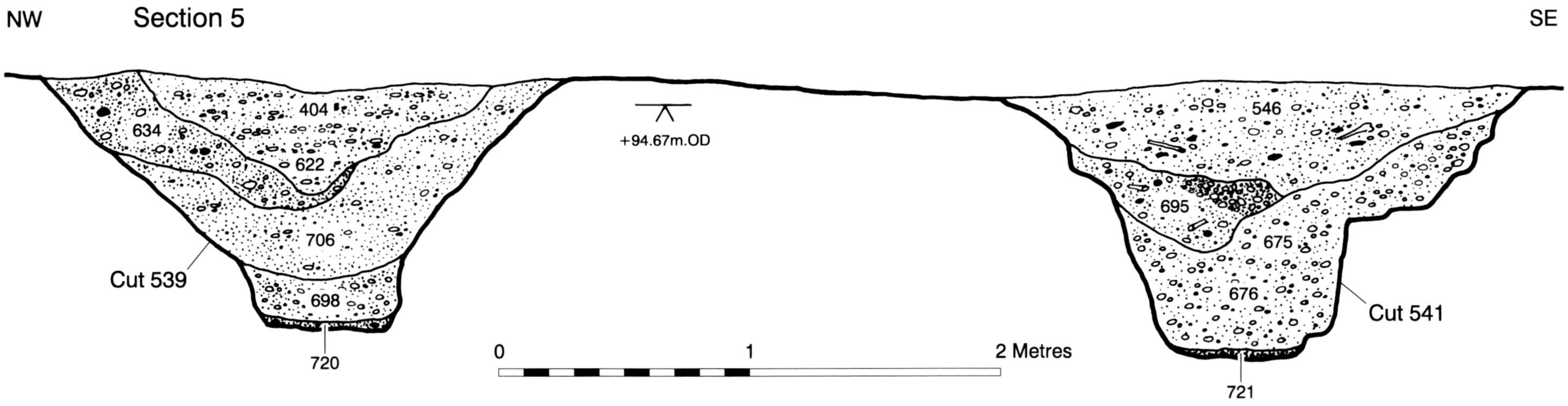

Fig 13. Eastling Down: Section 5. Scale 1:25.

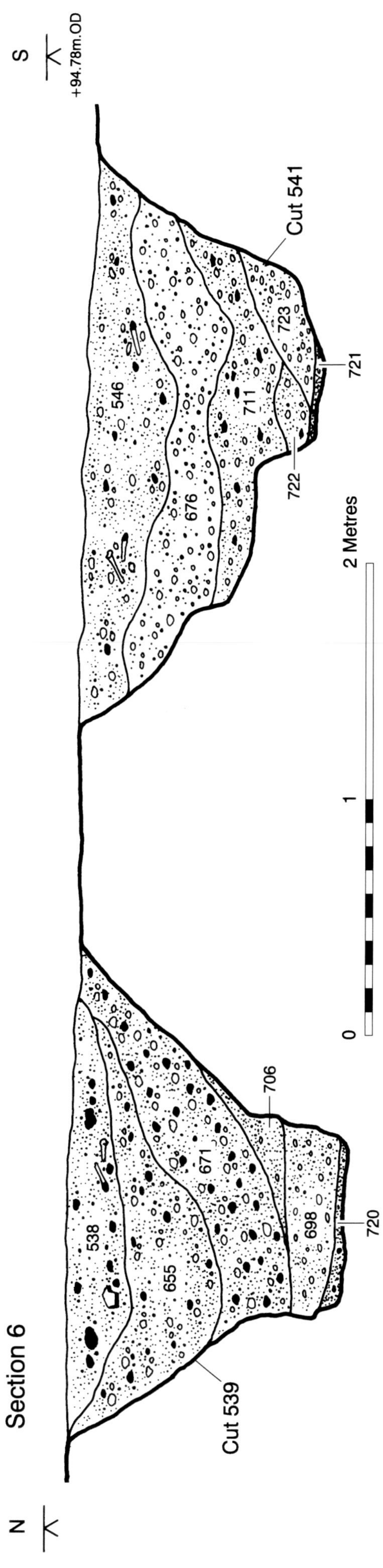

Fig 14. Eastling Down: Section 6. Scale 1:25.

quantity of cremated human bone (*see* p 63). The material may have derived from a disturbed cremation or 'placed' deposit, also predating Phase 2. Animal bones recovered from the upper ditch fill included fragments of roe deer and, unusually, a horse tooth (*see* p 66).

'Placed' deposit in the ditch

Cutting weathered chalk deposits in the north-east side of the ring-ditch in sector 2 within the lowest levels of overlying loam (context 690), was a shallow, subcircular, bowl-shaped pit (683), 0.30m in diameter, cut to a depth of 0.15m. The feature was filled with discoloured chalk and dark grey silt, rich in charcoal (context 680). The deposit provided a fragment of cremated human bone, fragments of unburnt human bone (*see* p 63), an animal bone, probably pig (*see* p 66), three struck flint flakes, six burnt flints, seven limpet shells, terrestrial snail shells and fossil shells of *porsphaera globularis*. The shallow pit was taken to represent a 'placed' deposit, the contents of which contained cremated and unburnt human bone, food waste (animal bone and marine shell) and pyre debris (charcoal and burnt flint). Charcoal in the fill proved to be *Prunus* sp (sloe) and *Quercus* sp (oak) (*see* p 73) and the species of terrestrial snails suggested that the area may have been somewhat overgrown at the time the feature was cut and filled (*see* p 71).

Phase 2: the rebuilt mound and the earliest intact burial

Following construction of the primary burial mound a long period of weathering may have taken place with the mass of the mound slumping or 'migrating' to infill the surrounding ditch. In Phase 2, a new ditch was cut to surround the mound. Only the northern half of the ditch survived; the southern half was re-cut in Phase 3 with only fragmentary traces of the early ditch surviving the re-cutting. During Phase 2, at least one 'crouched' burial, that of a child, was interred in a grave cut into the backfill of the primary ditch in sector 4, presumably before the old mound was remodelled, if such an event occurred. It is possible that the mound was not substantially enlarged, rather the new ditch, with wider arc to the south, was perhaps cut to define a flat, south-facing annexe to the pre-existing mound, with the first of a series of new burials interred within it.

The new ring-ditch (Figs 5 and 7)

A new ditch (540) was cut to surround the early burial mound. To the north, in sectors 7, 8 and 1–3, the ditch was positioned to follow the line of its predecessor which may still have been visible. To the south in sectors 3–7, the ditch was substantially re-cut in Phase 3, but its southern edge was identified.

The northern arc of the ditch was cut into natural chalk outside and between 0.30–0.80m distant of the primary ditch. The ditch was between 0.75–1.50m wide, cut with steeply sloping sides and flat base to an average depth of between 0.80 and 0.90m. The flat sump was 0.35–0.60m

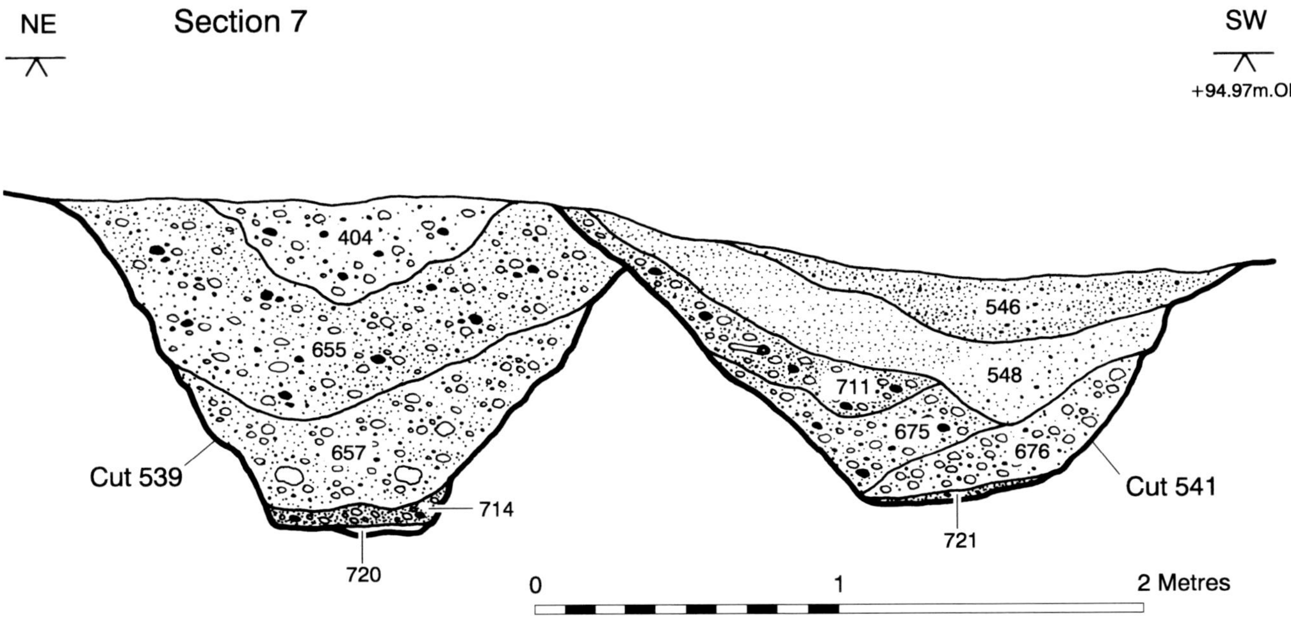

Fig 15. Eastling Down: Section 7. Scale 1:25.

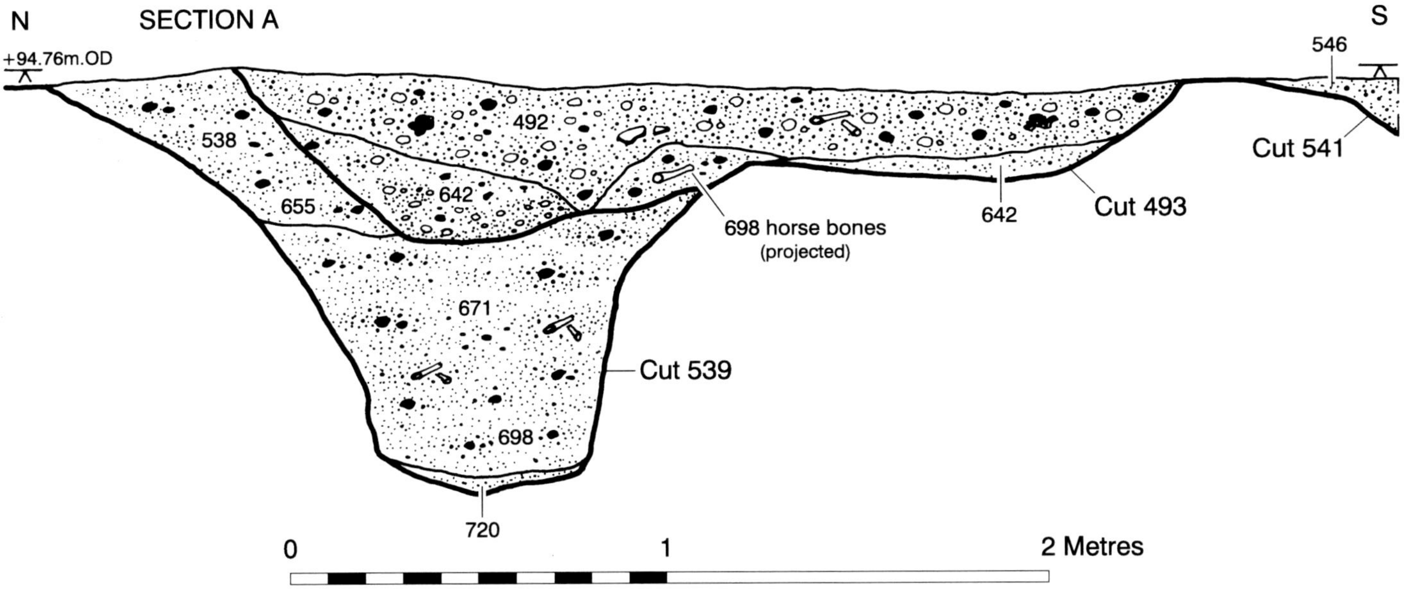

Fig 16. Eastling Down: Section A (Ditch 539 and Pit 493). Scale 1:20.

wide. At this time the complete ring-ditch was perhaps oval-shaped, measuring externally 20.55m east–west by 25.20m north–south.

Traces of the outer edge of the Phase 2 ditch were identified to the south (701). In sectors 4 and 5 this took the form of a step in the leading (southern) edge of the later Phase 3 ditch (Fig 12, section 4). In sector 5 however a more substantial section of ditch edge was identified, together with a compact chalk and loam upper fill (context 702) which provided no finds. The southern arc of the Phase 2 ditch was positioned approximately 3m from the outer edge of the primary ditch, suggesting that either the early mound had either 'migrated' to the south, with the ditch aligned to follow the mass of the mound, or that the ditch was deliberately cut well to the south of the mound to flank a narrow southern annexe between the southern tail of the primary mound and the inner edge of the new ditch.

The early mound was presumably increased in size with chalk and soil generated by the excavation of the new ditch. Although an important burial may have been the impetus for the construction of an enlarged mound, no burial was found in or near the centre of the new monument. Whilst a burial may have been located within the mass of the mound and left no trace, alternatively, the mound may have been rebuilt to extend and perpetuate the earlier use of the site as a place of ceremony associated with funeral rites, with new burials located not in the mound but within a flat annexe formed to the south side of the enhanced mound.

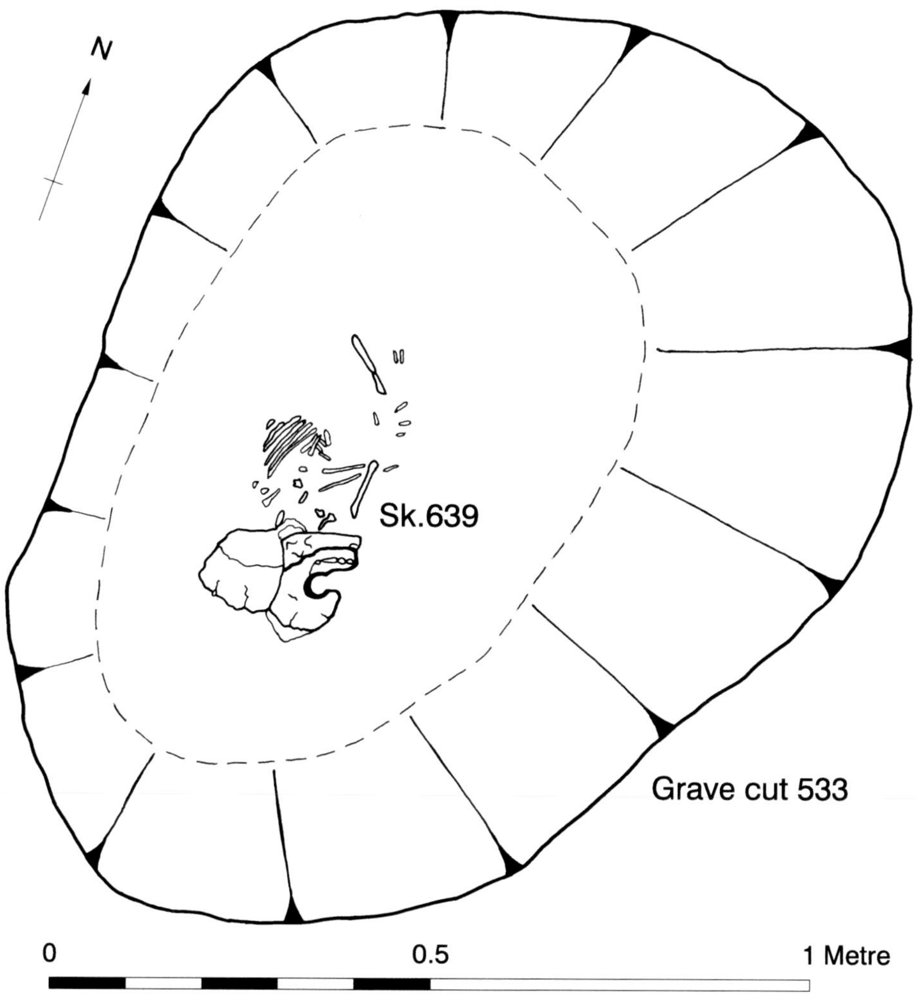

Fig 17. Eastling Down: SK 639 and Grave 533. Scale 1:10.

The early burial, Grave 533 (Fig 17; Pl 4)

Perhaps associated with the rebuilding of the barrow and the formation of a possible southern annexe was a grave (533) containing a poorly-preserved crouched inhumation of a young child (SK 639) aged approximately eight months (*see* p 60). The body had been laid in a crouched position on its right side, facing south-west, with left arm extended in front of the body, forearm bent upward towards the face. The grave cut to a depth of 0.35m into the uppermost fills of the primary ring-ditch in sector 4, was oval-shaped, aligned roughly north-east to south-west and measured 1.30 by 0.90m. The grave fill of grey-brown marl and loam with chalk lumps (contexts 532 and 639) provided four limpet shells and an intrusive rabbit bone, indicating that the grave fill had been disturbed. Although the shells may have been a by-product of the burial ceremony they may be residual, incorporated into the primary mound at the time of its construction and reworked during the cutting and filling of the grave.

Bone from skeleton 639 provided a radiocarbon date for the burial; 2265–2260 cal BC and 2220–1910 cal BC (lab no 141269, Table 2).

When compared with other burials on the south side of the mound, this is the earliest dated inhumation or cremation associated with the monument. Although it is quite possible that the burial predates the rebuilding of the mound, the interment had to have taken place after the primary ditch had been filled and therefore perhaps at a time just before the mound was rebuilt. Although there is insufficient evidence for certainty, the burial and the rebuilding of the mound have been included in Phase 2, with the date of the burial tentatively providing a *terminus ante quem* for reconstruction of the mound.

Pl 4. Eastling Down: SK 639, Grave 533.

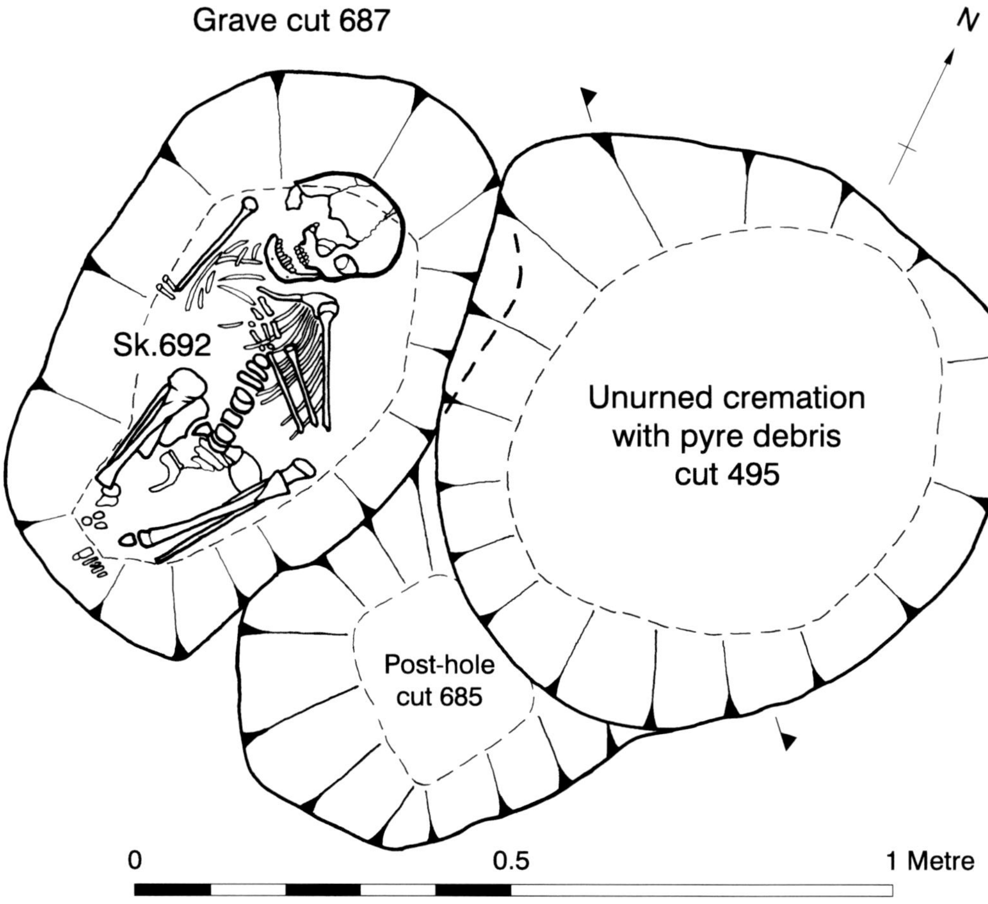

Fig 18. Eastling Down: SK 692, Grave 687, Post-hole 685 and cremation pit 495. Scale 1:10.

Post-pit (Fig 18)

Some 2m south-east of Grave 533 was a possible post-pit. The pit (685), 0.50m in diameter and 0.26m deep was cut by a later inhumation (687) and a cremation burial (495). The pit with steeply-sloping sides and rounded base was filled with chalk marl and chalk lumps (context 577). There were possible traces of a post-ghost in the lowest part of the fill, indicated by a fine grey silt-clay, suggesting that a timber post approximately 0.10m in diameter may have rotted *in situ.*

It is possible that the post-pit may have contained a marker. Although the pit provided no datable finds, later-dated features cut the post-pit, suggesting a Phase 2 attribution for the feature and a possible association with Grave 533.

The ditch fills (Figs 9, 12 and 19 Sections 1, 4, 8; Fig 20, Section B)

The earliest deposit at the sump of the ditch in sectors 7, 8 and 1–3 was of a compact weathered loamy chalk (contexts 674, 709, 738 and 739) 0.05–0.08m thick, representing a construction trample or an early weathering of the ditch edges. The primary fill provided a small number of intrusive rabbit bones (Table 9), and a few worked flints including an end scraper, but no pottery.

Capping the basal deposit was a 0.25–0.40m deep compact mixture of small chalk lumps and pale-brown chalk marl. The layer (contexts 662, 663, 694 and 708) may have accumulated from the weathering of ditch edges and erosion of the mound, perhaps over a protracted period. The deposit contained a number of flint flakes and a single worn potsherd of Peterborough Ware.

The upper fill of the ditch was a compact brown chalk-loam containing chalk flecking and small rounded nodules of chalk (contexts 402, 545 and 715). The deposit, 0.25–0.40m deep, may have developed slowly as a consequence of natural weathering of the ditch sides and perhaps of the mound. The layer provided a single potsherd of Peterborough Ware and three of Beaker (p 58), together with a number of struck flint flakes (some burnt). Worked flint implements included a number of scrapers including FN 1225 from context 545 (Fig 27). All the finds were taken to be residual, probably deriving from weathered mound deposits.

Phase 3: the southern annexe, later burials and 'placed' deposits

The burial monument was remodelled in Phase 3 with a substantial horseshoe-shaped ditch cut to the south of the barrow in sectors 3–7. The wide and deep ditch with rounded

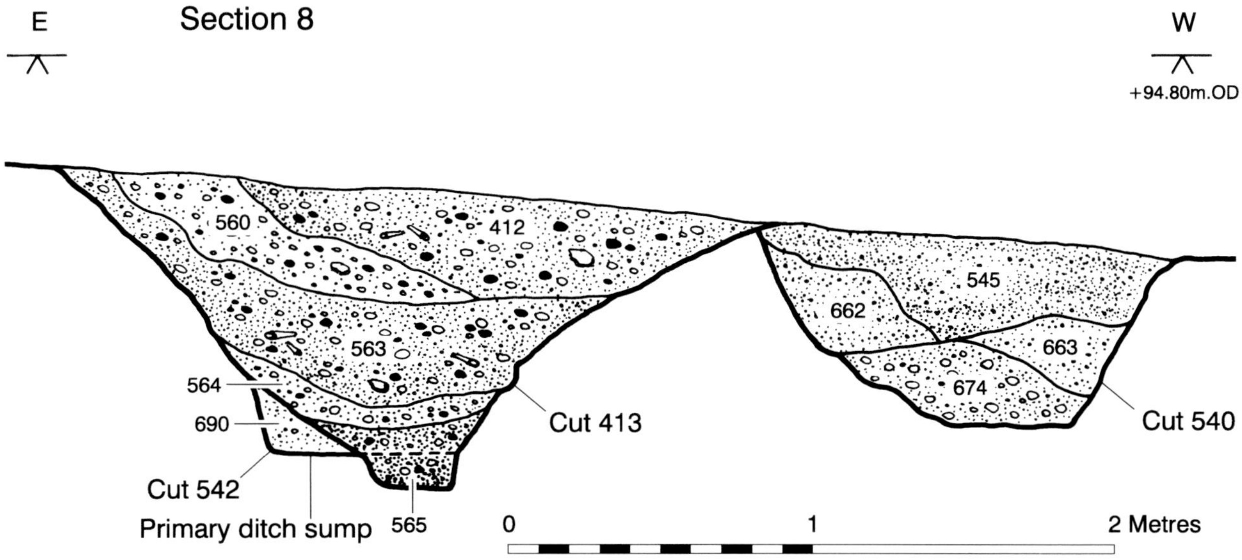

Fig 19. Eastling Down: Section 8. Scale 1:125.

terminals to the east and west almost entirely removed the remains of the Phase 2 ring-ditch in sectors 4–6 and cut into the early ditch in sectors 3 and 7. The identifications of the Phase 3 ditch terminals was not made during the excavation, but has been deduced from feature relationships in the post-excavation process. Excluding Grave 533 allocated to Phase 2, the annexe created by the new ditch was associated with a six crouched inhumation burials and two cremations. There were in addition, possible 'placed' deposits within each of the ditch terminals. Two further undated but probably contemporary 'placed' deposits were found in pits cutting the northern outer ring-ditch in sectors 1 and 2.

The ditch for the southern annexe (Figs 5 and 7; Pl 5)

The southern ditch (541) was cut from a mid-way point against the east and west sides of the Phase 2 mound, intersecting and cutting through the Phase 2 ring-ditch (540) and into the Phase 1 ditch (539/542). No trace of the Phase 2 ditch remained save for a short section of outer edge (701)

Pl 5. Eastling Down: general view following excavation, looking north-west. Scale 1m.

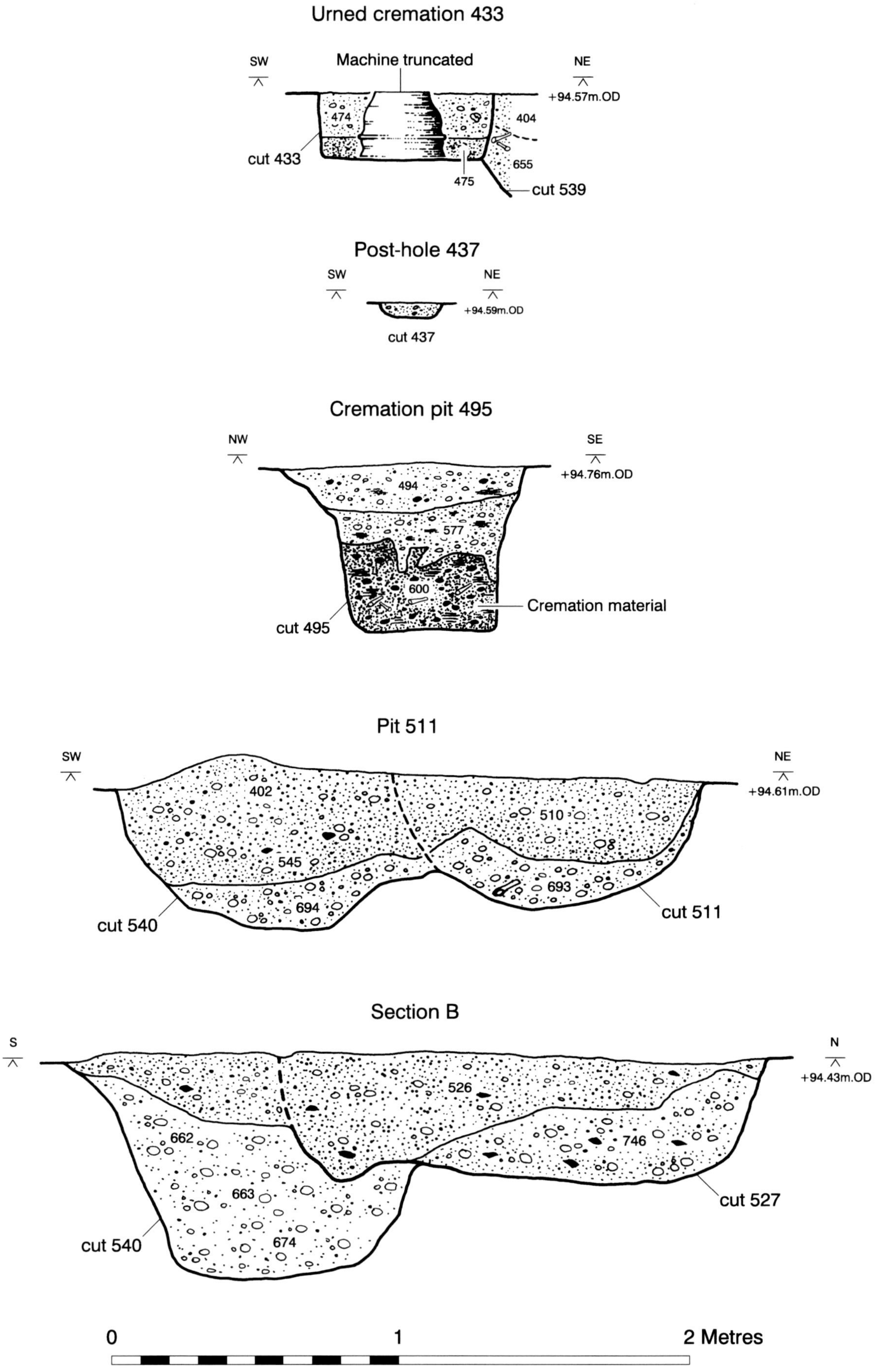

Fig 20. Eastling Down: Cremation 433, post-hole 437, cremation pit 495, pit 511 and Section B (ditch 540 and pit 527). Scale 1:10.

identified in sectors 4 and 5 and deposits of intact upper fill (context 702). The northern part of the Phase 2 ditch may have remained visible at this time, though mostly filled with debris from a decaying mound.

The Phase 3 ditch was on average 2m wide and 1.0m deep but irregularly cut. The eastern and western terminals were 2.75 and 2.55m wide and a central section of the ditch (sectors 5 and 6), due south of the mound was up to 2.6m wide. Generally steep-sided with a flat base, the ditch was cut up to 1.5m deep. The central, southern part of the ditch appeared to have been formed from at least three large, intercutting lobes. The scars, most evident at the base and sides of the ditch, perhaps reflect one or more phases of ditch re-cutting. The rounded and steep-sided eastern terminus in sectors 3 and 4 (719) was found to cut the earlier ditches; the western terminus in sectors 6 and 7 (658) was cut into the Phase 1 ditch but was in turn cut by a later boundary ditch (413). The irregularities in the sides and base of the cutting may perhaps have been formed during repeated episodes of ditch clearance, possibly associated with new interments. In addition to episodes of clearance of ditch sediment and vegetation, deliberate quarrying of chalk from the ditch sides may have taken place to dress or 'whiten' the mound to make the monument more visible in the landscape (see Grinsell 1975, 18).

The early ditch fills (Figs 12–15, sections 4–7)

At the base of the ditch was a 3–5cm thick deposit of crushed chalk (context 721) which was probably a construction trample or 'rapid' silt which developed soon after the ditch had been cut or cleared for the final time. The primary deposit provided no finds.

Capping the primary fill was a banded deposit of weathered chalk and chalk silt, taken to represent erosion of the ditch sides by weathering and perhaps vegetation. The deposit (contexts 675, 676, 682, 705, 711, 722, 723 and 736) of grey-brown chalk marl and loam mixed with discoloured chalk on average 0.35–0.45m thick provided three Peterborough Ware potsherds (including two conjoining sherds) and two of Beaker (*see* p 55). The deposit also provided worked flints including two end scrapers and a chisel-shaped transverse arrowhead (Fig 28, FN 1065) from context 675 as well as a small collection of animal bones (Tables 9 and 10) and marine shell (cockle and limpet).

The inhumation and cremation burials

Six inhumation burials in five graves, an 'urned' cremation burial, a pit cremation and four possible 'placed' deposits may have been interred during Phase 3. All of the burials have been radiocarbon dated; the 'placed' deposits have not been dated.

Three inhumations and a cremation in a Collared Urn were of early Bronze Age date (439 (SK 566), 729, 537 and 433). Three inhumations dated from the middle Bronze Age (687, 439 (SK 623) and 479). The latest-dated burial was a cremation or 'placed' deposit found in a pit (495) cutting an earlier grave (687) in sector 4. The feature was dated to the later Bronze Age.

The burials were in three groups, located in sectors 4, 5 and 6. A single burial was found cutting the early ring-ditch in sector 4. Four burials, including two skeletons in one grave and a cremation in a Collared Urn were found in sector 6. The remaining grave was located between the two groups in sector 5.

The eastern group

The eastern group of burials includes the crouched inhumation of a child (533) dated earlier than the other burials and tentatively included in Phase 2 (*see* p 25), and a second crouched inhumation of a child (687) dated later in the early Bronze Age. The latter grave was cut by a pit (495) containing cremated human bones (a cremation or a 'placed' deposit) dated to the late Bronze Age.

Grave 687 (Fig 18; Pl 6)

The badly preserved remains of the burial of a child (SK 692) was recovered from a grave found cutting the fill of the early ring-ditch. The grave, cut by a later cremation burial (495), was oval-shaped, measuring 0.82m east–west by 0.50m north–south. The grave aligned north–south was

Pl 6. Eastling Down: SK 692, Grave 687, looking north. Scale 0.5m.

cut to a depth of 0.30m with steep sides extending down to a flat, roughly rectangular base. The grave contained a homogenous fill of grey-brown loam and dirty chalk (contexts 686 and 691) which provided a single flint flake and nineteen shells of *porsphaera globularis*, a common chalk fossil. According to the excavator a number of the fossil shells, which disintegrated during excavation, were pierced, suggesting the possibility that collectively they may have formed a primitive necklace.

The burial was that of a child, aged approximately eight years (*see* p 60). Unusually, the child was laid on its back, with head to the north-east and tilted to face west. The legs were tightly flexed. The left upper arm was at an angle to the body, the forearm bent back across the rib cage with the hand resting high on the chest. The right upper arm lay parallel to the body with forearm at right angles, resting vertically against the side of the grave. Fossil shells concentrated near the skull may have been utilised for a necklace. Similar fossil shells were recovered from other burial contexts (Grave 537 and 'placed' deposit 683) but were not pierced.

One possible explanation for the extraordinary posture of the burial is that the child may have died in a fire and that the effects of this made it impossible to lay out the burial in a conventional manner. This was the only burial laid with head to the east. All the other burials were laid with head to the west or north-west. The earliest burial (533) a short distance to the north was aligned with head to the south-west. Skeleton 692 provided a date of 1737–1531 cal BC (lab no UBA20689, Table 2).

The western group of burials

The western group of burials comprised two graves with children, including one grave with two differently dated burials. A third substantial, deep grave contained an adult. A cremation burial of an adult contained within an urn and a nearby post-hole also formed part of this group.

The double burial, 439 (Fig 21; Pl 7)

Grave 439 was subcircular, aligned long axis north-west to south-east. The grave measured 1.30 by 1.05m was cut with steep, near vertical sides and flat base to a depth of 0.56m. The grave fill (context 438) of light to medium-brown loam and small chalk rubble contained two skeletons buried one over the other, with grave fill separating the interments. There was no sign of a later cut in the grave fill which otherwise provided five struck flint flakes, animal bones and a cockle shell.

The primary burial (SK 623) was of a child aged approximately five years laid on its right side, head to the north-west, facing south-west, with legs tightly flexed. The left arm was laid parallel with the body, with the forearm flexed and across the waist. The right upper arm lay parallel with the front of the body. At the foot of the grave (north-east end), and lying above the base of the grave in grave fill capping the skeleton, was the broken but nearly complete remains of a small undecorated Food Vessel - an open handled bowl of early to middle Bronze Age date (*see* p 54). Bone from the child provided a radiocarbon date of 1520–1280 cal BC (lab no 130971, Table 2).

Over the pelvis of the child but separated from the early burial by a layer of soil was the fragmentary remains of the skull of a neonate, no more than a month old (SK 566). A few fragments of bone recovered from the upper grave fill by sieving were also from the burial, which was in a badly decomposed state. Bone from the skull of the later burial provided a radiocarbon date of 1955–1670 cal BC (lab no 141268, Table 2).

The radiocarbon dates indicate that the burials are not contemporary; the earliest burial seals a later-dated interment. One possible explanation for this may be that Grave 439 partially or wholly removed an earlier burial with perhaps an accompanying Food Vessel. The vessel was perhaps broken and was included in the lower grave fill capping the body with the remains of the neonate placed in the upper fill of the grave after the interment had taken place. Although this interpretation may be correct there was no indication of an earlier grave cut suggesting the superimposition of two graves.

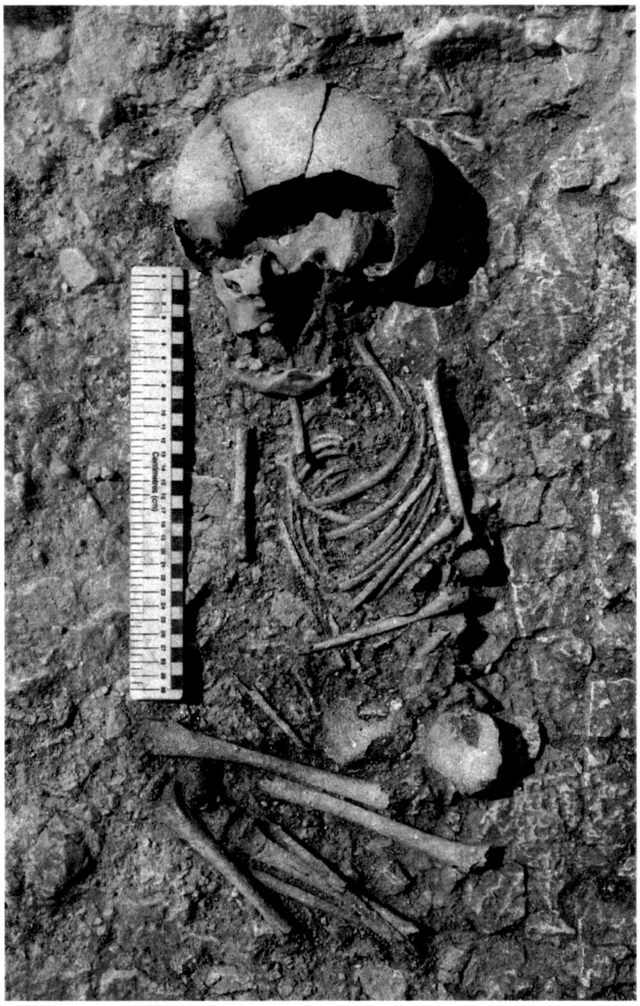

Pl 7. Eastling Down: SK 623, Grave 439, looking north-west. Scale 0.30m.

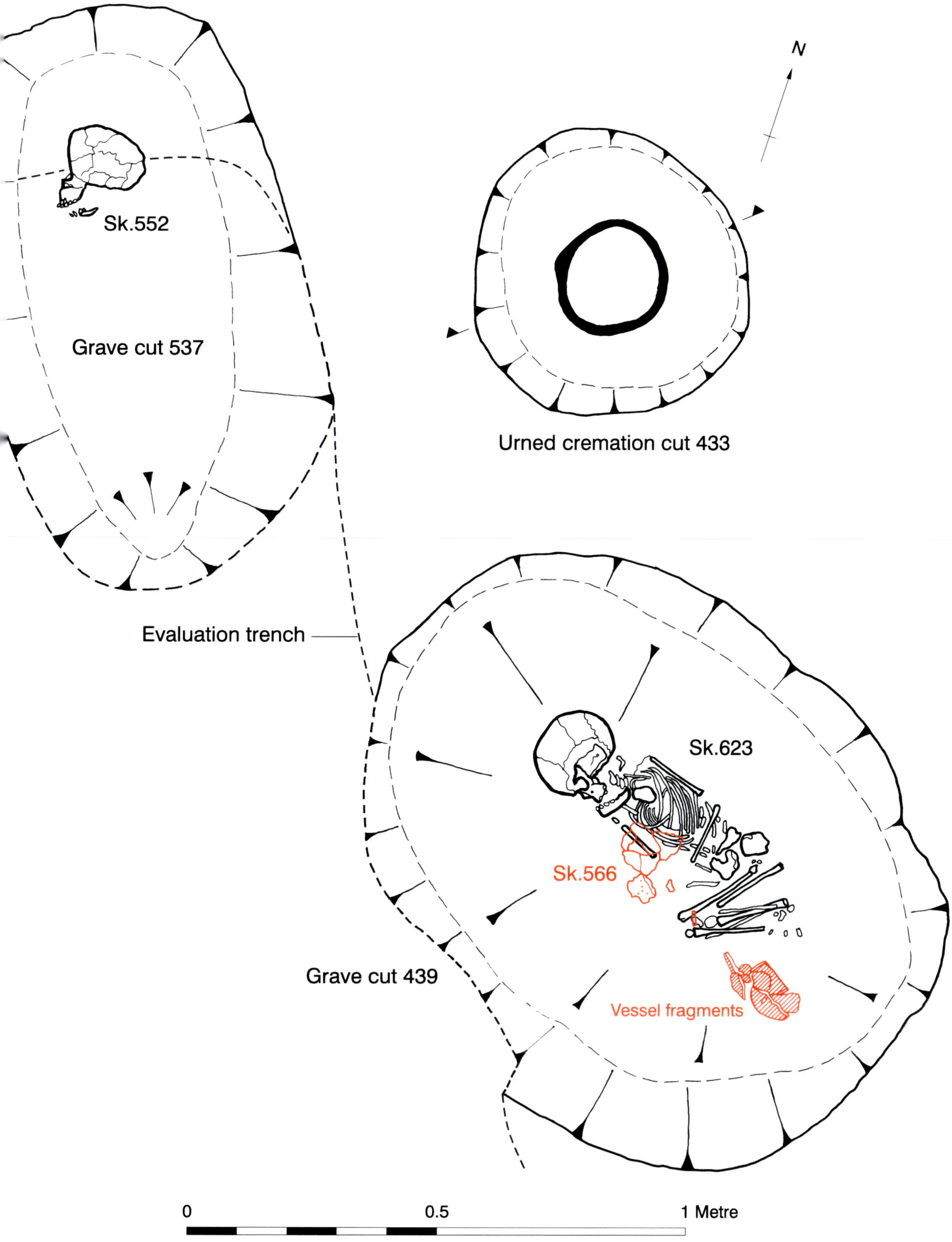

Fig 21. Eastling Down: SK 552, Grave 537; double burial SK 523 and SK 566; and urned cremation 433. Scale 1:10.

Pl 8. Eastling Down: SK 557, Grave 537, looking north-west. Scale 0.50m.

An alternative explanation might be that the early burial may originally have been contained within the Food Vessel and buried elsewhere, perhaps nearby, and deliberately re-interred with the later burial as part of the burial rite. The vessel may have been deliberately emptied and broken early in the backfilling of the open grave (the vessel was incomplete). The vessel contents were then perhaps placed in the upper fill of the grave after the interment of the child had taken place.

A further more remote possibility might be that the neonate had been 'stored' in a domestic household or shrine, perhaps in a mummified state within the Food Vessel, as a revered ritual object. Then, after perhaps 400 years, the foetus was finally buried within the grave of a recently deceased child.

The double burial is an enigmatic discovery; the gap of over four centuries separating the interments, with the early burial over the latter and the presence of a near complete early vessel on the base of the grave are difficult to interpret and other explanations may need to be sought.

Grave 537 (Fig 21; Pl 8)

Approximately 0.40m north of the double burial was the grave of a third child. The grave (537) cut to a depth of 0.38m in undisturbed chalk between the ring-ditches was aligned north-west to south-east and measured 1.15 by 0.70m. Grave fill (context 536) was a pale-brown chalk-loam with few inclusions and no additional finds. The skeleton (SK 552), aged between 2 to 3 years, was poorly preserved, with only part of a skull found laying on its right side, positioned at the north-west end of the grave (*see* Pl 8). Bone from the burial provided a radiocarbon date of 1878–1636 cal BC (lab no UBA20691, Table 2).

Grave 729 (Fig 22; Pls 9 and 10)

The burial of an adult male (SK 730) was contained within a substantial grave (729) measuring 2.70 by 1.80m aligned long axis north-west to south-east. The grave was cut with shallow sloping sides and flat base to a depth of 0.56m through the fills of the early ring-ditch. The burial had been contained within a wooden coffin (context 741) measuring 1.85 by 0.75m indicated by soil stains and chalk rubble. Within the grave was a single fill (context 728) of redeposited chalk and mid-brown loam heavily discoloured with pale grey powdered chalk and small abraded chalk lumps. The fill provided two potsherds of Peterborough Ware (*see* p 56) and three of possible Beaker. Intrusive animal bones, including badger and rabbit (Table 10), were present, together with fragments of burnt daub and carbonised oak (*see* p 73), burnt flints and nearly 300 struck flints, including two end scrapers, a piercer and four cores (*see* p 45). The presence of such a large quantity of residual worked and burnt flint,

Pl 9. Eastling Down: SK 730, Grave 729, looking north-west. Scales 0.30 and 1m.

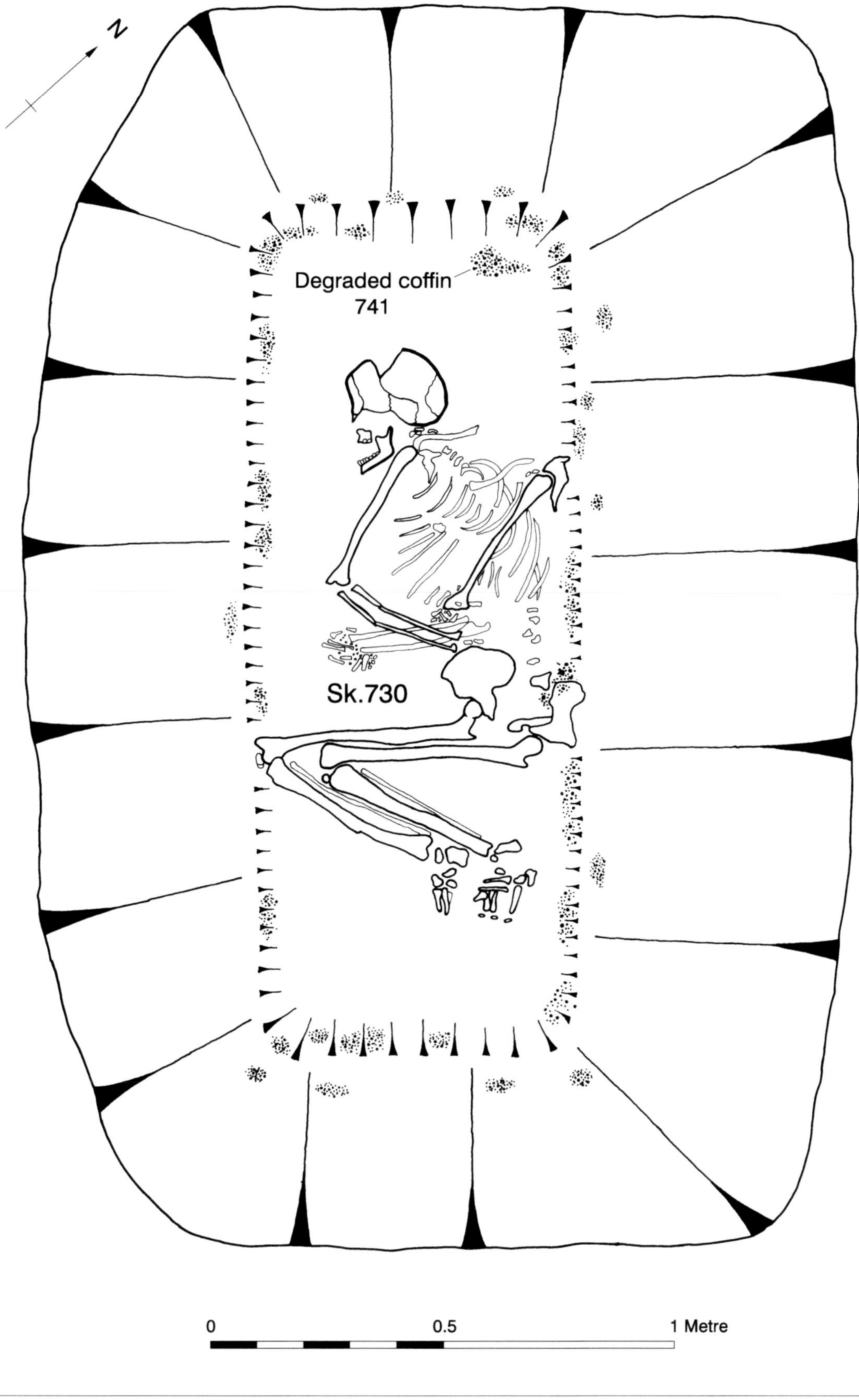

Fig 22. Eastling Down: SK 730, Grave 729. Scale 1:10.

Pl 10. Eastling Down: SK 730, Grave 729, looking north-west. Scale 0.30m.

daub, animal bones and the early potsherds is highly unusual but given the size of the grave, its position cutting the inner ring-ditch and the quantity of early 'midden' incorporated in the ring-ditches (*see* p 43), the presence of the material might be explicable. It remains a possibility that at least a proportion of the material may have been deliberately included as part of the funerary ritual.

The skeleton, aged between 30–35 years (*see* p 60), was found lying on his right side facing south-west with head to the north-west. The upper legs were drawn up at right angles to the spine so that the knees and pelvis were in contact with the coffin. The lower legs were bent back, with feet aligned to the axis of the body. The spine was bent forward; the left arm and shoulder blade were detached and lay against the north side of the coffin. The right arm lay forward of the body with forearm crossing over the left forearm. The right hand overlay the pelvis and the left was forward of the body. Bone from the burial provided a radiocarbon date of 1920–1625 cal BC (lab no 141270, Table 2).

Cremation 433 (Fig 21; Pl 11)

A cremation burial was located between graves 439, 537 and 729, forming part of a tight cluster of burials. The cremation was contained in an inverted Collared Urn in a circular steep-sided pit (433), 0.57m in diameter and 0.23m deep. The cremation pit cut into the edge of the primary ring-ditch (539) was almost filled with the urn, but the sides were packed with clay-loam and powdered white chalk (context 475). The pit fill provided no finds.

The cremated bones were those of a mature adult (*see* pp 61–2) and were accompanied by unidentified fragments of animal bone and an unburnt pair of bone tweezers (*see* pp 58–9). Although by no means common, when similar objects have been found they have usually been associated with male burials. The burial urn, though damaged was a substantially complete Collared and decorated Urn of Longworth's Secondary Series, South-East style (Fig 32, no 19), generally dated 2000–1500 BC. Cremated bone from the burial was dated to 1964 –1756 cal BC (lab no UB18136, Table 2)

Post-hole (Figs 7 and 20)

A post-hole (437) was located 0.25m south of Grave 439. The post, 0.20m in diameter and some 0.05m deep, was filled with a fine, grey silt with inclusions of small rounded chalk nodules (context 438), possibly suggesting that a post up to 0.20m in diemater had rotted *in situ*. The post may have been sited to mark one of the nearby burials. Another possible marker was associated with Grave 533 (*see* p 26).

Pl 11. Eastling Down: cremation burial contained in inverted Collared Urn during excavation, looking north-west. Scale 0.30m.

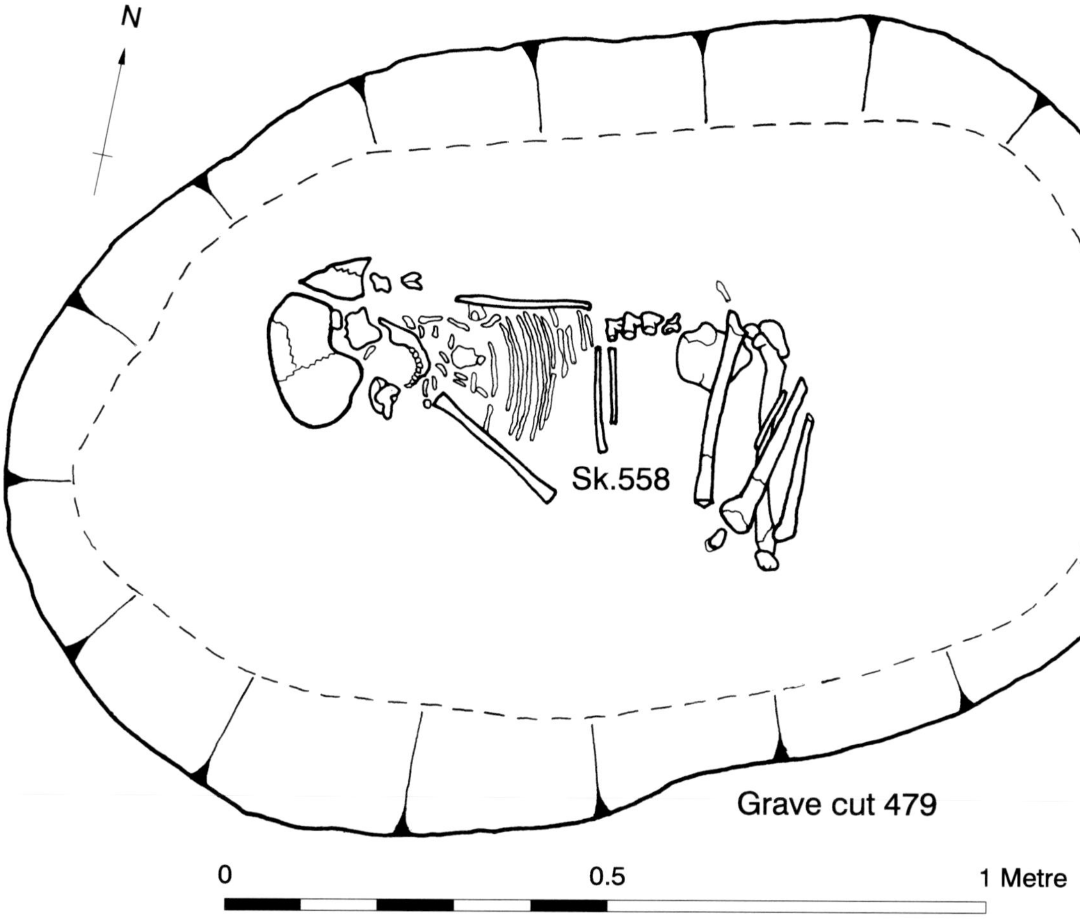

Fig 23. Eastling Down: SK 588, Grave 479. Scale 1:10.

The central burial

Grave 479 (Fig 23; Pl 12)

The burial of an 11 or 12 year old child (SK 558, *see* p 61) was located in an isolated position in the southern part of the mound (sector 5), mid-way between the two groups of burials. The oval-shaped grave aligned roughly east–west and measuring 1.60 by 1.05m was cut into natural chalk just inside the primary ring-ditch and 3.4m north of the Phase 3 ditch. The burial was positioned on the east–west centre line of the mound. No finds were recovered from the rubble chalk fill of the grave (contexts 478, 557 and 559).

The child was laid on its right side, head to the west, facing south, with legs tightly flexed at right angles to the spine. The left arm was parallel to the body with forearm at right angles and extending forward. The right upper arm was laid at an angle and forward of the body. Skeleton 558 was dated to 1515–1120 cal BC (lab no 130970, Table 2).

The 'placed' deposits

Four possible 'placed' deposits were associated with Phase 3 use of the mound. A small pit containing human bone and pyre debris was found in each of the terminals of the Phase 3 ditch in sectors 3 and 7 and human bone was recovered from two adjacent pits found cutting the infilled Phase 2 ring-ditch in sectors 1 and 2. The 'placed' deposits have not been dated.

Pl 12. Eastling Down: SK 730, Grave 729, looking north-west. Scale 0.30m.

Placed deposit 737 (Fig 7) took the form of a small shallow pit identified in the intermediate fills (contexts 722, 723 etc) of the western terminal of the Phase 3 ditch during the removal of a baulk separating sectors 6 and 7. The subcircular pit 0.13m in diameter and 0.05m deep was filled with a deposit of charcoal and burnt reddish-brown loam containing 16g of cremated human bone, including skull fragments, a child's finger bone, fragments of cockle shell and a roe deer bone. The deposit also contained charcoal (*see* p 73), burnt flints and a transverse arrowhead (Fig 28, FN 1016).

Placed deposit 724 was a small, shallow circular pit, some 0.15m in diameter found cutting the intermediate weathered chalk fill (context 705) of the eastern terminal of the Phase 3 ditch in sector 3. The pit contained fragments of human bone, including part of a femur.

Two oval-shaped pits (527 and 511) appear to have been cut when the ditch was partially or fully infilled. Both pits contained human bones on the base of pit and may have been 'placed' deposits associated with some form of funerary ritual or rite.

Pit 527 (Figs 7 and 20) was located against the northern edge of the Phase 2 ditch. Cut with steep, near vertical edges and a flat base, the pit was 3m long, 1.25m wide and 0.52m deep. The pit was filled with redeposited chalk and a grey-pale brown chalk loam (contexts 526 and 746) which contained 10g of eroded human bone, including a fragment of femur (p 61). A single unidentified animal bone, nine flint flakes, one burnt flint and a waisted core tool (Fig 29, FN 855, context 526) were also recovered from the fill.

Pit 511 (Figs 7 and 20) was located against the outer edge of the Phase 2 ditch on the south-east side of the mound. The pit, 2.71m long and 1.20.m wide, was cut with sloping sides and rounded base to a depth of 0.41m. The pit fill (context 510) of redeposited chalk and chalk marl provided no datable finds but 4g of eroded human bone was recovered from the basal fill (context 693).

The late cremation or 'placed' deposit 495 (Figs 7 and 18; Pl 13)

An irregular subcircular pit 0.82m in diameter and 0.57m deep was cut through the north-east corner of Grave 687 in sector 4. The pit had shallow sloping sides and a flat, circular base, some 0.50m in diameter. The lowest 0.40m of the pit had near vertical sides. The pit contained three fills of which the lowest (context 600) was of cremated bone and pyre debris, comprising a 0.21–30m thick layer of compact, grey-black carbonised wood, burnt soil (with a few fire fractured flints) and cremated human bone. The capping fill (context 577), a 0.09–0.20m thick layer of orange-brown clay flecked with chalk and carbon, also contained cremated human bone. The clay, the only material of this kind from the excavation, may have been garnered from a natural ice wedge in the underlying chalk. The uppermost fill, (context 494) a grey-brown chalky clay mixed with flint and chalk nodules, contained animal bones.

The burial contained 271g of bone, of which 228g occurred in the primary cremation deposit (600), along with 88g of carbonised wood. The remainder of the bone occurred in the pit's clay sealing layer (577) or the graded boundary between the two deposits. The bones were of an adult but the quantity of bone recovered was unusually small for an average adult cremation, whilst the quantity of pyre debris was surprisingly high. It is possible that such incomplete skeletal material and the large quantity of carbonised wood perhaps suggests the ritual disposal of cremation pyre debris, rather than a formal cremation burial (*see* pp 44–5, 63).

Pl 13. Eastling barrow: pyre debris and cremated bone in pit 495, looking north-west. Scale 0.30m.

The carbonised wood recovered from context 600 contained charcoal of *pomoidea* which appears to have been fuel used for the cremation process (*see* p 73). The carbonised wood provided a radiocarbon date of 920–795 cal BC (lab no 141271, Table 2).

The late ditch fills (Figs 12–15, sections 4–7)

The primary fills of the Phase 3 ditch in sectors 3 to 7 were capped by a weathered deposit (context 695) tipping steeply to the centre of the ditch from the sides. The deposit, identified in all sectors was capped by an extensive and ubiquitous deposit of pale brown chalk-loam (496, 546, 548 and 681) on average 0.4–0.6m deep. The deposit contained residual potsherds of Grooved Ware, Peterborough Ware and Beaker (all from context 546) together with a substantial collection of struck flints including 112 flakes, four blade fragments and ten cores, including a globular type (Fig 26, FN 357) and a class B bi-polar type (Fig 26, FN 356). Flint tools included a polished axe fragment (Fig 28, FN 1062), four end scrapers, one end and side scraper and a possible fabricator (Fig 28, FN 1227d). All the tools were recovered from context 546 in sectors 4, 5 and 6. The same context also provided some 10g of human bone (*see* p 61). The capping layer appeared to have been formed over a considerable period, perhaps partly by weathering and erosion of the mound, but also by other agencies including vegetation and perhaps agriculture. Two medieval potsherds dated AD 1175–1225, recovered from the uppermost fill of the ditch, suggested that the ditch remained visible in the landscape into the medieval period.

Phase 4: the late Iron Age feature

Phase 4 comprised a single Iron Age pit or small 'sunken' building cut into the primary ring-ditch on the south side of the mound.

The late Iron Age pit or 'sunken' building (Fig 16, Section A)

A substantial pit (493) was located cutting the primary ring-ditch in sector 3. The pit, aligned east–west at the centre of the south side of the mound was positioned close to the internal edge of the Phase 3 ditch. The feature, with near vertical sides and flat base measured some 4.1m east–west by 2.5m north–south and was cut 0.24m into the fills and south side of the ring-ditch. The base of the pit was defined by a thin layer of powdered chalk (context 698), probably a construction trample or floor deposit, capped by a 0.07 to 0.10m thick layer of discoloured and compacted chalk (context 642), similar to deposits sealing the base of the ring-ditch. Sealed by this layer and resting on the trample at the centre of the feature was a cache of horse bones, comprising long bones and part of a skull of an adult horse, together with some sixty-two unidentified cattle-sized fragments that may have belonged to the same animal (*see* p 67). The uppermost fill of the pit (context 492) was a uniform layer of pale brown chalk-loam containing no finds.

The horse bones provided a radiocarbon date of 364–201 cal BC (lab no UBA16780, Table 2), placing the deposit in the mid-to-late Iron Age.

An alternative interpretation of the feature might be that it formed the footprint of a 'sunken' building, set slightly below the contemporary ground surface. The deposit of compacted chalk may have been a rough floor with the horse bones placed on it, set centrally within the structure. No post-holes, beam slots or other structural features were found to support the interpretation and the function of the feature remains unclear.

Whatever the interpretation of the feature, the horse bones appear to have been deliberately positioned within it, suggesting that they may have formed a 'placed deposit' or ritual offering. If the interpretation is correct, then although no longer used for formal burial for at least 600 years, the mound may have retained a special and perhaps revered status for surrounding inhabitants in the later Iron Age. The deposition of the horse bones may therefore represent a last tangible ritual act associated with a monument that was by then perhaps over 2,000 years old.

Post-holes south of the barrow (Fig 8)

Two post-holes (477 and 535) found cutting into natural chalk some 5.50m south-east of the ring-ditch may have been cut during the prehistoric period. Both features were 0.33m in diameter and cut between 0.10 and 0.22m deep. The fill of 535 (context 534) yielded an undiagnostic, but probably prehistoric potsherd.

Undated possible post-holes south of the barrow

A dispersed group of ten possible post-holes was recorded at the southern extremity of the excavation, some 36m south of the ring-ditch. Most of the features were subcircular, measuring on average between 0.15 to 0.30m in diameter and cut to an average depth of 0.05–0.10m. The holes were filled with chalk loam and provided no chock-stones or finds. There were three isolated post-holes (451, 471 and 459) and two groups of posts. The first of these was located in the south-west corner of the excavated area (457, 447, 445 and 449), and the second (463, 465, 467 and 469) some 6m to the east of the first. None of the posts formed a coherent structure.

With two other post-holes (477, 535) located closer to the barrow, this dispersed group of features tentatively suggests the presence of some form of settlement activity south of the barrow. The date and nature of that activity remains unproven.

Phase 5: the Roman ditch and later activity

Phase 5 features comprised a single large V-shaped ditch (Pl 14) that cut across the north-west edge of the mound. The ditch probably formed part of an early Roman field system or an estate boundary.

Pl 14. Eastling Down: Roman boundary ditch, section 8, looking south-west. Scales 0.5m and 1m.

The Roman ditch (Fig 7; Fig 9, Section 1; Fig 19, Section 8)

Cutting across the north-west edge of the monument was a north-north-east to south-south-west aligned ditch (413). The ditch, probably forming a major field or possibly an estate boundary, was cut on average 1.85m wide. Ditch width increased at the point of intersection with the primary ring-ditch, where it was at its maximum of 2.50m. The ditch, cut between 0.75 and 1.50m deep with steeply sloping sides and flat base, was on average 0.35m wide. The primary fill was of weathered chalk (context 565), a deposit which probably formed rapidly after the ditch was cut. The layer provided no datable finds. The primary fill was capped in places by a 30–50mm thick layer of clean frost fractured chalk (context 564) which provided four potsherds dating from the later first or early second century AD. Elsewhere the primary fill was sealed by a substantial 0.40–0.50m thick layer of banded brown chalk-loam (contexts 560 and 563) yielding residual prehistoric flints including a transverse arrowhead (Fig 28, FN 667a) and a rod (Fig 28, FN 667b) both from context 560 (*see* p 50), and a few residual Iron Age potsherds and pottery of the first to the mid third centuries AD. The deposit also provided a fragment of burnt human bone, possibly part of a fibula (*see* p 63), recovered from sector 7 where all four ditches intersect. The cremated bone may therefore be residual from a cremation burial or 'placed' deposit associated with any of the earlier phases of the monument. The deposit also contained a few fragments of horse pelvis and teeth. The capping fill (context 412) of pale brown chalk-loam, in places 0.40m thick, provided Iron Age and Roman potsherds together with a middle Anglo-Saxon potsherd dated *c* AD 750–850 and early medieval potsherds dated *c* AD 1075–1125 and *c* AD 1175–1225.

The ditch, probably cut in the late first or early second century, was in use until at least the mid third century. The ditch was almost certainly accompanied by a bank perhaps supporting a hedge to form not only a visible boundary but a division defining land ownership, acting as a physical barrier. It was not possible to determine which side of the ditch the bank may have been located, but the ditch had clearly been positioned to respect the mound and it is likely that the monument formed a prominent feature in the local landscape and was used as a marker for the laying out of the boundary.

There are no cropmarks in the immediate area to suggest that the ditch formed part of a field system, although there is evidence for ancient fields in the vicinity (see Fig 2). The substantial size of the ditch and the lack of evidence for an accompanying field system suggests that the ditch defined a significant boundary, perhaps that of a Roman estate. It has been noted above (p 6) that the south-west to north-east aligned boundary is parallel to an existing road located to the west (Fig 24). The lane to Ashley, slightly sunken and undoubtedly of some antiquity, intersects with the Dover to Richborough road approximately 2km to the north-east of the present site. It is possible that at least part of the present lane may be of Roman origin and that the boundary ditch and the road are contemporary features.

The ditches defining both mound and boundary remained 'open' for a considerable period, with latest finds in their uppermost loam fills dating into the early medieval period.

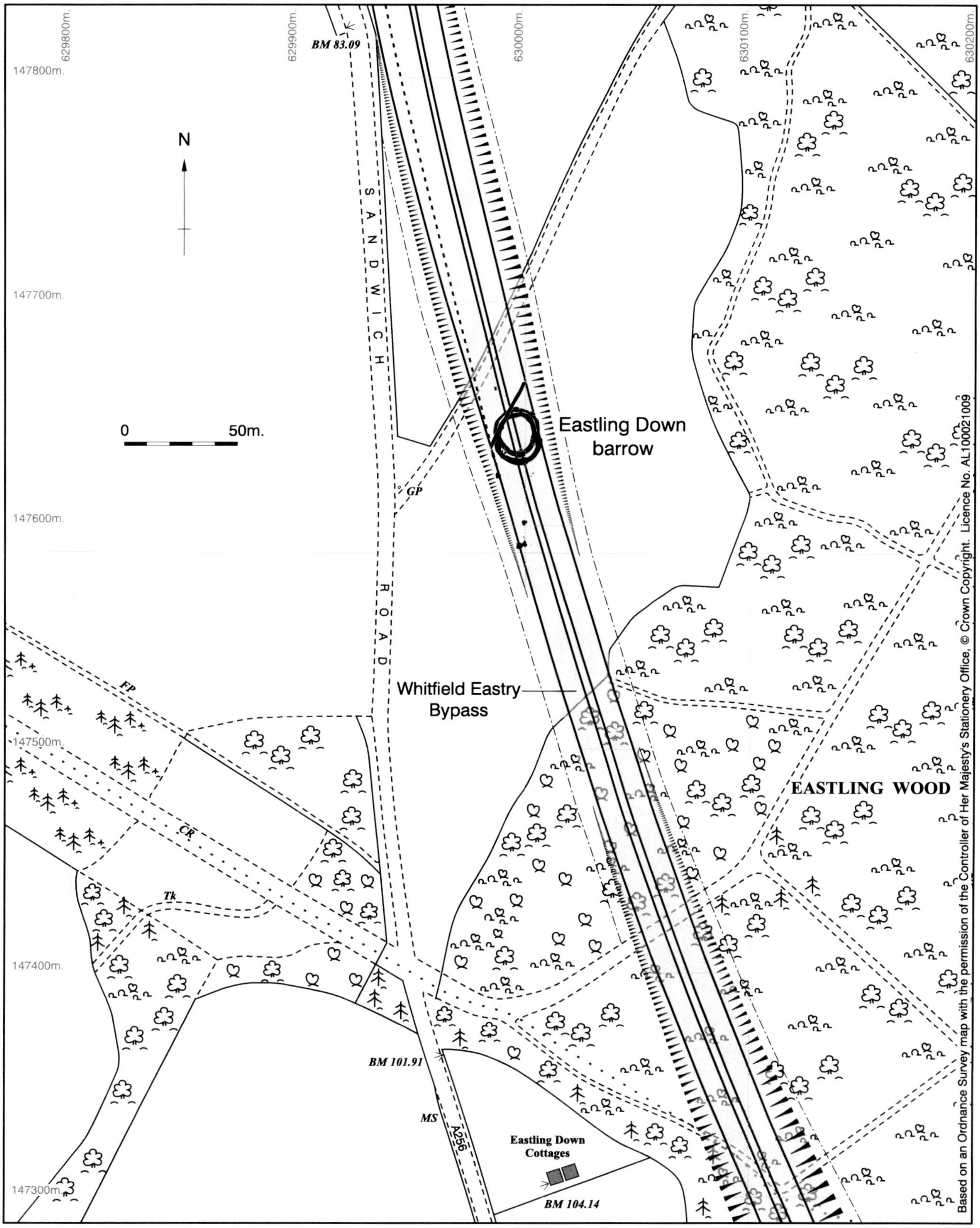

Fig 24. Eastling Down: Roman ditch and road.

The burial mound and the bank of the boundary may have survived as visible features in the landscape for much longer.

Phase 6: the animal disturbances and recent features

Phase 6 deposits and features comprise a complex of intercutting burrows, runs and chambers associated with a rabbit warren. Other burrows, perhaps belonging to a badger sett, were also present. The majority of the features were identified in two zones within the footprint of the ring-ditches. Some disturbance to the upper ditch fills almost certainly occurred but this was not identified during the excavation. A number of animal disturbances and features, including tree 'throws' outside the barrow have also been included in this period.

The animal disturbances (Figs 7 and 25; Pl 15)

An area of interconnected, irregular pits and gullies measuring some 5.60m east–west by 3.70m north–south, cut between 0.10m and 0.65m deep, was recorded east of centre of the barrow. The disturbances (contexts, 486–91, 498–509, 512–23, 544, 553–56, 604–5, 643–4, 649–50, 656, 660–61, 665–9), generally filled with a loose, loamy chalk rubble, yielded six prehistoric potsherds broadly dating from the later Neolithic period to the early Bronze Age (*see* p 54), seventeen worked flints, including a possible burin (Fig 28, FN 323,context 490), six eroded fragments of human bone (neonate or juvenile bones, *see* p 61), thirty-seven neonate pig bones, seven neonate sheep bones, two foetal cattle bones (*see* p 67) and a surprising number of wild animal bones, including badger, rabbit, vole, mole, shrew, mouse and amphibian (*see* p 68). The presence of a small amount of human bone in the fills of the interconnecting gullies and hollows, (probably the passages, galleries and nests of a rabbit warren and perhaps a badger sett) suggest that burrowing animals may have dislocated one or more burials or 'placed' deposits.

A second, less intense area of disturbance was identified in the western part of the barrow (contexts 406–09, 414–31, 434–35, 480–85, 551, 561 and 562). The burrow fills yielded two fragments of human bone, a number of animal bones and small number of worked flints, including an obliquely-pointed tool (Fig 28, FN 312g, context 417).

Animal disturbances were also identified between the ring-ditches in sector 2 (contexts 524–5), in the uppermost deposits of the primary ring-ditch in sector 4 (contexts 635, 735 and 740), between the ring-ditches in the same sector (context 631–2) and immediately west of the barrow (411), in sector 6 cutting ditch 413. These features provided no finds.

Features outside the barrow (Fig 8)

A group of undated features was located outside the monument footprint.

Pl 15. Eastling Down: rabbit burrows under excavation, looking south-west. Scales 0.5m and 1m.

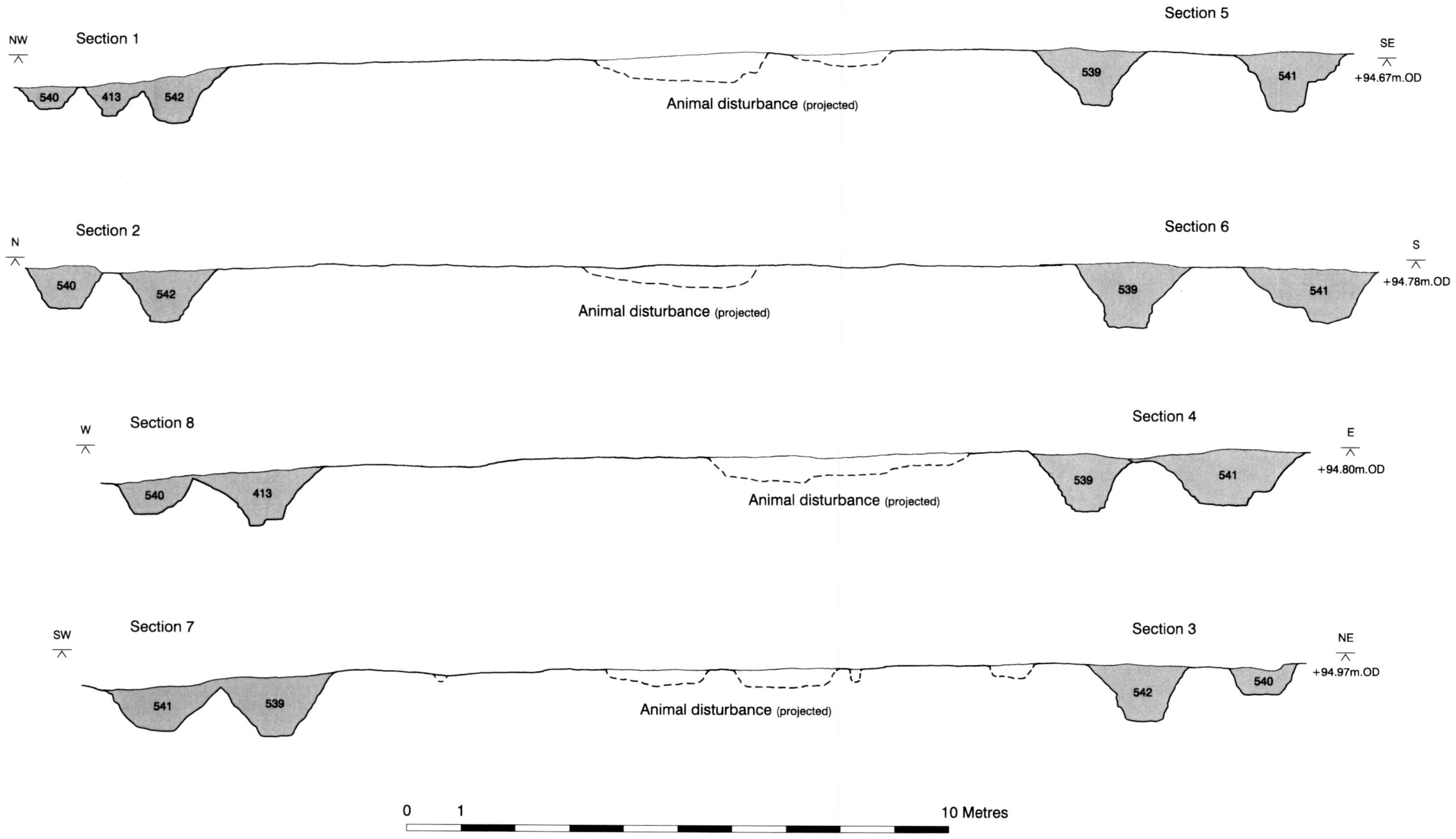

Fig 25. Eastling Down: barrow profiles. Scale 1:100.

Possible 'tree-throws'

A large, irregular, shallow disturbance in the chalk measuring some 4.50m east–west by 3.00m north–south, with a maximum depth of 0.20m (451, 455 and 461), was located at the southern end of the excavated area. The feature, filled with mid-brown chalk-loam with frequent chalk lumps (contexts 460, 454 and 450) comprised three interconnected, lobed, bowl-shaped depressions with an uneven base. The fills provided no datable finds and appeared to comprise a discoloured, redeposited natural. The feature may have been formed by a substantial tree that had been uprooted by natural processes.

A second possible 'tree-throw' (473) was located 7m to the north of the first, and two others (443 and 441) were identified south-west and west of the barrow. All three features contained similar characteristics and fills to feature 461 and have also been interpreted as disturbances to the natural chalk caused by uprooted trees.

Modern feature

A machine-cut pit (401) 0.80m wide, 1.35m long and 1.05m deep was located to the north of the barrow. The pit, aligned north–south and extending beyond the excavated area, contained modern debris, including corrugated tin and may have been a geo-technical test pit cut to provide technical data for road construction.

Discussion of the excavated evidence

The remains of approximately nine Bronze Age burials and five 'placed' deposits containing human bone were recovered from the surviving remnants of the Eastling Down barrow. If the fragments of human bone recovered from the fill of animal burrows beneath the footprint of the mound is included in the accounting (two primary burials - both children), then burials associated with the barrow can be increased to at least eleven. Other fragments of human bone recovered from the ditch fills may further increase the sum of finds and placed deposits recovered from the monument to nineteen. This represents a remarkable number of interments for a funerary monument in Kent and constitutes one of a number of significant aspects for an otherwise modest-sized tumulus in an unremarkable location.

It is not just the number of burials that is surprising, but the chronological range of interments and 'placed deposits', arguably spanning at least two millennia. Alongside the three main phases of construction activity that have been identified, continuity of use (with wide gaps) is indicated by dated burials. These suggest that, following on from primary mound construction, the first burial (533, p 25) occurred at the very end of the Neolithic period, with a second group of interments (cremation 433 and burials 439, 729 and 537, pp 30–4) taking place in the early Bronze Age and a third group (687, 439, pp 29–30 and 479, p 35) in the middle Bronze Age. A final burial (cremation 495, p 36) took place in the late Bronze or early Iron Age, with a possible votive offering (698) of a horse interred on the site in the late Iron Age (*see* p 37). This clearly suggests that the mound was not only visible in the landscape throughout the entire period, but held a special significance for those occupying the land, and was used albeit intermittently, for the burial of their dead and particularly, but not exclusively, for the burial of children.

It has been assumed that the first monument was a burial mound surrounded by a ring-ditch. This may not have been so, and a case for a 'flat' enclosure, defined by the primary ring-ditch, has been made above (p 16). Evidence for an earlier 'open' monument is slim, and relates solely to the presence of earlier cultural material in the primary and later ditches. The case for a primary mound and not an 'open' enclosure is based on a number of factors. Firstly, a lack of evidence for a formal causeway interrupting the ring-ditch. Secondly, there were no recognisable features within the enclosure, other than animal disturbances, to suggest that ritual activities may have taken place there ('placed' deposits, for example) and thirdly, the primary ditch fills appear to have been filled from the interior of the enclosure and not from an external bank, as would perhaps have been the case had the enclosure been 'open'. The lack of any surviving intact soils over natural chalk makes a definitive interpretation difficult, but given the combination of factors, then the early cultural material may have been an accidental or deliberate inclusion during mound construction, and the presence of the material in primary and later ditch fills therefore a by-product of mound erosion. On balance then, it is likely that the first monument was a round barrow and not an 'open' enclosure.

That a mound accompanied later phases of the monument is certain, as it remained a significant landmark into the Roman period and beyond and would not have been attractive to rabbits and badgers in the more recent past. Similarly, although no trace of mound deposits survived the plough, a slightly raised mound of truncated natural chalk was identiable in 1977 and subsequently. This suggests that a long history of ploughing had taken place lowering the surrounding level of natural chalk and leaving a slightly less eroded plateau of chalk which had been protected for centuries by a covering mound (see Ashbee and Dunning 1960, fig 19). This phenomenon has been observed on a number of other barrow sites in east Kent (eg at St Margaret's at Cliffe; Parfitt and Corke 2005).

Although it has not been possible to date the construction of the first mound with any accuracy, the earliest-dated burial (533) found cutting the infilled primary ring-ditch provides a *terminus ante quem* date for the commencement of Phase 2 activities of 2265/2220–1910 cal BC (*see* p 25 and Table 2). Given that the not insubstantial ring-ditch for the first mound had been filled with eroded soils and chalk from a mound that may have slumped or 'migrated to the south (and generally) over time, one must provide for sufficient duration for this to have happened before Grave 533 was cut. On this basis it is tentatively suggested that the first mound was constructed in the Chalcolithic or late Neolithic/early Bronze Age period, perhaps around 2,200 BC.

Pl 16. Eastling Down: general view following excavation, looking north-west.

Overall, the barrow excavation yielded a significant quantity of worked flint (1,735 pieces), pottery (350 potsherds) and animal bones (695 fragments), most deriving from the ring-ditches. A large proportion of this material was residual, pre-dating construction of the primary mound. Included in the assemblage was burnt flint and daub from fired structures. Most of this material was recovered from the primary ring-ditch, and slightly less from the later ditches.

There are two possible explanations for the quantity of residual material. The first mound may have been constructed on or very near a settlement site (the small number of undated post-holes located south of the mound, may be evidence for nearby settlement activity, *see* p 37), with residual occupation debris accidentally incorporated into the mound, to gradually erode-out of the mound into the primary and later ditches. Alternatively, it is possible that residual 'midden' may have been imported to the site, perhaps from a more distant settlement (probably that belonging to the mound builders) and deliberately included in the mound structure as part of a ritual process. A modest proportion of the finds assemblage from the base of the ditches and from burials is likely to have been a product of funerary ritual. This is perhaps most apparent in the ceramic assemblage with near complete pots from Grave 439 and Cremation 433 and a small number of potsherds that may have been residue from feasting or other burials lost to erosion (*see* p 54).

There was no trace of a primary inhumation or cremation burial or burials associated with the first monument. Animal burrows were extensive however and human bones were recovered from burrow fills, tentatively suggesting the remains of two children may have formed part of a badly disturbed, primary interment. However, the centre of the barrow was sufficiently clear of disturbance to suggest that unless graves had been totally truncated by ploughing, primary burials may not have been located in that position but east of centre, where disturbance by burrowing was most intense.

The footprint of the primary mound was some 165 square metres in extent, surrounded by a ditch at least 2m wide and 1m deep cut with steep, near vertical sides and a flat base, on average 0.50m wide. The cutting of the ditch, (52m long) would have produced approximately 78 cubic metres of spoil to form the mound. Allowing for perhaps 40 per cent bulking and a hemispherical shape for a mound extending to the inner lip of the ditch, the chalk mound may have been approximately 1.2m high at the centre. Given that the mound contained quantities of residual finds from soils garnered from elsewhere, one might suppose that the mound may have been built to a greater height. The presence of a high primary mound might also explain why the mound deposits began to erode and slump into the surrounding ditch, to the extent that 'migrating' mound deposits may have eventually filled the ditch, requiring the cutting of an entirely new external ring-ditch in Phase 2.

All of the excavated interments were south of the mound. Although other burials may have been interred elsewhere in the mound and subsequently lost to erosion, surviving evidence suggests that the second-phase ditch was cut to enclose a greater area of ground south of the mound, perhaps as a purposely-formed annexe for new burials. This modification perhaps occurred in the period 2265/2220–1910 cal BC when Grave 533 was cut. Other burials perhaps followed (433, 439 and 729) over the period 1964–1636 cal BC (*see* pp 30–4 and Table 2).

Sometime after this, perhaps before the date of burial 687 (1737–1531 cal BC; lab no UBA20689, Table 2), the final phase ditch was cut south of the mound, with at least three burials (687, 439 and 479) taking place thereafter (including a double burial described above pp 30–2). These burials together with 'placed deposits' in the ditch terminals and in the pits north of the mound all appear to date between 1737 and 1120 cal BC.

Terrestrial snail shells recovered from a 'placed' deposit in the terminal of the Phase 3 ditch (683) and from a column sample taken from Section 6 (Fig 14), indicated that the surrounding landscape was of woodland and that, although the vicinity of the mound may have been 'open' there were times when the barrow may have also been covered with vegetation (below, p 72).

A final burial or 'placed' deposit was interred in the southern annexe (495) in *c* 920–795 cal BC.

The burials constitute an interesting collection of at least eight young children, an adult inhumation and two adult cremations. The most curious was the double burial in Grave 439, where a burial lying at the base of the grave (SK 623) was dated much later than a second burial (SK 566) interred in grave fill above it. Lying on the base of the grave was a near complete Food Vessel that is more likely to have accompanied the second, earlier-dated burial than the underlying interment. The circumstances that led to such a curious inversion of burials and pot are discussed above (pp 50–2), but the possibility that the earlier burial (a neonate or foetus) may have been 'stored' in the vessel and kept in a domestic household or a 'shrine' as a sacred object and eventually buried with SK 623 is a speculative but interesting interpretation of the evidence. The sequence of events that led to the Food Vessel being broken on the floor of the grave, alongside the burial, with the foetus buried in grave backfill, would suggest the enactment of some form of complex graveside ritual.

The other burial worthy of special note, is SK 692 in Grave 687. This was again a child, but unusually not buried in a crouched position. All other burials, even the foetus and the adult male in a coffin (the only burial for which a sex was confirmed) were crouched and buried on their right sides, heads to the west, facing south, south-west or south-east. SK 692 was buried on its back, with lower and upper limbs tightly flexed, head to the west, facing north-east (below, p 30). It has been suggested that the child may have died in a fire, or that *rigor mortis* had taken place before the body was formally laid out for burial. The burial has been dated to the middle Bronze Age and may be linked chronologically with graves 479 and 439 that are somewhat later, but follow a pattern of interment adopted by earlier burials (graves 533, 537 and 729). Formal and perhaps traditional burial practice is witnessed by all burials except SK 692. Clearly this suggests that the burial of SK 692 is for reasons unknown to us, both unusual and perhaps special, although, as has been suggested below (p 61), the position of the head may merely indicate that the burial was female. If all other burials were male (including cremation 433), then this too indicates that the barrow was of greater significance to the local rural community than its size and position suggest.

The two cremation burials, one of the earliest burials (433) and the latest (495), are of interest. The first was buried in an inverted tripartite collared urn (p 54, Fig 32, No 19) within a small pit, tightly cut to fit the urn, in a group of three burials dated to the early Bronze Age. The pot contained 1346g of cremated bone and a pair of unburnt bone tweezers (*see* pp 58–9). There was sufficient evidence from the cremated bone to suggest that the burial was that of an adult male. The presence of the bone tweezers, believed to be a male item, supports the identification.

Wood ash from the burial, presumably from the funerary pyre, included oak and hawthorn or apple. Terrestrial snail shells were of shade-loving species, suggesting that at least part of the mound may have been overgrown with vegetation at this time.

The second cremation (495), a much later burial, perhaps of the late Bronze or early Iron Age, was buried in a pit close to a group of earlier burials, near the eastern terminal of the southern Phase 3 ditch. There appeared to have been no formal container, as the cremated bone, though concentrated in the base of the pit, was also mixed with overlying fills, the whole capped by a sealing deposit of clay. Only 271g of cremated bone was present, together with 88g of carbonised wood. The cremated bone (of an adult male) constituted but a fraction (perhaps 10 per cent) of the quantity and weight of an average cremation, whilst the amount of carbonised wood was exceptionally large. This suggested that the interment was either a burial where only token or carelessly collected remains from the funerary pyre were buried or a 'placed' deposit of pyre debris. In this case, larger bones from the pyre may have been collected for burial elsewhere.

The fuel ash recovered with the cremated bone was of hawthorn or apple; snail shells were of shade-loving species, again suggesting that at least part of the mound supported a mantle of vegetation.

The presence of up to five 'placed' deposits is an unusual feature of the Eastling Down barrow. At least two of the deposits (680 and 724), the first located at the base of the primary ditch and the second recovered from the eastern terminal of the Phase 3 ditch, contained carbonised wood, perhaps pyre debris, mixed with small quantities of cremated and unburnt human bone. The first provided identifications of sloe and oak and the second hawthorn or apple as possible fuel ash, whilst 'flot' from both deposits yielded terrestrial snail shells that indicate a mound shaded by vegetation. The positioning of two placed deposits, one in each terminal of the third-phase ditch and the burial of fragments of unburnt and somewhat eroded human bone in comparatively large pits on the north side of the mound appear to represent ritual acts whose significance can now only be guessed at.

If the interpretation of horse bones (context 698) as a votive offering on the floor of a large pit or small sunken building (493) is correct, then final ritual use of the monument may have taken place in the period 364–201 cal BC. A similar dated burial, but of a complete horse, was found within a contemporary cemetery at Mill Hill, Deal (Parfitt 1995a, 146–7)

The mound remained visible well into the Roman period and appears to have been used as a landmark for the laying of a Roman estate boundary defined by a substantial ditch and perhaps a bank. Cropmarks identified by aerial photographs to the north and north-east of the present site (Fig 2) may be for contemporary cultivated fields, whilst a nearby lane, set parallel to the boundary, perhaps preserves the line of a Roman road which may have also formed an estate boundary. Terrestrial snails from a column sample taken through the ditch fills clearly indicated that a radical change in vegetation took place in the Roman period to one of 'open' countryside dominated by grassland (*see* pp 71–2). The combined evidence suggests a managed landscape with well defined boundaries, routeways and a mix of pasture and arable farming.

The upper loam fills of the latest ring-ditch and the estate boundary contained pottery dating into the early medieval period. Terrestrial snails recovered from the same deposits were of medieval and modern origin, confirming that both features were 'open' and visible into at least the medieval period. A remnant of the burial mound and perhaps the bank associated with the boundary survived into more recent times, with the monument still visible in the growing crop and as a negative earthwork until the by-pass was built.

The finds

The flint assemblage

Tania Wilson

Methodology

All flintwork recovered from the barrow was recorded and catalogued, each piece being measured and weighed and its dimensions measured according to accepted standards (Saville 1980, 16). The record includes the types of raw material used, the types of artefacts present and their completeness and condition. In addition, the analysis of scar patterns, striking platforms and hinge terminations was undertaken in order to ascertain flintworking techniques.

The assemblage

Ninety-seven per cent of the flintwork came from stratified contexts associated with or immediately adjacent to the barrow, approximately 50 per cent being recovered from the ring-ditches and 20 per cent from the Iron Age ditch which intersected them. The remainder were fairly evenly distributed throughout other features, with only a small number occurring within burials and most of these within the backfill of burial 729 (p 32). Excepting the latter, none of the flintwork was considered to have been deliberately buried as grave goods or directly associated with burials. Six kilograms of burnt, unmodified flint, probably 'pot-boilers', was also recovered from ditch fills.

Excluding the unmodified burnt flint, the flint assemblage comprised a total of 1,735 pieces. These have been summarised by type in Table 3. Approximately 45 per cent of the assemblage was incomplete or had suffered post-depositional damage and about 2 per cent of the collection was burnt. The majority of the material bore heavy white patination, with several calcium carbonate encrusted pieces also occurring. The heavy patination made determination of the types of flint difficult but where identification was possible, three main types were observed: a black semi-translucent flint with a buff cortex, a pale brown-grey semi-translucent flint with a buff cortex and glauconitic (Bullhead) flint, also with a buff cortex.

The assemblage was divided into two groups, debitage (including blades), and implements. The first group made up 93.5 per cent of the total.

Identification	Quantity
Blades	112
Chips	5
Chunks	12
Cores and struck lumps	41
Flakes	1450
Hammerstones and hammerstone fragments	3
Retouched pieces	112

Table 3. Eastling Down: flint artefacts.

Debitage

A total of 1,450 pieces definable as debitage and weighing 19kg was recovered. The debitage comprised flakes and blade-like flakes, along with a small number of core trimming, core rejuvenation flakes and other knapping debris in the form of sixteen chips (the term 'chip' is used here to describe complete flakes of 15mm or less in length). The striking platforms of the flakes, including blade-like flakes and blades (see below), were generally plain, with only thirty-four flakes and three blades with dihedral/facetted butts. Fifty-seven per cent of the flakes were complete (see Table 4 for the dimension summary). Altogether, 158 blade-like flakes (11 per cent of the debitage) are present, 44 per cent of which were complete.

	0–9mm	10–19mm	20–29mm	30–39mm	40–49mm	50–59mm	60–69mm	>70mm
Length	0	2	11	26	27	18	10	6
Breadth	0	6	27	31	22	9	4	1

Table 4. Eastling Down: complete flint lakes and chips.

	Class A	Class B	Class C	Fragment	Struck nodule/lump
Quantity	14	6	20	2	0
Total weight	2152	667	2602	82	0
Average weight	154	111	130	41	0

Table 5. Eastling Down: flint cores by class.

Cores

Forty-three cores (including the hammerstone, see below) were present, forming 2.5 per cent of the flintwork assemblage. They were divided into five types: Class A (single platform), Class B (two platforms), Class C (three or more platforms), struck nodules, lumps and fragments (see Table 5 for quantities and weights of the different core types). The cores included keeled-edged, and single-, two- and multiple-platform core types, along with single examples of the sub-discoidal type, a possibly failed Levallois type and a core worked from opposite ends. Several cores appeared to be of unskilled workmanship. The maximum dimensions of complete cores ranged from 38mm to 137mm, the average being 66mm. Several cores were still covered with large areas of cortex and one example retained 50 per cent. With the exception of one particularly small unstratified example (Fig 26, FN 199), none had been thoroughly worked. Selection of both nodules and naturally shattered lumps for use as cores was indicated.

Fourteen of the cores (*c* 33 per cent) were Class A (single-platformed), six (*c* 14 per cent) were Class B (bi-polar or two platforms) and twenty (*c* 48 per cent) of Class C (three or more platforms). A wide range of core forms were represented, from globular types (eg Fig 26, FN 357, context 546) to flatter examples, with other cores including the unstratified sub-discoidal example (Fig 26, FN 583) and another unstratified find of possible Levallois type (Fig 26, FN 26b). Of the Class B bi-polar type, one had been rotated through 90° to continue flaking, and another (Fig 26, FN 356, context 546) had blade-like removals detached from opposing ends. One complete hammerstone (Fig 26, FN 1219, context 538) weighing 85g and probably re-used as a core was also recovered, as were two flakes which had probably been detached from other hammerstones. It is noteworthy that no randomly struck nodules were represented within the assemblage, suggesting that systematic flintworking more typical of the Mesolithic or Neolithic was represented, rather than the often *ad hoc*, casual flintworking of the Bronze Age (Edmonds 1995).

Blades

Overall, 112 blades were collected, 23 per cent of which (twenty-six pieces) were complete. Fourteen (12.5 per cent) were possibly serrated, but it was not clear whether the serration was deliberately produced or resulted from utilisation damage. Only one of the blades was silica-glossed (considered to result from cereal harvesting, see Champion *et al* 1992, 127).

Implements

The total of 112 retouched pieces (here defined as implements), comprised a broad range of types (see Table 6) and represented 6.5 per cent of the flintwork assemblage as a whole.

Type	Quantity
Arrowhead	3
Axe fragments, ground and polished	4
Bifacial retouched pieces	4
Fabricator	1
Flaked flake	2
Retouched flakes/blades	14
Knife	1
Laurel leaf	1
Miscellanious retouched pieces	2
Notch	3
Plane	1
Points	12
Rod	2
Scraper	60
Waisted core tool	2

Table 6. Eastling Barrow: retouched flint pieces.

Scrapers were the most common implements, the total of sixty representing 53.5 per cent of the retouched assemblage. The predominance of scrapers was of chronological significance in suggesting that a large part of the flintwork assemblage derived from the later Neolithic 'scraper-dominated industries' (Holden and Bradley 1975, 85–103), although earlier Neolithic elements also appear to have been present within the assemblage (see 'Chronology' below).

Scrapers

Forty-one scrapers (68 per cent of the retouched pieces) were complete, the scrapers fairly evenly split in terms of type between end-retouched and end-and-side retouched types; the overall ratio being 57:43 in favour of the former.

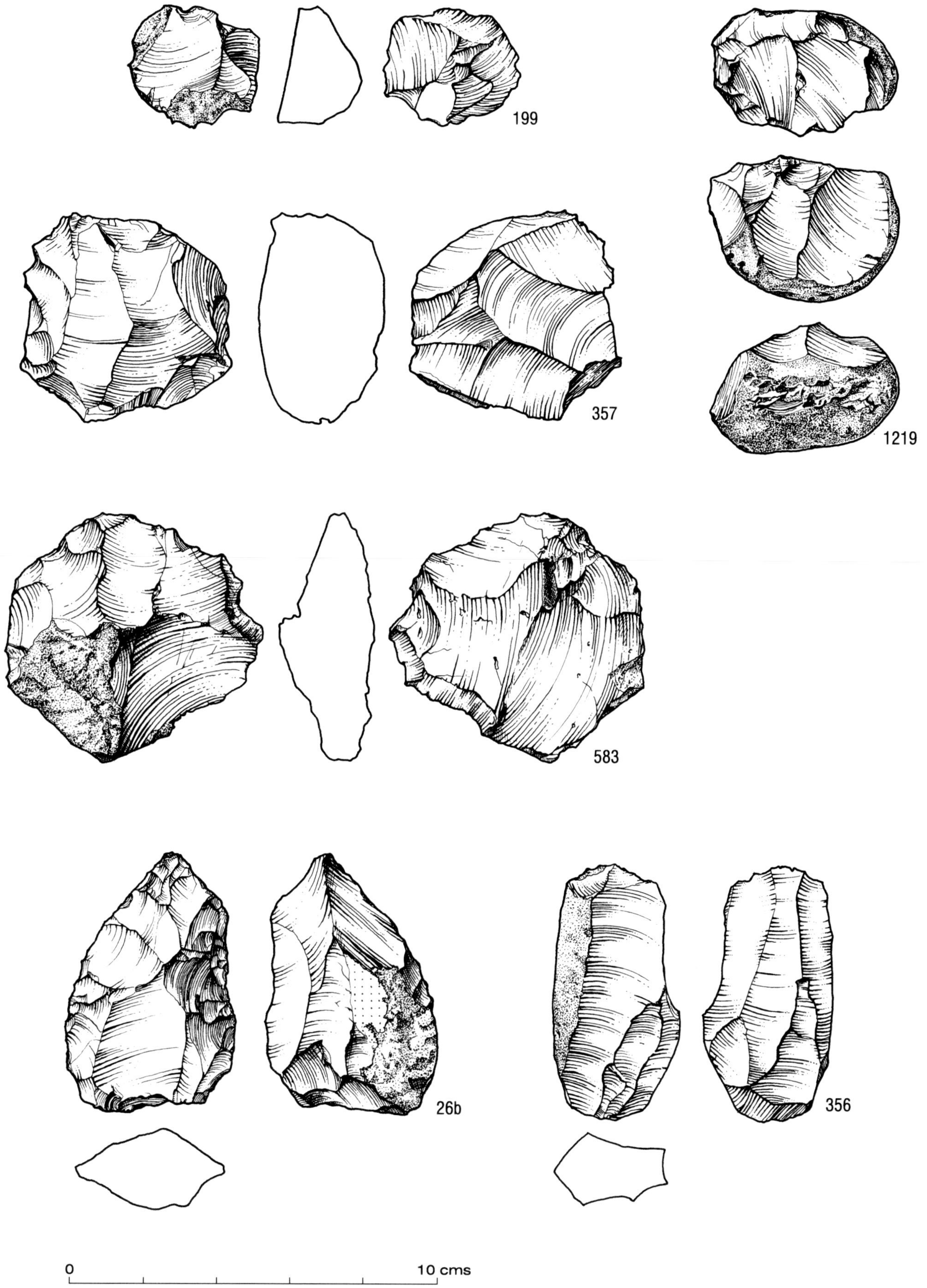

Fig 26. Eastling Down: cores and hammerstones. Scale 2:3.

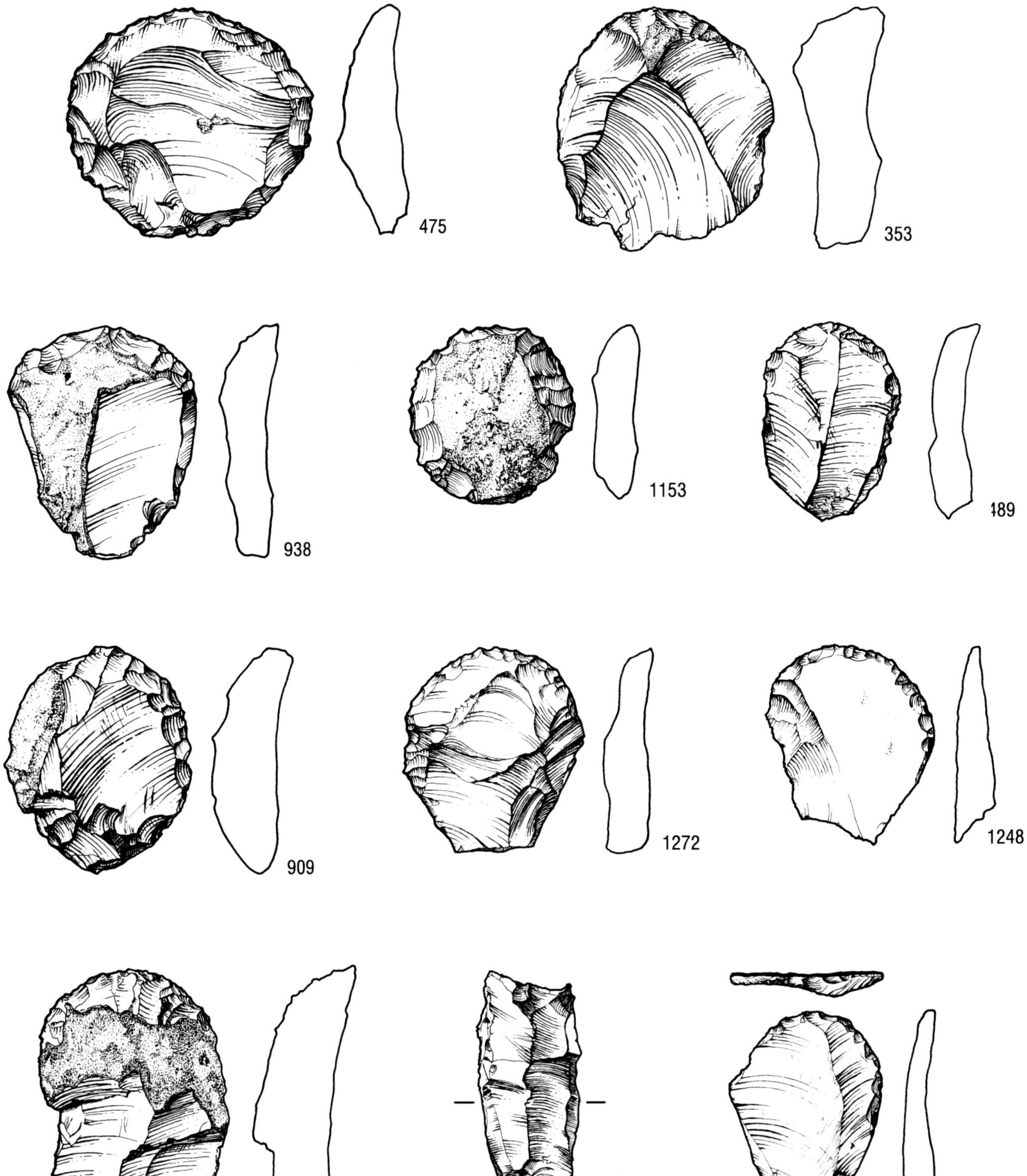

Fig 27. Eastling Down: scrapers. Scale 2:3.

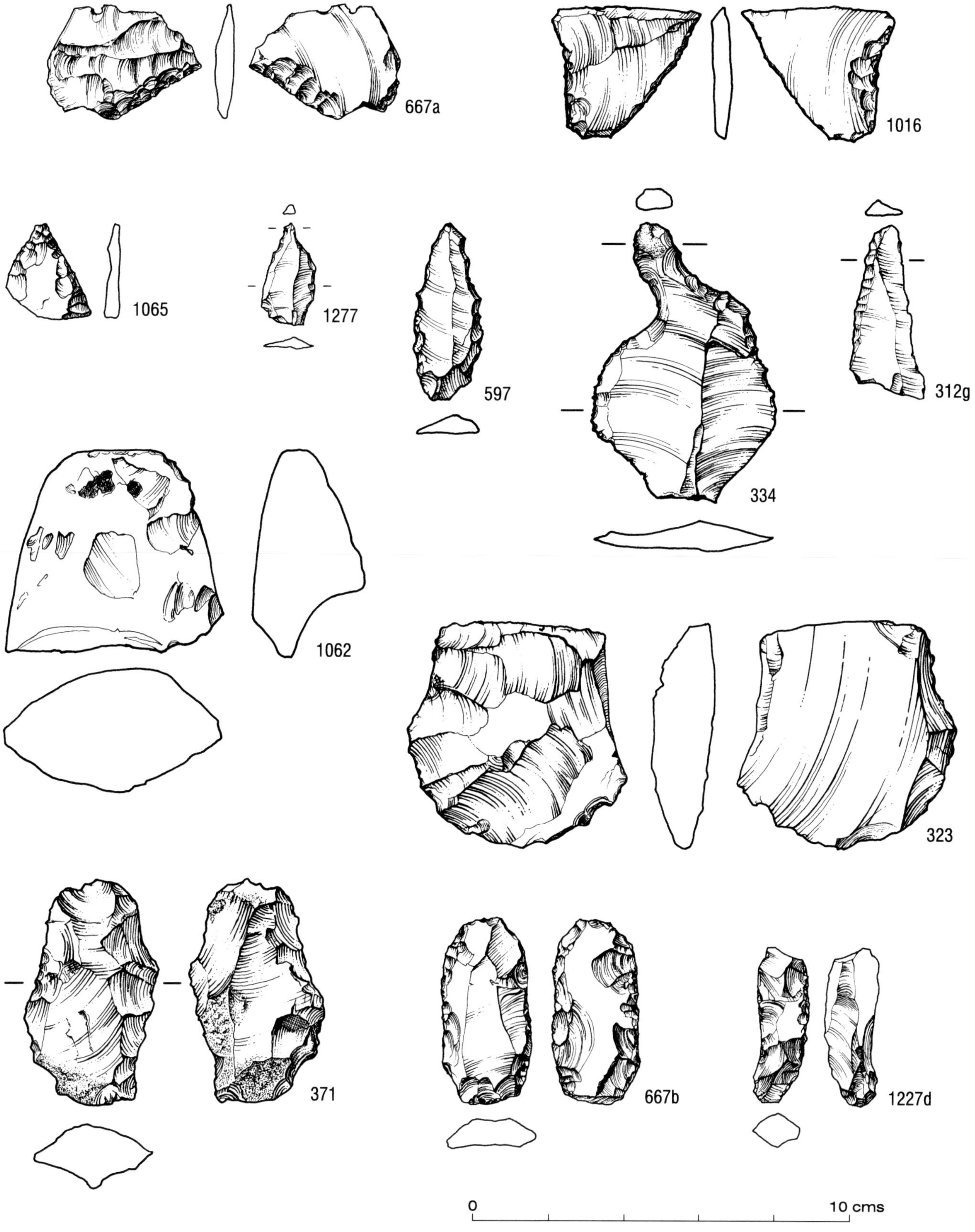

Fig 28. Eastling Down: retouched pieces. Scale 2:3.

	0–9mm	10–19mm	20–29mm	30–39mm	40–49mm	50–59mm	60–69mm	>70mm
Length	0	0	0	2	34	34	17	13
Breadth	0	0	8	19	49	19	5	0
Thickness	17	73	10	0	0	0	0	0

Table 7. Eastling Down: complete flint scrapers.

Of the end-and-side types, a preference was shown for end-and-side retouched scrapers with retouch on one side. A wide selection of shapes and sizes were represented (see Fig 27), with the average length, breadth and thickness being 56mm, 44mm and 13mm respectively (see Table 7). In addition, two scrapers displayed evidence for abrupt retouch at the distal end of large blades (see Fig 27, FN 479, context 672). Two concave scrapers were also represented, one of which (Fig 27, FN 1252a, context 620) had a slightly concave area of retouch at the distal end of a blade-like flake. An end retouched scraper (Fig 27, FN 1225, context 545) of particular note had been ground smooth at the distal end.

Arrowheads

Three possible transverse arrowheads (Fig 28, FN 667a, context 560; FN 1016, context 737; FN 1065, context 675) were recovered, two of which were incomplete. The first example (FN 667a), which was incomplete and appeared to be unfinished, had a single straight edge formed by shallow bifacial flaking and may have snapped during manufacture. The second (FN 1065) appeared to be the tip of an oblique arrowhead with retouch restricted to one surface only. The third example (FN 1016) was a complete chisel arrowhead with bifacial flaking along one side.

Points

A total of twelve pieces within the implement group were classifiable as points, representing a broad range of forms varying from delicate types (eg Fig 28, FN 1277, context 712) with retouch at the distal end, to more extensively worked pieces (eg Fig 28, FN 597, context 538). One piece (Fig 28, FN 334, context 538) had an elongated point formed by two concave areas of retouch. Another, classified as an obliquely blunted point (Fig 28, FN 312g, context 417), had an abrupt retouch on the left-hand side at the distal end. At the other end of the range was a heavier example (FN 513, context 706, not illustrated), made using a naturally shattered lump with the point formed by bifacial flaking.

Polished axe

A large fragment from a ground and polished axe (Fig 28, FN 1062, context 546) represented the butt end of an axe with flattened sides. It was unclear whether three flakes bearing similarly ground and polished areas on their dorsal surfaces were detached from the same axe or whether further axes were represented.

Other tools

Also recovered were four miscellaneous bi-facially retouched pieces varying in style from a flat example (Fig 28, FN 323, context 490), possibly part of a burin (a flake or blade modified into a chisel-like implement), to a fragment of a flat nodule which had been flaked around three quarters of its circumference. Other bifacially retouched pieces included a fabricator (a tool of unknown purpose) and two implements classified as rods, these being long, thin dihedral flakes or blades (see above). One example of a rod (Fig 28, FN 667b, context 560) had been formed on a blade retouched along both sides; the other (Fig 28, FN 371, context 547) was formed on an elongated fragment with a thick section. The possible fabricator (Fig 28, FN 1227d, context 546) had features in common with the second rod but was much more slender. The absence of a tip on the fabricator meant that there was no evidence of wear.

Two flakes from which further flakes had been struck were also recovered. One was a shattered fragment, the second a flat piece with flakes detached from both the dorsal and the ventral surfaces. Another piece with bifacial retouch was evident in a possible knife fragment (Fig 29, FN 417a, context 620). An incomplete laurel leaf, possibly an arrowhead, (Fig 29, FN 367, context 547) was retouched over approximately half of each surface, with about a quarter of one surface with its cortex remaining having similarly been retouched.

The implement assemblage also included three possibly deliberately notched flakes, one with a notch formed about half way along the right-hand side, one with a notch on the distal end and one with two notches on the left-hand side. The notches on these pieces were irregular, however, and may have resulted from later damage. Two waisted core tools (Fig 29, FN 416j, context 670 and FN 855, context 526) were made using naturally shattered lumps, with both having retouch concentrated to form the 'waist'. Also present was a plane (Fig 29, FN 596g, context 538) formed on a flake with the cortex remaining at the distal edge and a small number of miscellaneous retouched pieces consisting largely of limited areas of retouch on both flakes and blades.

Technology

The Eastling Down barrow located on the Upper Chalk dip slopes, was close to a ready source of raw material. Where the cortex on the flintwork from the barrow can be observed, it is generally hard and weathered, implying that the selected raw material was exposed as nodules on the surface in the

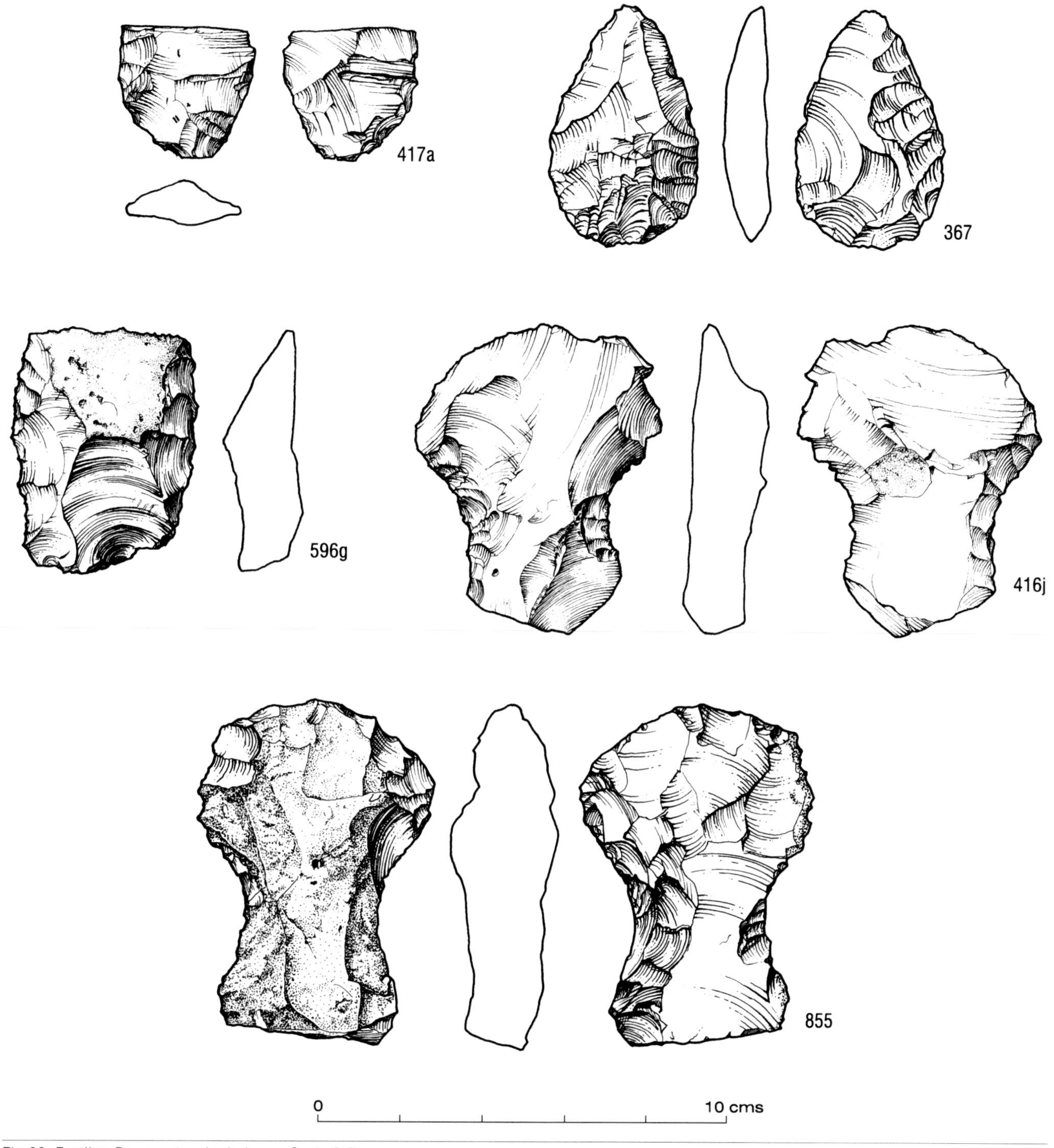

Fig 29. Eastling Down: retouched pieces. Scale 2:3.

vicinity of the site. In addition, naturally frost-shattered nodules, presumably also nearby surface finds, were selected for use.

Both flake and blade production clearly took place on or near the site, with hard hammer percussion being used throughout. However the production of blades appears to have been relatively small scale, with only 112 blades (6.5 per cent of the total assemblage) and one core with blade removals being recovered. In contrast, blade-like flakes are well represented, making up 83.5 per cent of the total assemblage.

The cores from which the flakes and blades derived are divisible into a single platform type and multiple platform types. In general, none had worked beyond the point of usefulness and several retain areas of cortex and, in the case of the single platform type, are relatively sparsely flaked These factors suggest an uneconomical approach to flintworking which probably reflects an abundance of raw material.

Some of the material displays characteristics consistent with pre-determined knapping strategies. For example, a small number of pieces with platform abrasion and dihedral or faceted striking platforms and some displaying evidence of core trimming and rejuvenation suggest that care was taken to achieve a desired product. Furthermore, the flat core and the Levallois-type core are considered to result from specialised tool production, the latter probably being used to create blanks for the production of transverse arrowheads (Gardiner 1987, 27).

In contrast to assemblages from the other Kentish sites, for example at Monkton (Wilson 2008), the present barrow assemblage produced a substantially greater proportion of retouched pieces definable as implements, with scrapers representing the dominate type, but with a wide diversity of other types also being present. In general, the scrapers had been formed on blanks which were almost as wide as they are long, but there is no common blank type for the other implements and in some examples the flintworkers simply took advantage of fortuitously-shaped fragments. Due to the amount of patination, it is not possible to determine if specific types of raw material were selected for certain implement types.

Chronology

Distinctive forms such as the waisted core tools, the planes, the laurel leaf, the transverse arrowheads and the polished axe fragments suggest a Neolithic date for the assemblage as a whole. Further chronological refinement is provided by the large numbers of blades, blade-like flakes and end-on-blade scrapers. These, in association with the above forms, suggest that an early to middle Neolithic element was dominant (Healey 1988, 46), although in this respect the presence of an obliquely blunted point is problematic, such pieces being conventionally attributed to the Mesolithic (blades and blade-like flakes may similarly be attributable to that period). As previously discussed, the high percentage of scrapers points however to a probable later Neolithic date for a large proportion of the assemblage (Holden and Bradley 1975, 85–105) and it is therefore likely that the obliquely blunted point's resemblance to an earlier form is coincidental. A less likely interpretation is that part of the assemblage dates to the late Mesolithic/early Neolithic period.

On balance then, the great majority of flintwork recovered from the barrow is likely to date from the middle to the late Neolithic, although little can be considered to be late enough to be contemporary with the use of the site for ritual burial and must be considered to be residue from earlier settlement activity. Such an interpretation is supported by the high incidence of breakage and post-depositional damage within the assemblage.

Approximately 6.5 per cent of the struck flints at the barrow are retouched and definable as implements, in contrast to sites such as Bury Hill and Offham, both in Sussex, where such pieces form 1.3 per cent and 0.3 per cent of the assemblages respectively (Tucker 1986, 39), and Area 9 at Monkton where retouched pieces form 0.7 per cent (Wilson 2008). The subject material therefore relates more closely to sites such as Hurst Fen, Suffolk, where implements form between 5 per cent and 6 per cent of the assemblage (Clark 1960, 214), Broome Heath, Norfolk where they form 5 per cent (Wainwright 1972, 66–7) and Street House at Loftus, Cleveland, where they form 7.5 per cent (Healey and Jelley 1988, 182–202). With regard to the latter two, similarities with the Eastling implement types and proportions are also apparent, with scrapers comprising the dominant tool type and polished axes, laurel leaves, transverse arrowheads, notched and serrated flakes being represented in either one or both.

Overall, the evidence suggests that, with the possible exception of material within the fill of Grave 729 and the fills of other burials associated with the barrow, most or all of the barrow's flintwork assemblage resulted from domestic/industrial activity associated with a Neolithic settlement situated on or near the barrow site and probably predates the construction of the barrow. It is also possible that small-scale flintworking had previously taken place on or near the site as part of early and middle Neolithic occupation activity. Similar activity during the late Mesolithic/Neolithic cannot be precluded.

The pottery

Alex Gibson

Including a semi-intact inverted tri-partite Collared Urn (burial 433), a total of 350 potsherds was recovered from the barrow. With the exception of the Collared Urn and twenty-five conjoining sherds from a pierced-lugged cup of Food Vessel type (Grave 439) most are considered to be residual, occurring within the ring-ditch fills, with smaller numbers in grave backfills and in the fills of a late ditch which intersects with the north-west part of the barrow. Nine sherds were recovered in association with worked flint and traces of eroded human bone in a disturbed area within the barrow interior. These sherds are also residual.

Only 62.5 per cent of the total ceramic assemblage is identifiable in terms of type and period, this representing a total of 202 sherds. These are divisible into four broad groups on the basis of their presumed date and postulated relationship with the barrow. The first group comprises middle and later Neolithic wares considered to pre-date the use of the barrow and/or to be contemporary with the raising of the first mound (Phase 1). The second group comprises late Neolithic and Bronze Age wares considered to be contemporary with construction of the barrow and perhaps a rebuilding of the barrow (Phases 1 and 2). The third group comprises later Bronze Age wares associated with a later rebuilding of the barrow and a number of inhumation and cremation burials (Phase 3). The fourth group comprises prehistoric and Roman wares thought to post-date the use of the barrow and probably introduced onto the site as a result of manuring. The groups are further divisible into sub-groups on the basis of type to provide the following (the percentage of each type relative to the identifiable sherds as a whole is also provided):

1 Middle and later Neolithic wares thought to pre-date and/or to be contemporary with the first phase barrow (Phase 1)

a 33 sherds of Peterborough Ware (16.5 per cent)
b 3 sherds of Grooved Ware (1.5 per cent)

2 Late Neolithic and Bronze Age wares considered contemporary with two phases of barrow reconstruction (Phases 2 and 3)

a 22 sherds of Beaker (11 per cent)
b 27 sherds of Food Vessel, including 25 from same vessel (13.5 per cent). However, as the latter derive from a single vessel placed in a grave, a more meaningful percentage for this group is probably 1.5 per cent
c 10 sherds of Urn-type ware (5 per cent)
d 1 near-complete Collared Urn (0.5 per cent)
e 26 miscellaneous Neolithic and/or Bronze Age wares (13 per cent)

3 Later Bronze Age wares associated with the final phase barrow (Phase 3) and the latest-dated burials.

a 6 sherds of later Bronze Age (Deverel-Rimbury) type (3 per cent)

4 Prehistoric and Roman wares post-dating the use of the barrow associated with the uppermost fills of the latest ring-ditch and a Roman boundary ditch (Phases 4 and 5).

a 8? sherds of late Bronze/early Iron Age type (4 per cent)
b 1? sherd of mid to late Iron Age (0.5 per cent)
c 4 sherds dating generally from *c* 900 BC to *c* 50 BC (2 per cent)
d 2? sherds of pre-Conquest 'Belgic' ware (1 per cent)
e 56 sherds of first-/early second-century Roman wares (28 per cent)
f 2 sherds of mid second-/third-century Roman wares (1 per cent)

Using the above percentages of datable ceramic groups as rough indicators of occupation or other activity, it appears that a significant proportion (18 per cent) of that activity took place during the Neolithic. In the instance of the Eastling Down barrow, this period may conveniently be considered to predate burial 533 (2265 BC–2260 cal BC and 2220 BC–1910 cal BC; lab no 141269, Table 2), this representing an acceptable transitional Neolithic/Bronze Age date as well as a reliable *terminus ante quem* for the building of the first barrow (Phase 1). A further implication is that the Phase 2 barrow ditch was cut in the late Neolithic or early Bronze Age. However, only residual Peterborough and Grooved Ware was recovered from the ditch fills.

As discussed elsewhere in this report, the flintwork, burnt flint, burnt daub, animal bone and sea shells are suggestive of Neolithic domestic occupation activity associated with a settlement which pre-dated the barrow. Such activity is likely to be represented most strongly in the ceramic record by the 16.5 per cent of Peterborough Ware, dating from *c* 3500 BC – *c* 2900 BC and 1.5 per cent of Grooved Ware, dating from *c* 3000 BC to *c* 2400 BC.

Neolithic wares thought to pre-date and/or contemporary with the Phase 1 barrow

The Peterborough Ware recovered from Eastling Down barrow appears to be of predominantly or exclusively Mortlake style, thought to date in south-east Britain from *c* 3500 BC – *c* 2900 BC, as indicated by a 'T'-sectioned rim-sherd with oblique maggot decoration and potsherds displaying horizontal and dimpled bird-bone impressions (Fig 30, Nos 1 and 5). Indeed, twisted cord and bird-bone decorations predominate within this group, distinguishing it from the more simply decorated Ebbsfleet-style.

At the time of writing, there are some eleven Peterborough Ware find spots in Kent, with Ebbsfleet and Mortlake styles being the best represented and the later Fengate style occurring more rarely. All three styles occurred at Baston Manor (Philp 1973, 5–19) and Mortlake sherds have been documented from Caesar's Camp, Folkestone (Pitt-Rivers 1882, 429–65); Castle Hill (Gibson 1994); Chalk Hill, Ramsgate (Hearne *et al* 1995, 239–354) and St Richard's Road, Deal (Gibson 1995). In the vessels from these sites decoration is variously by bird-bone impression (Baston Manor), by twisted cord impression (St Richard's Road, Deal and Chalk Hill, Ramsgate) and by fingertip impression (Chalk Hill). Incised decorated wares recovered from the Baston Manor site are not paralleled at the Eastling Down site and are generally rare in the rest of Kent.

Only three residual sherds of Grooved Ware were recovered from the Eastling Down barrow, one being undecorated and two being decorated with diagonal broad grooves. One of the latter (Fig 30, No 7) has a concave bevelled rim with a slight internal ridge and all pieces have grog inclusions. The paucity of Grooved Ware on the site is typical for Kent, where it is recorded from only seven other find spots: East Malling/Snodland (Greenfield 1960, 58–72; Wainwright and Longworth 1971), St Richard's Road, Deal (Gibson 1995), Holywell Coombe (Gibson 1998, 265, 297), Lord of the Manor (Gibson 1993), the Lyonesse surface of Lydden Valley (Halliwell and Parfitt 1985, 39–43) and possibly Ringwould (Woodruff 1880, 43–6). The rarity of this ware in Kent is in contrast to Essex, where it occurs more commonly. Indeed, the Kentish material may be derived stylistically from Essex, as it is generally of the Clacton sub-style. Grooved Ware is thought to date from *c* 3000 BC to *c* 2400 BC. As the Clacton subtype is thought to date to the earlier part of the third millennium BC (Garwood 1999), the presence of the three residual Grooved Ware sherds on the Eastling Down site suggests an association with the postulated settlement predating the barrow, rather than with the barrow itself.

Late Neolithic and Bronze Age wares considered contemporary with the rebuilding of the barrow

Twenty-two sherds from a maximum of nineteen Beakers were recovered from the monument. Again, these sherds are predominantly small, residual and for the most part have no reconstructable profiles. Currently, the date-range for Beakers is thought to be *c* 2400 BC to *c* 1700 BC (Needham 1996, 121–40). One piece recovered from the Eastling Down barrow (Fig 31, No 12) is from a flared Beaker neck with well-defined horizontal grooving and may be from a stylistically-late form.

Unlike Beakers, Food Vessels, like Food Vessel Urns (see below) can be seen to have developed from the indigenous ceramic tradition, being directly related to Peterborough Ware (Gibson 1986, 35). Food Vessels date to the early and mid Bronze Age, this being consistent with the two radiocarbon dates (1955 BC–1670 BC and 1520 BC–1280 BC; Table 2) derived from Grave 439, which contained the sherds of a nearly complete Food Vessel (Fig 32, No 15). However, as the vessel was probably originally associated with the primary burial (*see* p 30), the earlier date is probably the more reliable indicator. The vessel has the form of an open-handled bowl and is similar to a miniature food vessel from Kingston Deverill, Wiltshire (Annable and Simpson 1964, no 552), although the latter has vertically-perforated lugs as opposed to the horizontally-perforated lugs of the Eastling Down example.

The Eastling Down Food Vessel has a rim diameter of 105mm, a base diameter of 65mm and a height of 80mm. The rim is simple and rounded and the base is flattened rather than flat, suggesting that the lower part of the pot had been pinched. Externally, there are two opposed and horizontally-perforated lugs, one of which had broken off, showing them to have been applied rather than raised. The body is otherwise plain, this contrasting with the Kingston Deverill example, the upper part of which is decorated with twisted cord impressions. Impressions from fingernails and a length of twisted cord had been left on the inner surface near the intact lug and almost certainly occurred accidentally whilst the pot was being built. The fabric is medium-hard and grog-filled. A sherd from another probable Food Vessel was recovered from the central area of animal disturbance (487) (Fig 32, No 16), which, as previously discussed, is thought to have contained fragments of two juvenile, perhaps primary, burials. This sherd is decorated on its outer surface with six circular stabbed impressions, each of 3mm diameter and is tempered with sparse fine white crushed calcined flint.

Ten sherds of general urn type were also recovered from the barrow. As they occurred on a sepulchral site it is reasonable to assume that they derived from disturbed urned cremations. The residual presence of the urn sherds in the Eastling Down barrow may therefore indicate that an unknown number of urned cremation burials may have been lost to erosion, animal disturbance and plough attrition. The presence of nine urn sherds within the fill of the primary ditch (four from a basal deposit 697, and five from uppermost fills, 538, 547 and 622) in Sectors 4 and 5 provides evidence to suggest that other burials may have existed or that feasting took place, and that final infilling of the barrow ditch may have been rapid. The radiocarbon date of the inhumation inserted in part in the backfilled area (Grave 533, skeleton 639) of 2265 BC–2260 BC and 2220 BC–1910 cal BC (Table 2) again provides a useful *terminus ante quem* for the redeposition of these sherds. All of the urn sherds are grog tempered and are too small to permit profile reconstruction, or, indeed, precise diagnosis. All but two are undecorated, one having traces of fingernail impressions on the outer surface (Fig 32, No 18) , another having a single incised line, also on the outer surface (Fig 32, No 17).

A single semi-intact tripartite Handled Collared Urn was recovered from burial 433 (Fig 32, No 19) (see above for a detailed description of this burial). Collared Urns, like Food Vessels and Food Vessel Urns, are thought to have derived from Peterborough Ware, particularly the Fengate sub-type. Collared Urns also retain the decorative tradition of Peterborough Ware in the form of incision, twisted, whipped and plaited cord and stabbed impressions. The combed impressions which also commonly occur are probably a borrowing from the Beaker decorative tradition.

Cremated bone from the burial provided a radiocarbon date of 1960–1750 cal BC. As a general ceramic type Collared Urns are considered to date from *c* 2000 BC to *c* 1500 BC, but the example recovered from the Eastling Down barrow is probably of the South-East style of Longworth's Secondary Series (Longworth 1984), which agrees well with the radiocarbon date. Indeed, its manner of decoration (ten lines of evenly-spaced horizontal twisted cord decoration on the collar and the marking of the boundary between the neck and the belly with a horizontal row of finger-tip impressions) is reminiscent of a Collared Urn found at Stodmarsh, Kent and classified by Longworth as of Primary Series (*ibid*, no 800). A vessel from Southend on Sea (*ibid*, 540) shares the collar concavity and narrow neck of the Eastling Down urn although its body is more barrel-shaped.

The Eastling Down Collared Urn has a concave collar of 80mm vertical width and a rim of 270mm diameter. Beneath the collar, the neck or 'cavetto zone' is narrow (vertical width 50mm) and has a diameter of 320mm. Atypically for Collared Urns, which occur across the British Isles, the Eastling Collared Urn has two handles which were applied horizontally. Each handle is decorated with two thin lines of horizontal twisted cord impressions. This represents a merging of the Collared and Handled Urn traditions.

Below the neck of the Eastling Down urn is a sharply-angled shoulder leading to a virtually straight-sided 'belly'. The boundary between the neck and the belly of the vessel is marked by a horizontal row of evenly-spaced subrectangular finger-tip impressions. The belly itself is undecorated. The vessel's fabric, which is grog-tempered, was up to 15mm thick. Although the base is missing, the reconstructed profile indicates a diameter of 90mm.

Later Bronze Age wares associated with the final phase barrow and associated burials (Phase 3) *Tim Allen*

The later radiocarbon dates for two of the burials in Phase 3 (Grave 439, inhumation 623, 1520 –1280 cal BC; Grave 479, inhumation 558, 1515–1120 cal BC; Table 2) indicate a date within the regional currency of the middle Bronze Age Deverel-Rimbury tradition. This tradition was probably a native development of a Europe-wide phenomenon called the Urnfield Culture. It is characterised by a change in burial style and the establishment of flat urnfields in the south of Britain, notable examples being Ardleigh, Essex (Erith and Longworth 1960) and at Kimpton, Hampshire (Dacre and Ellison 1981). In Britain, urnfield cemeteries are thought to occur from the thirteenth to the eighth century (Cunliffe 1975, 26–7). The adoption of this new burial style is not considered to have resulted from large-scale demographic change but from a process of acculturation as new ideas and ritual practices were assimilated by indigenous populations (Coles and Harding 1979, 367). Indeed, in many instances, and probably in the case of the Eastling Down barrow, long-established barrow sites containing crouched inhumations were subsequently used for urned and unurned cremations (eg pit 495) in what appears to have been a native modification of Urnfield-style burial practise. Elsewhere, such as Monkton in Thanet, Deverel-Rimbury burials took place in barrows (Barrows 9 and 10) apparently constructed for that purpose (Clark and Rady 2008, 43–4) and seemingly representing a hybridisation of a traditional and a new burial style. Similarly suggestive of hybridisation in terms of ceramic culture are the bucket-shaped, barrel-shaped and globular Deverel-Rimbury vessels which, as mentioned above, clearly developed from British late Neolithic/early Bronze Age prototypes, rather than from continental imports.

Although no potsherds contemporary with the later inhumations were recovered from their backfills, six thick-walled and coarsely-gritted sherds of probable Deverel-Rimbury type were recovered from the barrow's upper ditch fills and may have derived from vessels associated with disturbed burials of mid to late Bronze Age date.

Prehistoric and Romano-British wares post-dating the use of the barrow

The majority of sherds within this group are thinner walled and have manufacturing characteristics more typical of first millennium BC ceramic types, and therefore probably post-date the formal use of the barrow. One coarseware bodysherd from ditch 413 has surface rustication typical of eastern Kent's early Iron Age tradition (*c* 550 BC – *c* 350 BC). Some of the remainder probably also belong to this period but eight or so more coarsely gritted examples may belong to the preceding late Bronze/early Age (*c* 900 BC – *c* 600 BC). Some largely undiagnostic sherds can only be dated broadly from *c* 900 BC to *c* 50 BC. The small size and generally weathered condition of many of these sherds suggest that they derived from later prehistoric field manuring.

A further sixty-nine sherds were recovered from the uppermost fills of the ring-ditches and from the intersecting ditch, including two 'Belgic'-style grog-tempered sherds dating from *c* 50/25 BC, the rest dating to the Roman period, probably no later than *c* AD 175/200. The proportionally large amount of the Roman-period material (34 per cent), which again may have occurred on the site as a result of agricultural manuring, suggests the presence of a nearby Roman-period farmstead. Following the end of the second century AD, land use appears to have changed, perhaps to pasture, as there was a virtual absence of pottery on the site from later periods.

In addititon to the ceramic material recovered from the barrow, sixty-eight sherds were recovered from the fills of ditch 413. Of these, fifty-four sherds were of late Iron Age, un-Romanised and Romanised 'Belgic'-style and early Roman type (a further fifteen Roman sherds were recovered from the upper fills of the ring-ditches). As forty-seven of the sherds recovered from the ditch's uppermost fill dated to the early Roman period, a late pre-Roman Iron Age or early Roman date is proposed for the intersecting ditch.

Also comprising part of the ceramic assemblage are forty-five fragments of burnt daub weighing 12g in total and occurring residually, like the great majority of the potsherds, within ditch and grave fills. Although an origin for this material cannot be proposed with confidence, it may have derived from wattle-and-daub structures or from bonfire or clamp kilns. Whatever its origin, the burnt daub can be assumed to have been brought to the site for a specific purpose because clay deposits in a pure and usable form do not occur naturally in the immediate area. It was notable that twenty of the burnt daub fragments occurred within deposit 728, which also contained charcoal fragments, seven Neolithic/early Bronze Age potsherds, thirty-four flint pot-boilers and 147 worked flints, including ten blades (one serrated), twenty-two blade-like flakes, a bladelet, two end scrapers, a piercer, three chunks and four cores. Deposit 728 was the grave fill for the encoffined adult inhumation (729), and it therefore appears possible that these materials represent debris from funeral feasting associated with this burial as well as earlier residual materials incorporated into the backfill.

Illustrated vessels

Peterborough ware

1 Hard well-fired sherd from the concave neck of a Peterborough bowl. The fabric has light brown surfaces and a dark-grey core. It contains finely crushed inclusions. The outer surface is decorated with a horizontal row of bird-bone impressions. Context 517.

2 Single rim sherd in a dark, friable and abraded fabric with some grog inclusions. The surfaces are grey-brown and the core is black. The rim is simple and rounded and is

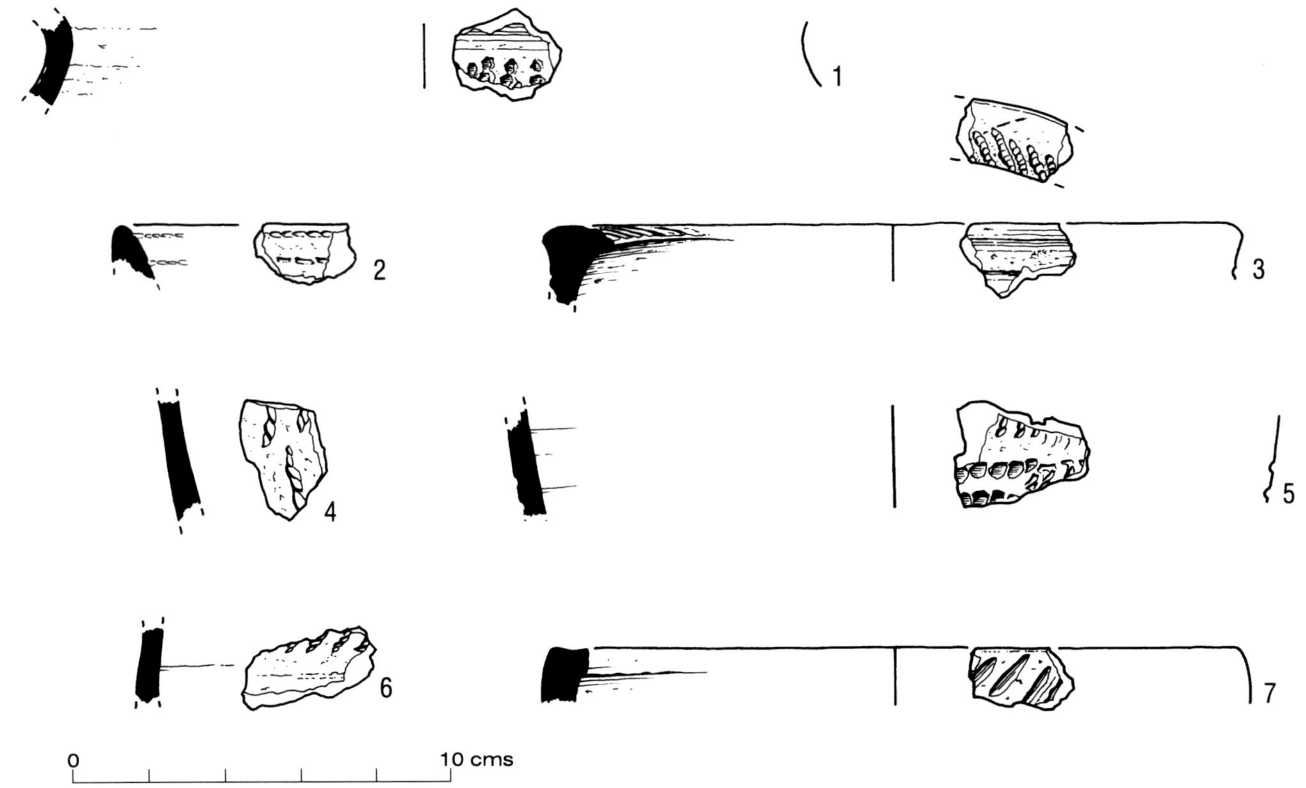

Fig 30. Eastling Down: middle and later Neolithic pottery. Nos 1–6 Peterborough Ware; No 7 Grooved Ware. Scale 1:2.

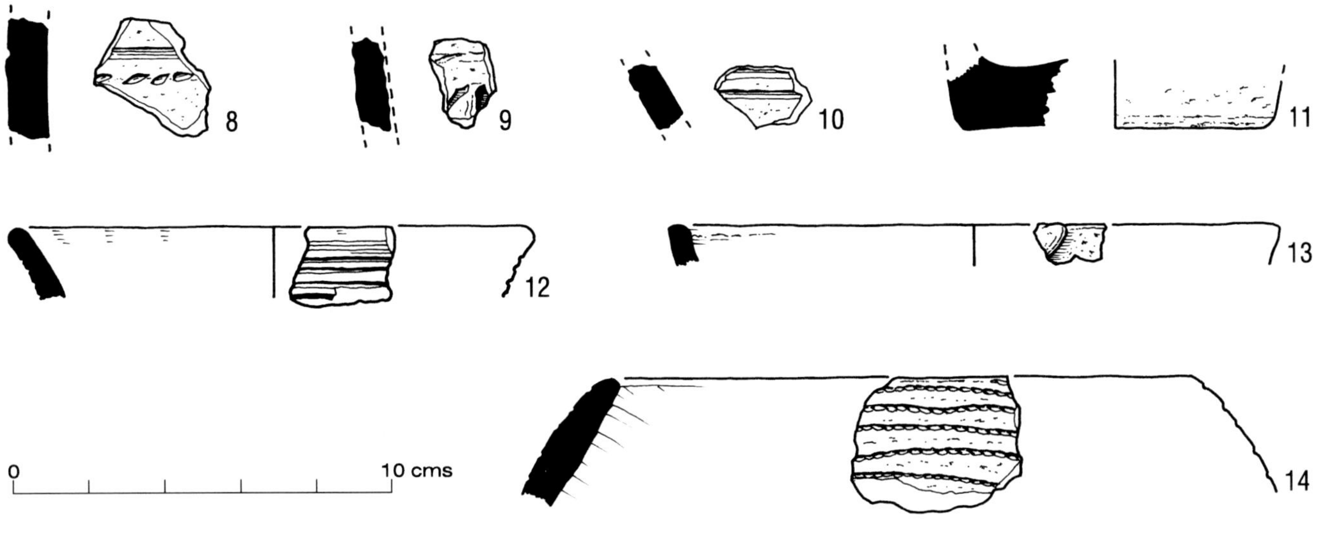

Fig 31. Eastling Down: early Bronze Age pottery. Nos 8–14 Beakers. Scale 1:2.

decorated internally with two horizontal lines of twisted cord impressions. Context 538, section 6.

3 Single calcined flint-filled rim sherd with light brown surfaces and a black core. The rim has a rounded top with internal lip and the top of the rim is decorated with whipped-cord impressions. Mortlake style. Context 545, section 1.

4 Two sherds, the larger has coarsely crushed flint inclusions. The outer surface has slight dimples, possible bird-bone impressions. Context 546, section 5.

5 Hard well-fired sherd in a slightly laminated fabric with reddish-brown outer surface, and a black inner surface and core. It has finely crushed sand and grog inclusions with some sparse calcined flint. The outer surface is decorated with three horizontal lines of close-set bird-bone impressions. Context 705, section 3.

6 Hard well-fired sherd in a slightly laminated fabric with reddish brown outer surface, and a black inner surface and core. It has finely crushed sand and grog inclusions with some sparse calcined flint. The outer surface is decorated with a horizontal line of whipped-cord impressions. Identical to 5 above. Context 728.

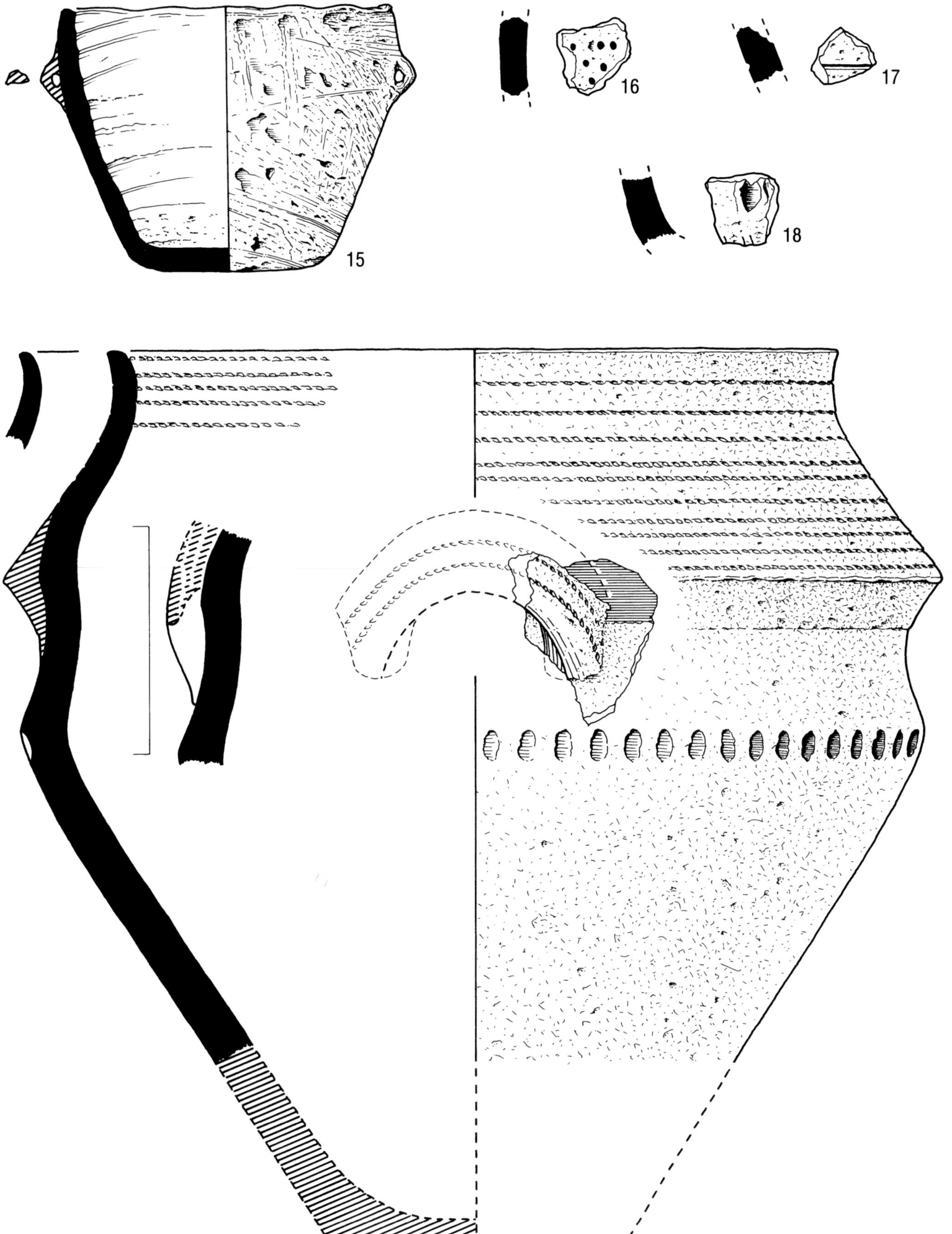

Fig 32. Eastling Down: early Bronze Age pottery. Nos 15–16, Food Vessel; Nos 17–18 Urn; No 19, Collared Urn. Scale 1:2.

Grooved ware

7 Rim sherd in a well-fired fabric with finely crushed grog inclusions, brown surfaces and a black core. The rim has a concave bevel and a slight ridge internally. Externally the decoration comprised four diagonal broad grooves. Context 546, section 4.

Beakers

8 Single sherd in a fairly hard fabric with light brown surfaces and a dark grey/black core. The fabric contains grog inclusions and the outer surface is decorated with a row of fingernail impressions below and incised line. Context 490.

9 Single grog-filled sherd with a light brown outer surface, black core and with the inner surface missing. There are traces of fingernail impressed decoration on the outer surface suggesting Rusticated Beaker. Context 545, section 1.

10 Single grog-filled sherd with a light brown outer surface, black core and inner surface. There are traces of a single incised line on the outer surface. Possibly Beaker. Context 545, section 8.

11 Single shell-filled base sherd with a red-brown outer surface, black core and inner surface. Undecorated, possible Beaker. Context 545, section 1.

12 Single rim sherd in a hard, well-fired dark grey-brown fabric with finely crushed calcined flint inclusions. The fabric has well-finished surfaces and averages 6mm thick. The rim is rounded, slightly everted and decorated externally with three horizontal incised lines starting at a distance of 8mm from the rim. Context 620.

13 Context 671, section 6. Single fine rim sherd in a grog-filled fabric. The rim is simple and rounded with a pellet of clay on the outer surface suggesting that the vessel has been decorated with fingernail impressions with attendant raised pellets.

14 Rim sherd in a hard well-fired fabric with a reddish brown outer surface and with a black inner surface and core. The fabric appears to contain grog inclusions and has some slight carbonaceous encrustations on the inner surface. The rim has had a diameter of *c* 180–200mm and is simply rounded. Five horizontal lines of twisted cord impressions decorate the outer surface. Rather thick for Beaker, possibly Collared Urn, though the rim form is unusual for this class. Context 690, section 2.

Food Vessel

15 Small open vessel with a rim diameter of 105mm, a base diameter of 65mm and a height of *c* 80mm. The fabric is grog-filled, medium hard and with light brown surfaces and a black core. The rim is simple and rounded and the base is flattened rather than flat suggesting that the lower portion of the pot has been pinched. Externally there are two opposed lugs, each perforated horizontally. One of these lugs had broken off leaving join scars indicating that the lugs are applied rather than raised. Save for these lugs, the pot is undecorated though there are two fine fingernail impressions on the inner surface near to the intact lug. Context 438.

16 Single sherd in a medium hard fabric, 8mm thick and with a light brown outer surface, black core and inner surface. The fabric contains sparse finely crushed calcined flint. The outer surface is decorated with six circular stabs, each with a surface diameter of 3mm. Probably Food Vessel. Context 487.

Urn

17 Single soft light brown sherd with black inner surface and core and with finely crushed grog inclusions. One broad incised line decorates the outer surface. Context 538, section 5.

18 Single soapy sherd with finely crushed grog inclusions and in a well-fired fabric with a light brown outer surface, black core and inner surface. There are traces of fingernail impressions on the outer surface. Probably urn but possibly rusticated Beaker. Context 538, section 6.

Collared Urn

19 Tripartite Collared Urn in a light brown, soft, friable fabric with abundant grog inclusions. Base missing but rim diameter 230mm. Decorated on the 80mm deep concave collar with ten or eleven rows of horizontal twisted cord lines. The neck is undecorated but the sharp shoulder is decorated with a single row of subrectangular-oval impressions, probably bird-bone. The fabric is 15mm thick. Context 433.

The bone tweezers (Fig 33)

Tim Champion

Bone tweezers are known from a number of early Bronze Age grave contexts in southern Britain, especially in Wessex. Proudfoot (1963, 424–5 with references) lists twelve examples, to which can now be added those from Ford, Laverstoke, Wiltshire (Musty 1969, 99 and 102); Oakley Down, Dorset (White and Reed 1970, 163); Radley, Oxfordshire (Barclay and Halpin 1997, 141, 148, 235); and the example from Eastling Down. A broken bone object, almost certainly the perforated top of such a pair of tweezers, has also been found much further north, at Carsington Pasture, Derbyshire (Harding and Beswick 2005, 11 and fig 5). The provenance and distribution of this type of object are remarkable. They are known only from burial contexts, all but one of which were cremations. Of the total of sixteen, or probably seventeen, examples, fourteen are from Wiltshire and Dorset. One comes from Radley in the Upper Thames Valley, only a short distance north of the main concentration, while the present example and the fragment from Carsington Pasture are the only outliers to this otherwise very clustered distribution. There is also a single example from a settlement context at Fort Harrouard, Eure-et-Loire, France (Gerloff 1975, 122 and 125–6).

The tweezers are probably made from the bones of sheep or goat, though only at Radley is there a certain identification (Barclay and Halpin 1997, 148). They are often highly polished, so much so that they were once thought to have been made of ivory. They vary somewhat in length, from about 40mm to 70mm. They also vary in form: the most complex have a constricted neck between the two arms and a disc-like head, with grooved decoration on the arms; others have rather cruder variants of the constricted neck, but without the decoration, while the simplest have no shoulders or neck. They are perforated horizontally, as though for suspension or attachment; the constricted neck and horizontal perforation of the Carsington Pasture fragment makes its identification almost certain. The present example

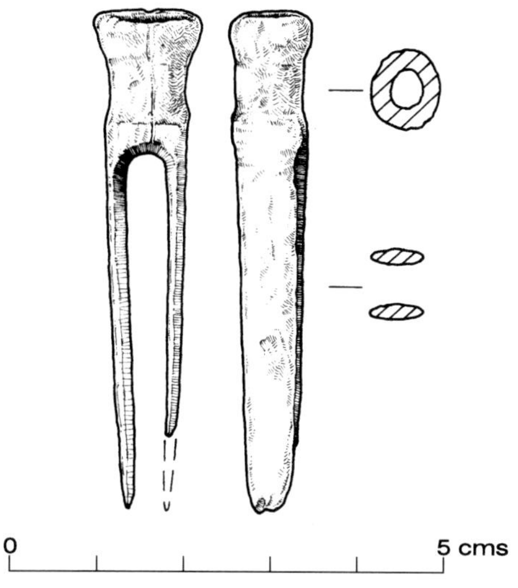

Fig 33. Eastling Down: bone tweezers from fill of urn, context 432. Scale 1:1.

falls well within the known size range, and has the constricted neck known on most other examples, but without decoration.

The graves containing the tweezers fall roughly into four groups. One group comprises seven of the more richly furnished graves, including associations with bronze daggers and bone pins; there are five graves which contained dagger, pin and tweezers, for example Winterbourne Stoke G4 and Wilsford G56 (Gerloff 1975, pl 47 C and D). These weapon associations are predominantly with daggers of the Camerton-Snowshill series, the distinctive characteristic of the Wessex II graves; the only exception is at Radley, where the association is with a knife-dagger of less determinate date. Another group of associations comprises two graves which contained beads of jet, amber and faience together with the tweezers: Kingston Deverill 9 and Bloxworth 4a (Clarke *et al* 1985, 291 and fig 4.97). These graves should be assigned to Gerloff's Aldbourne series, which contained cremations with a range of beads and other ornaments, but were less richly furnished than the Wilsford series and were broadly contemporary with the Camerton-Snowshill series of weapon graves (Gerloff 1975, 197–214). The third group of graves (Handley Hill 24, Wimborne St Giles 22b, Amesbury 11, Upton Lovell 2d, Carsington Pasture and now the present site) contained only the tweezers and an urn in addition to the ashes, while the fourth group (Laverstoke and Oakley Down) lacked even the urn.

The Eastling Down grave therefore fits well in the group of less well furnished graves with tweezers. With the exception of Carsington Pasture, which included a Biconical Urn, the only known ceramic associations of the tweezers are with Collared Urns. We can now add Eastling Down to the examples from Bloxworth 4a and Handley Hill 24 listed by Longworth (1984, 61).

The function of these objects remains enigmatic. They are traditionally referred to as tweezers, and are generally thought to have had a depilatory function. White and Reed (1970, 163) speculated that they could have been used to remove the fragments of cremated bone from the pyre remains. Thomas (1966, 6) has argued that the shape of their terminals would have made them ineffective as tweezers, especially for removing hairs. He compared them in form to old-fashioned clothes-pegs, and suggested that they would have served to attach something to the clothing. The regular association of the tweezers with pins suggests that they did indeed play some role in the decoration of the clothing; in the Edmondsham grave the pin and the tweezers were deposited together, separately from the cremated bone and the dagger, while at Radley the pin, tweezers and knife-dagger were deposited together, possibly in a leather container (Barclay and Halpin 1997, 145).

The tweezers have been generally thought of as a male item, but more because of the association with presumably male objects such as the daggers than because of certain osteological identifications. The burial at Carsington Pasture was certainly that of an adult male over the age of fifty (McKinley 2005). More tentative identifications of the sample of cremated bone buried at Radley (Barclay and Halpin 1997, 143), with a knife-dagger and pin, and at Oakley Down (White and Reed 1970) suggest that both may also have been the burials of adult males. If Gerloff was correct, however, in her identification of the Wilsford and Aldbourne series of graves with ornaments as the female equivalents of the male weapon graves, then tweezers could also have been used by, or associated with, females.

The bone tweezers are an important addition to the range of exotic or unusual artefacts found in early Bronze Age graves in Kent with strong links to the better known burials of Wessex (Champion 2004). These include objects of gold, amber, jet, faience, and now bone, as well as distinctive ceramics such as the incense cups. Taken together, these comprise a well-defined regional group of rich early Bronze Age burials, with its focus in east Kent.

The bone

Human bone

Trevor Anderson† and Tim Allen

Numerous Bronze Age barrows have been recorded in Kent (Grinsell 1992) and these probably include examples with origins in the late Neolithic. A detailed inventory indicates that thirty cremations and fifty-seven inhumations dated to the Bronze Age have been discovered in Kent in the last 130 years (Bristow 1998, vol 2: 217–20, 225, 233, 363 and 393). Several sites were excavated without the benefit of modern archaeological techniques (Brent 1866; James 1899; Payne 1884; Rawlings 1872; Woodruff 1874; 1880) and certainly very little of the skeletal corpus (now unavailable) was subjected to detailed osteological analysis (Mays and Anderson 1995).

Many sites in Kent contain a single isolated inhumation (Anderson 1994; Cruse and Harrison 1983; Grinsell 1992; Minter and Herbert 1973; Oakley *et al* 1967; Parfitt 1986; Payne 1884; Perkins and Gibson 1990; Tester and Gaiger 1951; Willson 1985). However, in recent years, only the excavations at Monkton (Bennett *et al* 2008); North Foreland, Broadstairs (Perkins and Macpherson-Grant 1981) and Lord of the Manor, Ramsgate (Macpherson-Grant and Perkins 1977) have revealed multiple burials (*see* p 73), with the majority of those at Monkton being generally less well-preserved. Consequently, the inhumations at Eastling Down comprise a significant proportion of those known in Kent. Coupled with the detailed examination to which the human bone material has been subject, the Eastling Down human bone assemblage is therefore of clear importance in Kentish palaeo-osteological research.

The complete skeletons

There were six originally complete sketetons in addition to a fragmented foetal skull (566) buried (in association with the sherds of a complete Food Vessel) above an articulated skeleton in Grave 439. This provides a total of seven discrete inhumations (Table 8). The skeletons, six of which failed to reach adulthood, are represented by incomplete long-bones and fragmented crania. In the majority of cases, hands, feet, ribs and spine have not survived, or, at best, are represented by eroded fragments. Based on dental development, an age estimation was possible for the majority of the sample. Sub-adult ages range from foetal to 11–12 years (Table 8).

Based on cranial and pelvic morphology, the only adult (730), an articulated burial within a coffin or wood-lined grave (741), was male (Ferembach *et al* 1980). Degree of dental attrition, suture closure and pelvic indicators suggest that age at death was *c* 30–35 years. The bones are quite gracile, suggesting a slim build. Based on the maximum length of the right femur and fibula, stature was assessed as 1.754m or 5ft 9¼in (Trotter and Gleser 1958).

The only evidence of pathology on any of the skeletons is pitting and porosity within the eye sockets of an eight month old child (639), a condition known as cribra orbitalia. The orbits of a 5 year old (623) and an 8 year old (692) were available for examination and proved normal. 'Cribra orbitalia' is a term coined by Welcker in 1885 from the Latin word *cribrum*, meaning sieve or strainer, because of the sieve-like appearance of the sockets in advanced cases. The lesions, the result of diploid expansion, are generally considered to result from iron deficiency (Carlson *et al* 1974; Cybulski 1977; Fornaciari *et al* 1982; Hengen 1971). It must be stressed that other factors apart from poor diet can lead to iron deficiency (Von Endt and Ortner 1982; Walker 1986), perhaps the most common being parasitic infestation (Hengen 1971; Kent 1987).

There is no evidence of skeletal pathology in the 8 year old child (692). However, the unusual burial position, flexed upper limbs and tightly contracted lower limbs, may indicate severe burning or a period of prolonged unconsciousness prior to death. A body subject to intense burning, either while alive or after death, displays contraction of the limb bones (Camps 1968, 87–8), with the flexion of the upper limbs resulting in the so-called 'pugilistic attitude' (Simpson 1964, 129, fig 94). Such contraction caused by heat stiffening is permanent and it is very difficult to alter the position of the limbs after the episode of burning. Limb rigidity with marked contraction of the joints can also occur during long periods in a comatose state (Margaret Doe, pers comm). In the present case, however, there is no evidence for any burning on the skeleton. The damaged skull is reconstructable and severe warping or deformation due to extreme heat is not evident. Nor is there evidence of disuse atrophy on the bones or any dental evidence for malnutrition or prolonged sickness. In addition, the bones were fully articulated, indicating that re-interment had not taken place, as is occasionally the case in Bronze Age contexts (Russel 1990; Stone 1938; Taylor 1933; Taylor and Woodward 1985; Vatcher 1960). On balance, it would appear that the marked symmetrical contracture of the lower limbs probably resulted from human manipulation after death.

If the limbs were deliberately positioned to fit the body into the confined space of Grave 687, it is probable that the burial occurred several days after death. *Rigor mortis* normally sets in between two and four hours after death, occurring first in the face and progressively spreading to the neck, the upper limbs, trunk and finally to the lower limbs (Camps 1968, 87–8). In the majority of bodies in temperate climates, *rigor mortis* takes thirty-six to forty-eight hours to pass off, and some rigidity may remain in the lower limbs for up to five days (Camps 1968, 88). Unlike heat stiffening, *rigor mortis* does not result in marked contracture but, until it passes off, the limbs remain immovable. This would suggest that the bodies placed in the crouched position in the Eastling Down barrow may have remained unburied for up to five days and that a period of 'laying out' or similar preceded all or most crouched burials of the late Neolithic and early Bronze Age, including those at Eastling Down. It was probably during this period that ceremonial feasting took place, as suggested by the evidence within the backfill of Grave 729 (*see* pp 32–4).

SK No	Sex	Age	Comment
552	?	2-3 yrs	Badly eroded cranial fragments and teeth
558	?	11-12 yrs	Incomplete cranium; long bone shafts and pelvic fragments. Localised defect on labial surface of upper right central incisor, probably the result of trauma to the deciduous tooth..
566	?	foetal	Badly eroded cranial fragments.
623	?	*c* 5 yrs	Incomplete cranium; long bone shafts and pelvic fragments. The teeth are lightly worn.
639	?	*c* 8 months	Badly eroded cranium; humeral shafts; shoulder and vertebral fragments. Cribra orbitalia.
692	?	*c* 8 yrs	Badly eroded cranium; humeral shafts; shoulder and vertebral fragments. Widespread deposits of calculus. Crowding of upper and lower incisors (imbrication).
730	M	30-35 yrs	Stature: 1.754m. Practically complete; long bones rahter eroded. Spine incomplete and fragmentary. Widespread calculus.

Table 8. The human skeletons from Eastling barrow.

Based on a sample of thirty-six deciduous teeth and sixty-six permanent teeth, there is no evidence of *ante-mortem* loss, caries or enamel hyperplasia. Two individuals, the adult (730) and the 8 year old child (692), display widespread calculus deposits. The latter also display slight crowding of the upper and lower incisors. The lack of dental attrition in the 5 year old (623) suggests that this child had consumed a soft diet. Loss of enamel was noted on the labial surface of the upper right central incisor of an 11 or 12 year old child (558), suggesting that facial trauma involving the deciduous incisor had occurred when the child was perhaps 2 to 4 years old.

The high sub-adult mortality evident in the barrow argues that the local population was particularly unhealthy. An incidence of iron deficiency has already been noted and the lack of dental attrition on the teeth of the 5 year old (558) may suggest a sickly child fed on a soft, gruel-based diet. It is possible that several children succumbed to acute infection, which would not be indicated by skeletal evidence. A similar high sub-adult mortality rate is known from Overton Hill in Wiltshire (Brothwell and Powers 1966) and at Ladies Mile, Patcham, Sussex (Holleyman and Yeates 1960). Both sites contained six inhumations, with only one on each site reaching adulthood. In the former, four children died in their first year (Brothwell and Powers 1966). The youngest child, who died at *c* six months, also displayed cribra orbitalia (*ibid*). At Amesbury, also in Wiltshire, sub-adult mortality of 55 per cent (5:9) was recorded (Brothwell and Powers 1967). A barrow containing only juvenile urned and pit cremation burials is known at Upton Pyne, near Exeter (Pollard and Russell 1969, 49–78).

With the exception of the adult male inhumation (729), there is no osteological evidence within the Eastling Down skeletons to indicate gender. However, where such evidence is available in other barrows of this period, particularly in Wessex, male inhumations appear to have been placed predominantly with their skulls pointing northward and females with their skulls pointing southward (Fowler 1967, 33). Assuming a similar shared alignment according to sex at Eastling Down, this would suggests that five of the six intact inhumations in Eastling Down were of males, as they shared the same alignment as the adult male skeleton. It should also be noted that a great degree of cultural and, presumably, ritual diversity had come to prevail during the Bronze Age and that a great degree of local and regional variation probably occurred.

Bone from disturbed graves or 'placed' deposits

A total of 74g of bone of this type, mostly small eroded fragments, was recovered from the barrow, 10g of which was recovered from animal burrows close to the centre of the primary barrow. Of this collection some 5g was largely undiagnostic but probably human (414, 1g; 418, 1g; 498, 1g; 508, 1g and 514, 1g). The remainder included parts of a radius (504, 1g), a child's diaphysis (unfused) ulna (509, 1g), a child's frontal skull bone (649, 2g) and parts of another child's skull (656, 1g), all suggesting that at least two neonate and/or juveniles burials were represented. Although badly disturbed with only small fragments surviving, the position of the bones close to the centre of the mound suggests that they may be the residue of primary interments.

A total of 14g of probable human bone fragments was recovered from the uppermost fill of the primary ditch, comprising an eroded femur (538, 20g) and two widely spaced fragments (547, 3g and 654, 1g). The presence of this material suggests that at least one disturbed satellite burial may be represented, this post-dating the construction of the mound, but pre-dating mound reconstruction and the cutting of Grave 533.

Some 10g of human bone was also recovered from the uppermost fill of the Phase 3 ditch (546), a deposit which contained material dating into the medieval period.

Human bone was recovered from a shallow elongated oval pit (683) cutting the basal fill of the primary ditch in Sector 2. Some 10g of bone fragments was recovered from the pit fill (680) together with 1g of burnt bone. A small quantity of carbon was also present, perhaps suggesting that the bone and burnt bone may have been a 'placed' deposit.

Human bone was recovered from two pits found cutting the Phase 2 ditch on the northern side of the mound in Sectors 1 and 2 (527 and 511). The basal fill of the first of these (526) provided 10g of bone including part of a femur (8g); the basal fill of the second (693) contained 4g of eroded bone. The pit fills, which contained no other finds, may have been cut solely for disposal of the human bone and may also have been 'placed' deposits

The basal fills of the eastern terminal of the Phase 3 ditch (in sector 3) was cut by a small shallow subcircular pit (724) containing, grey-black carbon-rich soil with 10g of human bone, 7g of which was a probable femur. The pit with human bone appears to represent a further 'placed' deposit. A deposit of cremated bone (737) in a shallow pit (722) found in a near identical stratified position in the western terminal of the same ditch (sector 6 baulk) has also been interpreted as a possible 'placed' deposit.

Burnt bone fragments from a cremation urn and a cremation pit

A cremation burial in an inverted urn (Pl 17) was located within the south-western burial group in sector 6. The fill of the cremation urn (432) contained 1346g of burnt bone and a pair of bone tweezers (*see* p 58). The urn was of tripartite collared type and had been placed in an inverted position in a pit (433) cutting the primary ring-ditch. The base (the top of the inverted urn) was found to have been removed probably by ploughing. A total of 42g of burnt bone was recovered from the fill of the pit (474, 475). This included two maxilla fragments, a fragment of skull and a fragment of rib, all of which may be assumed to have derived from the urn.

Following the lifting of the urn, its contents were removed for examination, this being done in seven spits, each of 46mm thickness. The basal spit (that is, the lowest spit when the urn was in its original inverted position)

was given the number seven, the top the number one. The majority of the bone, 54 per cent (729g) was recovered from Spits 6 and 5. Overall, 61 per cent of the bone by weight was identifiable. The average weight of each identifiable fragment is 2.26g. Cranial and axial elements and bones of the upper and lower limbs are represented by 21.2 per cent, 23.4 per cent, 24.6 per cent and 30.8 per cent by weight, respectively. Similar figures: 18.2 per cent, 23.1 per cent, 20.6 per cent and 38.1 per cent have been obtained from modern complete adult cremated bodies (McKinley 1989).

The majority of the bone is mostly white, hard and highly fragmented, although in Spits 3–6 a small number of bones are blue/black in colour. Lightly burnt lower spine as well as larger dark blue fragments of pelvis and leg bones occurred in spits 5 and 6 and conjoining fragments were present in Spits 4, 5 and 6, with eight fragments of the same bone (a tibia) occurring in Spits 3, 4, 5 and 6. The reconstructed tibia weighs 84g and is 240mm long. All spits contained teeth or parts of teeth, with a total of twenty-two dental fragments representing nineteen different teeth. In one case, part of a tooth root in Spit 5 was found to join with fragment in Spit 6.

No bones or teeth are duplicated, indicating that only one cremated individual is represented. The absence of unfused bones and unformed tooth roots suggest this was a fully-grown adult, as does the presence of fused bones fragments such as hand phalanges (Spits 1, 3, 6, and 7), iliac crest of pelvis (Spit 6), proximal tibia (Spit 7), distal tibia (Spit 4), distal fibula (Spit 6) and foot phalange (Spit 5). None of the identifiable bones displays characteristics clearly indicative of gender. Two supra-orbital fragments are insufficiently complete to examine for brow-ridge development, prominent brow ridges being a common male characteristic. The small odontoid peg found in Spit 4 may be considered a female characteristic but this is contradicted by the well-developed muscle marking on the femur and the relatively large size of the patella, both male characteristics. However, on balance, this evidence, along with the presence of the tweezers accompanying the burial (*see* p 59), perhaps suggests the burial was of an adult male.

The only sign of pathology was noted on the fragments of right tibia from Spits 5 and 6. On reconstruction, the mid-shaft of the tibia displayed definite striae and slight porosity. This so-called periosteal reaction is typical of chronic bone infection (Ortner and Putshcar 1985, fig 186).

The bone within cremation burial 433 was uncalcined and of solid consistency, such that scratching left no mark, suggesting that the temperature of the pyre was between 400^0 and 750^0 (Holck 1987, 131–2). The exfoliation of the tooth crowns indicates that the temperature was probably in excess of 500^0 (Buikstra and Goldstein 1973, 23). Although the white bone fragments were all burnt effectively in a well-oxygenated environment, the larger fragments from the spine and the dark blue fragments from the pelvis and lower limb from Spits 5 and 6 appear to have been subject to less intense heat. It is therefore possible that these bones were displaced to the periphery of the funeral pyre when the pyre collapsed. The recovery of several small hand bones suggests that, during the cremation process, the hands had been placed over the chest. In this position, they would be protected by the 'heat shadow' of the body (Holck 1987, 160).

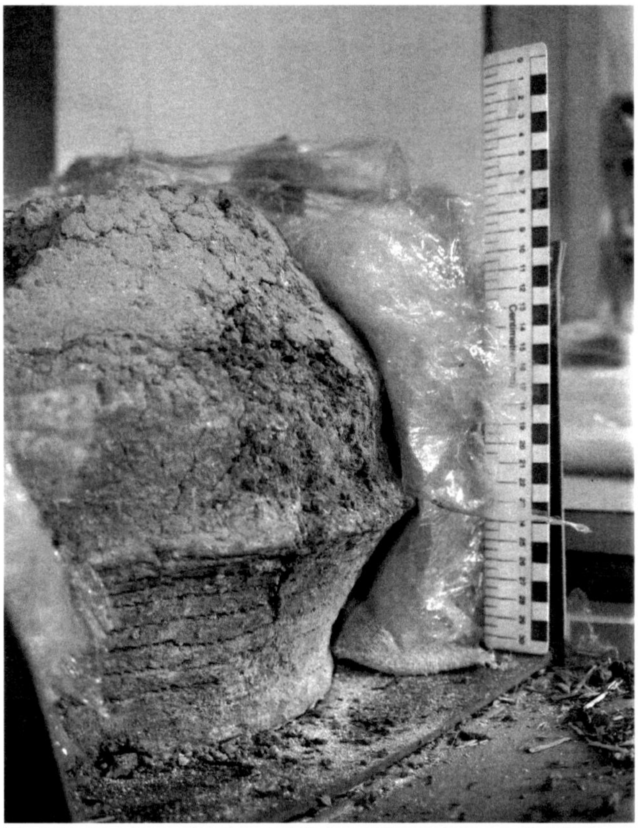

Pl 17. Eastling Down: the inverted Collared Urn under excavation in the lab.

Even in modern, high-temperature cremations, bone shafts of up to 250mm in length survive, prior to being crushed mechanically (McKinley 1989). Research has also revealed that the bones of cremated bodies for the most part retain their form as long as they remain undisturbed (Buikstra and Goldstein 1973, fig 16). It therefore appears that the majority of bone breakage associated with prehistoric cremations was mechanical, occurring when the pyre collapsed or, either deliberately or accidentally during the subsequent collection of the burnt bone.

The 1346g of bone within the urn compares to an average weight of bone of 2.5kg produced by modern adult cremations, where the range falls between 1.6 and 3.6kg (McKinley 1989). The bone recovered from the urn therefore represents between 40 per cent and 84 per cent of the predicted adult weight. As discussed in above, there is no evidence that particular skeletal elements are either under- or over-represented, suggesting that the shortfall is the result of selective and/or careless collection of the bone from the cremation site.

The pit cremation

Cremation pit 495, in the south-east group of burials, located in sector 4 was excavated in two halves, each half being divided into seven spits. The pit contained a total of 271g of bone, of which 228g, including two ear ossicles (a malleus and an incus) occurred in the primary cremation deposit (600), along with 88g of carbonised wood. The remainder of the bone occurred in the pit's clay sealing layer (577) or the graded boundary between the two deposits. The majority (63 per cent) of the fragments are white externally and display dark blue colouration internally. A little less than 20 per cent are completely white and a similar percentage are charred and discoloured rather than burnt.

The bone was too fragmentary to establish sex. By weight, 6 per cent is smaller than 5mm in length, the majority (59 per cent) is between 20–50mm and only 16 per cent is over 50mm in length. Visible cranial sutures suggest that the cremated bones are those of an adult under 50 years old. Vertebrae and long-bone shafts are notably absent from the 146g of identified bone (55 per cent of the total), some 66 per cent (96g) of which comprises skull fragments. This is in strong contrast to the predicted figure of 18.2 per cent for cranial elements in complete adult cremations (McKinley 1989). Also, the recovered bone within the pit represents only 7 to 17 per cent of the expected weight for an adult cremated body (*ibid*). Such marked under-representation is unusual, although an earlier example in association with fragments of a collared urn is known at Street House, Loftus in Cleveland (Parker 1988). In the case of Eastling Down, the under-representation may be due to extremely careless collection or preferential selection. However, it is possible that such incomplete skeletal material does not represent evidence for formal burial as it was accompanied by large quantities of carbonised wood, perhaps suggesting the (ritual?) disposal of cremation pyre debris following the removal of the long bones and vertebrae, rather than a formal cremation burial. An example of this practise is known at Guiting Power 111, Gloucester, where the bones missing from a central cremation burial containing an adult and full-term foetus/neonate were buried in a nearby pit (McKinley 1997).[1]

The above would appear to be a rare example of the examination of Bronze Age pyre debris, as opposed to cremation burial, in Kent. However, recent work has shown that such debris is often associated with Bronze Age barrows (McKinley 1997), is frequently found in the backfill of cremation graves (*ibid*, Parrington 1978) and occasionally occurs, as at Twyford Down, Winchester, as deposits over cremation graves or in barrow ditches (McKinley 1997). The latter is probably the case in Eastling Down barrow, as discussed above (p 35). Previously, surface spreads and formalised deposition of pyre debris have probably been confused with cremation pyre sites (*ibid*). At Burghfield, Berkshire, two pits, one containing an adult female cremation, the other containing pyre debris examples have been excavated (Butterworth and Lobb 1992) and a separate pit for cremation debris is also known at Guiting Power 111, as previously mentioned (McKinley 1997).

Burnt bone from disturbed cremations or 'placed' deposits

This group consists of 20g, a small amount of which was recovered from the upper loam fill of the inner ditch in sector 4 (538, 2g; 618, 1g). Although the fragments were found close to cremation pit 495 they are stratigraphically earlier and must have derived from another burial, perhaps a satellite cremation or 'placed' deposit originally located within the primary barrow mound that was perhaps eroded out of the mound and dispersed into the upper ditch fill.

A single gram of cremated bone was recovered from a small pit containing 6g of unburnt bone (680, above) found cutting the basal fill of the primary ditch in sector 2 and thought to have been a possible 'placed' deposit.

The largest deposit of cremated bone in this category, weighing some 16g, was recovered from a shallow depression or pit (737) found at the base of the western terminal of the Phase 3 ditch in a baulk separating sectors 6 and 7. The bone, off-white in colour, was mixed with clay-silt and carbon-flecked crushed chalk. Although the material may derive from a cremation burial, perhaps disturbed during the cutting of the late ditch, or by episodic clearance of the late ditch, it is also possible that this was a 'placed' deposit matching a 'placed' deposit of unburnt bone (724) located in a similar position in the eastern terminal of the same ditch.

A fragment of burnt human bone, possibly a fragment of fibula, was recovered from an upper loam fill (560) within a Roman field boundary ditch in sector 7. The boundary was cut through all three barrow ditches at this point and the cremated bone could have derived from a cremation burial or 'placed' deposit in any one of the ditches or the associated barrow mound against the north side of the monument.

Animal bone

Robin Bendrey

Animal bones were recovered by both hand-recovery (Table 9) and bulk sampling (Table 10) and from all phases of activity at the site:

Phase 1: the primary mound
Phase 2: the second mound and early burial
Phase 3: the re-cut ring-ditch and later burials
Phase 4: the late Iron Age feature
Phase 5: the Roman ditch and later activity
Phase 6: animal disturbance

Methodology

The assemblage was identified and recorded using the diagnostic zones of Dobney and Reilly (1988). If it was not possible to identify a fragment to species an animal-size

1 For a detailed study of the possible significance of the ritual burial of human remains and their apparent disposal as rubbish see Brück 1995, 257–64.

category was awarded, for example cattle-sized, otherwise it was labelled indeterminate. The assemblage has been identified with the aid of a comparative osteological reference collection, and a number of publications (Amorosi 1989; Bailon 1999; Boessneck 1969; Callou 1997; Gleed-Owen 1998; Hillson 1986; Lawrence and Brown 1973; Prummel 1987a; 1987b; 1989; Vigne 1995).

Bones identified to sheep and sheep/goat are shown separately in Table 9 and as there are no fragments identified to goat in the assemblage, sheep and sheep/goat are considered in the text and other tables together as sheep. The equid remains in the assemblage have been positively identified to horse, *Equus caballus*, using the enamel patterns on the occlusal surfaces of the cheek teeth (Baxter

	Phase 1	Phase 2	Phase 3	Phase 4	Phase 5	Phase 6	Total
Mammal							
Pig, *Sus* sp domestic	16	2	1	1	2	56	78
Cattle, *Bos* sp domestic	27	6	15		10	8	66
Sheep, *Ovis* sp domestic	1				2	3	6
Sheep/Goat, *Ovis/Capra*	3	1	2		4	5	15
Horse, *Equus caballus* sp domestic	1			46	3		50
Dog, *Canis* sp domestic	1						1
Red deer, *Cervus elaphus* L	1						1
Roe deer, *Capreolus capreolus* L	3		1			1	5
Hare, *Lepus* spp			1			1	2
Badger, *Meles meles* L	2					33	35
Fox, *Vulpes vulpes* L						1	1
Rabbit, *Oryctolagus cuniculus* (L)	13	11				13	37
Mole, *Talpa europaea* L	1					18	19
Cattle-sized	35	11	41	62	19	27	195
Sheep-sized	21	3	5		4	50	83
Indeterminate	35	6	26		4	25	96
Amphibian							
Common toad, *Bufo bufo* L	1					2	3
Toad, *Bufo* sp	1					2	3
Frog/Toad, anuran						1	1
Total	162	40	92	109	48	246	697

Table 9. Eastling Barrow: summary of hand-recovered animal bone (number of fragments).

	Phase 3			Phase 6		
	NISP	cf	rf	NISP	cf	rf
Pig, *Sus* sp domestic	6	1	0.1	3	3	0.3
Cattle, *Bos* sp domestic	9	3	0.4			
Sheep, *Ovis* sp domestic	4	1	0.1			
Roe deer, *Capreolus capreolus* L				1	1	0.1
Badger, *Meles meles* L	1	1	0.1			
Fox, *Vulpes vulpes* L				1	1	0.1
Rabbit, *Oryctolagus cuniculus* (L)	1	1	0.1			
Mole, *Talpa europaea* L				2	2	0.2
Water vole, *Arvicola terrestris* (L)				1	1	0.1
Bank vole, *Clethrionomys glareolus* (Schreb)	6	1	0.1	3	3	0.3
Field vole, *Microtus agrestis* (L)				4	2	0.2
Vole, cricretidae spp	1	1	0.1	4	1	0.1
Wood/Yellow-necked mouse, *Apodemus* spp	1	1	0.1	3	2	0.2
Common shrew, *Sorex araneus* L				2	2	0.2
Shrew, Soricidae spp				1	1	0.1
Mouse/Vole, Myomorpha	4	4	0.5	10	4	0.4
Common toad, *Bufo bufo* L				21	4	0.4
Toad, *Bufo* sp				23	5	0.6
Common frog, *Rana temporaria* L.				1	1	0.1
Frog, *Rana* sp				1	1	0.1
Frog/Toad, anuran				64	7	0.8
Slow worm, *Anguis fragilis* L				7	3	0.3
indeterminate	50	7	0.9	240	9	1.0
Total	83	8	1.0	392	9	1.0

Table 10. Eastling Barrow: bulk sampled bone, quantified by number of identified fragments (NISP), context frequency (cf) and relative frequency (rf). Context frequency is a count of the number of contexts that contain a taxon, and the relative frequency is the number as a proportion of the total number of bone-producing contexts (O'Connor 1985).

1998; Eisenmann 1986). Cattle, pig and sheep mandibular toothwear data have been recorded following Grant (1982). The few measurements from the cattle and pig bones indicate that the animals were domestic, and there were no other fragments which were large enough on visual examination to suggest wild cattle or wild boar.

Quantification of the hand-recovered assemblage is done by the number of identified fragments (NISP). The small size of individual assemblages (Table 9) often limits the strength of conclusions that can be drawn from this material. Material from the sieving programme (Table 10) is also quantified by context frequency and relative frequency (O'Connor 1985). Table 12 provides a breakdown of the bones identified to pig, cattle and sheep, by the number of fragments (NISP), and the distribution of perinatal (foetal and neonatal) bones, which are particularly common in the assemblage.

Preservation and taphonomy

The assemblage was largely characterised by poor preservation, with heavy erosion and root etching recorded on the surfaces of the bones. Root etching on archaeological animal bones is thought to be caused by acid excretion from plant roots or fungi associated with decomposing plants (Lyman 1994, 475–7). The degradation of the bone surface has probably obscured much information, for example there are no records of direct butchery marks from the assemblage, and only two fragments had evidence of being gnawed by a carnivore. The bones are generally friable.

The bones of badger, rabbit and mole (Tables 9 and 10) are characterised by a very good state of preservation, in contrast to the bulk of the assemblage that is generally poorly preserved. The differences in quality of preservation indicate that the latter group are of greater antiquity, and

Taxon	Pig						Cattle						Sheep					
	1	2	3	4	5	6	1	2	3	4	5	6	1	2	3	4	5	6
cranium						5												1
mandible	3					5	2					1						
loose teeth	7	1			1	11	21	6	7		8	4	2	1			3	
vertebrae						4												
scapula						5												2
humerus	1	1	1			6	1		1				1					3
radius	2					2			2			1	1		1			
ulna					1	3			1									
pelvis						2												1
femur				1		2			2		1							
tibia	1					5			1									
astragalus	1					1												
calcaneum	1						1				1							
metacarpal						1									1		2	
metatarsal						2	1		1			1					1	1
metapodial							1					1						
1st phalanx																		
2nd phalanx						1												
3rd phalanx						1												
Total NISP	16	2	1	1	2	56	27	6	15		10	8	3	1	2		6	10
perinatal bones (N)	3					37						2	1					7

Table 11. Eastling Barrow: skeletal element representation for pig, cattle and sheep (NISP), also showing the distribution of perinatal bones.

Taxon	Phase	Context	Mandibular toothwear scores						
			dP2/P2	dP2/P3	dP2/P4	M1	M2	M1/2	M3
Pig	6	690			(alv.)	E			
		649		(alv.)	(a)				
		487		(pr.)	(a)				
		420		(pr.)	(c)				
		428		(alv.)	(c)				
Cattle	1	697					k		k
		671			(g)				
		547							k
	2	545						f	
	3	546						g	
	5	560							g
	6	509		pr.					
Sheep	1	672				g			
		547						e	

Table 12. Eastling Barrow: mandibular teeth, dental age data following Grant (1982) (for premolars, deciduous teeth (dP2-dP4) denoted in brackets; 'alv.' indicates alveolus; 'pr.' indicates present).

that the former group, all burrowing animals, are intrusive (the rabbit only became established in Britain during the medieval period, although there do appear to have been some earlier attempts at introductions from the Roman period (Sykes and Curl 2010)). The bones of these species, therefore, are not of anthropogenic origin and are not discussed in relation to the prehistoric use of the site. The possibility that they may have introduced other bones to the site as food waste is discussed below. It is not clear, from the state of preservation, whether the fox bone is intrusive or not. Due to the remains of these burrowing animals, we must be aware of the possible movement of remains (bioturbation) within the sequence of phased deposits.

Phase 1: the primary ditch

A small and generally poorly preserved assemblage was recovered from ditch fills assigned to Phase 1 (late Neolithic/early Bronze Age) activity. Table 12 highlights the number of loose teeth in the ditch deposits, particularly those of cattle. This may be related to the process of assemblage formation of the material, for example if some of this material has been redeposited from elsewhere (*see* p 66); teeth are robust elements and will preferentially survive when other less dense material is destroyed. One notable aspect of this assemblage is that it represents a relatively wide range of taxa for the small sample size (see Bendrey 2007, fig 3.7).

Cattle and pig are the most common domestic taxa (Table 9). There are a small number of neonatal bones present in the sample, including three pig bones (contexts 671, 712 and 690) and one sheep (context 706). Ages at death of animals can also be estimated from a small quantity of tooth eruption and wear data (Table 12). A single pig mandible had the first molar (M_1) erupting through the bone of the mandible at death, suggesting an age somewhere in the first six months of life for this individual (Ma 2008; Silver 1969, 297). The few cattle teeth point towards mostly mature animals: one mandible had both M_3 and M_1 at Grant wear stage k and a further loose M_3s had a wear stage of k (Table 12). The two M_3s at Grant stage k indicate animals kept into old age for secondary products such as traction, milk or breeding.

Two fragments of roe deer antler (contexts 538 and 671) and one of red deer (context 622) are present. The presence of a roe deer mandible (context 655) suggests this animal may also have been hunted for its meat. The badger, rabbit and mole bones probably represent intrusive burrowers.

A single horse tooth came from the uppermost fill of Phase 1 ditch (context 538). The tooth ($M^{1/2}$) came from an animal aged 8½ to 11½ years at death, based on its crown height measurement (Levine 1982). This find is of potential significance due to its date, as horses were rare in earlier Bronze Age Britain and their status in the Neolithic is currently uncertain (Bendrey 2012; 2010a; Bendrey *et al* in press). The latest direct date for the horse in the Mesolithic of Britain is on a find from Cavall's Cave, Wye Valley, Herefordshire, which dates to the later seventh millennium BC (Bronk Ramsey *et al* 2002). The question of whether there was survival of horse populations in Britain through the Mesolithic and Neolithic, or whether horses become locally extinct only to be re-introduced later as a domestic animal by human agency, has been much debated (eg Bendrey 2010a; Grigson 1966; Kaagan 2000). Although horse is known from a number of Neolithic sites from Britain (eg Grigson 1966), direct dating of these finds has tended to return later dates (Bendrey *et al* in press; Kaagan 2000). A find that had been considered as an early domestic horse is the skull from Grimes Graves, which was originally dated to the late Neolithic/early Bronze Age by a conventional radiocarbon determination (Clutton-Brock and Burleigh 1991); however, a recent AMS determination on this find places it in the Roman period (Higham *et al* 2007). There had also been a good biogeographical case for a Beaker-period introduction of domestic horse into Ireland, with the earliest Holocene horse bones being found in association with Bell Beaker pottery at the passage tomb of Newgrange (van Wijngaarden-Bakker 1974); however, radiocarbon dating of two of these bones has now placed them in the first few centuries AD (Bendrey *et al* in press). With the re-dating of the Grimes Graves skull, there is now a gap in the record of direct dates for Britain between the later seventh millennium and the later second millennium BC (Bendrey *et al* submitted), which marks the later Bronze Age for the earliest directly dated evidence for the re-introduction of the horse. However, there are horse remains dated on stratigraphic grounds earlier than the later Bronze Age, including finds from elsewhere in east Kent (eg Bendrey 2008a), and the horse tooth from the Phase 1 ditch deposit at Eastling Down, perhaps pre-dating 2200 cal BC (according to its stratigraphy), could potentially derive from one of Britain's early domestic horses (although we need to be wary of the dangers of bioturbation on a single find).

Phase 2: the second mound and early burial

The small Phase 2 zooarchaeological assemblage derives from ditch fills, apart from a single rabbit bone from context 532 (the fill of Grave 533). A further ten rabbit bones from this phase (also intrusive) derive from context 674. These are consistent with being from a single very young individual. As with the assemblage from the Phase 1 ditch fills, the Phase 2 bones are generally poorly preserved and dominated by loose teeth fragments (Table 11).

Phase 3: the re-cut ring-ditch and later burials

As in the earlier assemblages, loose teeth are well-represented in the Phase 3 assemblage and the bulk of the material is poorly preserved. All the material identified to species derived from ditch fills from this phase; bones from non-ditch deposits (contexts 434 and 526, placed deposits) consists of a small quantity of very poorly preserved, unidentified material. Again cattle bones are the most frequently recorded (Table 9), although given the poor conditions of preservation, the greater robusticity of cattle bones may mean that they are being preferentially preserved. Roe deer is represented by a single hand-excavated fragment of shed antler from context 737 (and therefore represents a collected specimen, not a hunted animal).

Bulk-sieved samples from eight Phase 3 contexts also produced zooarchaeological material (Table 10). These confirm that cattle is the most common domestic animal, but that pig and sheep were also represented. Badger and rabbit bones (probably intrusive) were also recorded from Grave 729 (context 728). A range of microfauna, also recovered via the sampling programme (Table 10), will be discussed below.

Phase 4: the late Iron Age feature

A partial horse skeleton was recovered from a late Iron Age feature cut into the Phase 3 ditch (context 698). That the skeleton was not found in articulation (*see* p 37) and that large parts of the skeleton are absent, may indicate that it may have undergone some form of predepositional 'manipulation' (eg butchery, redeposition, etc). All the horse bones, and the sixty-two unidentified cattle-sized fragments from the same context (Table 9), exhibit a consistent colour and state of preservation, and all appear consistent with being from a single animal. A single pig femur is also present in this context.

Bones present include elements of the skull and jaw bones (including the left M_2, M_3 and M^2, and the right M^1, M^2 and M^3), several cervical, thoracic, lumbar vertebrae and ribs, the left and right scapula, the right radius and ulna, the left and right humerus, and the left and right pelvis. Measurements of the crown heights of the teeth give estimated ages, after Levine (1982, Appendix IIIa), of 9–10 years for the left M_2 and right M^3, and 10-11 years for both left and right M^2s and the left M^1. The animal, therefore, would have been about 10 years old at death. There is no evidence for cause of death or butchery on the skeleton.

On British Iron Age and Roman sites, evidence for the deliberate deposition of horse is recognised as both complete burials and disarticulated remains, and is identified in a range of contexts (eg Bendrey *et al* 2010; King 2005; Morris 2011). Meanings associated with the 'ritual' deposition of animal remains may be transmitted through the manipulation of body parts and also the location of deposition (Bendrey 2007, chapter 7). Animal burials may also be associated with 'rubbish' disposal (Hill 1995), and perhaps disease containment (eg Bendrey 2010b; 2008b). Whether or not the location of the horse, within the earlier Phase 3 ditch is of significance, is uncertain, although other such finds, that perhaps respect earlier monuments, are known from elsewhere (eg Amour-Chelu 1998; Bendrey *et al* in press). At about 10 years old the horse was an animal still in its prime, and if it was killed specifically for burial then it may represent the foregoing of an item of significant value.

Phase 5: the Roman ditch and later activity

The Phase 5 zooarchaeological assemblage all derived from the fills of the Roman ditch. It is a small assemblage, and again generally poorly preserved and dominated by loose teeth (Tables 9 and 11). Three horse fragments (two loose teeth and a pelvis fragment) came from the Roman ditch. One tooth, a worn upper deciduous premolar ($dP^{3/4}$), from context 560, produced an age estimate of between four months and three years of age for the death of the animal (Levine 1982, 245).

Phase 6: animal disturbance

Both a badger sett and rabbit warren had significantly disturbed the centre of the burial mound. Both these species are evidenced also by bones (Table 9), which by their state of preservation are clearly intrusive. A number of mole and fox bones are also probably intrusive (Tables 9 and 10).

This material also produced a large number of perinatal domestic animal bones, including thirty-seven neonatal and foetal pig bones (including four mandibles aged *c* 0–4 months at death (Ma 2008; Table 12)), seven neonatal sheep bones and two foetal cattle bones (Table 11). This material is discussed in detail below, as is the microfauna recovered by both bulk-sampling and hand-recovery (Tables 9 and 10).

Discussion

Natural and anthropogenic bone accumulations

To understand the origins of the zooarchaeological material recovered from Eastling Down barrow we need to consider the role of intrusive burrowing animals in the mound, and their potential as natural bone accumulators. This is particularly relevant in discussion of the origins of the high number of perinatal remains in the assemblage.

Badgers will scavenge carrion, and may also kill lambs (Neal 1986, 125–31). Neal (1986, 125) states, however, that whereas foxes habitually take prey back to their earth when they have cubs, badgers do not do this as they suckle their cubs for 3–4 months, by which time they are able to forage for themselves. Badgers typically eat their prey on the spot, and although it is extremely unusual, it is known for badgers to take food back to the sett. Neal (1986, 124–5) reports a case in which a new born calf had been found dragged into the main entrance of a sett still alive. Such behaviour is very rare, usually when such carrion as a still born farm animal is eaten it will be eviscerated where it is found (Neal 1986, 131).

Amongst the neonatal material, evidence of gnawing is only recorded on one fragment, an ulna from Phase 6 (context 649) and in general the material does not exhibit the marks suggestive of having been accumulated by small carnivores (Mallye *et al* 2008). Also, none of the bones exhibit the degradation of the surface that would indicate that they had passed through the digestive tract of a carnivore. Stallibrass (1990, 153) reports that sheep-sized bones recovered from fox scats are small and unidentifiable 'crumbs'. The state of preservation of the bones, therefore, argues against them being accumulated by mammalian carnivores, and for their deposition through human agency, either as natural casualties from breeding or as deliberate deposits. However, in contrast to this interpretation, the concentration of the bulk of these finds in the features identified as animal burrows could argue that their origin may indeed be intrusive. The material from the internal features exhibits a better state of preservation than that from the ditch deposits, and the perinatal bones occasionally exhibit better preservation than other bones from the same context. Variation in and between contexts, however, has made it difficult to make any clear overall distinctions.

The perinatal remains

As stated, there is a significant presence of perinatal bone in the assemblage, making up 51 per cent of the hand-recovered pig bones, 38 per cent of the sheep, and 3 per cent of the cattle bones (Table 11). Both foetal and neonatal bones are represented in the material, based on unfused diaphysis lengths (Prummel 1987a; 1987b; 1989), with foetal remains being represented in the pig and cattle assemblages.

The presence of perinatal bones is often taken to infer breeding animals in the vicinity of a site. Mortality frequencies for young domestic animals can be high, with modern figures in England and Wales of up to 20 per cent in piglets and 11 per cent in lambs (Baker and Brothwell 1980, 13; see also Mellor and Stafford 2004), and may fluctuate according to various factors, such as disease or climate. Foetal mortality may have a number of causes, including potential abortifacient pathogens that affect domestic livestock (Givens and Marley 2008).

The material is spatially concentrated in the features within the barrow, and a smaller number of remains are recovered from the Phase 1 ditch fills (detailed above). As discussed, it is notable that much of the perinatal material is more or less associated with those remains of burrowing thought to be intrusive to the archaeological levels. This leads to two possible conclusions: 1) the perinatal remains are carnivore scavenged remains (probably by badgers) from breeding populations of domestic animals contemporaneous with later carnivore activity at the site; 2) burrowing animals dug into and disturbed stratified archaeological deposits containing these perinatal remains. As discussed above, the lack of marks of carnivore damage on the material argues against the first interpretation. If it is the second, then we need to consider how these remains may have entered the archaeological record. Perinatal remains representing a 'background' mortality signature of breeding animal populations would not survive so visibly unless the carcasses were being deliberately deposited (as perinatal remains are delicate and particularly susceptible to taphonomic attrition). As Serjeantson (2011, 74) argues:

> Skeletons and part-skeletons of neonatal and very young piglets, calves and lambs ... are often thought to be natural deaths, but there is no reason why such casualties should be carefully buried out of the reach of dogs. These newborn animals may be better considered as some kind of sacrifice or offering. A rite in which the firstborn calf or lamb was sacrificed to ensure fertility is known widely from ethnographic studies.

One 'functional' possibility might be that mortalities caused by infectious disease may have been buried as a form of disease containment, as certain abortifacient pathogens, such as *Brucella* spp, have economic implications for farmed herds (being responsible for infertility and drops in milk production, as well as abortions), but also represent potential infection risks to contiguous animal and human populations (Bendrey *et al* 2008; 2011; Schlafer and Miller 2007). However, the 'functional' disposal of such remains at a mortuary barrow site perhaps seems unlikely, and an interpretation in which these young animals were included as deliberate, 'ritual', deposits may be preferred.

Microfauna ecology and local environment

A number of small vertebrates are present in both the hand-recovered and bulk sampled assemblages (Tables 9 and 10), these have potential for informing on the local environment of the site.

Water, bank and field vole are all recorded from the bulk samples (Table 10). The current habitat of the water vole is mainly on well vegetated banks of lowland rivers, ponds, canals and drainage ditches (Stoddart 1977, 199), but archaeological evidence shows them occupying a wider range of habitats, often far from water (O'Connor 2000, 128–9). Bank voles prefer areas with thick cover, and are abundant in deciduous woodland and scrub (Flowerdew 1977a, 178). The habitat of the field vole is mainly rough, ungrazed grassland (Evans 1977, 189).

Specimens recorded as *Apodemus* spp may have derived wood mouse, *Apodemus sylvaticus* (L), or the yellow-necked mouse, *Apodemus flavicollis* (Melchior), but overlap in size range for these two animals prevents identification of these remains to species. The wood mouse has an extremely varied habitat, occurring wherever there is the cover of trees, shrubs or rocks, and also in hedgerows, field and gardens (Flowerdew 1977b, 210–2). The yellow-necked mouse mainly inhabitats woods, hedgerows and field edges (Corke 1977, 217–8).

The common shrew will occur in most habitats as long as there is plenty of ground cover present (Corbet 1977, 50).

All the amphibian bones from the bulk samples (Table 10) derive from samples taken from areas of animal burrowing disturbance (Phase 6). Common toad and common frog have been identified, and material simply identified to toad and frog probably derives from these two species, respectively. Common toad bones were also recovered from the hand-recovered material, from Phases 1 and 6 (Table 9). Toad bones are more common than those of frog, and as toads prefer a drier habitat than frogs then this may suggest quite a dry environment. Toads however, may hibernate in disused burrows of mammals (Smith, 1951, 107) or in loose rubble (O'Connor 2000, 126) and so may enter the archaeological record by failure to survive the winter.

Slow worms, also present in Phase 6 samples (Table 10), live in a wide variety of habitats. They favour dry country, but are equally at home on heaths, in hedgerows, in open woodland and in gardens (Smith 1951, 173). Smith (*ibid*) also notes that the slow worm is a regular burrower and spends a good deal of its time underground.

The possibility that these remains represent badger prey needs to be considered before any conclusions can be drawn. Badgers will eat all the small mammals recorded, and also eat toads, frogs and slow-worms (Neal 1986, 122–30). The number of rabbit bones recorded (Table 9), and the presence of neonates suggests that rabbits were living and breeding in a warren on site. Badgers will eat very young rabbits, but they are eaten whole and the bones can be completely digested (Neal 1986, 110). The small vertebrate bones are generally well preserved, not exhibiting the surface corrosion (by digestive acids) or fragmentation recorded from bones in carnivore scats (Lyman 1994, 204–6; Stallibrass 1990, 153–5). The small vertebrate assemblage therefore probably largely represents animals that lived and died around the barrow, indicating a local environment that was probably quite dry, with plenty of nearby ground cover, and possibly near woodland or scrub (contemporaneity of all remains with the archaeological features is hard to prove as some burrowing species are present).

Conclusions

Archaeological investigations at Eastling Down barrow produced a small, but diverse, faunal assemblage. It is evident that different parts of the assemblage have undergone differing taphonomic pathways. In general the material from the internal features of the barrow tends to be better preserved than that from the ditches. This could be, to a large extent, due to slower assemblage formation rates in the ditch deposits, exposing the material to greater taphonomic attrition and resulting in a poorer quality of preservation and assemblages dominated by loose teeth (Table 11). The internal features of the barrow, and to some extent the ditches, have been disturbed by burrowing animals, the intrusive bones of which are evident in the assemblages (Tables 9 and 10). Movement of these burrowers within the site may also have moved earlier archaeological remains and it is perhaps best that the location of some finds are treated with caution, such as the possible early domestic horse tooth, and also the few perinatal pig and sheep remains from the Phase 1 ditch (Table 11). It is also not completely clear whether burrowing carnivores introduced prey skeletal material (microfaunal remains and perinatal remains of domestic animals) into the archaeological record of the barrow. However, the dearth of characteristic marks of carnivore gnawing and digestion, and a consideration of badger ecology, would suggest that these are not accumulations of prey remains. This means that the perinatal pig, sheep and cattle bones could represent a deliberately deposited assemblage into the internal features of the barrow, as some form of ritual of offering, which would be a find unusual for this period (Serjeantson 2011) and of significant interest.

Environmental evidence[2]

Mark Robinson

Molluscs

Two column samples were analysed; one associated with the Phase 3 ditch flanking the south side of the barrow (Section 6) and the second from a Romano-British boundary ditch that cut the north-west side of the barrow (Section 8). In addition to the column sample from the barrow ditch, shells were also examined from the flots from grave fills, cremations and 'placed' deposits in the barrow.

Methods and results

The samples were analysed following the methods of Evans (1972, 445). One kilogram of each sample was broken up in water; any shells which floated poured off onto a 0.5mm mesh and the residue sieved down to 0.5mm. The dried flots and residues were sorted under a binocular microscope for molluscan remains, which were identified with reference to the collections of the Oxford University Museum of Natural History. The results have been tabulated for each sequence in Tables 13 and 14. The tables give the minimum number of individuals represented by the fragments in each sample. *Cecilioides acicula* was excluded because it is a species which burrows deeply. Nomenclature follows Kerney (1999).

The barrow ditch (Feature 541) (Fig 34)

The southern outer ditch of the barrow (Phase 3) in sector 5 (Section 6, see Fig 7) had been cut about 1m deep into chalk bedrock. The filling of the ditch subdivided into three phases: primary fill (Contexts 705, 711,721,722, 723, 736, and 737); deposits associated with erosion of the ditch sides and mound (Contexts 675, 676 and 702) and subsequent chalk-loam accumulation in the ditch (Contexts 496, 546, 548, 659 and 695).

The molluscs from the primary fill of the ditch (90+cm and 80–90cm) were mostly open country species but there was also a major shade-loving element. The concentration of shells was low. The most numerous species was *Vallonia costata*, which greatly outnumbered *V Excentrica*. This was probably a result of the rupestral habitat presented by the unstable, chalk rubble sediments in the ditch. The shade-loving species did not comprise a full woodland fauna, *Carychium tridentatum* in particular being absent. Neither, however, was it the restricted shade-loving fauna of rock-rubble habitats for it included species such as *Aegopinella pura* and *Clausilia bidentata*. Many of these shells were in a damaged state and it is thought likely that they had been amongst soil belonging to a former woodland phase which had been eroded into the ditch.

2 The reports on molluscs and carbonised plant remains were only taken to assessment.

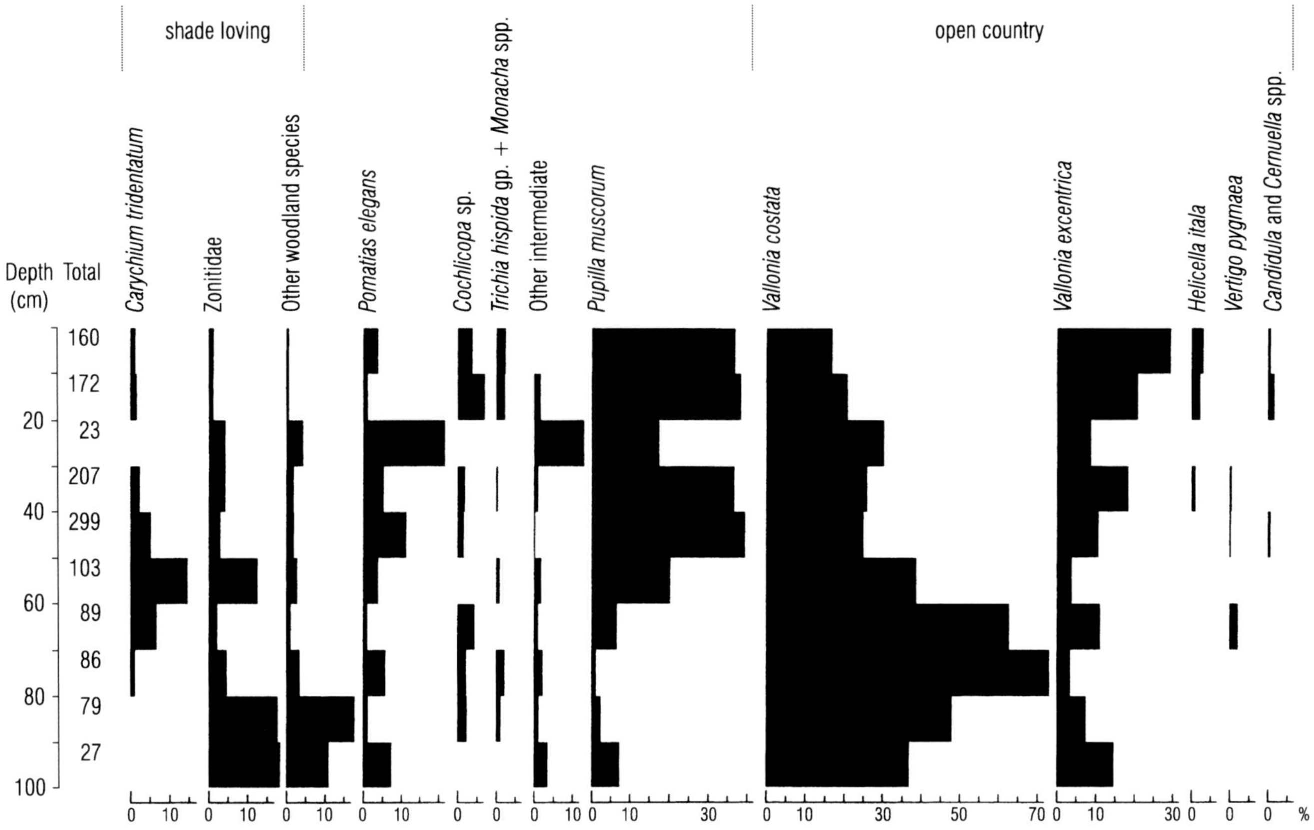

Fig 34. Eastling Down: molluscs from the southern outer ditch (541).

Context	721	676	695			546				
Depth (cm)	90+	80 90	70 80	60 70	50 60	40 50	30 40	20 30	10 20	0 10
Pomatias elegans (Müll)	2	1	5	1	4	34	11	5	2	6
Acicula fusca (Mont)		1			2	3	1			
Carychium tridentatum (Ris)			1	6	15	16	5		3	2
Cochlicopa sp		2	2	4		5	4	1	12	6
Vertigo pygmaea (Drap)				1		1	1			
Vertigo sp				1						
Pupilla muscorum (L)	2	2	1	6	21	118	76	4	66	59
Vallonia costata (Mull)	4	13	16	23	20	44	24	3	16	14
V excentrica Sterki	2	2	1	4	2	19	17	1	16	21
Vallonia sp	8	29	49	39	22	44	51	5	40	39
Acanthinula aculeata (Müll)						2	1			
Ena obscura (Müll)		2								
Punctum pygmaeum (Drap)		2	2							
Discus rotundatus (Müll)		3								
Vitrina sp	3			1						
Vitrea sp	1	9	2	1	7	1				1
Nesovitrea hammonis (Ström)						1	5		1	
Aegopinella pura (Ald)	2	2			1	3	3			
A nitidula (Drap)		1	2	1	5	4	1		1	1
Oxychilus cellarius (Müll)	2	2								
Limax or *Deroceras* sp									1	
Clausilia bidentata (Ström)		6	1		1	1	2	1	1	1
Candidula gigaxii (Pfeif						2			1	1
cf *Cernuella virgata* (da Costa)									2	
Helicella itala (L)							2		4	5
Monacha cartusiana (Müll)							1		3	4
Trichia hispida gp		1	2		1				1	
Cepaea sp	1	1	2	1	2	1	1	1	1	
Arianta or *Cepaea* sp							1	2	1	
Total	27	79	86	89	103	299	207	23	172	160

Table 13. Eastling Down: snails from the ditch.

Context	565	564	563		560		412	
Depth (cm)	70 75	50 60	40 45	30 40	20 30	15 20	10 15	1 10
Pomatias elegans (Müll)	1	1	3	3	3			5
Carychium tridentatum (Ris)					4			
Cochlicopa sp	1		7	2	11	1	2	
Vertigo pygmaea (Drap)	2		2	2		1	3	2
Vertigo sp			1			1		3
Pupilla muscorum (L)	28	4	73	40	70	7	58	64
Vallonia costata (Mull)	5	4	17	13	29	5	16	11
V excentrica Sterki	13	4	19	11	6	4	21	13
Vallonia sp	14	6	30	13	54	8	25	17
Punctum pygmaeum (Drap)	1						1	1
Vitrina sp		1						
Nesovitrea hammonis (Ström)					1			
Aegopinella pura (Ald)					2			
A nitidula (Drap)							1	
Clausilia bidentata (Ström)					1			
Monacha cartusiana (Müll)	3		1	3	3			
Trichia hispida gp	10		5	5	1	2	1	1
Candidula gigaxii (Pfeif)							1	
Helicella itala (L)	9	1	3	4	3		8	6
Cepaea sp			1		1		1	1
Arianta or *Cepaea* sp						1	2	
Total	87	21	162	96	189	30	140	124

Table 14. Eastling Down: Iron Age snails.

The next two samples of the column (Samples 70–80 and 60–70cm) were from rubble which had probably eroded from the ditch sides and from the mound. *Vallonia costata* again predominated but the proportion of shade-loving species was much reduced. The appearance of Carychium tridentatum was possibly due to some herbaceous vegetation becoming established amongst the spills of chalk. Snail concentrations remain low.

The top sample from the weathered rubble (Sample 50–60cm) and the first two samples from the subsequent fill to the ditch (Samples 40–50cm and 30–40cm) gave evidence for conditions becoming somewhat more stable. Shell concentrations increased and the proportion of *Pupilla muscorum* rose at the expense of *Vallonia costata* to become the predominant species. The majority of the shells from these samples were appropriate to short-turfed grassland, perhaps with some bare patches. However, *Pomatias elegans* was sufficiently well represented to suggest ares of loose soil into which it could burrow. Some of these deposits could have been derived from nearby cultivation. The proportion of shade-loving species rose again in this part of the sequence. While *Carychium tridentatum* could have found suitable conditions amongst tussocks, members of Zonitidae such as *Aegopinella nitidula*, and other woodland species including *Acicula fusca*, were also present. It is possible that some woodland survived in the vicinity of the barrow. Two examples of *Candidula gigaxii* from Sample 40–50cm were possibly intrusive because this species is generally regarded as a medieval introduction.

Shell numbers were very much reduced in Sample 20–30cm, which possibly reflected an episode of rapid sedimentation. The top two samples from the column (Samples 10–20cm and 10–0cm) contained similar open country molluscan assemblages. *Pupilla muscorum* was again the most numerous species but *Vallonia excentrica* outnumbered *V Cosata*, *Pomatias elegans* and shade-loving species were scarce. The immediate environs of the barrow were perhaps open grassland. The occurrence of shells of alien Helicellinae including *Candidula gigaxii* would suggest a medieval or recent date for these sediments. *Monacha cartusiana* was present in the top two samples.

Flots from two 'placed' deposits

Two contexts stand apart in containing a majority of shells from shade-loving molluscs including the true woodland species *Acicula fusca* (context 680, a 'placed' deposit in the base of the Phase 1 ditch and context 724, a 'placed' deposit in the Phase 3 ditch, *see* Fig 7 for location). The more numerous shade-loving species in these samples included *Carychium tridentatum*, *Discus rotundatus*, *Aegopinella pura* and *A Nitidula*.

These and other contexts (cremation 433 and cremation pit 495), though not ideal for molluscan analysis because they have a high potential for containing shells reworked from earlier deposits, do however raise the possibility that some scrub or trees had become established on the barrow in the early Bronze Age and again in the middle and late Bronze Age.

The Roman ditch (Feature 413; Section 8) (Fig 35)

The ditch was cut across the north-west side of the barrow and extended about 0.75m into the chalk bedrock (Fig 7). Ditch fills consisted of three bulk layers of clay-loam (basal 565, middle 563 and upper 412) alternating with two layers of chalk loam (lower loam 564 and upper loam 560).

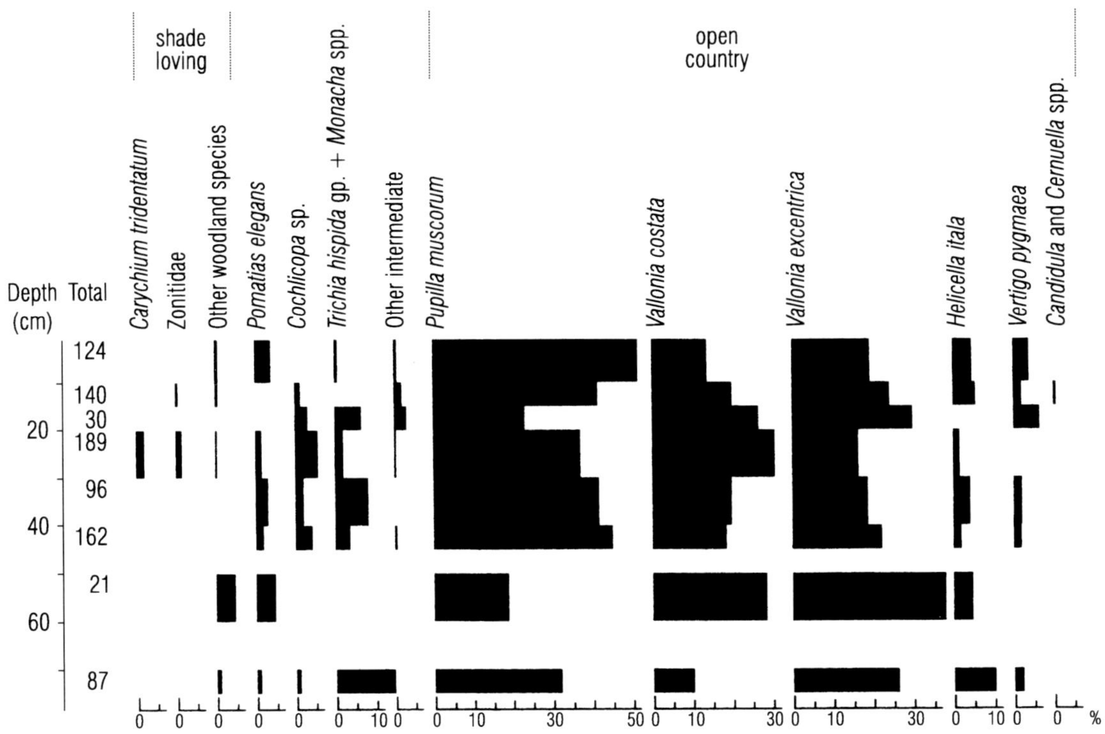

Fig 35. Eastling Down: molluscs from the Roman ditch (413).

Dry-ground, open-country molluscs predominated throughout the sequence, with *Pupilla muscorum* being particularly numerous. *Vallonia costata* and *V Excentrica* were also abundant. There were some changes in the proportions of the different species in the column but they do not seem to have been of major interpretative significance. The concentration of shells was, however, related to the rate of sedimentation. Sample 50–60cm, from the lower rubble layer, and Sample 15–20cm from the upper rubble layer, both had very much reduced numbers of shells in comparison with the other samples. The molluscan fauna would be appropriate to short-turf, dry grassland with some bare patches, but could also have occurred under conditions of Roman cultivation. It is possible that the majority of sediment in the ditch, including the chalk rubble layers, had been derived from the erosion of the barrow mound and perhaps a bank that probably accompanied the boundary ditch.

Conclusion

Clearance of the landscape around the barrow may have been of only limited extent by the early Bronze Age with woodland probably surviving in the vicinity of the barrow into the later Bronze Age. Although the immediate environs of the barrow may have remained open, some scrub or tree growth possibly occurred on the mound itself.

Conditions in the Roman period seem to have been very open and it is likely that some sediment in the ditches derived directly from cultivation.

The southern outer ditch of the barrow and the Roman ditch do not seem to have been completely filled until the medieval period or more recently, conditions remaining open.

Carbonised plant remains

During the excavation of the barrow twenty-three samples, largely taken from inhumation burials and 'placed' deposits and ranging from 4–37 litres in size were taken for charred plant remains.

The samples were floated onto a 0.5mm mesh and the dried flots scanned at x10 magnification for charred plant remains. Charcoal was present in seven of the flots. Representative fragments of charcoal were broken in the appropriate planes and examined at up to x400 magnification for full identification. The results are given in Table 15. In addition two seeds of *Crataegus* cf *monogyna* (hawthorn)

	Context	494	577	600	680	686	724	728
	Sample volume (l)	12	8	15	19	37	9	21
Prunus sp	sloe etc	-	-	-	+++	-	-	-
Pomoideae indet	hawthorn, apple etc	+	++	+++	-	++	+	-
Quercus sp	oak	-	-	-	+	-	-	+

Table 15. Eastling Barrow: charcoal.

were found in Context 724 (a 'placed' deposit located in the base of the east terminal of the Phase 3 ditch), but charred seeds were otherwise absent.

A very small quantity of *Quercus* sp (oak) charcoal was found in Context 728 (the fill of Grave 729, containing adult inhumation SK 730 dated 1920–1625 cal BC; Table 2).

All the other charcoal was from three features (cremation pit 495, contexts 494, 577, 686 and 600 (dated 920–795 cal BC; Table 2); 'placed' deposit 680 in the primary ring-ditch, dated to the early Bronze Age and 'placed' deposit 724, in the Phase 3 ditch dated to the middle Bronze Age) and apparently represented the fuel used in pyres.

Contexts 494, 577, 600 and 686 all contained a considerable quantity of Pomoideae (hawthorn, apple etc), with Context 600 alone yielding about 0.5kg of charcoal from a 15 litre sample. Context 686 was the fill of an adjacent feature (Grave 687) cut by the cremation pit. Carbonised wood recovered from the grave fill was almost certainly from cremation pit 495. Context 680 contained *Prunus* sp (sloe) charcoal with a very little *Quercus* sp. The two seeds of hawthorn in Context 724 were more likely to have been in branches used for fuel than to represent collected wild food.

It is possibly of significance that the majority of the charcoal from the cremations was from hawthorn or sloe which are thorny shrubs, rather than from oak. This might suggest that fuel was derived from a largely cleared landscape.

The Eastling Down barrow in context

John Hammond

Any attempt to contextualize the occurrence of a late third millennium BC ring-ditched monument, or to extract meaning from its intermittent use as a repository for human remains, presents considerable challenges. Not least because the form in which Eastling Down presented itself in the modern era was demonstrably different from that created by the architect-builders or even as seen by the generations of people who put it to use. When excavated, it had endured more than 4,000 years of change, wrought on it by a combination of human agency, taphonomic processes and environmental attrition. Consequently, only fragmentary and decaying remnants of the monument's cumulative iterations survived and now even those have been consumed by mattock, trowel and spade.

Such a sequence of creation, modification, eventual abandonment, decay and destruction is not unusual and would barely be worth mentioning if it were not for the fact that the biography of this particular monument is manifestly quite extraordinary. For a start, it seems to have been constructed during the earliest florescence of the round barrow tradition, at a time now being referred to as the British Chalcolithic (Sheridan 2012) and it remained intermittently active from that point on, throughout the entire Bronze Age and beyond. No other known Kentish 'barrow' has such a long evidentially attested use-life (Hammond 2010, 58–70), nor is there one which contains such a large assemblage of predominantly infant and child human burials.

These facts alone are sufficient to make this circular monument worthy of close scrutiny, but there are other anomalous characteristics which also demand attention: the most apparent being its elaborate morphology, along with the asymmetrical burial depositions and the absence of Beaker inhumations – a Chalcolithic/early Bronze Age burial tradition that is endemic to such early monuments. It is also important to address the question of how Eastling Down fits in to the prehistoric sacred landscape of east Kent, southern Britain as a whole and even the near continental English Channel region.

Cemetery barrows

One of the most distinctive features of Eastling Down is the number of burials it contains. There were at least eleven, which is a larger number than has yet been found in any other Kentish barrow (Hammond 2010, 137–58). Elsewhere in England, although not on the near continent, monuments with larger burial groups have been excavated, such as at Barnack, Cambridgeshire (Donaldson 1977; Fig 43). At least twenty-four burials were located within its concentric double-ditched circuit. Woodward refers to such monuments as cemetery barrows (2002). She suggests that these may have been constructed intentionally as communal burial places, where it was anticipated that funerary rites would take place generation after generation. This may go some way to explain why Eastling Down apparently had no central burial and why some areas were devoid of human depositions.

If such barrows were intended to house multiple burials this raises an interesting possibility. It is generally considered that the communal funerary rites of the Neolithic gave way to single occupancy round barrow burials and thus signalled a shift towards the growth of individual status within society (Thomas 1999). However, the concept of communal round barrows seems to suggest that personhood or individual identity may have been no more significant to the early Bronze Age population than it was to the people who preceded them.

A notable exception to this is the group who practiced Beaker funerary rites. During the nascent Beaker period flat-grave burials and modestly proportioned single occupancy crouched inhumation barrows prevailed. This type of funerary tradition may owe its immediate antecedence to the Corded Ware burial practices which predominated in north-eastern Europe during the early part of the third millennium BC (Lanting and Van de Waals 1972). Numerous examples of such burials can be found throughout Kent but especially in Thanet at such places as Monkton-Mount Pleasant, Ramsgate (Clark 2008), St Peters, Margate (Minter and Herbert 1973) and Manston Runway Approach (Perkins and Gibson 1990). Inclusion within such graves of one or more objects from a range that has been dubbed the Beaker package clearly indicates that identity and status was important to these people.

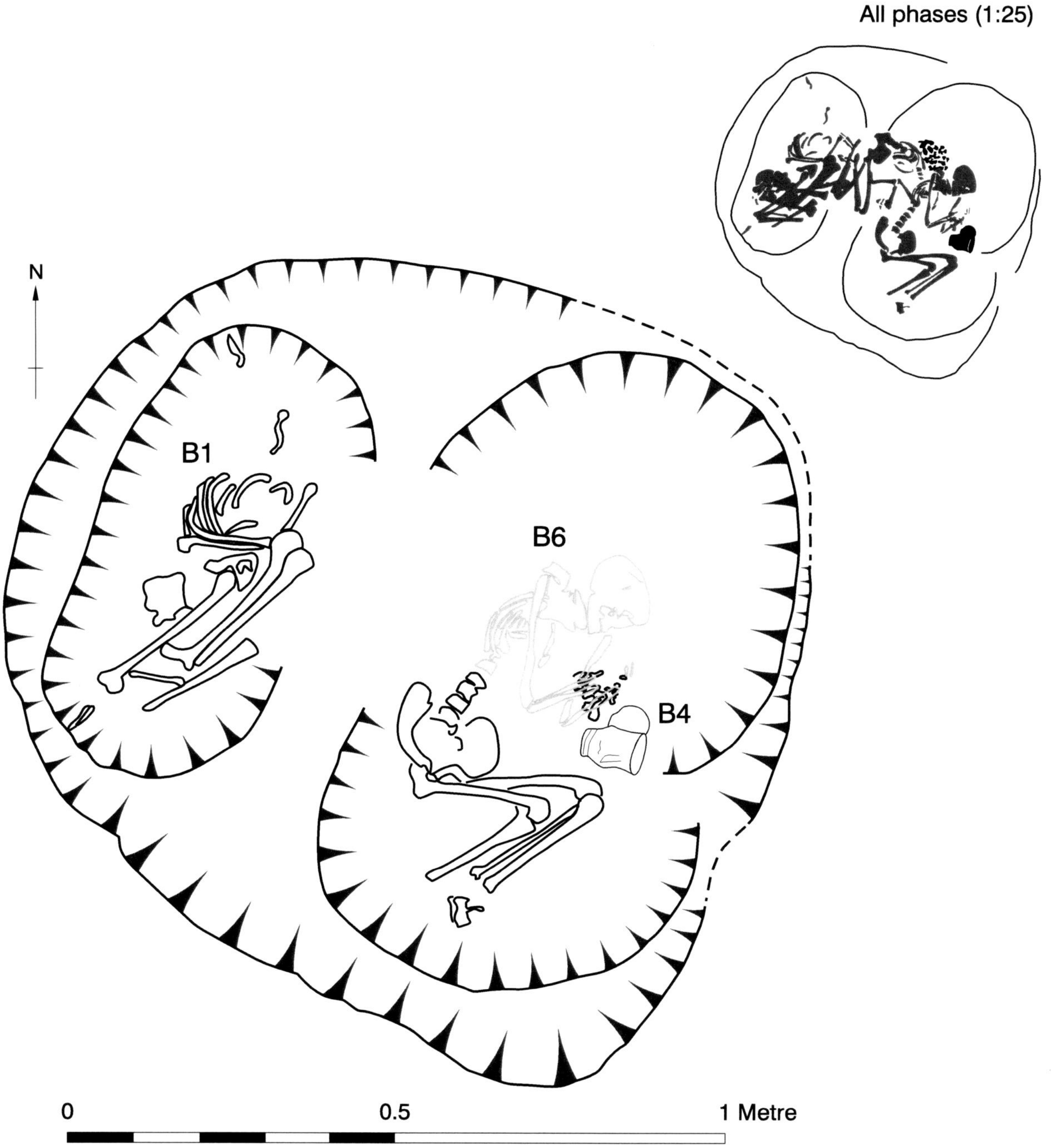

Fig 36. Primary burials at South Dumpton Down, a Beaker (B6), an infant (B4) and an adult male (B1), later joined by three adult crouched inhumations (inset) (after Perkins 1999). Scale 1.10.

Beaker burials are not always found in isolation. Some barrows with multiple human depositions also include them. One such was discovered at South Dumpton Down, near Ramsgate. This was a single ring-ditched monument containing six crouched adult inhumations and one infant, deposited over a 200 year period starting at around 2135 cal BC (Perkins 1999). The burials appear to have been placed one on top of another in a series of grave reopening events; but the primary deposition is most likely to have been the Beaker burial which is within its own pit, cut into the natural chalk subsoil and may therefore predate the construction of the mound and ring-ditch. It is of a man in his early twenties, possibly accompanied by the infant (Fig 36). However, at Eastling Down, and at a number of similar multi-phased complex monument sites Beaker burials do not appear to feature in the depositional sequence. This is not to imply that Beaker activity is entirely absent from such sites as sherds of rusticated domestic Beaker pottery are often found. However, these are distinct from the characteristic vessels that accompany burials.

A unique feature of the Eastling Down burial assemblage is the predominance of sub-adult interments. Even the disarticulated bone found within the bioturbated central area was largely that of children or infants. It is difficult to explain why this was so. Mizoguchi's (1993) quantative analysis of Bronze Age mortuary practices in the Yorkshire Wold demonstrates that when they occurred these burials were almost always secondary to adult inhumations, usually a male. Barrows where an infant or child was the primary interment make up only 3 per cent of the sample. This makes the apparent exclusivity afforded to children at Eastling Down all the more remarkable, especially as the only confirmed adult inhumation, a man in a wood-lined grave or coffin, took place centuries after the primary child burial.

Practically nothing is known about the role and status of children in early Bronze Age society or indeed how they were considered by their parents, other blood relatives and the wider community. The fact that at least some were afforded burials identical to those of adults suggests that in life they were regarded as fundamentally the same. It is also important to remember that being buried in a barrow or circular monument was in itself an exceptional event. It has been estimated that little more than 2 per cent, one person in forty-four, were afforded this type of burial (Allen 1965). As this was evidently a minority rite it follows that some form of selection must have been taking place. The inclusion of sub-adults within this selection may therefore imply the existence of inherited status, perhaps through membership of a distinctive clan, family or sect (Brück 2000).

Another intriguing aspect of the depositional record at Eastling Down is the length and number of temporal gaps between successive burial episodes, raising questions of community, clan or family memory and tradition. From first to last the burials span a remarkably long period of time, somewhere in excess of thirty-six generations of people. Up to a point, this issue was explored by Last (1998) in the context of barrows at Market Deeping and Barnack in Cambridgeshire, both comparable to Eastling Down except that the burials took place over a much shorter period of time. Even so, he concluded that each burial phase was sufficiently separated in time from the previous for it not to be fresh in the mind. He argued that, whilst the act of

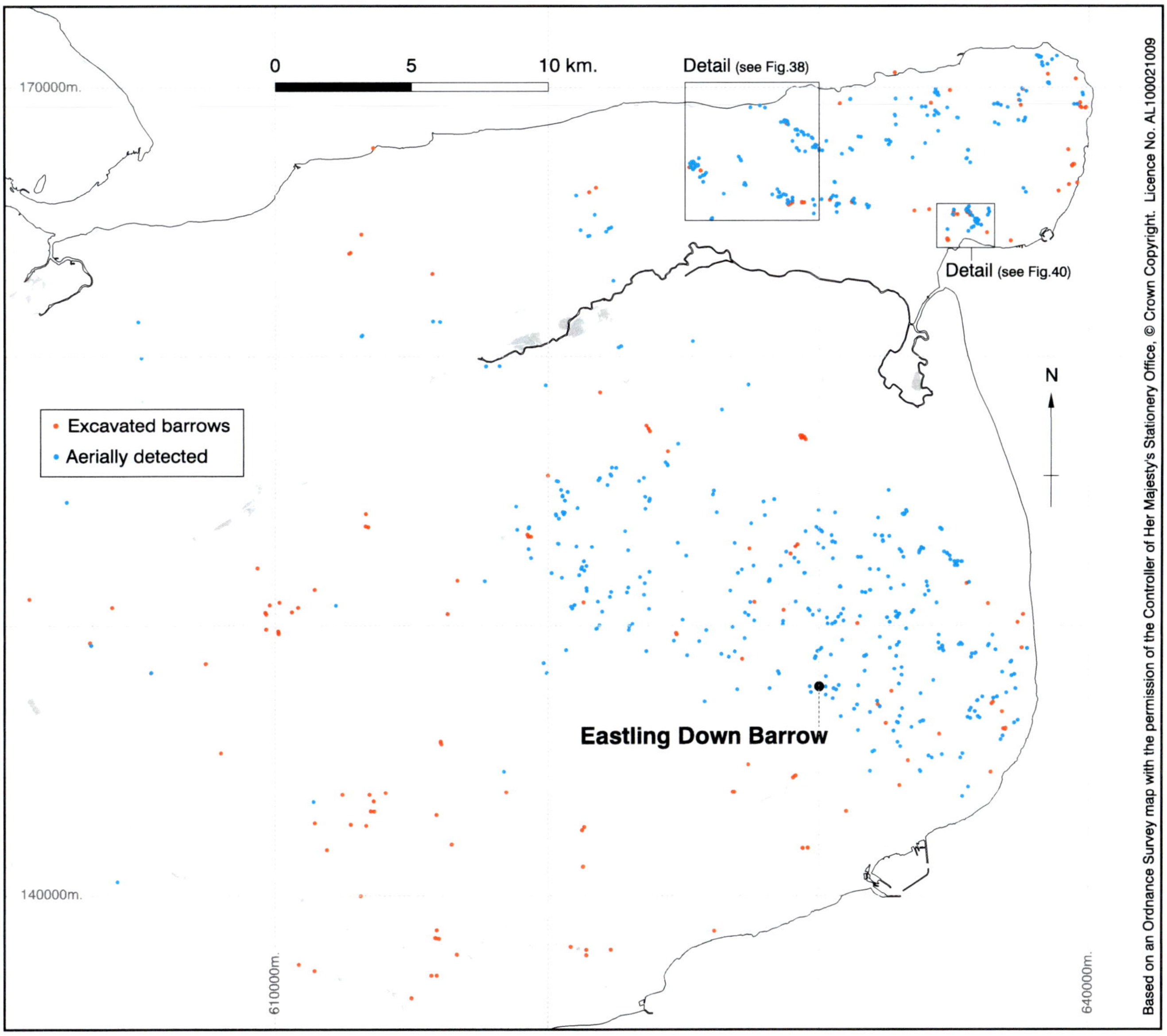

Fig 37. Distribution of known barrow sites in East Kent. Scale 1:250,000.

Fig 38. Cluster analysis of barrow distribution on the western flank of the Isle of Thanet (see Fig 37 for location).

periodically reactivating the barrow was intrinsically a continuation of traditions established by the ancestors, the positioning of individual burials and grave groups was deliberately structured to emphasise differences from those who had gone before.

It is possible to apply this interpretation to Eastling Down, especially in regard to the burial group in the south-west quadrant, which consisted of Grave 729, the adult male; the double burial in Grave 439, the urned burial 433 and burial 537. However, this still does not explain why the monument went through alternating periods of use and disuse. It has been asserted that during the early Bronze Age there was a preoccupation with concepts of circularity (Field 1998, 323), as in the cycle of the seasons and the movement of heavenly objects; and that round barrows and ring-ditches were physical manifestations of this obsession. It is therefore possible that this cosmologically bound doctrine dictated the periods of time when monuments of this kind should be active; but why in this case that also resulted in so many children being singled out for burial may never be known.

Founder monuments

Another concept that has been applied to multi-phased or aggrandized barrows with early inception dates is that of 'founder' monuments. These are defined as focal points around

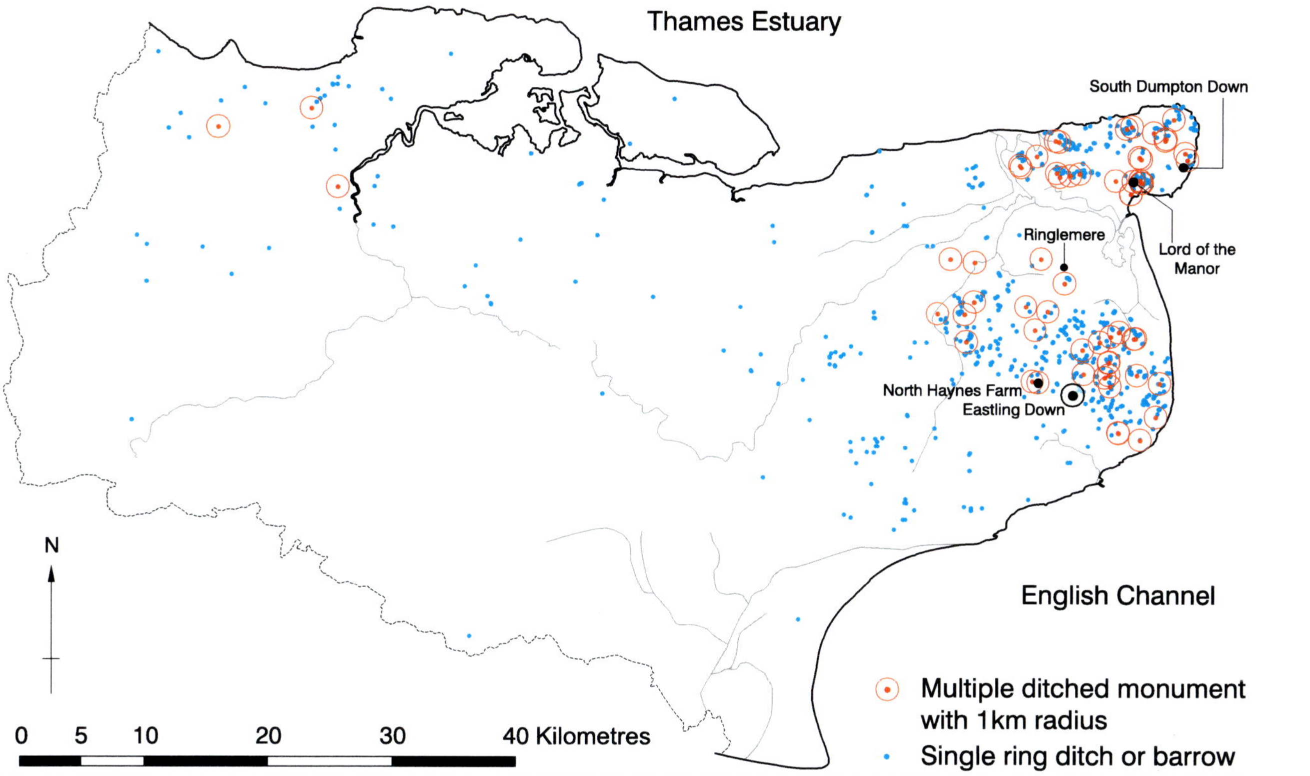

Fig 39. Distribution and disposition of barrows and ring-ditches across Kent. Multiple-circuited monuments are shown in red with a 1km territorial buffer encircling them. Scale 1:625,000.

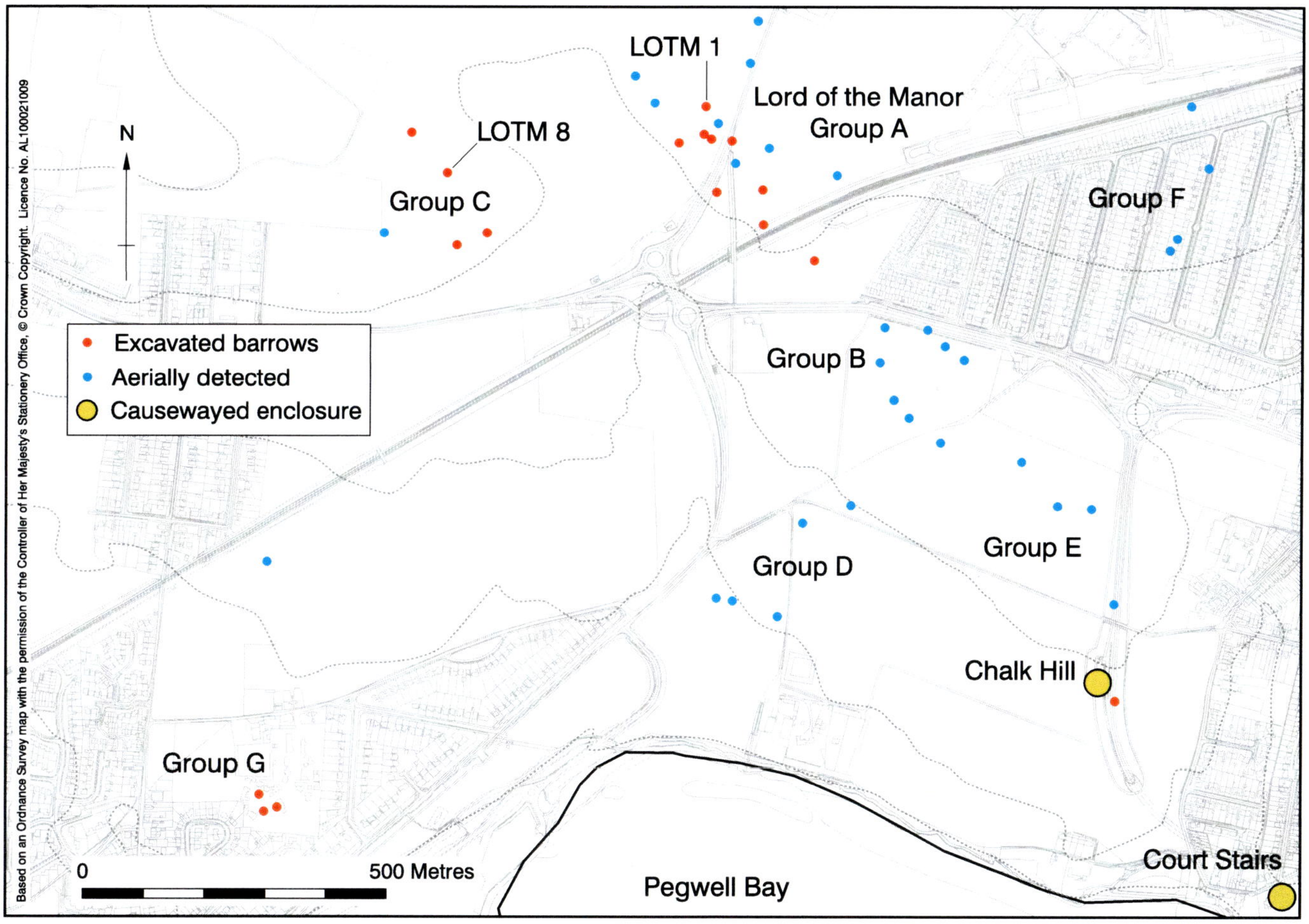

Fig 40. Lord of the Manor sacred funerary landscape overlain onto the modern map of the area. For location see Fig 37. Scale 1:12,500.

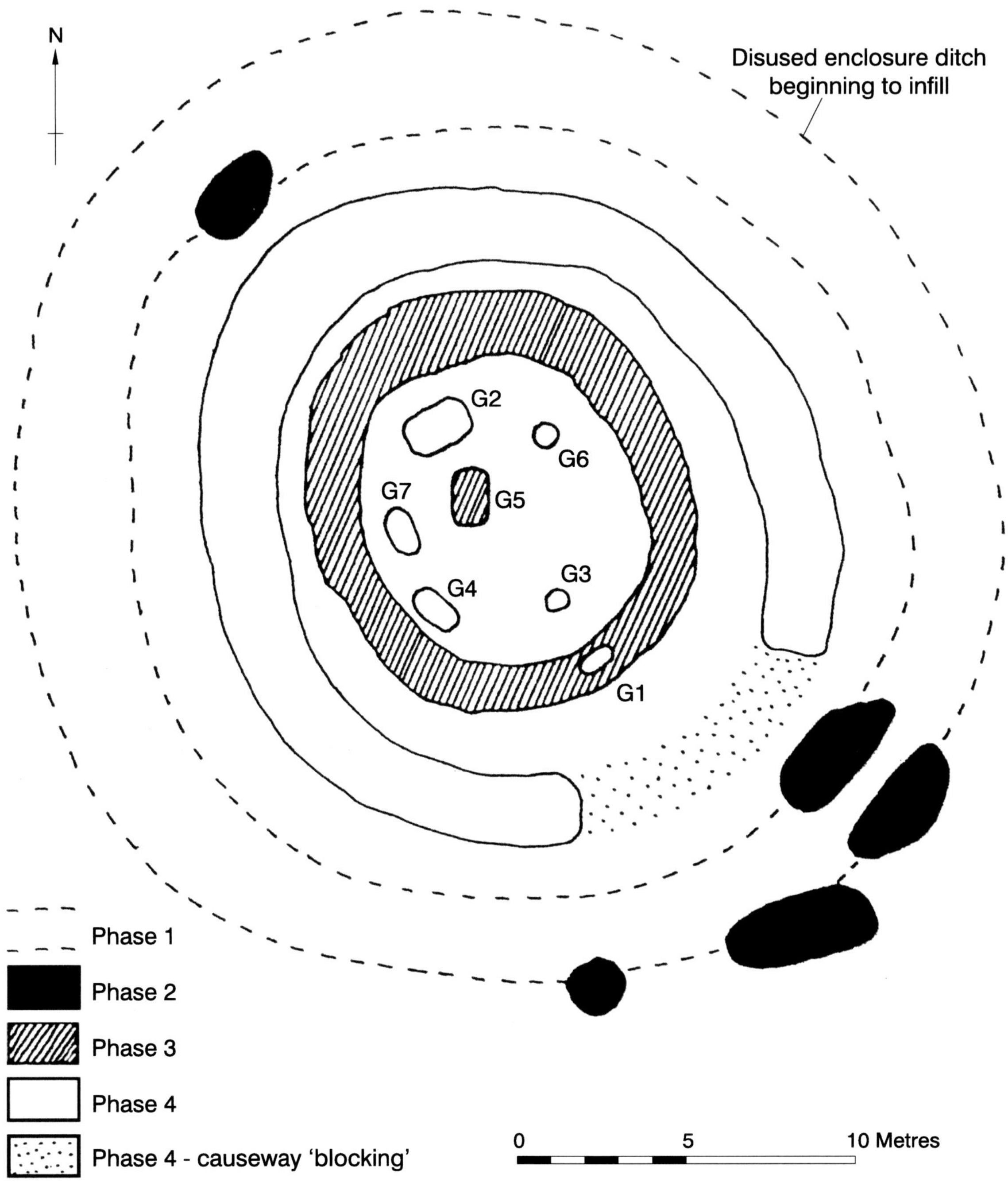

Fig 41. Phase plan of Lord of the Manor (LOTM) 1 showing the burial positions G1-G7 (after Macpherson-Grant 1977). Scale 1:200.

which barrow cemeteries evolved. Perkins (1999) invoked this notion in his unpublished thesis which explored the barrow landscape of Thanet. It is also an idea which finds favour with some scholars in northern France, Belgium and the Netherlands (Fokkens 2012; Ampe *et al* 1996; Piningre 1990).

At Eastling Down it can be shown through aerial photographic analysis that at least ten ring-ditches lie within a 1.6m radius (Fig 37), all presumed to be Bronze Age barrows - and it is known that at least one more is hidden within the copse that directly flanks the barrow on its eastern side (Grinsell 1992). Other more tightly clustered groups can be found scattered throughout the entire area. In fact, nearly 150 examples of dispersed, nucleated or linear barrow cemeteries have been identified in Kent (Fig 38), 204 in the north-eastern French coastal region and 180 in Belgian Flanders. Many of these groups appear to include complex, often multi-circuited and probably multi-phased, barrows. Indeed, analysis has shown that on average 60 per cent of these clusters in all three areas include at least one such monument (Hammond 2010, 211–19) (Fig 39).

However, this is far from proof that such spatial associations are the result of a deliberate intention to respect particularly aggrandized or complex monuments. In order to make such a claim it would be necessary to demonstrate that a presumed 'founder' monument dates to earlier than the structures around it and such evidence has not yet been forthcoming, except perhaps at the impressive linear cemetery of Barrow Hills, Radley, Oxfordshire (Barclay and Halpin 1997; Fig 43), although even there the dating sequence is incomplete.

As it stands, the evidence from Barrow Hills (Garwood 1997) does not support the concept that it is the larger more complex structures that should be interpreted as founder monuments. It seems to point to a relatively small and modest ring-ditch (611) being the first circular monument. It is described as a hengi-form structure incorporating the cremated bones of an infant. This was followed chronologically by barrow 4a, containing a single Beaker inhumation, and then by barrow 3, which consisted of a single ring-ditch, apparently containing a solitary central adult inhumation. Barrow 12 came next and was the only multi-phased and aggrandized monument within the cluster. It lay to the west of the main cemetery and consisted of a double ring-ditch enclosing at least seven burials: three child inhumations and four adult cremations. The inner circuit was constructed sometime between 2300–2100 BC, which is up to 200 years after ring-ditch 611, but broadly concurrent with Eastling Down. Its outer ditch and bank was added no more than 200 years later, replacing the silted-up and backfilled inner; physical alterations which also closely parallel Eastling Down.

In east Kent the best comparable evidence is found at Lord of the Manor (LOTM), which is located on the south-eastern flank of the Isle of Thanet, overlooking the entrance to the Wantsum Channel (Figs 40 and 43). Unfortunately, whilst nine out of the seventeen barrows in the main LOTM group 'A' have been excavated, the results have never been fully analysed or published. Despite this there is sufficient data to discern similarities between Eastling Down and LOTM 1, a

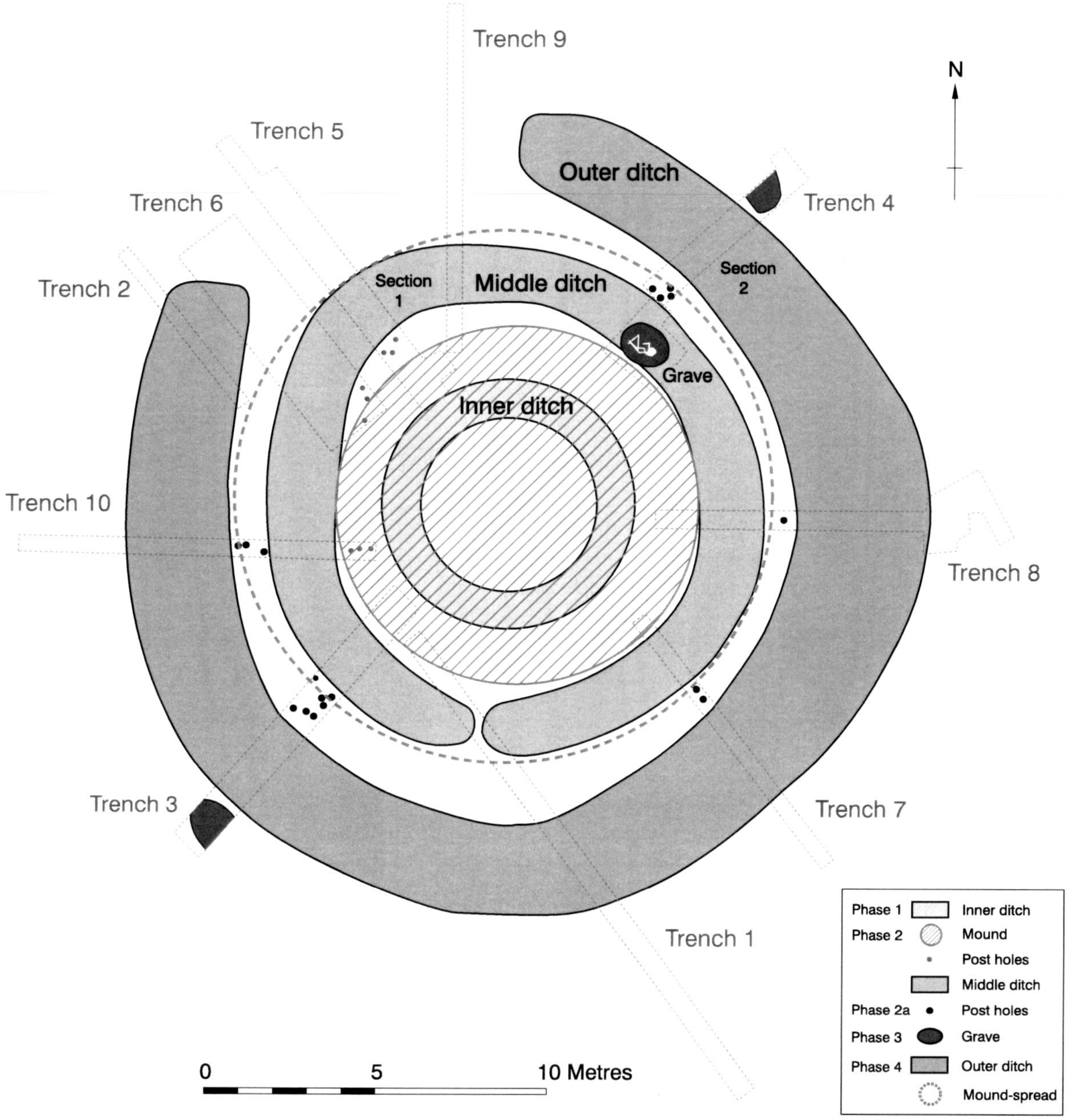

Fig 42. The multi-ringed complex circular monument located at Haynes Farm, Eythorne, 3km north-west of the site of Eastling Down. Scale 1:200.

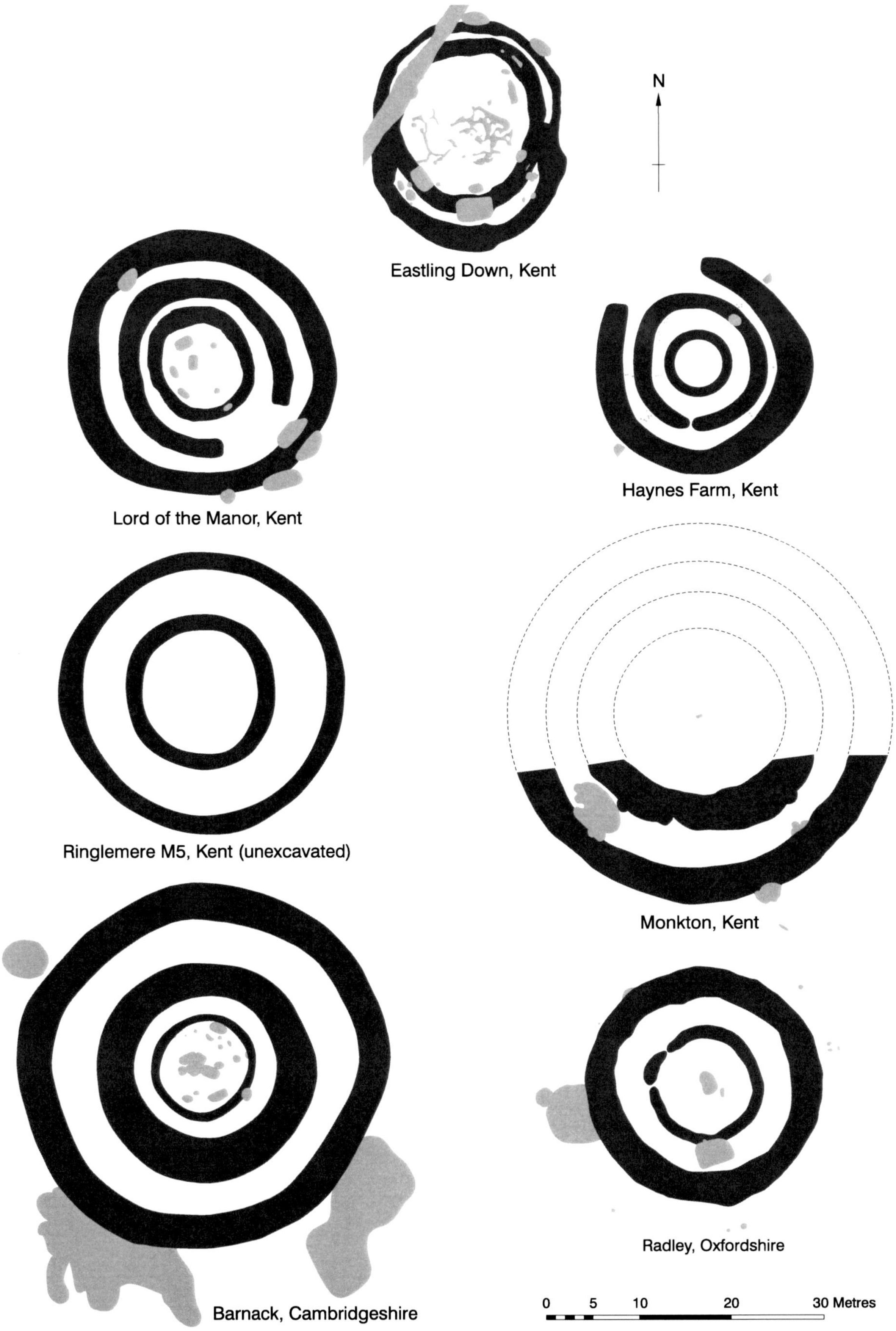

Fig 43. Eastling Down barrow compared with similar multiple circuited, multi-period complex monuments. Scale 1:625.

multi-phased barrow with multiple burials. For a start, the primary construction date is said to be earlier than 2100 BC. It is also one of the few monuments in Kent where Grooved Ware pottery has been found, along with Ringlemere, which is a henge surrounded by a barrow cluster incorporating a double-ditched monument (Parfitt and Needham 2007, 48), Haynes Farm, Eythorne (Parfitt 2004) and the seven other sites referred to earlier by Gibson (*see* p 81).

The first phase construction of LOTM 1 consisted of a 30m diameter ring-ditch with an interior bank (Fig 41). It was devoid of burials and the only find of any significance was a discrete deposit of Grooved Ware sherds. There followed four phases of modification and aggrandizement resulting in two more ditch circuits within the interior and the deposition of six inhumations, two of which were children, and a single inverted urn cremation of a neonate. Excepting a flat Beaker burial that was on the south-eastern periphery of the monument, the earliest grave is dated to approximately 1800 BC and seems to have been a near centrally placed double crouched Beaker burial of a man aged around 35 years at death and a girl aged 16 (G5). The remaining burials took place during the following 200 years, after which the monument was apparently deliberately decommissioned, although other barrows in the cluster continued to be used for funerary purposes until around 1500 BC (Macpherson-Grant 1977).

Lord of the Manor has another multi-phased, multiple-ditched monument, designated as LOTM 8. Very little data is available on this beyond the fact that it seems to have contained a central male Beaker burial and was located directly opposite LOTM 1 on the western slope of a small coombe valley (Fig 40). It was originally constructed with a single modest 9 metre diameter ditch circuit, which became totally subsumed when a mound was raised and a new ditch circuit, measuring 28m diameter, was cut.

Monumental complexity

Multiple-ditched monuments account for an average of 10 per cent of all the known Bronze Age ring-ditches and barrows in Kent (Fig 39), a proportion which also holds true on the near continent (Hammond 2010, 248–9). However, not all of them are multi-phased. In fact, of those that have been excavated, half were constructed as double-ditched monuments from the outset. These include B1 Cliffs End, Ramsgate (Schuster 2010); Bradstow School, Broadstairs; King Edwards School, Broadstairs (Moody 2008); Prings Quarry, Halling (Cruse 1985); Whitehill Road, Longfield (Bull 2012) and B1 Thanet Earth (Jon Rady, pers comm). A distinguishing factor is that in general these single-phase monuments date later than the multi-phase variants.

Apart from those already described, there are two other multi-phased monuments known in Kent. The first is Haynes Farm, Eythorne (Parfitt 2004) which is located almost exactly 3km north-west of Eastling Down (Fig 42). As referred to above, this is also one of the few circular monuments in Kent where Grooved Ware pottery has been recovered; implying that ritual activity more commonly associated with the Neolithic was taking place in the vicinity. The earliest form of this monument consisted of an 8 metre (approx) diameter ring-ditch. It was later buried by the raising of a mound and the cutting of a penannular ditch circuit measuring 11.5m diameter. This ditch was then allowed to naturally silt up before a grave containing a crouched male inhumation, radiocarbon-dated to 1907-1639 cal BC, 3460±60 BP (Beta 129270), was dug into the fill of its north-eastern sector. Soon after this event a final outer penannular ditch measuring 20m diameter was cut. Due to the fact that the monument was only partially excavated it is not known if other burials are contained within.

The remaining multi-phased monument was discovered during investigations prior to road widening of the A253, Monkton-Mount Pleasant, on the Isle of Thanet (Bennett *et al* 2008). It consisted of two, near concentric, circuits the outer measuring an exceptionally large 42m diameter and the inner 24m diameter (Fig 43). Only about half the monument was excavated. No burials were found and no samples suitable for radiocarbon dating were recovered. However, the size, form and developmental phases of this monument have led to it being tentatively interpreted as a Neolithic henge (Clark 2008, 96–7).

Conclusions

That early Bronze Age circular monuments of all types were used for human burial deposition is self-evident, but it would be unwise to assume that this was the only motive for construction or even the originally intended primary function. In recent decades, as modern excavation methods have generated more detailed datasets and radiometrically derived dates, understanding has grown to the point where singular explanations of this kind now look overly simplistic (Bradley 1993; 2007; Woodward 2002; Barclay and Halpin 1997; Last 1998; Mizoguchi 1993; Barrett 1990).

Garwood (2007) compellingly argues that interpreting all so-called barrows as nothing other than burial mounds, whose purpose and meaning remained constant throughout their use-life, is to deny the complexity of human belief and its variability over time. Furthermore, he singles out monuments with primary construction phases that predate 2150 BC, such as Easting Down, as being more liable to have been deliberately located on sites that were already associated with ritual activities like ancestor worship, a credo that was ubiquitous during the Neolithic. As beliefs changed or were supplanted this was reflected in physical modifications to the form, appearance and use of these circular monuments, creating multi-phased, complex barrows complete with inhumation and cremation burials.

Such a process of interconnected metaphysical and material transformation can be compared to the broad morphology of religious buildings constructed during the past 1000 years or so, such as churches, chapels, temples and mosques. Each type of religious building displays gross similarities in overall design, created according to distinct sets of sacred architectural rules. In effect this makes them material manifestations of the philosophical differences which distinguish the different belief systems. Furthermore, within each of these types, individual buildings vary in inception date, phases of construction, materials, size, shape, elaboration, internal features and furnishings. To a large extent these more subtle variations in form can be seen to reflect changes over time in society, belief and practical application. Moreover, even though interments are undeniably a pervasive and commonly held feature few people would assert that such religious structures were built merely as places to bury the dead.

By comparing Eastling Down with other multi-phased, multi-ditched early Bronze Age circular monuments it has been possible to identify a significant number of commonly held attributes and a remarkable degree of temporal synchronicity in relation to the aggrandizement and major burial phases that were wrought on them. The very early initial construction dates and long – if intermittent – use-life, along with a higher than normal number of burials, is testament to the fact that this type of monument was exceptional. Most significant of all is that they were uniquely singled out for modification during the period 2100–1850 BC – which implies either a change to, or conversely the need for reinforcement of, the belief system they represented. Consequently, it could be inferred that they all held meaning and purpose in common.

At all of the cited monuments there are tantalising hints that early non-funerary activities may have been taking place either within or close by. In particular, at Eastling Down the occurence of Grooved Ware pottery can be taken as indicative of ritual use on the site either prior to construction or concurrent with the early monument. Aspects of the flint assemblage, especially the arrowheads, also point to late Neolithic activity in the immediate vicinity. In this context, the presence of neonate pig bone may also be significant. At Durrington Walls the remains of suckling pigs found in conjunction with arrowheads has recently been interpreted as evidence for seasonally determined ceremonial slaughter and feasting (Pearson *et al*, 2008). Whilst the depositional circumstances at Eastling Down are quite different it is still possible that a similar, although much smaller scale, ritual was being enacted here too. It is important to point out that a case is not being made for Easting Down to have started out as a Neolithic henge. Even allowing for the possibility that the earliest physical manifestation consisted of a penannular or causewayed ring-ditch, as the primary excavation archive implies, such a contention cannot be supported by the available evidence.

However, it is reasonable to assert that such evident commonality among so many multi-phase, multi-circuited, monuments suggests these are a distinct and previously undefined class of early Bronze Age ritual installation. It could even be argued that they came about as a direct response to the flat-grave or single burial round barrow tradition which arrived during the Chalcolithic; an attempt by the indigenous society to reinforce its cultural identity in the face of a compellingly attractive new doctrine. Monuments such as Eastling Down may have been intended to preserve and perpetuate the ancient communal burial traditions, previously made manifest through the construction of long barrows and chambered tombs, whilst at the same time allowing select aspects of the new belief system – epitomised by the Beaker burial tradition – to be adopted.

The incentive for the local population to embrace this novel credo was most probably its association with metal-making, which seems to have been an integral component of the Beaker philosophy. Gaining access to such arcane knowledge at a time when metal objects were rare and exotic items would undoubtedly have brought power, prestige and status to newly initiated cognoscenti. Such an ideology would therefore quickly gain more and more converts. Consequently, those who continued to favour the supremacy of the old doctrine may have felt compelled to re-emphasis its place within society. Hence there occurred a period of prolific burial depositions accompanied by aggrandizement and modification to monuments that remained dedicated to the indigenous traditional and ancient belief system. The result was Eastling Down and the other multi-phased, multi-circuited monuments that punctuate the barrow landscape as perceived today.

3
Watching brief discoveries at Tilmanstone

Jon Rady

The ring-ditch

In July 1996, during the watching brief maintained as road construction commenced (see p 5), part of a ring-ditch, presumably representing the remains of a ploughed-out round barrow, was exposed and recorded in a cutting to the east of Tilmanstone village, some 3.5km north of the Eastling Wood site.

The ring-ditch was located about half way down a long west facing slope at an elevation of about 50m OD (NGR TR 3063 5106), some 585m south-east of Tilmanstone parish church and 115m north-east of the 'Plough and Harrow' public house. Following the discovery of the feature it was noted that a circular cropmark immediately to the east of the road easement, represented by differential growth in a field of broad beans, exactly corresponded with the recorded circular segment of ditch.

During the roadworks, it was possible to dig a 10m length of the ring-ditch, but detailed examination of the enclosed area was impossible. The centre of the enclosure lay outside the road line and, in contrast to Eastling Wood, no associated burials were discovered at any point. Very little artefactual material was recovered from the site apart from a relatively small quantity of waste flint flakes and other debitage.

As recorded, the ring-ditch appeared to have an overall diameter of between 25 and 30m. The ditch, itself, was of a single phase, somewhere between 2 and 3m wide at the top, with a flat base and truncated V-shaped profile overall. The base was about 1m across and 1.40m deep from the bottom of the ploughsoil.

The primary fill of the ditch (layer 5) was a thin layer (0.01–0.02m) of dark brown, loosely compacted loam or clay loam with a granular texture. Inclusions of small chalk and flint were noted but there were no datable finds. The secondary fill (layer 4) was a slightly banded and very loosely compacted deposit of dirty white chalk fragments/rubble with voids and areas of conglomerated wash. Chalk fragments were generally small-medium with occasional flints also present. About 0.45m thick, this deposit probably represents the original erosion of the steep-sided chalk faces of the ditch. Again it produced no datable finds.

The chalk deposit was sealed by a relatively complex sequence of layers (3), consisting of alternate bands of chalk rubble and darker loamy and silty soils. This sequence, about 0.25m thick at maximum, probably represents general stabilization of ditch profile with intervening turf growth, followed by further less drastic erosion episodes followed by further consolidation. Also included was an overlying 0.20–0.30m thick deposit of very patchy silt and loam. This was riddled with animal and root disturbances and probably represents the final stage of consolidation and stability of the ditch profile, with the growth of turf and bushes or trees on

Pl 18. Tilmanstone ring-ditch. Section through ditch, looking north-east.

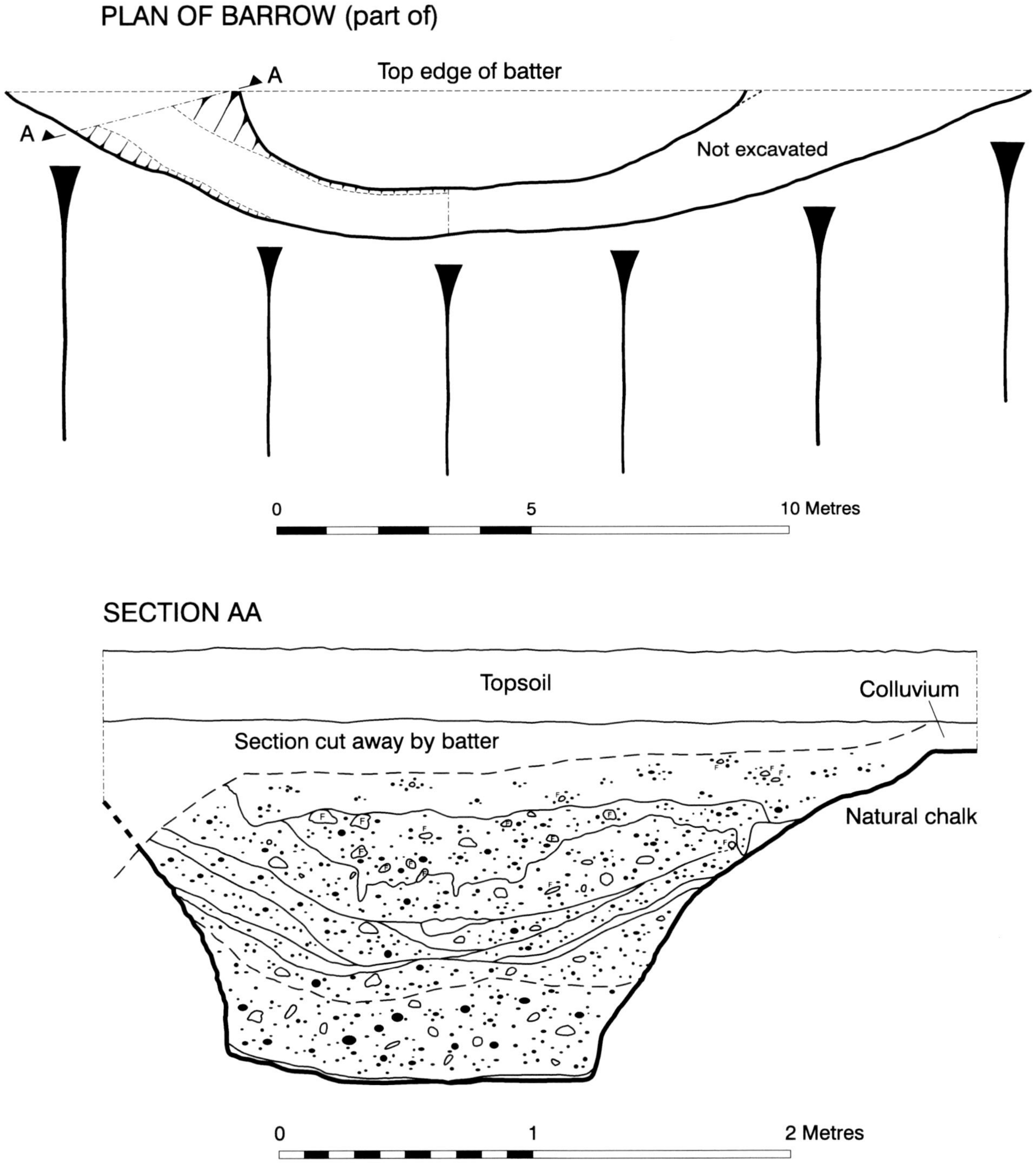

Fig 44. Tilmanstone: plan and section of ring-ditch. Scale 1:125 and 1:25.

the humic accumulations within the virtually backfilled ditch hollow. Final infilling (2), which may have commenced with deep ploughing activity over the last few hundred years was suggested by the final fill of colluvium, a mid orange-brown loamy clay, 0.40m thick over the centre of the ditch, but which appeared to extend beyond the ditch limits, where it was just over 0.10m thick.

Subsequent satellite imagery of the region (Google Earth 2007) confirms that less than half this monument was taken by the new road, the remainder showing as a clear cropmark in the south-west corner of a large arable field. Cropmarks of three more ring-ditches (one probably double ditched) occur on higher ground in the same field, some 350m to the north-east of the present site but none of these has been excavated.

The Beaker burial

About 400m to the north of the recorded ring-ditch, the new road cutting immediately south of the bridge works at Doves Corner revealed a probable Beaker burial. This apparently isolated feature was discovered along the top edge of the eastern side of the road cutting. Occupying a valley-side position at NGR TR 3057 5143, there was no surviving evidence to suggest that the burial had ever been covered by a barrow or enclosed within a ring-ditch.

Most of the pit containing the vessel had been removed by the machine prior to discovery, but a small portion remained. This contained an almost complete beaker, resting on the base of the cut. Overall, the feature appeared to be subrectangular in shape, extending westwards across the line of the road, with a flat base and vertical-sided profile about 0.40m deep from the base of the topsoil. The cut was about 0.70m wide and only 0.40m of its length survived. Some animal bone and possible human bone was also present within the pit. The filling itself consisted of a mid orange-brown loamy clay with abundant small–medium chalk, common small–medium flints and rare small charcoal and daub inclusions.

Attempts to expose the fragile pot *in situ* were not successful, so the vessel was lifted with its contents and some of the surrounding earth for cleaning under more controlled conditions in the lab.

Three sherds from the vessel were subsequently submitted to Dr Alex Gibson for comment; his report appears below.

The Beaker

Alex Gibson

The context of the discovery appears to be uncertain, but a flat grave is possible given the completeness of the vessel and the local parallels. The vessel has a rim diameter of 170mm and a base diameter of 78mm. It has an open profile, the rim diameter being the maximum, and a smooth belly profile though with the slightest hint of waisting just below the middle ladder motif. The rim is simple and rounded, the walls average some 7mm thick, the base is quite pronounced with a thickness of some 11mm. The total height of the pot is 97mm. Well-smoothed coiling bonding can be noted in the fabric and the vessel has tended to break along these lines of weakness.

The fabric is hard and well fired with abundant grog inclusions as well as some sparse calcined flint and some shell which, protruding from the surface, give the pink-brown, oxidised surfaces a slightly speckled appearance. The core of the fabric is black, the surface colouration failing to penetrate the fabric to a depth greater than 1mm.

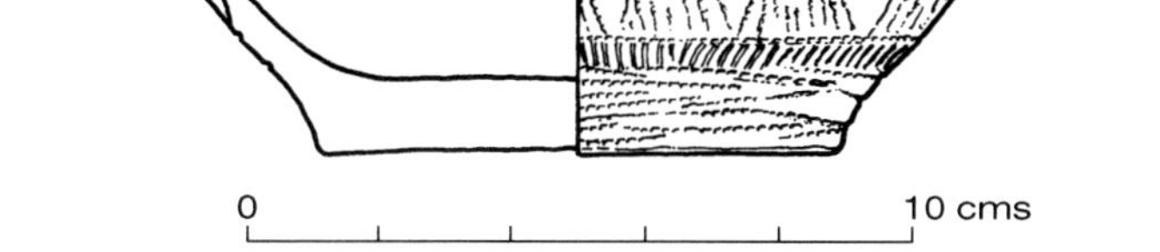

Fig 45. Doves Corner, Tilmanstone: Beaker. Scale 1:2.

The decoration has been executed with a toothed comb. It appears to have been done while the clay was still quite wet since the impressions are quite deep and the comb appears to have become clogged resulting in indistinct impressions. A curved-bladed comb with 10–14 teeth seems to have been used. Fingernail impressions have also been employed.

The decorative scheme, from the rim downwards, is as follows: top 6mm undecorated, followed by two encircling lines of comb impressions, the lower of which forms the upper margin of a ladder motif of slightly oblique fingernail impressions bordered below by another encircling line of comb impressions. Below this is a zone of filled chevrons, apex uppermost, defined by single combed lines and filled with short lengths of comb impressions set roughly vertically. This zone occupies some 28mm and is bordered below by another encircling line of fingernail ladder motif bordered above and below by two encircling lines of toothed comb impressions. Overlaps in the comb applications are clearly visible. A repeated zone of filled chevrons is set below this occupying some 25mm. This lower zone stands on a final row of fingernail ladder motif bordered above by a single encircling line of comb impressions and below by another single line followed by multiple short irregular horizontal lengths of combed lines.

None of the sherds submitted to the writer conjoined and it would have been logical to interpret them as representing the neck and base of a long-necked Beaker of Clarke's (1970) Developed or Late Southern groups (S^2-S^3). However, the vessel is reconstructable and can be seen to have an open bowl profile.

Beaker bowls, while common in Southern Europe (Harrison 1977; 1980), even including parallels with the chevron motif, are yet rare in Britain. The Polypod bowls from Inkpen Hill (Clarke 1970, no 26), and Newgrange (O'Kelly *et al* 1983, 72) are obvious exceptions, and the oft-cited open bowl from Knockadoon, Limerick, is by no means complete (Clarke 1970, no 1909), nor certainly reconstructable. Bowl forms, though generally closed, are found in Clarke's East Anglian group including one with chevron decoration from Syderstone in Norfolk (Clarke 1970, no 616). Other bowls tend to be either Peterborough or Food Vessel hybrids.

Bowls with classic Beaker decoration are, therefore, rare in the British Beaker repertoire, the best parallel being an open bowl from Lakenheath (Clarke 1970 no 930.1) though the parallel is not a close one. Parallels amongst necked vessels are easier to find at, for example, Manston (Perkins and Gibson 1990) or indeed from Monkton Minster, Grave 7114 (Gibson 1996, Beaker 2) or Grave 6409 (Gibson 1996, Beaker 1). In this light it is worth considering how many sherds have been interpreted as neck sherds from long-necked vessels rather than as bowls which, as this vessel indicates, clearly existed within the Beaker repertoire (see, for example, the 'neck' sherds from Fengate in Gibson 1980). The motifs employed are stylistically late in both Clarke's and Lanting and van der Waals's (1972) schemes which is unusual amongst the Kentish material which tends towards earlier style vessels.

4
Settlement at the Church Whitfield Crossroads

Keith Parfitt

Excavated structures and features

The investigated areas totalled around 8000m^2 in extent (Fig 4; Pl 19), with most of the 400 archaeological features excavated located in Field 8, north-east of the crossroads (Fig 46). Plough erosion of the natural chalk surface was found everywhere to have been severe and an unknown number of small features are likely to have been destroyed long before the excavations began. The features recorded have been arranged into five periods:

Period 1: Neolithic and early Bronze Age activity (residual flints and pottery; pit F103)
Period 2: early Iron Age settlement (boundary ditch, storage pits, Structure V and pit groups A–D)
Period 3: late Iron Age settlement (rectangular ditched enclosure; grave F146)
Period 4: Anglo-Saxon settlement (Structures I, III, IV, VI, VII and VIII)
Period 5: medieval and post-medieval activity (cow burial F897; roadside ditches)

Pl 19. Church Whitfield: initial clearance work in Field 8.

Period 1: Neolithic to early Bronze Age

A scatter of prehistoric struck flints was recovered from the ploughsoil and as residual material in many of the excavated features. The assemblage of just over 550 pieces comprises mainly waste flakes, with a number of cores, hammerstones and worked pieces, mostly scrapers. These would appear to be broadly datable to the Neolithic period (*see* p 132; Tables 27–31) and material of this general date is common across the downs in this part of east Kent (*see* p 5).

The earliest structural evidence for occupation is provided by an isolated pit located in the eastern part of Field 8 (F103; Figs 46 and 74). This was oval in shape measuring 0.70m (north-west–south-east) by 0.48m (north-east–south-west). It was just 0.14m deep with steep sides and a dished base. The light grey-brown clay loam filling produced a number of calcined flints, single shells of limpet and oyster and several fragments of red deer antler (Table 47). A sample of the antler gave a radiocarbon date of 3380±50 BP (cal BC 1765–1530, 2 sigma; Beta 142012; see Table 64), implying an early Bronze Age date for its filling.

Further evidence for early Bronze Age activity, perhaps more or less contemporary with the pit, is provided by three worn, residual sherds of Beaker pottery recovered from the filling of the late Iron Age enclosure ditch in Field 9 (*see* pp 136–7; not illustrated).

Taken together, these various discoveries suggest that there was at least casual, intermittent habitation around the excavated site during the Neolithic and early Bronze Age periods.

Period 2: early Iron Age settlement

Following the early Bronze Age activity, the site seems to have lain unoccupied for at least the next millennium. Evidence for renewed settlement is provided by a boundary ditch, together with a number of pits and probably a four-post structure (Structure V). Collectively, these remains have been designated Period 2 (Figs 46 and 47), although it seems likely that there are at least two separate phases represented here. The associated pottery, which has some interesting continental parallels, is dated to the early Iron Age, from the fifth to mid fourth century BC (*see* p 139; Figs 79–83; Tables 33–39).

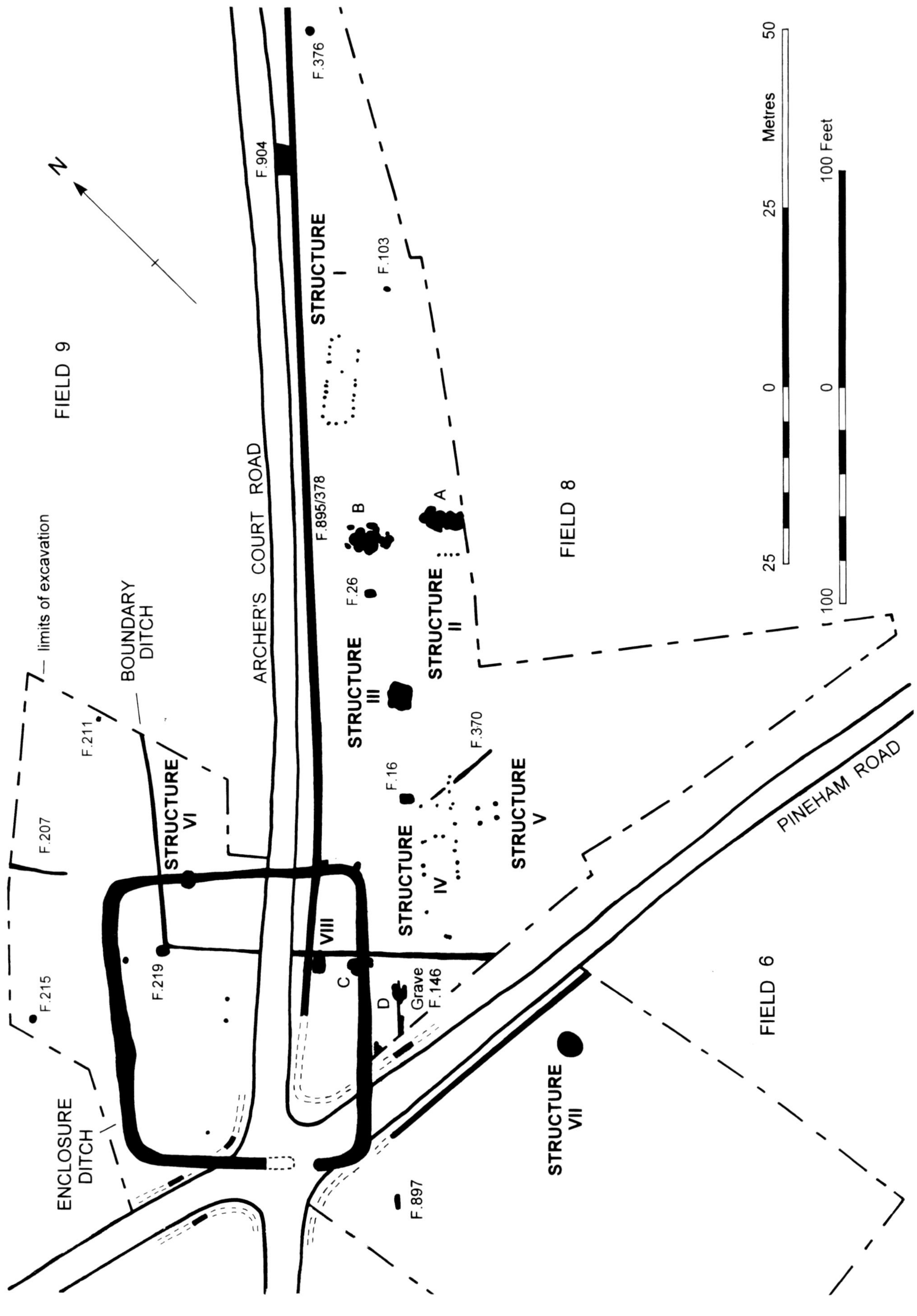

Fig 46 . Church Whitfield: general plan, showing all excavated features.

The pits located fall into two types; singles (F14, F16 and F26) and intercutting pit clusters (pit groups A, B, C and D). Two of the single pits yielded significant assemblages of pottery and animal bone. The pit clusters produced only small amounts of material. The four-post structure (Structure V) yielded no datable finds and has been assigned to this period purely on its positioning and morphological grounds.

Boundary ditch F205 and F10/F209

A shallow, L-shaped ditch (F205 and F10/F209) was traced running across Fields 8 and 9 (Figs 46, 47 and 48). The two separate arms, joining at an angle of around 100 degrees (Pl 20), appeared to define the western quarter of a larger enclosure that extended well beyond the limits of the excavation (Fig 47). The ditch contained pottery datable to the early Iron Age but it had been heavily truncated by later ploughing and there was no surviving evidence for any associated bank or palisade. Inside the enclosed area, three pits containing early Iron Age pottery (F14, F16 and F26) and the single four-post structure (Structure V) are likely to be contemporary, suggesting that the ditch originally bounded a farmstead.

The north-west arm of the boundary ditch (F205) was traced for just over 30m across Field 9. Some 24m from the corner of the enclosure the ditch re-aligned to a slightly more northerly heading but there was nothing to suggest this had any special significance. As surviving, the maximum width of the ditch was 0.75m, with a maximum depth of 0.27m. It had steep sides and a flat base (Fig 48, Sections 89 and 91). The soil and chalk filling produced forty-one potsherds (Table 34), together with a quantity of animal bone (Tables 47 and 49), a number of calcined flints and several residual prehistoric struck flints.

The south-west arm of the ditch (F10/F209) was traced for about 45m. It was best preserved along the southern edge of Field 8 where it was 0.85m wide and 0.36m deep. Again, the sides were sloping and the base was flat or dished (Fig 48, Sections 33 and 87). The soil and chalk filling produced thirty-three potsherds, including a piece of red-finished ware (Tables 34 and 36). Animal bone was also recovered (Table 47), together with calcined flints and a few more residual struck flints.

Pit F14

This small, bowl-shaped pit had been cut through by the east corner of the Period 3 enclosure ditch (Figs 47, 56 and 58). It was oval in shape and measured a minimum of 1.10m (east–west) by 0.80m (north–south). The pit was 0.29m deep with sloping sides and a rounded base (Fig 58, Section 96). The dark brown chalky loam filling (Section 96, context 13) containing a few calcined flints and two flint-tempered potsherds datable to the early Iron Age (Table 34).

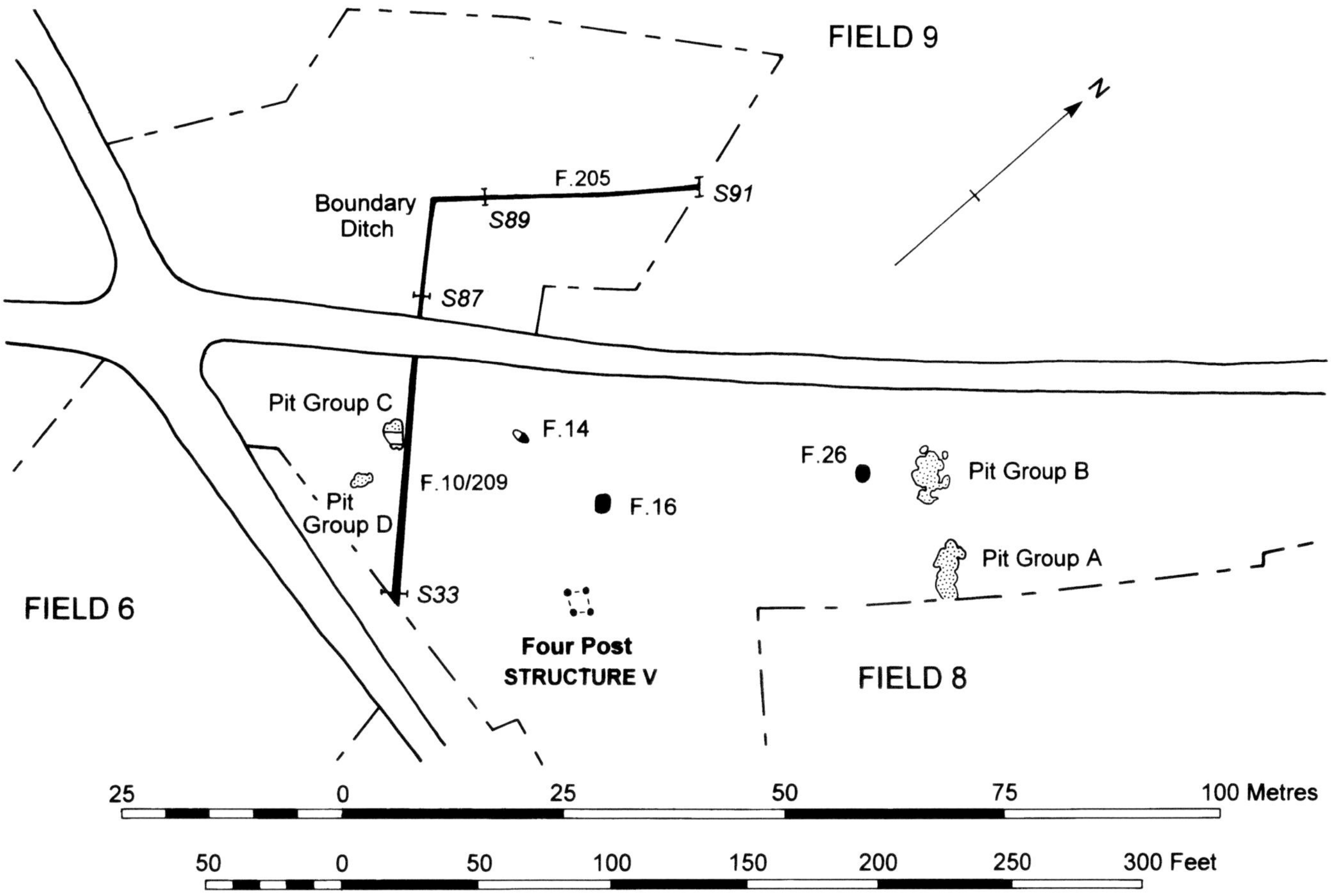

Fig 47. Church Whitfield: Period 2 features.

Pl 20. Church Whitfield: high level view of excavated features in Field 9, looking north.

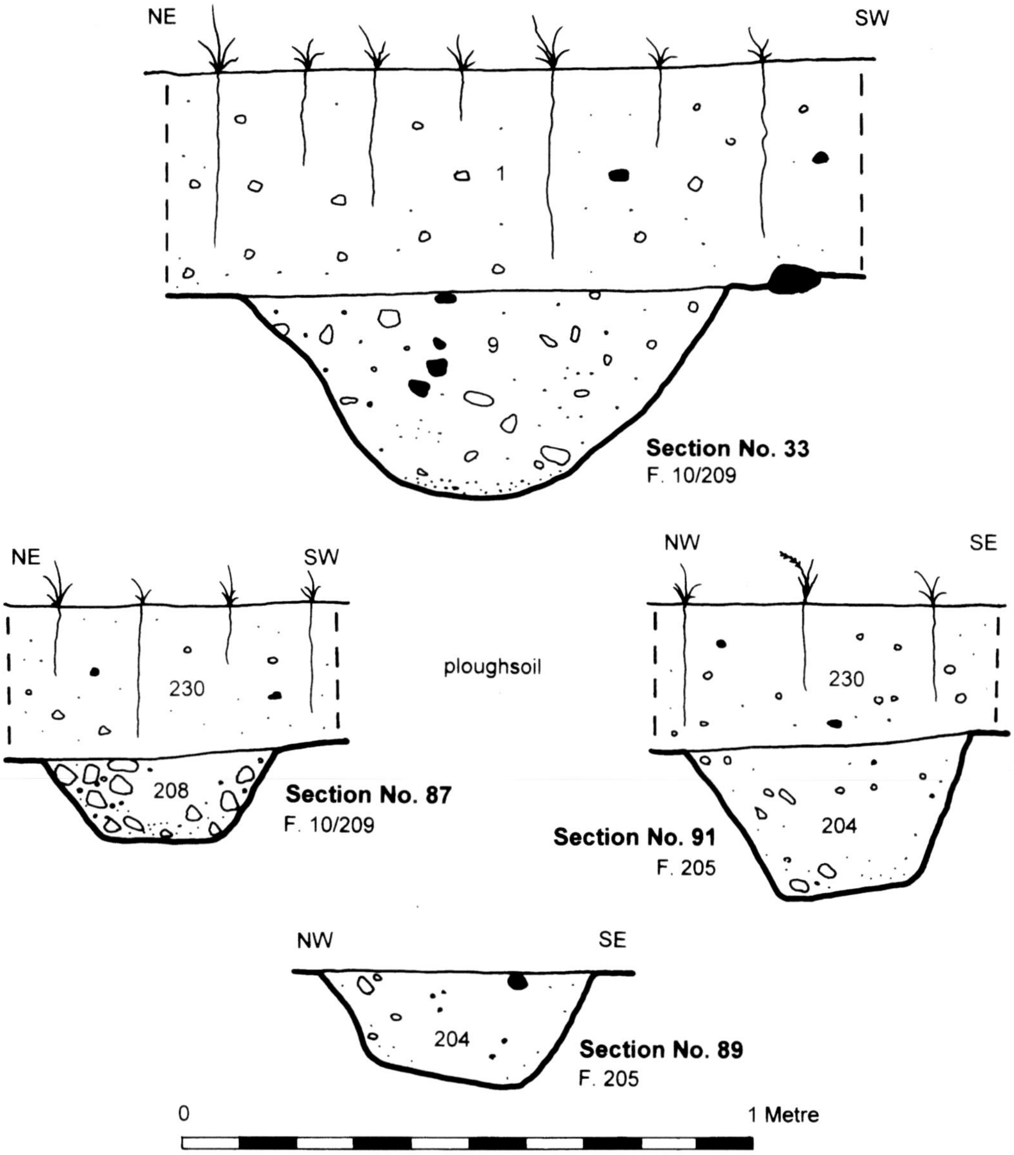

Fig 48. Church Whitfield: sections across Period 2 boundary ditch.

The purpose of this pit remains unclear. Its size and form is not typical of grain storage pits like F16 and F26 (see below) and the lack of finds implies that it was not extensively used for rubbish disposal. The fairly regular form, however, suggests purposeful excavation, rather than casual small-scale chalk quarrying.

Pit F16

This pit was subrectangular in shape and measured 1.96m (north-west–south-east) by 1.52m (north-east–south-west). As surviving, it was 0.50m deep with vertical sides (slightly undercut in places) and a flat base (Fig 49, Section 34). The filling consisted of a series of chalk and soil deposits which produced an important group of early Iron Age pottery (*see* pp 137–8; Table 33).

The primary filling, a thin layer of pure carbon (Fig 49, Section 34, context 134), perhaps related to *in situ* burning on the base of the pit. Above this were probable layers of deliberate backfilling (contexts 131, 132 and 133) containing burnt chalk and daub, chalk rubble, carbon specks and charred cereal grains (Table 62), together with seven early Iron Age potsherds (Table 33), several with a red-finished surface (Table 36). Sealing these deposits was a layer of yellow-brown silty loam (context 125) which contained a human skull fragment (Table 45), significant quantities of charred grain (Table 62), occasional daub fragments and fifty-eight potsherds (Table 33). These include further red-finished wares and polychrome-decorated fragments (Fig 79.1; Table 36). A sample of the charred grain gave a radiocarbon date of 2220±50 BP (cal BC 390–165, 2 sigma; Beta 142011; Table 64).

Wet-sieving of bulk samples from contexts 131, 132, 133 and 125 produced significant amounts of charred cereal grain and peas, all in an excellent state of preservation (Table 62). The cereal grains included emmer wheat, spelt wheat, six-row hulled barley, naked barley and possibly oats. There were also small bones from rodents, frogs/

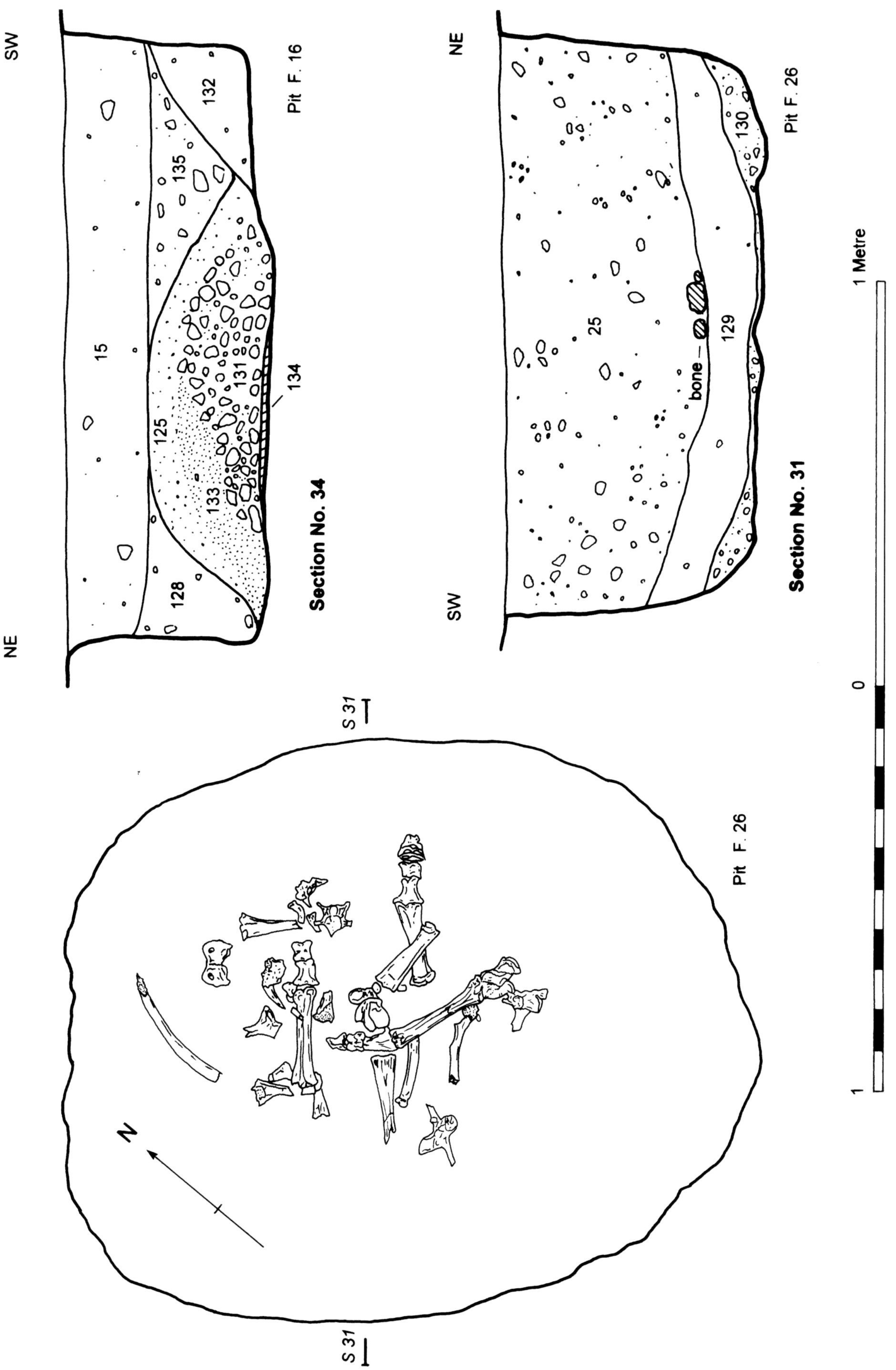

Fig 49. Church Whitfield: plan of probable placed animal bone deposit in pit F26. Sections of pits F16 and F26.

toads, shell fragments from mussel and oyster, and a single fish vertebra (*see* p 167; Table 61).

The final filling of the pit (Fig 49, Section 34, context 15) contained fragments of human leg bone (Table 45) and moderate quantities of animal bone (Tables 47, 49 and 53), including the articulated leg bones of a cow, perhaps representing a special, placed deposit (p 171). There were also a few fragments of sandstone, presumably from querns (FN 189 and FN 846, p 136; Table 32), together with seventy-seven potsherds (Table 33), these including more red-finished wares and polychrome decorated pieces, several of which can be joined with sherds recovered from context 125 below (Table 36).

Pit F26

This pit lay 30m north-east of F16 (Figs 46 and 47). It was oval in shape, measuring 1.70m (north-west–south-east) by 1.43m (north-east–south-west) and was 0.62m deep, with near vertical sides and an almost flat base. The filling (Fig 49, Section 31) produced further significant quantities of early Iron Age pottery (Table 33) and other material.

The primary filling (context 130) consisted of a thin deposit of burnt clay and carbon, containing two sherds of pottery. Sealing this was a deposit of grey-brown silty clay (context 129) which produced calcined flints, fragments of animal bone, shells of marine mollusc and four sherds of pottery. Lying on the slightly dished surface of this deposit were the articulated leg bones of a cow and a horse, again perhaps purposefully deposited (Fig 49, plan and Section 31; Tables 47 and 49). The upper two-thirds of the pit was filled with a single deposit of grey-brown loam incorporating frequent small chalk lumps (context 25). This probably represented largely natural silt but it also contained some domestic rubbish in the form of seventy-one potsherds (Table 33), quantities of calcined flint, a fragment of sandstone saddle quern (FN 1363; Table 32) and animal bone (Tables 47, 49 and 53).

Pits similar to F16 and F26 have been discovered on many Iron Age sites across lowland Britain and they are generally interpreted as grain storage pits. Once abandoned, they were often used for the dumping of domestic rubbish and this seems to have been the case at Church Whitfield. It is not clear whether the grain found in F16 represents part of its original contents or subsequently dumped waste. The range of species represented, however, probably indicates that this material is the collected sweepings of unwanted grain from a number of different sources. Groups of articulated animal bones similar to those recorded have also been regularly noted in pits on other Iron Age sites and these are now often regarded as representing ritually placed deposits (Grant 1984b; Cunliffe 1991, 517; Green 1992, 100–103; see also p 171).

Four-post structure (Structure V)

Structure V lay some 10m to the south-east of pit F16 (Figs 46, 47 and 71). Four large post-pits (F301, F304, F307 and F310), three containing traces of a post-pipe with flint packing, defined an almost square structure (Fig 50), measuring (using the post-pipe centres), 2.42m (north-west–south-east) by 2.22m (north-east–south-west). As surviving, the post-pits ranged in depth from 0.13 to 0.25m, with near vertical sides and flat bases (Fig 50, Sections 58–61; Table 16).

F No	Shape	Axis	Length (m)	Width (m)	Depth (m)	Pipe size (m)
F301	circular	-	0.70 diam		0.13	none
F304	oval	NW-SE	0.67	0.62	0.24	0.42 x 0.44
F307	oval	N-S	0.63	0.30	0.18	0.52 x 0.42
F310	oval	NW-SE	0.70	0.65	0.25	0.48 x 0.38

Table 16. Church Whitfield: details of post-holes, four-post Structure V.

Apart from a few residual prehistoric struck flints, no datable finds were recovered from any of the post-holes but the general form of the structure is well known from many excavated Iron Age sites across southern Britain. Such structures are normally regarded as representing timber-built, raised store-houses for grain. In this context the fairly close proximity of pit F16 is of interest, as this also probably originally stored grain. It is now generally accepted that such pits were employed for the bulk storage of seed-corn, with raised four-post structures containing bins, sacks or other receptacles from which the smaller quantities of grain needed for daily use could be drawn (Cunliffe 1991, 376). Other interpretations of four-posters are possible; it has been suggested, for example, that some could have served as exposure platforms for the dead (Ellison and Drewett 1971). It may be significant therefore, that human bones were recovered from pit F16, nearby (see above, Table 45).

Although a very well-known Iron Age type regionally, four-post structures have yet to be discovered in large numbers on the chalklands of east Kent. Locally, comparable remains have been recorded at Ringwould (Parfitt 1981) and Mill Hill (Parfitt 1990; Parfitt and Corke 2010), both near Deal. One of the post-holes in the Ringwould structure contained a sherd from a red-finished fineware bowl, broadly similar in date and form to the material associated with Period 2 on the present site (Parfitt 1981, fig 3.1; Middleton 1995, fig 18.1, site 11; table 18.1B).

The pit groups

Four groups of intercutting pits (pit groups A–D) were recorded in Field 8 (Figs 46, 47, 51, 52, 53, 54 and 56). Groups A and B were the most extensive and lay close together within the area probably enclosed by the boundary ditch (Fig 47). Smaller, but otherwise similar, pit groups (C and D) lay close together, outside the south-west arm of the boundary ditch. The somewhat limited dating evidence suggests that all these pit groups belong to the early Iron Age but if they are all roughly contemporary, it seems unlikely that they can be of the same date as the boundary ditch, since they lay both inside and outside the area it enclosed.

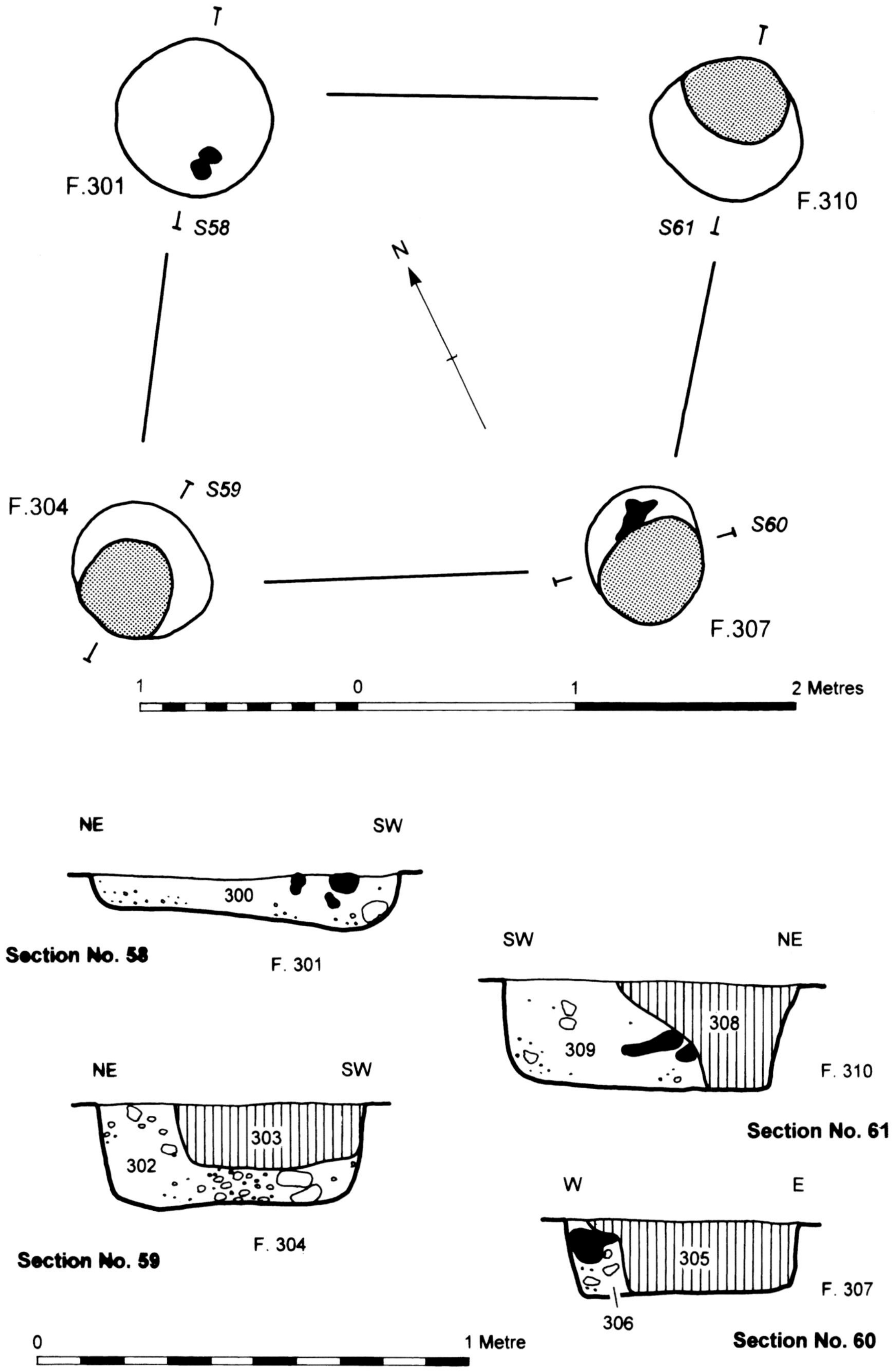

Fig 50. Church Whitfield: plan and sections of four-post structure (V).

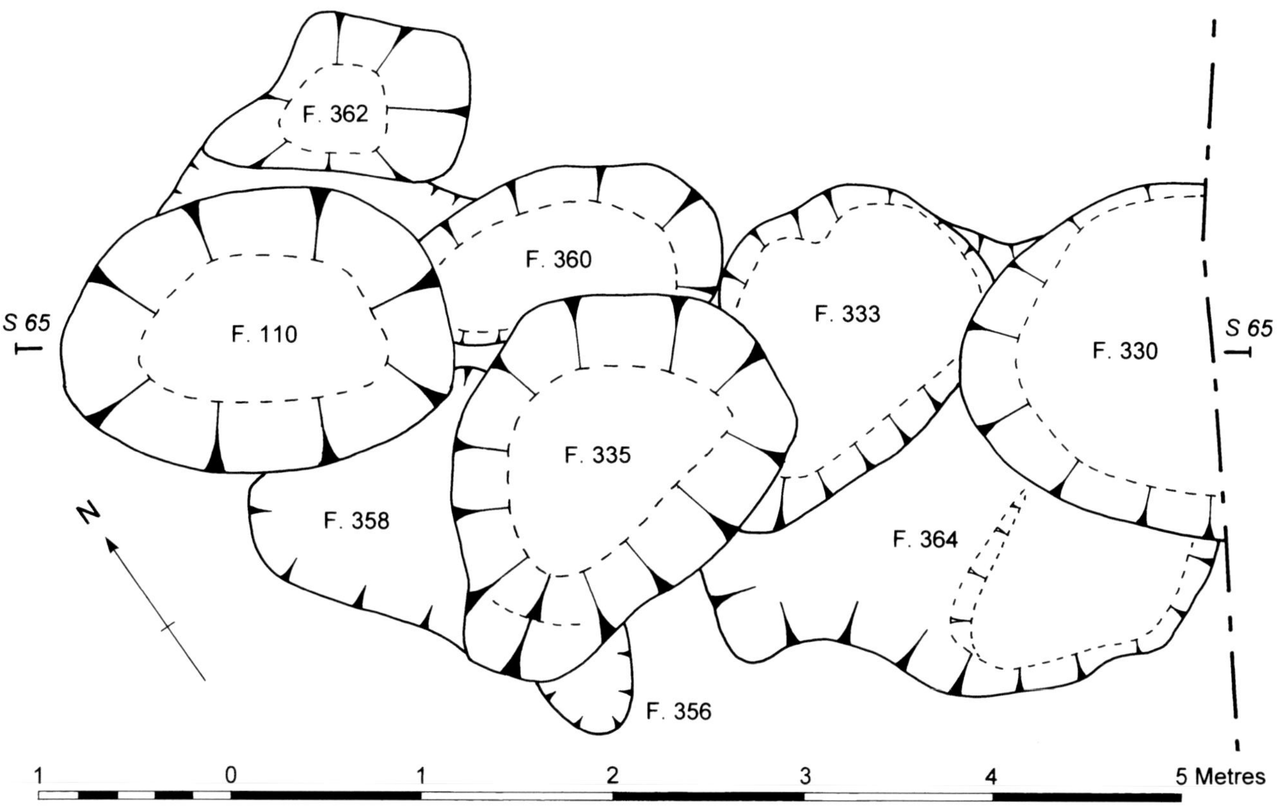

Fig 51. Church Whitfield: pit group A.

Pit group A

This group of shallow, irregular features consisted of at least nine intercutting pits and hollows of varying shapes and sizes, covering an overall area measuring a minimum of 6.00m by 2.50m (Fig 51). The individual pits were irregularly cut, usually roughly oval in shape and ranged in depth from 0.08 to 0.45m (Fig 54, Section 65); the deepest was F110. Their sides varied from steep to sloping and the bases were mostly undulating or flat.

It was clear that the individual features represented a series of separate excavations in which the earlier pits were largely filled before the later ones cut through them. The following sequence may be suggested from the stratigraphic evidence:

early:	F356, F358, F360, F364
middle:	F333
late:	F110, F330, F335
unphased:	F362

Most pits appear to have been left open for some time and to have largely silted up through natural weathering. A general lack of domestic rubbish contained within them tends to confirm this. Less than a dozen small, flint-tempered sherds, only broadly datable to the Iron Age period, were recovered from the entire complex (Table 34), together with a few fragments of animal bone (Tables 47 and 49) and a number of calcined flints.

A thin layer of brown loam (Fig 54, Section 65, context 109) sealed the upper fillings of all the pits and this produced further small amounts of domestic rubbish, including about a dozen sherds of Iron Age pottery (Table 34).

Some 3.50m to the south-west of these pits lay a row of four shallow circular post-holes (F115, F117, F119 and F121). These must relate to a timber structure (Structure II; Figs 46 and 74). No dating evidence was recovered; the posts might have supported some sort of protective fence or screen adjacent to the pit complex, but this is speculation.

Pit group B

This pit group was very similar in form and was perhaps roughly contemporary with pit group A (Figs 46 and 47). It was fully excavated and consisted of a cluster of eighteen partially intercutting features (Fig 52). The individual pits were generally either oval or subrectangular in plan and ranged in depth from 0.05 to 0.44m (Fig 54, Section 68; Pl 21). Their sides varied from steep to sloping and bases were most often slightly dished or flat.

As with pit group A, the chalk silt and soil fillings indicated that the pits formed a series of successive features (Fig 54, Section 68). The following sequence may be suggested from the stratigraphic evidence:

early:	F35, F45, F47, F347, F349
middle:	F34, F43, F342, F355
late:	F37, F41, F345
unphased:	F28, F30, F32, F39, F340, F366

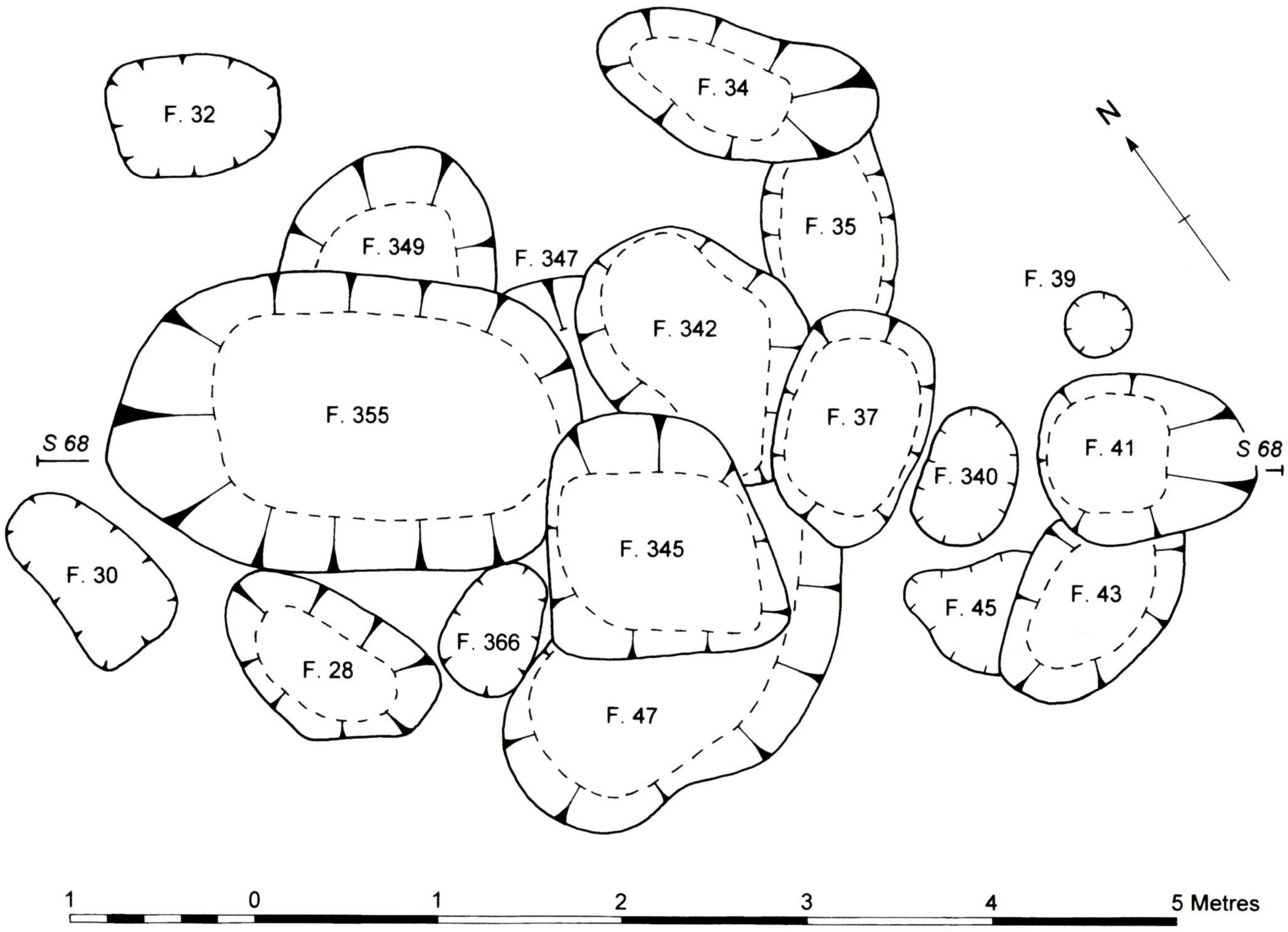

Fig 52. Church Whitfield: pit group B.

Pl 21. Church Whitfield: pit group B (Period 2) fully excavated, looking north-west. Scale 1m.

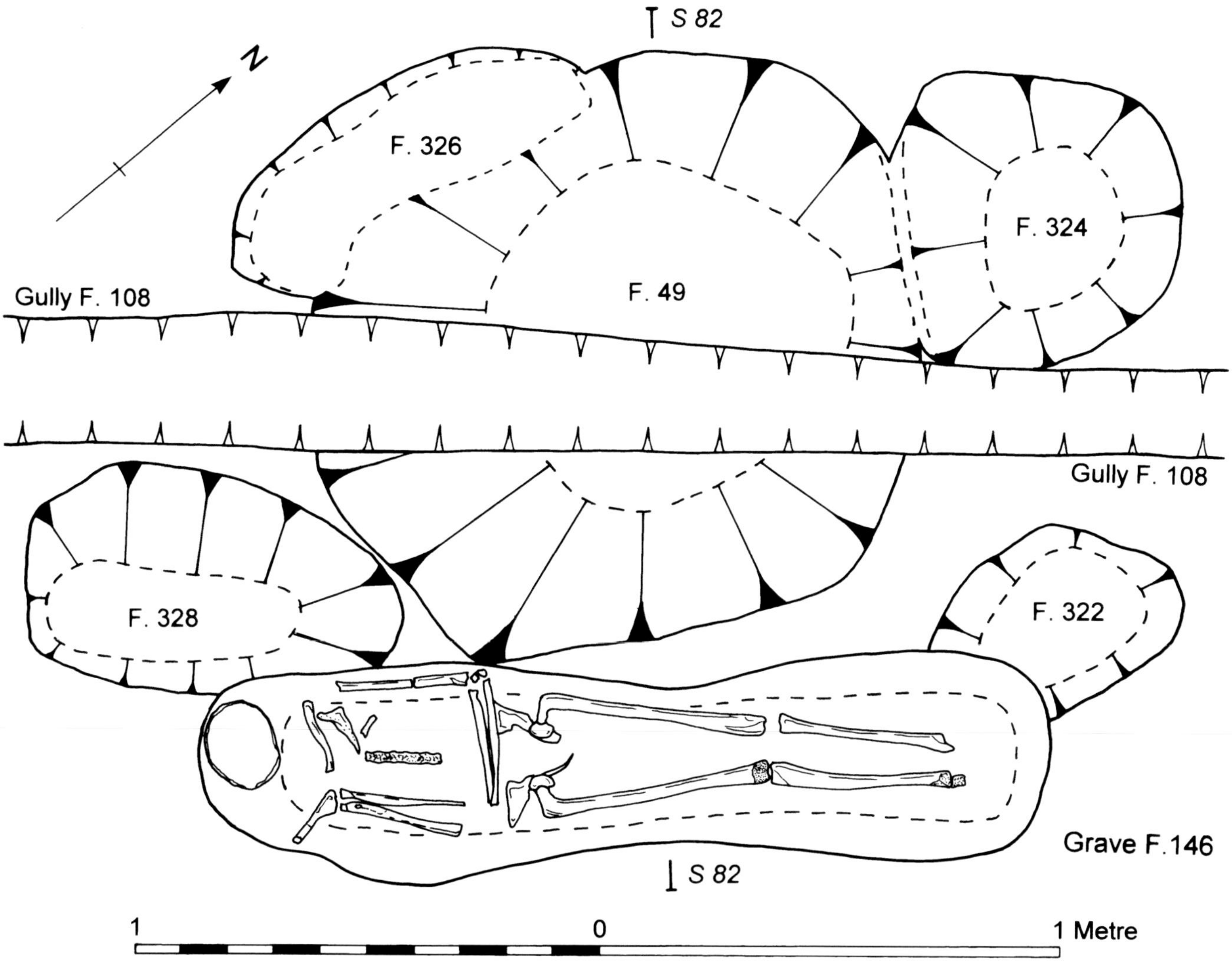

Fig 53. Church Whitfield: pit group D and grave F146.

Forty-six sherds of pottery datable to the early Iron Age were recovered from the fills (Table 34), together with a quantity of animal bone (Tables 47 and 49), significant amounts of calcined flint and a few residual prehistoric struck flints. Again, a final layer of brown loam sealed the upper fillings of the pits (Fig 54, Section 68, context 112) and this produced a further thirty-five early Iron Age sherds (Table 34), animal bone, significant numbers of calcined flints and residual struck flints.

Pit group C

This small group of five intercutting oval pits (F6, F8, F12, F199 and F314) was located immediately outside of the south-west arm of the boundary ditch, cut through by the late Iron Age enclosure ditch of Period 3 (Figs 46, 47, 56 and 58). The individual pits varied in depth from 0.14 to 0.60m and had steep sloping sides (Fig 58, Section 85). Pit F8 was the latest but the overall sequence could not be determined due to the damage caused by the later ditch.

The lower fillings within the individual features consisted mainly of weathered chalk rubble, again suggesting that these pits had been left open to silt-up naturally. The upper fills comprised a series of light brown loam deposits with chalk and some flint. A small quantity of domestic rubbish was present, mostly in the upper fills. This included four early Iron Age sherds, animal bone (Table 47), calcined flints and several residual prehistoric struck flints.

Pit group D

These five partially intercutting pits also lay outside the boundary ditch, close to pit group C (Figs 46, 47 and 56). Covering an overall area measuring about 2.50m (north-east–south-west) by 1.50m (south-east–north-west), the individual pits were generally ovoid in shape (Fig 53). They varied in depth from 0.13 to 0.45m, with steep to sloping sides and rounded or slightly dished bases (Fig 54, Section 82). The largest pit was F49.

Two of the smaller pits (F322 and F328) had been cut into by an inhumation burial (F146) assigned to Period 3, while a straight gully (F108), also assigned to that period, cut through F49 (Fig 53). The filling of the various pits effectively consisted of a single homogeneous deposit of

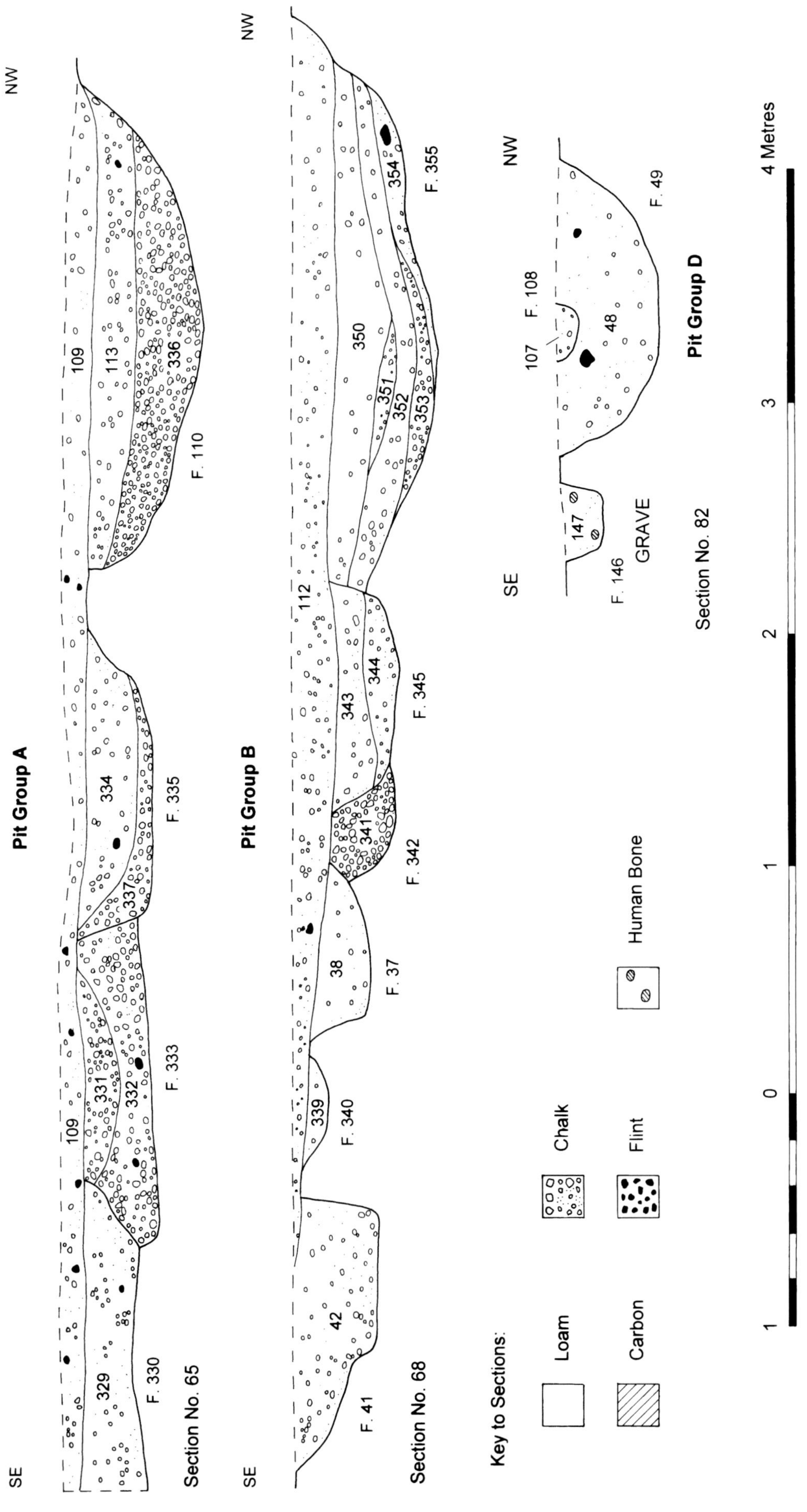

Fig 54. Church Whitfield: sections across pit groups A, B and D, and grave F146.

light brown loam with chalk and flint (Fig 54, Section 82). Six early Iron Age sherds were recovered (Table 34), along with calcined flints and some animal bone (Tables 47 and 49).

Discussion

From their generally shallow, irregular shape and variable size, it seems clear that pit groups A, B, C and D were not storage pits. The absence of obvious access points and trodden bases, together with their small size also indicates that they were not the so-called 'working hollows' that have been encountered on a number of Iron Age sites, such as Little Woodbury (Bersu 1940). The Church Whitfield pits probably represent shallow quarries where small quantities of chalk and perhaps flint had been casually dug over a period of time. The later pits, dug through the fillings of the earlier ones, however, could only have provided chalky loam.

Similar groups of shallow pits, interpreted as quarries, have been previously recorded at several other Iron Age sites, including Winnall Down (Fasham 1985, 41) and Cowdery's Down (Millett and James 1983, 169–72), both in Hampshire. Comparable Romano-British examples are also known, at Baldock, Hertfordshire (Stead and Rigby 1986, 47–50); Keston (Philp *et al* 1991), Mill Hill, Deal (Parfitt 1990) and more locally, near Maydensole Farm (Cross and Redding 2000, 5; see above; Fig 3).

The general lack of significant quantities of domestic rubbish within their fillings suggests that the present quarry pits were not situated within, or very close to, any contemporary habitation area. If so, it implies that the settlement site represented by the other Period 2 features was not then occupied.

Iron Age and Romano-British quarries elsewhere have often been interpreted as providing chalk for marling fields. Although situated on a shallow chalk-based soil, significant areas of heavier clay soil do occur near the present site (*see* p 2) and cultivation of these areas may have been assisted by marling. Quarried chalk might equally well, however, have been needed for cob walling or flooring in buildings.

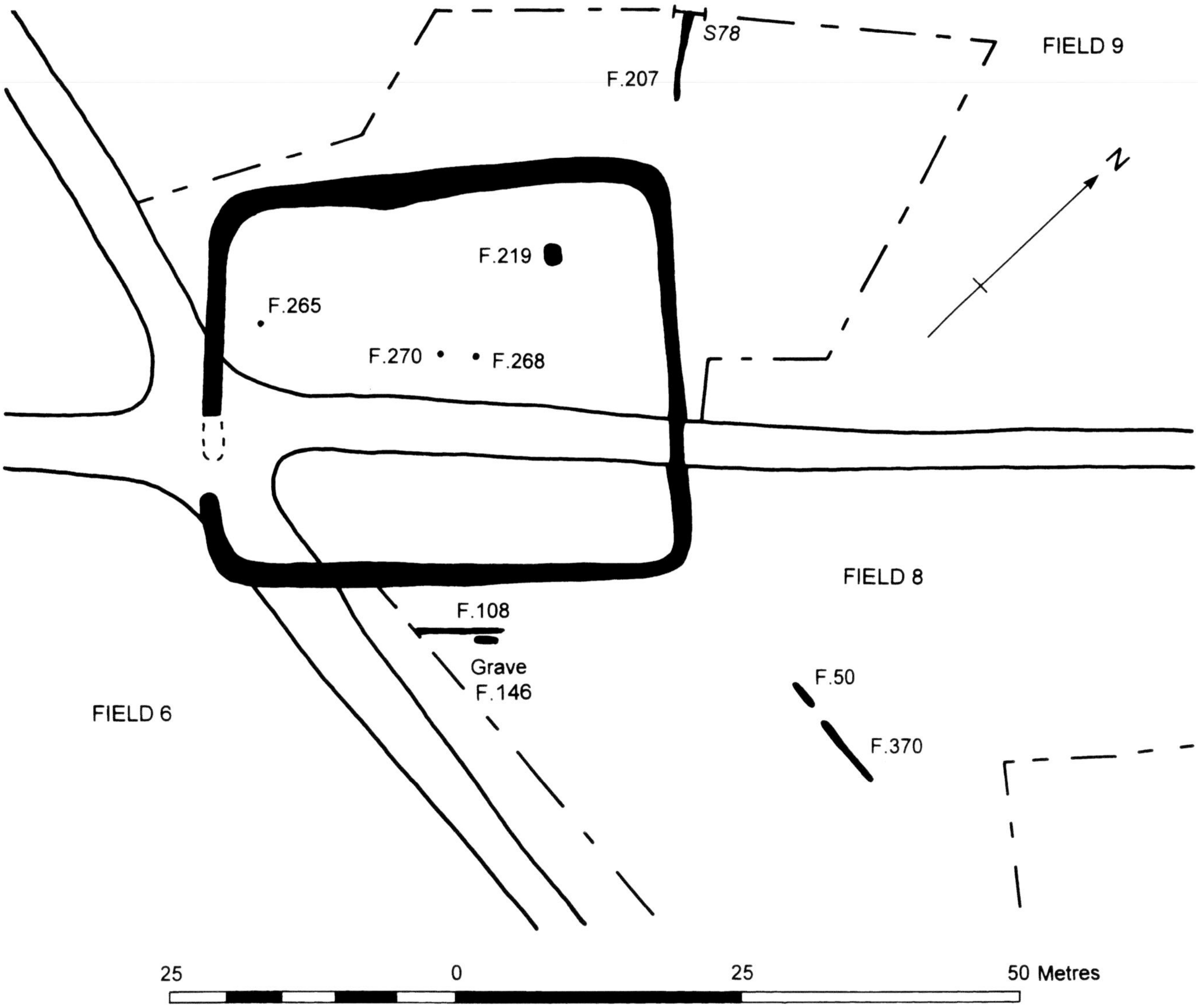

Fig 55. Church Whitfield: Period 3 farmstead enclosure and probably related features.

Other features

Two insecurely dated features located in Field 9, some distance north of the main excavation might also be tentatively placed within Period 2. Evaluation trench 23 (Fig 4 and Table 1) located the terminal of a curving chalk-cut ditch. Aligned east–west, this was about 1m wide and 0.60m deep, with sloping sides and a flat base. The lower filling contained two early Iron Age flint-tempered sherds.

A short distance further north, Evaluation trench 24 revealed a length of gully. This was 0.35m wide and 0.20m deep. There were no datable finds but it might have been contemporary with the nearby ditch. A larger area (Fig 4) was subsequently cleared adjacent to these features (Site 2 extension; Pl 20) but this failed to reveal any further remains, implying that the two features lay away from the main centre of activity. They may have formed parts of field boundaries.

Period 3: late Iron Age settlement

After the early Iron Age the excavated area seems to have lain uninhabited until sometime during the second century BC when a new farmstead was established (Figs 55 and 56). This was bounded by a substantial ditch which yielded large quantities of domestic refuse. Very few contemporary features had, unfortunately, been preserved within the enclosed area but outside a number of gullies (Figs 55 and 56, F108, F197, F207 and F50/F370) could have bounded associated fields or animal compounds. A single grave (F146), containing an adult male, probably represented the last resting place of one of the farmstead's inhabitants.

The main excavation exposed around half the enclosure (Figs 46, 55 and 56). During the new roadworks, removal of the existing tarmac revealed further, previously inaccessible, sections of its ditch and on the south-west side located the only entrance causeway. The size of the ditched area, less than 0.13 hectares in extent, suggests that the settlement originally accommodated just a single family unit.

The enclosure ditch

The enclosure ditch defined a reasonably precise rectangle with neatly rounded corners (Figs 46, 55 and 56; Pls 2 and 4). It measured internally some 39m (north-east–south-west) by 31–32.50m (north-west–south-east). There was no trace of any associated bank inside the ditch, although presumably one had formerly existed, being ploughed away in later centuries.

The filling of the ditch contained evidence of up to three subsequent recuts in its upper filling (F4, F201, F233 and F244; Figs 55, 56, 57 and 58; Table 17). Only the latest, however, extended around the complete circuit (third recut, F246, F247, F248 and F372). The earliest (first recut, F252) was confined to the north-west side, whilst the intermediate F253, appeared to represent localised redigging at the north corner.

The quality and quantity of the associated pottery, datable from the mid second to mid first century BC (Tables 35–37), warranted the complete excavation of all available lengths of the enclosure ditch. Some substantial groups of ceramic material were consequently recovered (Figs 84–91; Tables 40–42), together with significant amounts of animal bone (Tables 50 and 51) and other finds. A sample from the north-east arm of the ditch (F233) provided a land snail assemblage which shows that the Period 3 site lay in open country, without woodland (*see* p 175, Fig 100; Table 63).

North-west arm, F201	Filling
Primary	262, 225
Lower	261, 257, 224
Middle	256, 223
Upper	–
First recut, F252	249, 255, 260, 263
Second recut, F253	259
Third recut, F247	200, 254, 258, 271
South-west arm, F244	**Filling**
Primary	243
Lower	242
Middle	241
Upper	240
First recut, F252	249
Third recut, F246	239
South-east arm, F4	**Filling**
Primary	124
Lower	312, 123, 371
Middle	–
Upper	122, 374
Third recut, F372	3, 311
North-east arm, F233	**Filling**
Primary	138, 245
Lower	137, 217, 232
Middle	–
Upper	136, 250, 251
Second recut, F253	259
Third recut, F248	234, 216, 375

Table 17. Church Whitfield: context numbers relating to fills of Period 3 enclosure ditch and its recuts.

North-west arm (F201)

In Field 9 complete excavation of the north-west arm of the ditch was possible (Figs 54 and 55; Pl 22; Table 17). It had a total length of about 40m and at each end curved through a right angle to connect, respectively, with the south-west and north-east arms (see below). The original ditch (F201) had a V-shaped profile and was about 1m deep. It varied in width from 1.80 to 2.80m across the top (Fig 57, Section 108). Due to differential weathering of the sides, the widest section occurred where the ditch had cut through a large natural pipe in the chalk, filled by softer clay (Fig 56).

The ditch sides were generally convexly sloping, leading down to a flat, narrow slot-like base, between 0.10 and 0.30m wide (see sections, Fig 57). The general sequence of soil deposits filling the ditch consisted of a series of rapid silts, mostly of loose chalk rubble weathered from the sides of the ditch (Fig 57, Section 108, contexts 261

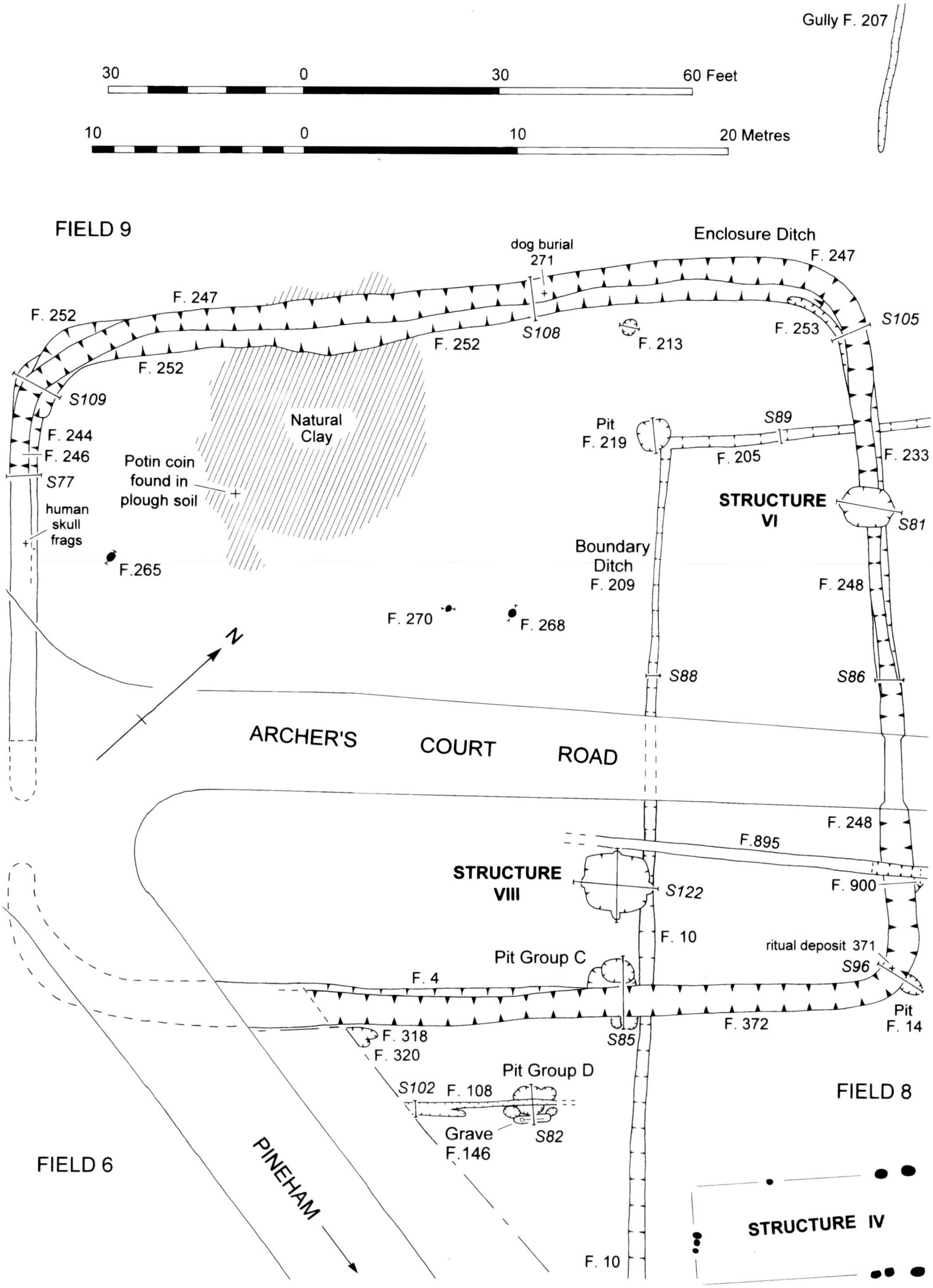

Fig 56. Church Whitfield: Period 3 farmstead enclosure and adjacent features.

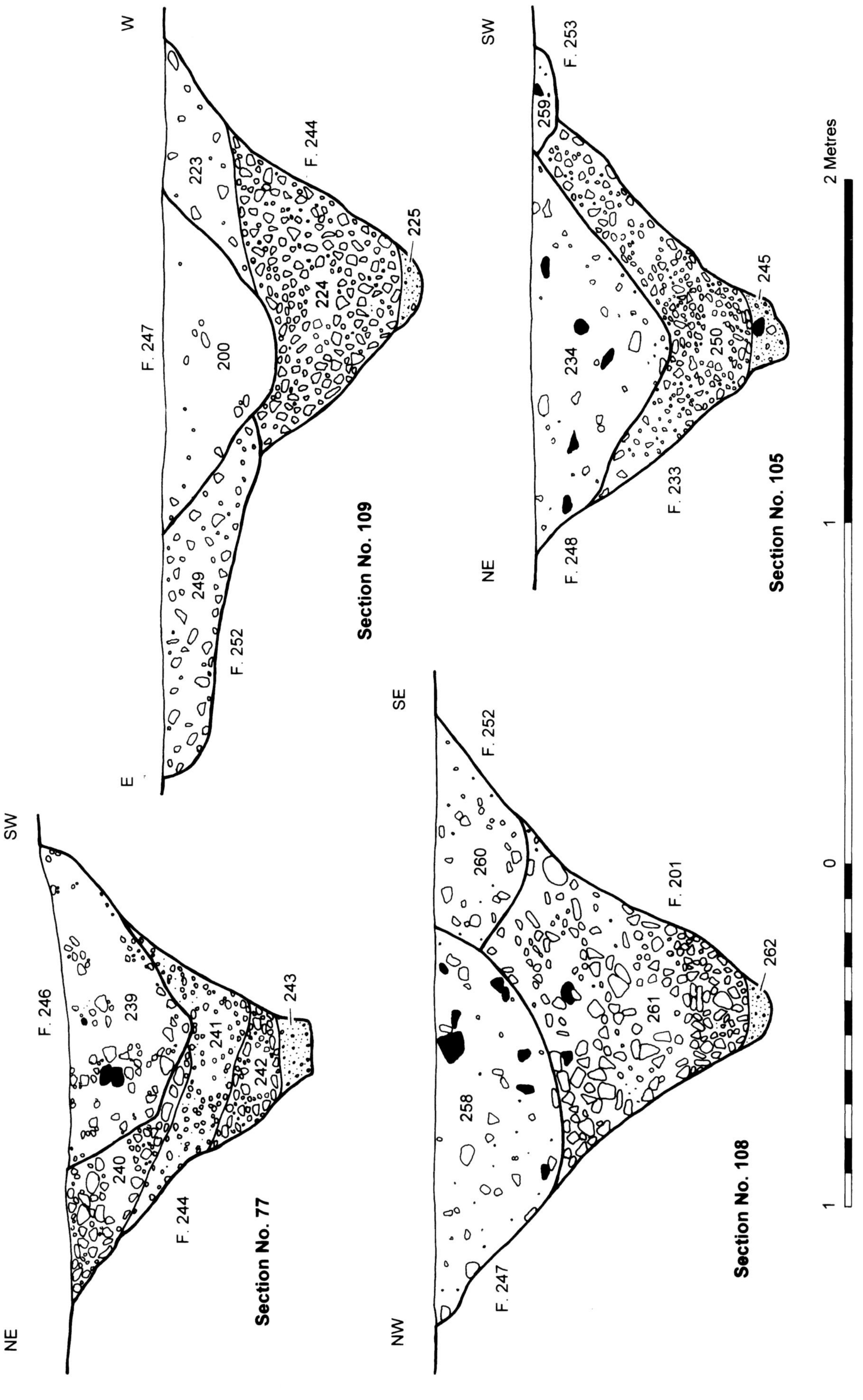

Fig 57. Church Whitfield: sections across Period 3 enclosure ditch (Sections 77, 105, 108 and 109).

and 262; see also Section 109, contexts 224 and 225; Table 17), giving way to secondary deposits of brown loam. These higher deposits contained significant quantities of domestic rubbish in the form of pottery (Tables 40, 41 and 42), animal bone (Table 51) and calcined flints. Most of the upper fill of the ditch, however, had subsequently been removed by three successive shallow recuts (F252, F253 and F247; Figs 56 and 57, Sections 105, 108 and 109).

Just over 200 sherds of pottery were recovered from the filling of the main ditch. These include three residual sherds of Bronze Age beaker (*see* pp 136–7) and some fragments of early Iron Age date, but more than two-thirds belong to the late Iron Age. A carbon residue on one piece from the middle filling (context 256) gave a radiocarbon date of 2080±50 BP (cal BC 200–AD 30, 2 sigma; Beta 141267; Table 64).

First ditch recut, F252

The earliest ditch recut (F252) was found to extend along the full length of north-west arm. It terminated at the north corner but continued a short distance around the west corner into the south-west arm, before ending (Fig 56). Ditch F252 had a maximum width of 1.95m and a maximum depth of 0.52m, with sloping sides. The brown loam fillings (Fig 57, Section 108, context 260; Section 109, context 249; Table 17) contained frequent small chalk lumps and some dumped domestic rubbish, including 339 potsherds (Tables 41 and 42) and a quantity of animal bone (Table 51). The bulk of the pottery is late Iron Age flint-tempered ware and includes a piece with curvilinear decoration (Fig 85.39). There are also thirty-five pieces of late Iron Age grog-tempered ware, together with a few residual sherds of early Iron Age date. Several pieces of sandstone were recovered (FN 849, 912 and 1209), together with a fragment of oolitic limestone (FN 1210; Table 32).

Second ditch recut, F253

At the north corner of the enclosure a short length of shallow gully (F253) filled with light brown loam and chalk (context 259) cut the filling of recut F252 (Fig 56). There was a rounded terminal at its western end but the gully was destroyed by a later, more extensive, ditch recut (F248) as it turned into the north-east arm (Fig 57, Section 105). Its full extent thus remains uncertain, but it seems to have been little more than a localised redigging of the ditch in this area.

Third ditch recut, F247

On the north-west side of F252 were clear traces of later redigging. This third recut of the ditch (F247) could be traced around the complete circuit of the enclosure ditch (as F247, F246, F372 and F248; Fig 56). Along the north-west side (F247), it ranged in width from 0.88 to 1.40m and was generally about 0.45m deep, with sloping sides and a rounded base. It was again filled with brown loam, chalk lumps and domestic rubbish (Fig 57, Section 108, context 258). More than 200 potsherds (Tables 41 and 42), mostly of late Iron Age date, were recovered together with several pieces of sandstone (FN 913, 1365 and 1366; Table 32) and a quantity of animal bone (Table 51). At one point in the central sector the body of a dog, lying on its left side, had been placed on the base of this recut (Fig 56, context 271;

Pl 22. Church Whitfield: Period 3 enclosure ditch and other excavated features, Field 9, looking west.

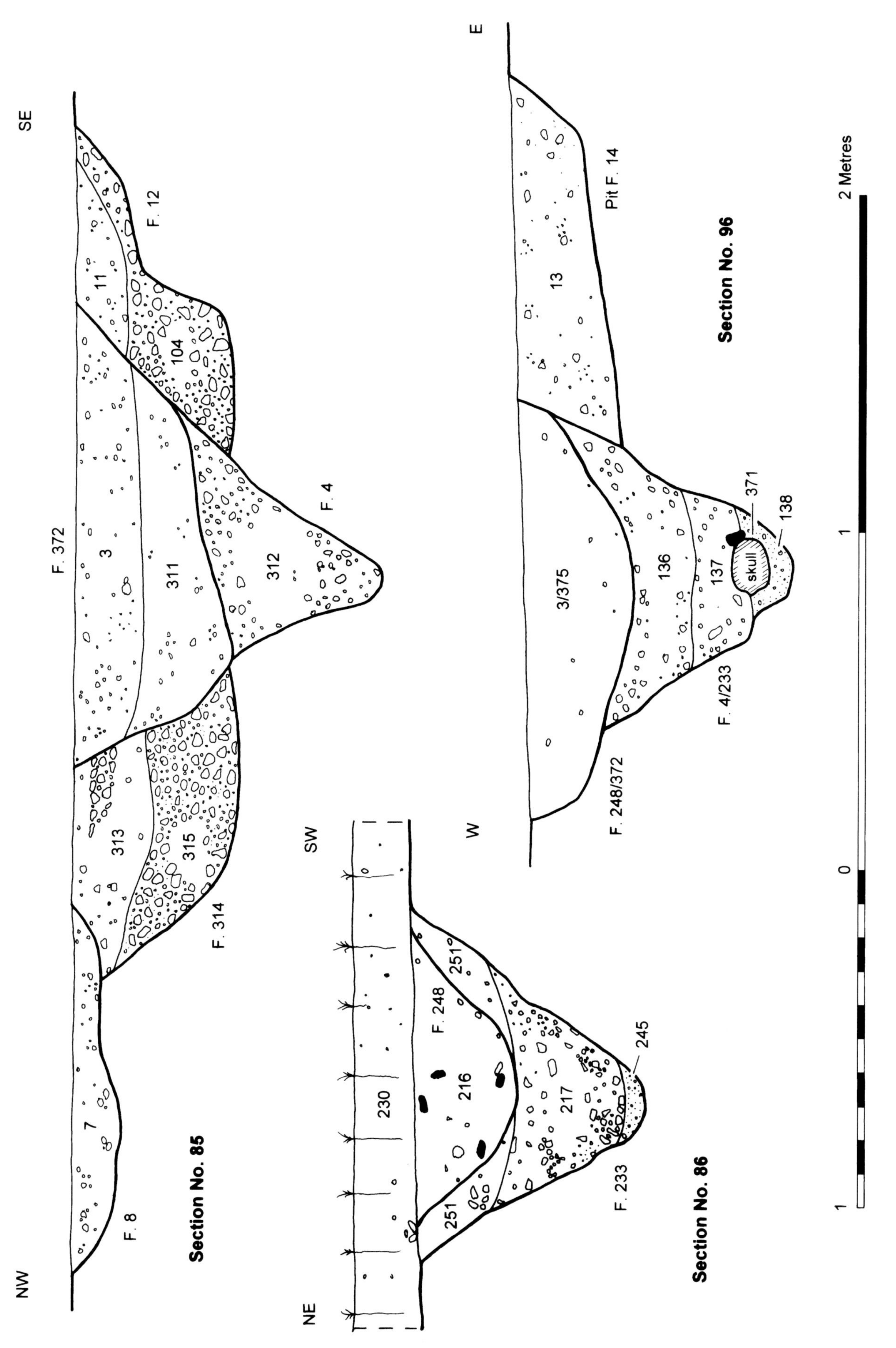

Fig 58. Church Whitfield: sections across Period 3 enclosure ditch, pit group C and pit F14 (Sections 85, 86 and 96).

see p 171). A bone from the skeleton gave a radiocarbon date of 2050±40 BP (cal BC 170–AD 45, 2 sigma; Beta 142010; Table 64).

South-west arm (F244)

Much of the south-west arm of the enclosure ditch lay under the modern crossroads and only a short length by the west corner could be examined in detail (Fig 56). Subsequent removal of the existing tarmac revealed more. Towards the south-east end, undug chalk appeared to mark the site of the only entrance into the enclosure (Figs 54 and 55).

Where undamaged, the ditch was again found to be V-shaped in profile with a width of about 1.35m across the top and a depth of 0.76m (Fig 57, Sections 77 and 109). It was filled with a series of layers of chalk rubble and brown loam (Section 77, contexts 240, 241, 242 and 243; Section 109, contexts 223, 224 and 225; Table 17), similar to those recorded in the north-west arm (see above).

Third ditch recut, F246

Dug into the upper filling of the main ditch, along its outer edge and cutting through the terminal of the first ditch recut (F252), the third recut was identified continuing round from the north-west arm (Fig 57, Sections 77 and 109, F246 and F247). It was 0.88 to 0.94m in width and about 0.37m deep with sloping sides and a rounded base. The filling was a brown clay loam containing chalk and flint (Section 77, context 239; Section 109, context 200). This yielded three late Iron Age sherds, animal bone (Table 51) and calcined flints. Several conjoining fragments of an adult human skull (frontal bone) were found in the top filling (Fig 56; p 59; Table 45).

South-east arm (F4)

About two-thirds of the total length of the south-east arm of the ditch was excavated in Field 8 (Figs 55 and 56) but its south-western end, together with the south corner, lay buried under the modern crossroads (Fig 56). Within the excavated area, the ditch (F4) cut through three earlier features, pit group C, the boundary ditch (F10) and a small pit (F14), all of which have been assigned to Period 2 (see above). Again, the enclosure ditch was V-shaped in cross-section (Fig 58, Sections 85 and 96), varying in width between 1.20 and 1.80m across the top. It was cut about 0.93m deep into the chalk. The filling consisted of a sequence of lower chalky silts (Section 85, context 312; Section 96, contexts 138, 137 and 136), overlain by deposits of brown loam (contexts 122 and 374, not illustrated), containing some domestic rubbish in the form of forty-two sherds of late Iron Age pottery, animal bone (Table 51) and calcined flints.

Third ditch recut, F372

As in the other arms, the upper filling of the ditch was found to contain evidence of a broad, late recut (here F372), continuing round from the north-east arm (F248). This was between 1.10 and 1.45m in width and 0.60m deep with sloping sides and a rounded base. It was filled by layers of brown loam with chalk and flint lumps (Fig 58, Section 85; contexts 3 and 311; Section 96, context 3/375) containing further significant quantities of pottery (Tables 41 and 42), calcined flint, animal bone (Table 51) and part of a human leg bone (Table 45), together with a fragment of shale (FN 534), an iron object (FN 20) and a piece of sandstone (FN 845; Table 32). The pottery recovered comprises 325 sherds, mostly of late Iron Age date, with some residual early Iron Age material.

North-east arm (F233)

With the exception of the truncated section running under modern Archer's Court Road, the complete length of this ditch was fully excavated (Figs 55 and 56; Pl 22). Removal of the road metalling subsequently confirmed that the ditch on this side (F233) had been continuous and unbroken by any entrance causeway. It cut two earlier features, an undated pit (Fig 56, F900) and the north-west arm of the Period 2 boundary ditch (F205; Pls 20 and 22).

The enclosure ditch had the standard V-shaped profile and varied from 0.90 to 1.50m in width across the top (Fig 57, Section 105; Fig 58, Sections 86 and 96; Fig 64, Section 81). It was up to 1m deep but had been severely truncated by the plough along the south-eastern edge of Field 9. The filling consisted of a typical sequence of lower chalk silts (Sections 81, 86, 96 and105, contexts 137, 138, 217, 232 and 245) and upper loam deposits (Sections 86, 96 and 105, contexts 136, 250 and 251), containing ninety-five sherds of pottery (Table 41) and further quantities of animal bone (Table 51) and burnt flints. Two fragments from a possible clay loomweight were also recovered from the upper filling (FN 409, *see* p 135).

Placed deposit, context 371

At the east corner, contained within the largely sterile primary filling of the ditch, was a group of closely associated objects that appear to represent a specific, placed deposit (Fig 56; Fig 58, Section 96, context 371). These comprised, a human cranium, a cattle humerus, a large irregular flint nodule and a small sherd of pottery (Pl 23). The objects seem to have been deliberately deposited here together shortly after the initial ditch silts had started to accumulate. The cranium (Table 45) was probably put in as a skull rather than a freshly severed head since the lower jaw is missing (*see* p 159); the cattle bone could represent a meat offering and probably significantly, the unworked flint nodule was of phallus-like form. The pottery fragment is a wall sherd in grog-tempered fabric. The cattle bone gave a radiocarbon date of 2120±40 BP (cal BC 350–310 or cal BC 210–AD 45, 2 sigma; Beta 142009; Table 64).

Second ditch recut, F253

The upper filling of the original ditch on this side again contained evidence of recutting (Fig 56). At the north corner

Pl 23. Church Whitfield: ritual deposit 371 in Period 3 enclosure ditch.

a short section of shallow gully extended round from the north-west arm (see above, F253; Fig 58, Section 105). This continued for about 3m along the north-east arm before being completely destroyed by the third ditch recut (F248, see below).

Third ditch recut, F248

The latest (third) recut of the ditch could be equated with that recorded in the south-east ditch (there F372) and with F247 in the north-west arm. In the north-east arm, this third recut (F248) varied from 0.50 to 1.48m in width. It was 0.43m deep with sloping sides and a rounded base. The filling consisted of brown loam with chalk and flint (Fig 58, Section 86, context 216; Section 96, context 3/375; Fig 57, Section 105, context 234), which produced further quantities of pottery (Table 41), animal bone (Table 51) and burnt flint, together with a few residual prehistoric struck flints. There were also several fragments of fired clay, one of which could be derived from a loomweight (FN 848, *see* p 135) and a number of pieces of sandstone (FN 847 and FN 1104; Table 32). The pottery totals well over 500 sherds and is mostly of late Iron Age date with some earlier residual material. The majority of the later sherds are flint-tempered and they include one with curvilinear decoration (Fig 85.39).

Features within the enclosure

Based on the evidence revealed at many other Iron Age farmstead sites across southern Britain, the principal feature of the interior of the present enclosure might well have been a substantial round-house, accompanied by a series of ancillary structures including storage pits and post-built granaries, etc. As exposed in Fields 8 and 9, however, the heavily-ploughed interior of the enclosure contained very few features that could be identified as being contemporary with it (Figs 55 and 56). Apart from a large natural pipe filled with Clay-with-Flints (Fig 56) and several small natural solution hollows, barely a dozen features lay within the enclosed area; several exposed during the roadworks could not be investigated. Of those excavated, some are certainly earlier and have been assigned to Period 2 (see above), whilst others are Anglo-Saxon or later. Potentially contemporary with the late Iron Age enclosure are just two pits (F213 and F219) and three post-holes (F265, F268 and F270; Table 18).

Pit F213

This was a roughly circular pit, 0.65m in diameter and 0.20m deep, with steep sides and flat base (Fig 56; Fig 59, Section 92; Pls 20 and 22). It was situated close to the inner lip of the north-west ditch and lay in an area that was probably originally occupied by any bank associated with the enclosure ditch. The filling (context 212) produced no finds.

F No	Shape	Axis	Length (m)	Width (m)	Depth (m)
F265	oval	NW-SE	0.44	0.28	0.10
F268	circular	-	0.29 diam		0.24
F270	oval	NW-SE	0.28	0.24	0.17

Table 18. Church Whitfield: details of post-holes excavated within the Period 3 enclosure.

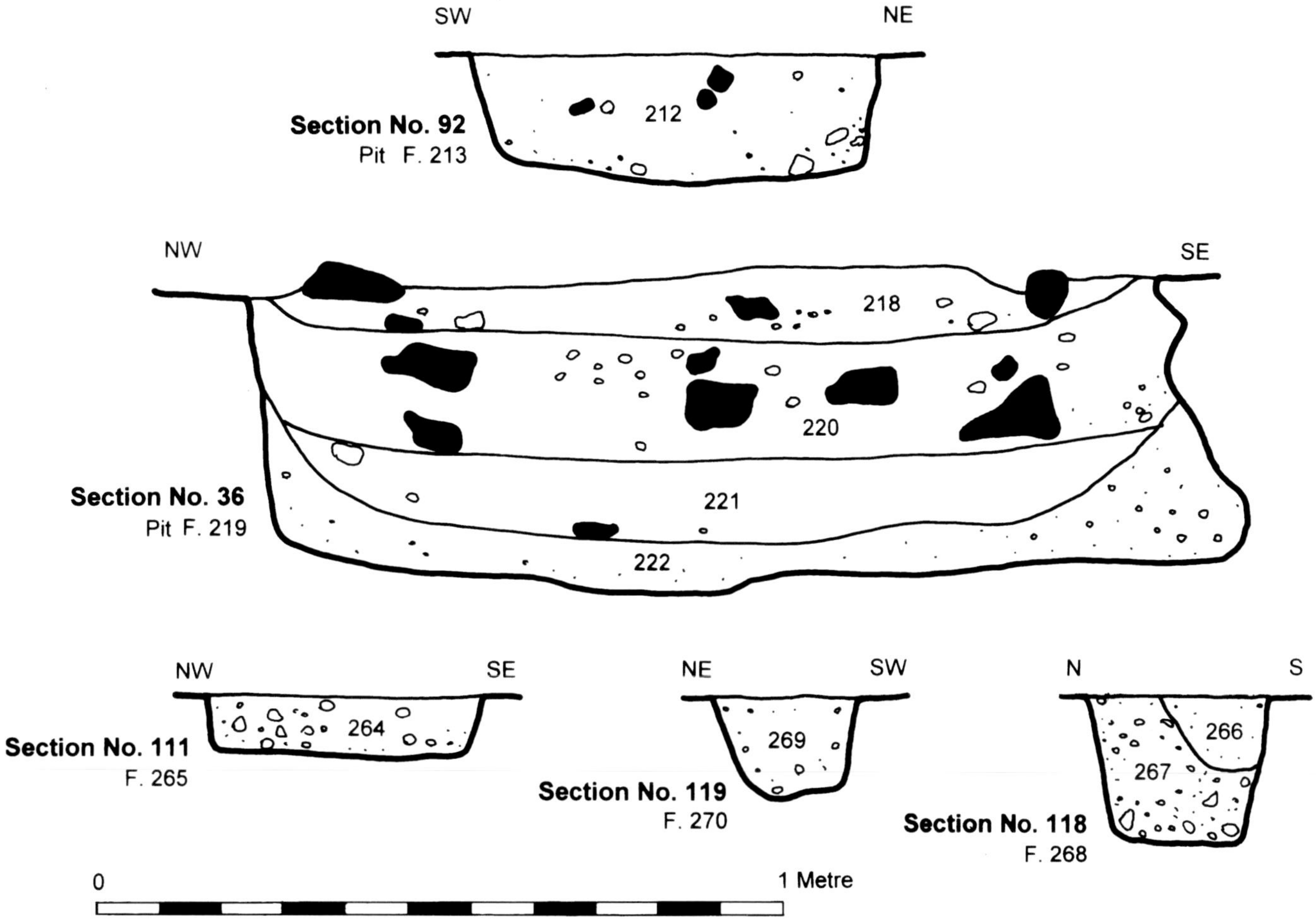

Fig 59. Church Whitfield: sections across features inside Period 3 enclosure.

From its position, unless it contained some sort of dedicatory offering deposited before the start of the construction of any bank, it probably relates to an earlier or later period.

Pit F219

This pit also lay towards the north-western side of the enclosure, not far from F213 (Fig 56). Cutting through the corner of the Period 2 boundary ditch, it was subrectangular in shape and measured 1.60m (north-east–south-west) by 1.45m (north-west–south-east). The pit was 0.49m deep with sides which varied from near vertical to undercut (Fig 59, Section 36). The base was flat and the fill comprised a series of brown clay loam deposits (Section 36, contexts 218, 220, 221 and 222), some containing large flint nodules. Small quantities of pottery (Table 43), animal bone (Table 47), calcined flints and residual prehistoric struck flints were recovered from the filling. Significantly, the lower filling (context 222) contained three late Iron Age sherds, whilst the upper filling (context 218) contained another fragment of a similar date. A few residual early Iron Age pieces, clearly derived from the Period 2 ditch, were also found (Table 43).

The overall size and shape of this pit is very similar to F16 and F26 assigned to Period 2, suggesting that it represents another grain storage pit. The pottery recovered, however, would seem to indicate that the present pit is later, presumably contemporary with the Period 3 enclosure ditch. The small quantities of domestic rubbish recovered from its filling suggest that it was not extensively used as a refuse dump when abandoned, whilst the large flint nodules it contained could suggest that there was an element of deliberate backfilling and consolidation.

Post-holes F265, F268 and F270

Three post-holes were found within the enclosure, all in Field 9 (Figs 55, 56 and 59; Table 18). Two (F268 and F270) lay close together near the centre, whilst the third (F265) occurred towards the western corner (Fig 56). None produced any datable finds. If they are contemporary with the Period 3 enclosure ditch, they must be indicative of the former presence of internal timber structures but little else can be deduced.

Perhaps significantly, F268 and F270 lay close to the exact centre of the enclosure, set some 2.70m apart (Fig 56). It is conceivable that they represent elements of a centrally positioned round-house of lightweight construction (cf Cunliffe 1991, 244–5), but they might equally well belong to other periods. Other features associated with the enclosure, especially shallow post-holes and stake-holes had, fairly certainly, been previously destroyed by the plough.

Late Iron Age features outside the enclosure

Several features found outside the main enclosure (Figs 46, 55 and 56; Pl 20) appear to be contemporary with it, although precise dating evidence is generally lacking.

Inhumation grave F146

A single inhumation burial lay a short distance to the south-east of the south-east arm of the enclosure ditch, just beyond gully F108 (see below), cutting into the edge of Period 2 pit group D (Fig 53; Fig 54, Section 82). The grave was aligned north-east by south-west, parallel with the enclosure ditch. It was 1.84m in length and between 0.34 and 0.49m in width. Contained within the grave was the moderately well-preserved skeleton of an adult male about 30–40 years old. The body was lying in an extended, supine position with arms bent (Fig 54). There were no grave goods but three flint-tempered sherds of pottery, broadly datable to the Iron Age, came from the general fill (Fig 54, Section 82, context 147). A sample of bone from the skeleton gave a radiocarbon date of 2230±60 BP (cal BC 400–155, 2 sigma; Beta 141266; Table 64), implying a mid to late Iron Age date.

The overall form of this burial is quite distinctive and can readily be paralleled by discoveries at the late Iron Age cemetery on Mill Hill at Deal, some 7km to the north-east. At that site, extended inhumation burials placed in characteristically narrow graves and very frequently without grave goods occurred from just before 200 BC into the first century AD (Parfitt 1995a). A comparable date for the present burial may be reasonably inferred on the evidence of the grave form, placing it within Period 3, although the broad radiocarbon date range might allow it to belong in Period 2 (see above).

On balance, it seems most likely that this burial represents one of the occupants of the Period 3 settlement, placed in a grave which had been dug just outside and parallel to, the main enclosure ditch. It is clearly a formal inhumation and may be contrasted with the human skull deposited in the enclosure ditch nearby (see above); and also with the seemingly casually discarded human remains found in other Iron Age features on the site (Table 45). Whether the grave formed part of a larger cemetery similar to that revealed on Mill Hill remains unclear. Certainly, no other graves were revealed in the excavated areas, but others could have been destroyed by the road to Pineham.

Miscellaneous features (Pits F318 and F320; Gullies F50/370, F108, F197 and F207)

Two adjacent shallow pits (F318 and F320) were located in Field 8, immediately outside the south-east arm of the main enclosure ditch (Figs 46 and 56). They were not fully excavated but had been previously noted in the 1982 pipe trench (*see* p 7). Pit F318 yielded a grog-tempered pot base (Table 43) and a few calcined flints.

Gully F50/F370

A poorly preserved and undated shallow gully (F50/F370) was found running east–west across Field 8 (Figs 46 and 55). All but its base had been destroyed by ploughing and it was clear that much of its course had been completely lost. It cut diagonally across the axis of the ridge and appeared to be heading directly towards the eastern corner of the main enclosure, perhaps implying that it was connected to it. The gully could possibly represent part of an ancillary compound situated on the southern side of the main enclosure, or perhaps it was a field boundary.

Gullies F108 and F197

Two more shallow gullies (F108 and F197) were revealed in Field 8, running parallel to the south-east ditch of the main enclosure, some 3.70m beyond its outer lip (Figs 46, 53, 55, 56; Fig 54, Section 82; Fig 74, Section 102). These appear to represent successive phases of a single feature which may have formed part of some sort of outwork beyond the main ditch. Gully F108 was the most extensive and appeared to cut pit group D assigned to Period 2 (Fig 53; Fig 54, Section 82). Its filling produced two sherds of pottery, one dated to the late Iron Age. Another large rim sherd of a similar date was recovered from the same feature when it was cut by the pipe trench in 1982.

Gully F207

Another gully (F207) was located in Field 9, north-west of the north corner of the main enclosure ditch, roughly continuing the line of its north-east arm (Figs 46, 55 and 56; Pl 20). It was aligned north-west by south-east and its south-east terminal lay some 7m from the main enclosure ditch. The gully was traced for a minimum distance of 7.60m and continued on beyond the limit of the excavation. Its filling of brown loam with some chalk and flint (Fig 74, Section 78, context 206) produced three sherds of late Iron Age pottery (Table 43). The gully might have formed part of a secondary enclosure situated on the northern side of the main compound. The gap between the gully terminal and the main ditch could represent a broad entrance.

Period 4: Anglo-Saxon settlement

The late Iron Age farmstead seems to have been abandoned before the end of the first century BC (*see* p 177). Despite the close proximity of a major Roman road, there was no clear evidence for any Romano-British occupation on the excavated site. However, a handful of pottery sherds, mostly of first- or second-century date, several Roman tile fragments and a worn coin of Faustina I (AD 138–141, *see* p 133), imply that there had been habitation at no great distance.

F No	Type	Shape	Axis	Length (m)	Width (m)	Depth (m)
III	Six-post	sub-rect	NE-SW	3.78	2.95	0.58
VI	Two-post	sub-rect	NE-SW	2.30	1.77–1.88	0.18
VII	Four-post	sub-square	NE-SW	3.40	3.30	0.40
VIII	Four-post	sub-rect	NE-SW	3.05	2.74	0.18

Table 19. Church Whitfield: summary of sunken-featured buildings, Structures III, VI, VII and VIII.

There was post-Roman occupation on the excavated site. Six structures datable to the Anglo-Saxon period provide important evidence for the presence of a farmstead or hamlet here during the late sixth and seventh century AD (Fig 60). The full extent of this was not established and it seems likely that further associated buildings lay beyond the limits of the excavation.

The structures examined included four sunken-featured buildings (*grubenhaüser*) of well-known Anglo-Saxon type (Structures III, VI, VII and VIII; Table 19), together with post-holes relating to two separate, surface-built timber structures (Structures I and IV). The dating for these plough-damaged wall-post buildings is extremely limited but the structural and circumstantial evidence allows them to be assigned to the Anglo-Saxon period with reasonable confidence.

Sunken-featured buildings: Structures III, VI, VII andVIII

Four sunken-featured buildings (SFBs) were fully excavated (Figs 46, 56 and 60–68), although two further possible examples (F904 and F1010) revealed during the roadworks could not be investigated. The excavated structures varied in details of size and construction method (Table 19). Structure III was situated in Field 8 between wall-post Structures I and IV. The SFB in Field 9 (Structure VI) lay some 30m to the north-west of Structure IV and had been cut into the top of the late Iron Age enclosure ditch, perhaps to take advantage of a slight hollow in the ground surface which might then still have survived. In Field 6, Structure VII lay 25m to the south of wall-post Structure IV, whilst Structure VIII was discovered during roadworks about 15m west of Structure IV.

Structure III

Structure III was the largest of the SFBs located. It was of 'six-poster' type (Figs 61 and 62; Pl 24; Table 20). The sunken area (F22) was subrectangular in shape, measuring 3.78m (north-east–south-west) by 2.95m (north-west–south-east) and was aligned with the main axis of the ridge. It was 0.58m deep with steep sides and a slightly dished base cut by numerous stake-holes. A narrow ledge in the middle of the north-west side could represent a step leading down into the building, hinting that the door lay on this side.

Surviving post-holes show that the building was originally supported by six substantial timber posts (Fig 61); the deepest of these post-holes (F143 and F150) were set in the middle of the south-west and north-east ends and were cut over 0.60m into the base of the sunken area. Lying on the main axis of the building, these must have contained the principal timbers. The four remaining post-holes, one set at each corner of the sunken area (F145, F189, F192 and F195) were shallower and must have contained less substantial timbers (Figs 61 and 62). The side of F195 showed clear marks from the iron mattock blade that had been used in its excavation. The blade was about 50mm wide. The filling of post-hole F143 produced three sherds of organic-tempered Anglo-Saxon pottery, together with a single residual sherd of early Roman Upchurch ware.

The base of the sunken area was cut by 224 stake-holes (Fig 61; Pl 24). These were clearly not all contemporary and they probably related to a number of separate internal structures. Most occurred in a roughly H-shaped area running down the centre and across the two ends of the building. A separate cluster of about thirty lay on the south-east side, with a lighter scatter on the north-west side. Some of the stakes here might have obstructed the possible entrance (see above).

The individual stake-holes ranged from 0.03 to 0.25m in depth and were generally filled with brown silty loam and chalk. One within the south-east group produced a small annular bead of yellow glass, which was unfortunately lost on site.

The stake-holes within the H-shaped cluster could include successive replacements of the supports for a central partition and timbers for the north-east and south-west walls of the sunken area; several reasonably convincing alignments can be observed (Fig 61). If the stake-holes towards the ends of the sunken area represent the wall lines however, the overall internal length of the building is reduced to about 2m and a gap is left between them and the edge of the sunken area. More probably these stake-holes do not mark the walls but represent several phases

No	Shape	Axis	Length (m)	Width (m)	Depth into base (m)	Notes
F143	oval	NE–SW	0.36	0.34	0.66	Post removed?
F145	oval	N–S	0.35	0.24–0.29	0.18	
F150	oval	NE–SW	0.41	0.31	0.64	Post removed?
F189	oval	NW–SE	0.41	0.31	0.32	
F192	oval	NW–SE	0.38	0.24	0.14	
F195	oval	NW–SE	0.44	0.25	0.32 (max.)	Mattock marks on north-west side

Table 20. Church Whitfield: post-hole dimensions, Structure III.

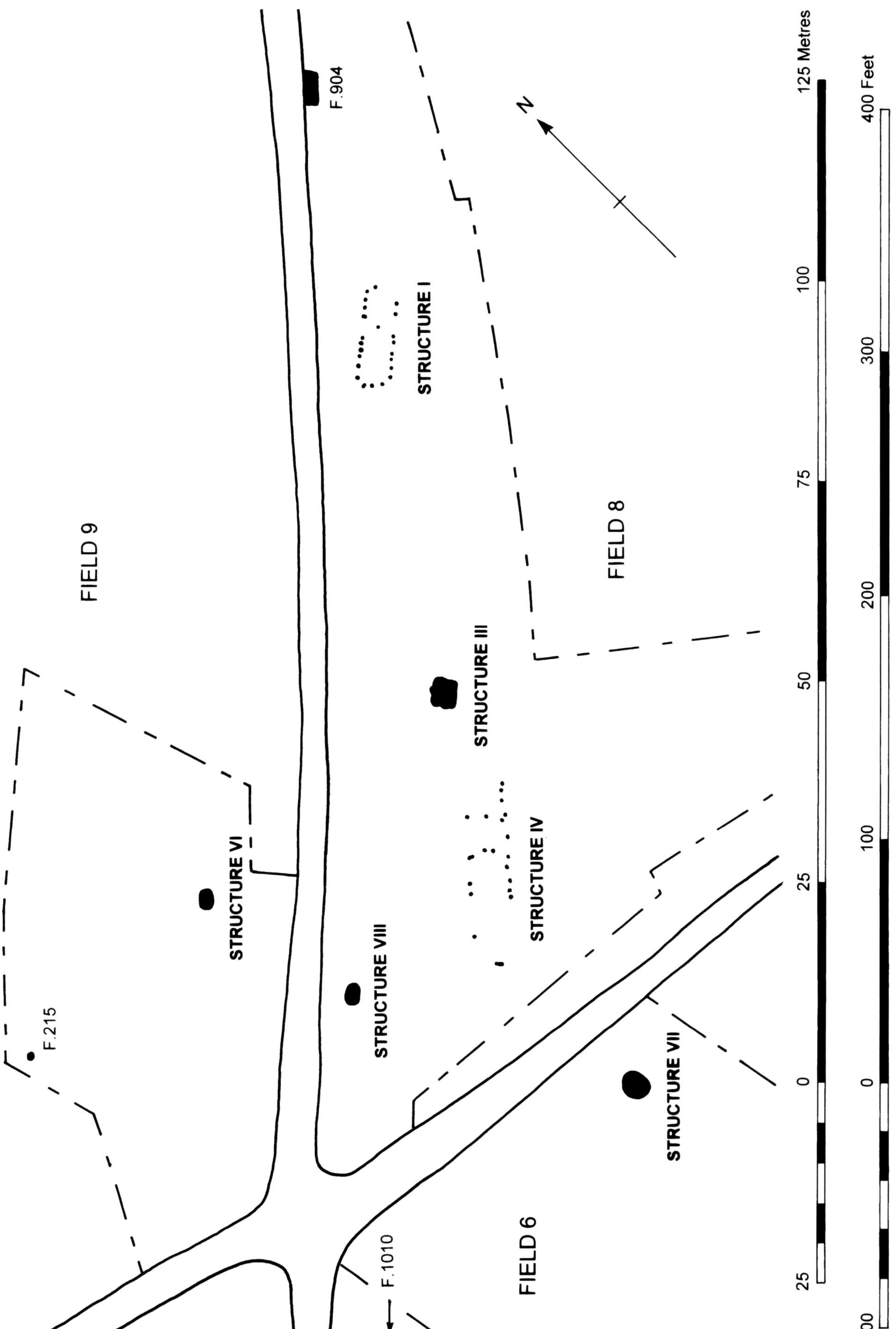

Fig 60. Chruch Whitfield: Anglo-Saxon structures and features.

Pl 24. Church Whitfield: Anglo-Saxon (Period 4) sunken-featured building, Structure III, looking south-west. Scale 1m.

of internal fitting, such as racking for drying or storage purposes, positioned just inside.

The sunken area was filled by deposits of soil and chalk with some flints. These were divided into an upper, middle and lower layer (Fig 62, Section 75, contexts 21, 139 and 140). The 0.13m thick lower filling (context 140), resting directly on the base, yielded fourteen pieces of Anglo-Saxon organic-tempered pottery, together with a few residual Iron Age and Roman sherds. Lying on the chalk surface, in the east corner was a large, triangular sandstone lump which appeared to have been used as a grinding stone (FN 911, pp 134–5 and Table 32). Several prehistoric struck flints, animal bone, a number of oyster shells and a copper-alloy object (FN 1110, *see* p 135) were also recovered. Wet-sieving of a bulk sample produced bird and fish bone, together with fragmentary shells of oyster, mussel, winkle, ?rough periwinkle and limpet. There were also eggshell fragments, probably from domestic fowl and goose, and a few charred grains, together with two small glass beads (FN 1109, *see* pp 133–4) and two iron fish hooks (FN 1108, *see* p 133).

The middle filling (context 139) produced a further nine organic-tempered Anglo-Saxon sherds. Again, there were also a few residual Iron Age and Roman pieces, together with animal bone, a number of limpet shells, a fragment of sandstone (FN 192, Table 32) and residual prehistoric struck flints. The upper filling (context 21) produced a further twenty-one sherds of Anglo-Saxon pottery (Table 44). Excepting one in a coarse sandy fabric, these are again all of organic-tempered wares. Residual Iron Age and Roman pottery was also present, together with a Roman tile fragment, animal bone, prehistoric struck flints, a chalk object (FN 191) and an iron object (FN 151, *see* p 135).

From the contents of its filling it is clear that the sunken area had served for small scale rubbish dumping after the building was abandoned, but its precise function when standing remains unclear. The stake-holes cutting the floor might have supported storage racks, perhaps for food. If the two iron fish hooks and the fish bones found in the lower filling do not represent subsequently dumped rubbish derived from elsewhere, they could suggest that the building had been used to store fish.

Structure VI

This small, two-post SFB was located in Field 9 (Figs 46, 55, 59, 62 and 63) and consisted of a subrectangular pit (F203), partially cut into the top of the north-east ditch of the late Iron Age enclosure (Pls 20 and 22). The pit was 2.30m in length and between 1.77 and 1.88m in width, the main axis being north-east by south-west. It was cut 0.18m into the underlying natural chalk and ditch fill, with steep sides and a flat base. The bottom of the sunken area showed no clear evidence for a trodden floor surface and there were no stake-holes or other features cutting it.

Large central post-holes (Figs 63 and 64, F236 and F238) had been cut into the north-east and south-west ends of the sunken area. F236 at the north-east end was sub-oval in shape and measured 0.42m (north-west–south-east) by 0.27m (north-east–south-west). It was dug 0.28m deep into

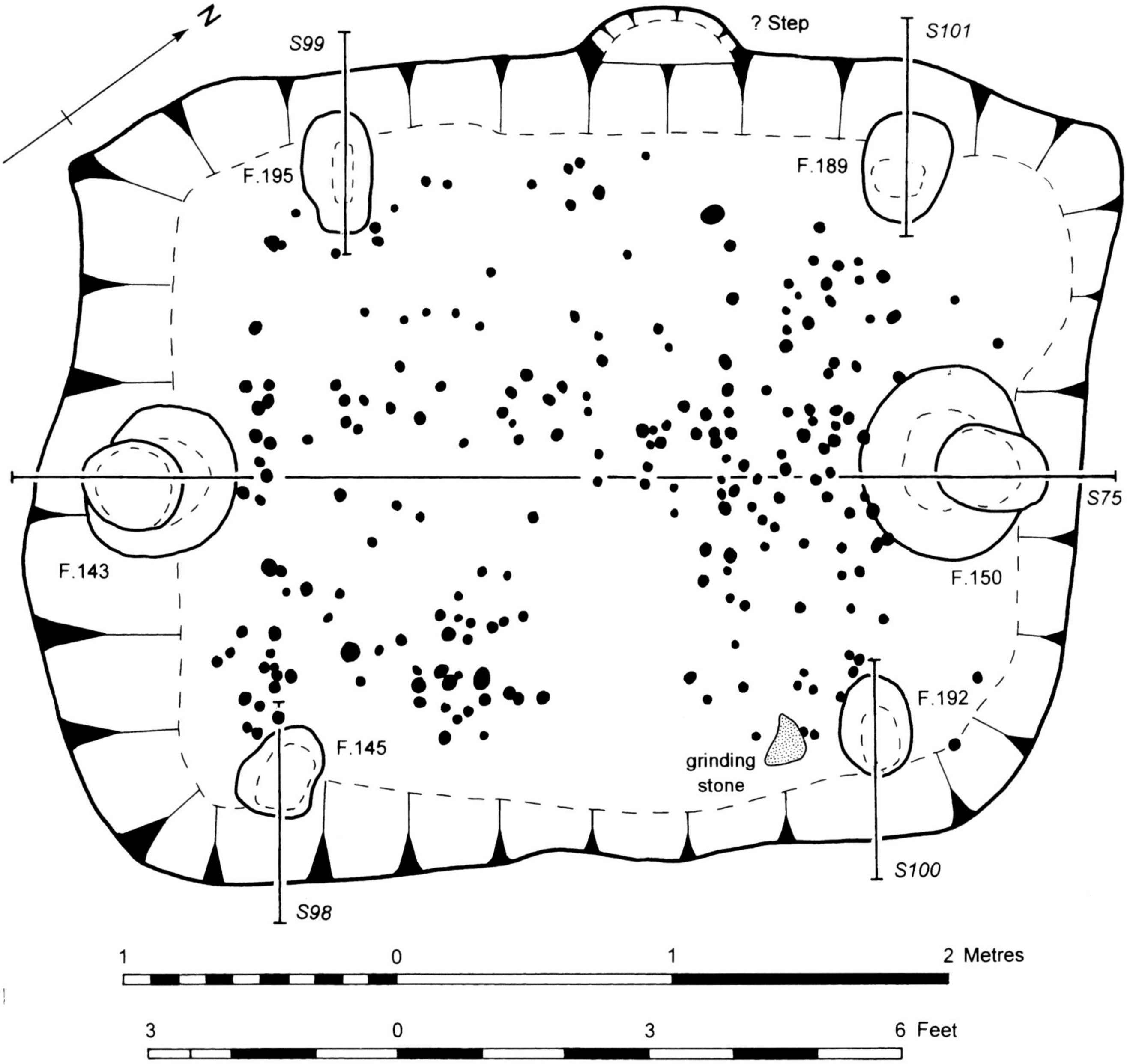

Fig 61. Church Whitfield: sunken-featured building, Structure III.

the base of the sunken area, with almost vertical sides and a slightly rounded base. The filling was a dark brown clay loam with occasional chalk lumps; a ring of six large flint nodules in the top must represent packing stones around the original wooden post. Two residual sherds of pottery were recovered from the filling, one Iron Age and one early Roman.

The post-hole at the south-west end, F238, was oval in shape and measured 0.45m (north-west–south-east) by 0.35m (north-east–south-west). It was dug 0.35m deep into the base of the sunken area, with near vertical sides and a slightly rounded base. The filling was a dark brown clay loam with occasional chalk lumps and half a dozen flint packing stones. This yielded two sherds of pottery, one residual Iron Age and the other Anglo-Saxon organic-tempered ware.

The brown clay loam and chalk filling of the main sunken area (Fig 64, Section 81, context 202/231) produced over 100 sherds of pottery, animal bone, prehistoric struck flints and a few pieces of burnt red clay, probably daub. Most of the pottery is residual Iron Age material, derived from the underlying enclosure ditch. Fourteen sherds, however, may be dated to the Anglo-Saxon period. Amongst these there is a single fragment of probable late Saxon shell-filled ware, which is likely to be intrusive (Table 44).

Structure VII

This SFB was located on the north-eastern edge of Field 6 adjacent to Pineham Road (Figs 46, 60, 65 and 66; Pl 25). The sunken area was subsquare (F380) and measured 3.40m (north-east–south-west) by 3.30m (north-west–south-east). It

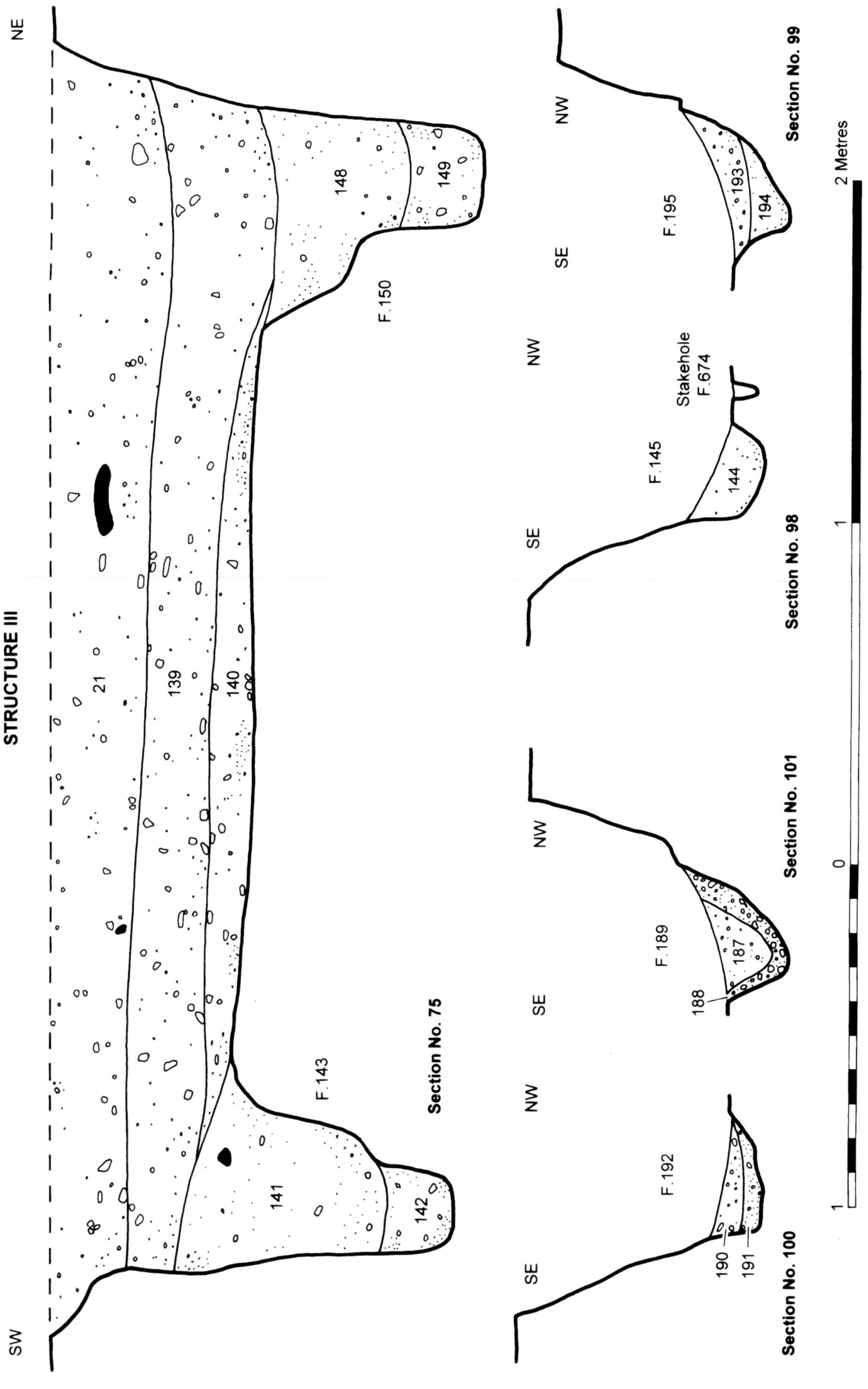

Fig 62. Church Whitfield: sections of sunken-featured building, Structure III.

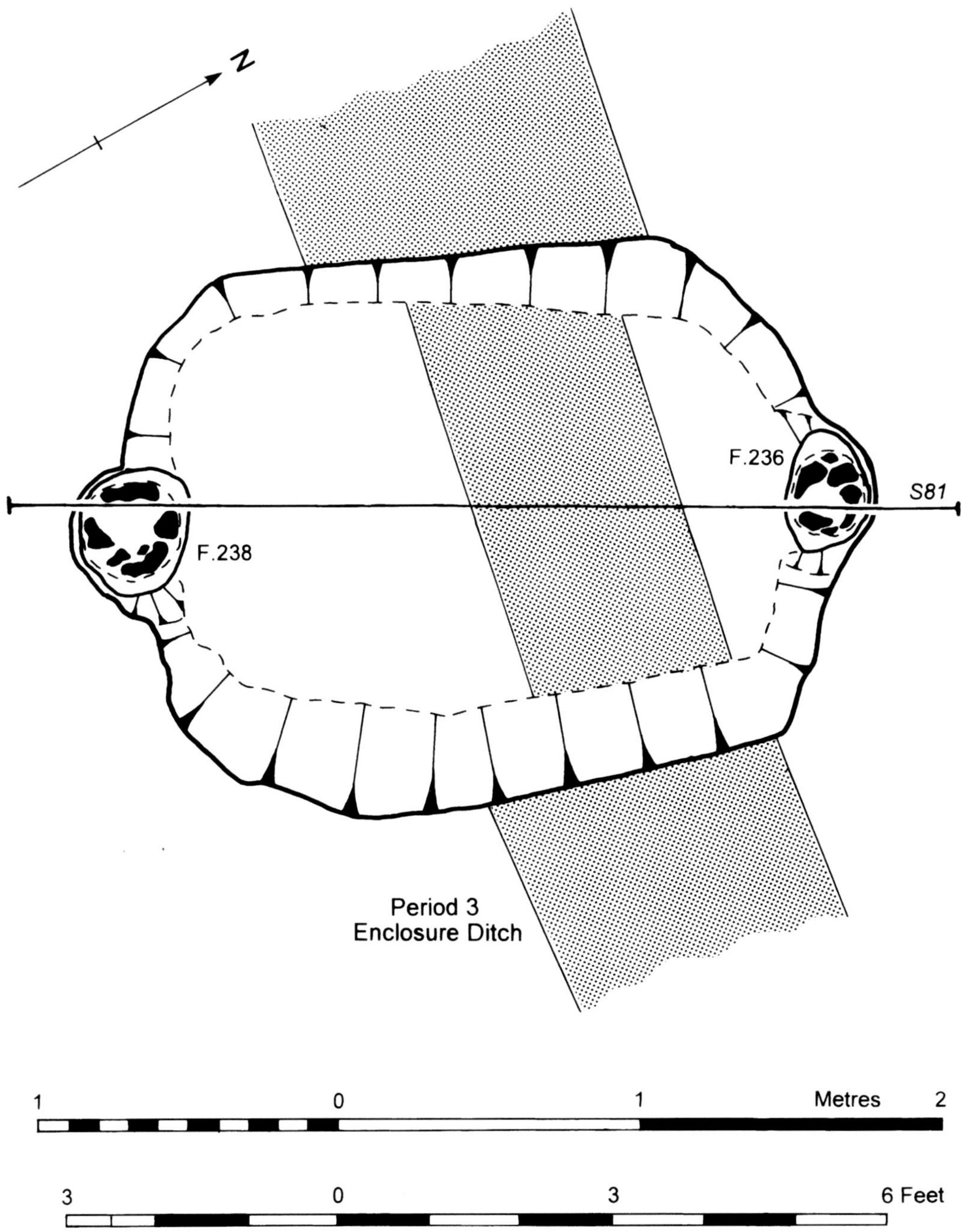

Fig 63. Church Whitfield: sunken-featured building, Structure VI.

was 0.40m deep, with sloping sides and a reasonably flat base. The structure represented was of a slightly unusual four-post type, having a single large post-hole set roughly in the middle of each of the four sides (F383, F386, F389 and F392).

The flat bottomed post-holes were all oval in shape, well over 0.30m across and cut 0.40m or more into the base of the sunken area (Table 21). F383 and F386 contained clear evidence of a post-pipe, whilst F389 and F392 contained large flint packing stones. Post-holes F383 and F392, set opposite each other, were slightly angled inwards, suggesting that they originally held sloping posts set between 10 and 13 degrees from the vertical (Fig 66, Section 114). Apart from a residual Iron Age sherd found in F392, no datable material was recovered from the post-hole fillings.

In the western corner of the sunken area a shallow, unfinished post-hole (F395) filled with a very compact brown chalky loam was located (Fig 66, Section 116, context 394). It seems clear that this post-hole had been dug in the wrong place and quickly backfilled before it had been fully excavated.

Cut into the base of the sunken area, close to the centre of the building, was a shallow, slightly irregular pit (F399). This was roughly oval in shape and measured 0.62m (north-west–south-east) by 0.48m (north-east–south-west). It was 0.09m deep and was filled with a brown loam containing much small chalk and burnt red clay fragments (Fig 66, Section 114; Pl 25). The burnt material could hint at the feature being a hearth or oven pit but there was no trace of any burning on its sides.

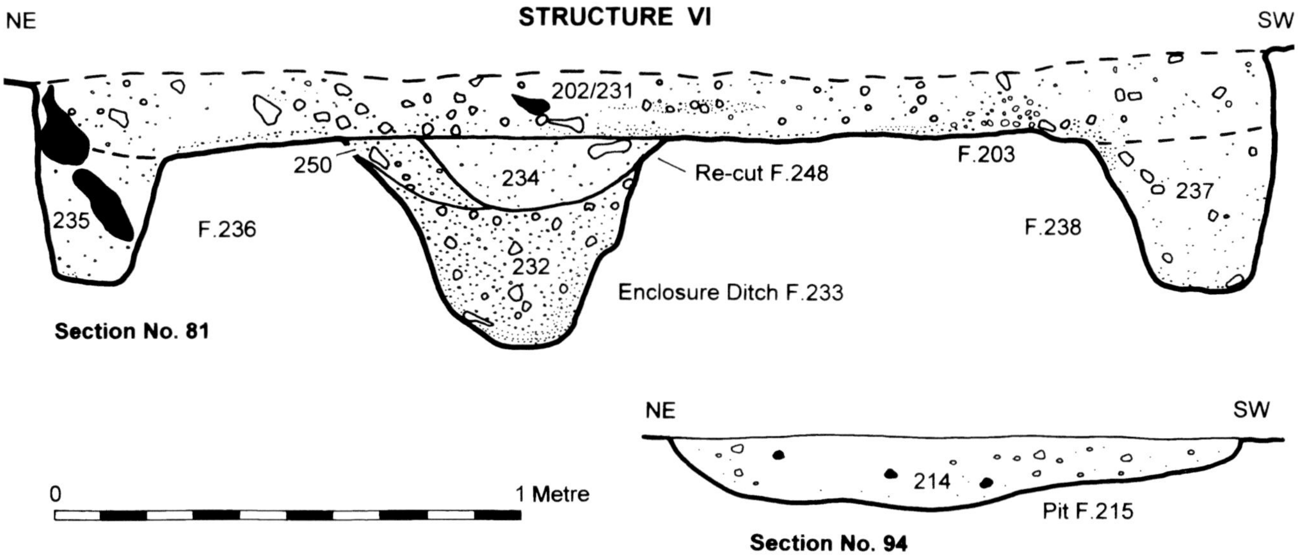

Fig 64. Church Whitfield: sunken-featured building, Structure VI and pit F215.

Pl 25. Church Whitfield: Anglo-Saxon (Period 4) sunken-featured building, Structure VII, looking north-east. Scale 1m.

F No	Shape	Axis	Length (m)	Width (m)	Depth cut into floor (m)	Notes
F383	oval	NE–SW	0.44	0.36	0.45	Post–pipe present
F386	oval	NW–SE	0.46	0.32	0.40	Pipe, 0.27 x 0.25m
F389	oval	NW–SE	0.55	0.39	0.45	Flint packing stones
F392	oval	NE–SW	0.36	0.34	0.51	Flint packing stones
F395	oval	E–W	0.45	0.38	0.14	Unfinished, builder's mistake

Table 21. Church Whitfield: post-hole dimensions, Structure VII.

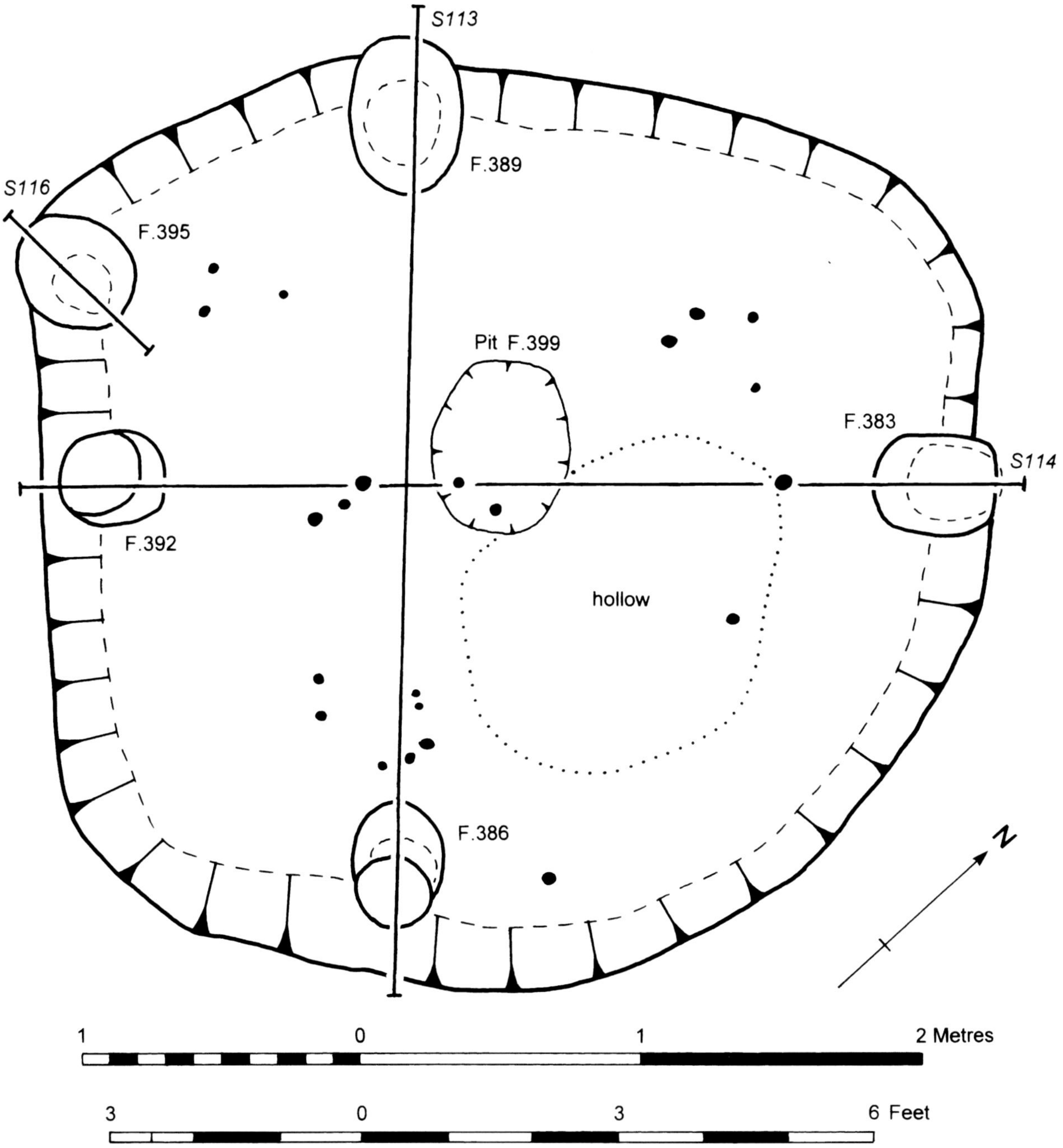

Fig 65. Church Whitfield: sunken-featured building, Structure VII.

Adjoining the eastern side of pit, F399 was a worn, shallow oval depression between 1.10 and 1.30m across and up to 0.12m deep (Pl 25). This may have been created by repeated activity occurring in this area, perhaps connected with the nearby pit. Alternatively, it may have formed just inside the entrance to the building. If so, the implication must be that the doorway was on the eastern side, between F383 and F386.

Small groups of stake-holes were recorded in the base of the sunken area towards the north, south and west corners. Another group of three occurred south-west of the central pit (F399) and two others cut the northern edge of this feature (Figs 65 and 66). Totalling twenty-two, these stake-holes were generally oval or circular in shape and ranged from 0.02 to 0.05m in diameter. They were between 0.03 and 0.11m deep, usually with steep sides and a rounded or pointed base (Fig 66, Section 114). The eastern quarter of the sunken area contained just two stake-holes. The exact purpose of the various stake-holes recorded remains unclear. They do not seem to relate to internal partitions but could be connected with other structures inside the building. They need not all be contemporary.

The main filling of the sunken area consisted of a brown clay loam with much small chalk (Fig 66, Sections 113, 114 and 116, context 379) and this produced half a dozen sherds of pottery, all but one of Iron Age or Roman date and clearly residual. A single sherd of organic-tempered ware was the only Anglo-Saxon piece recovered (Table

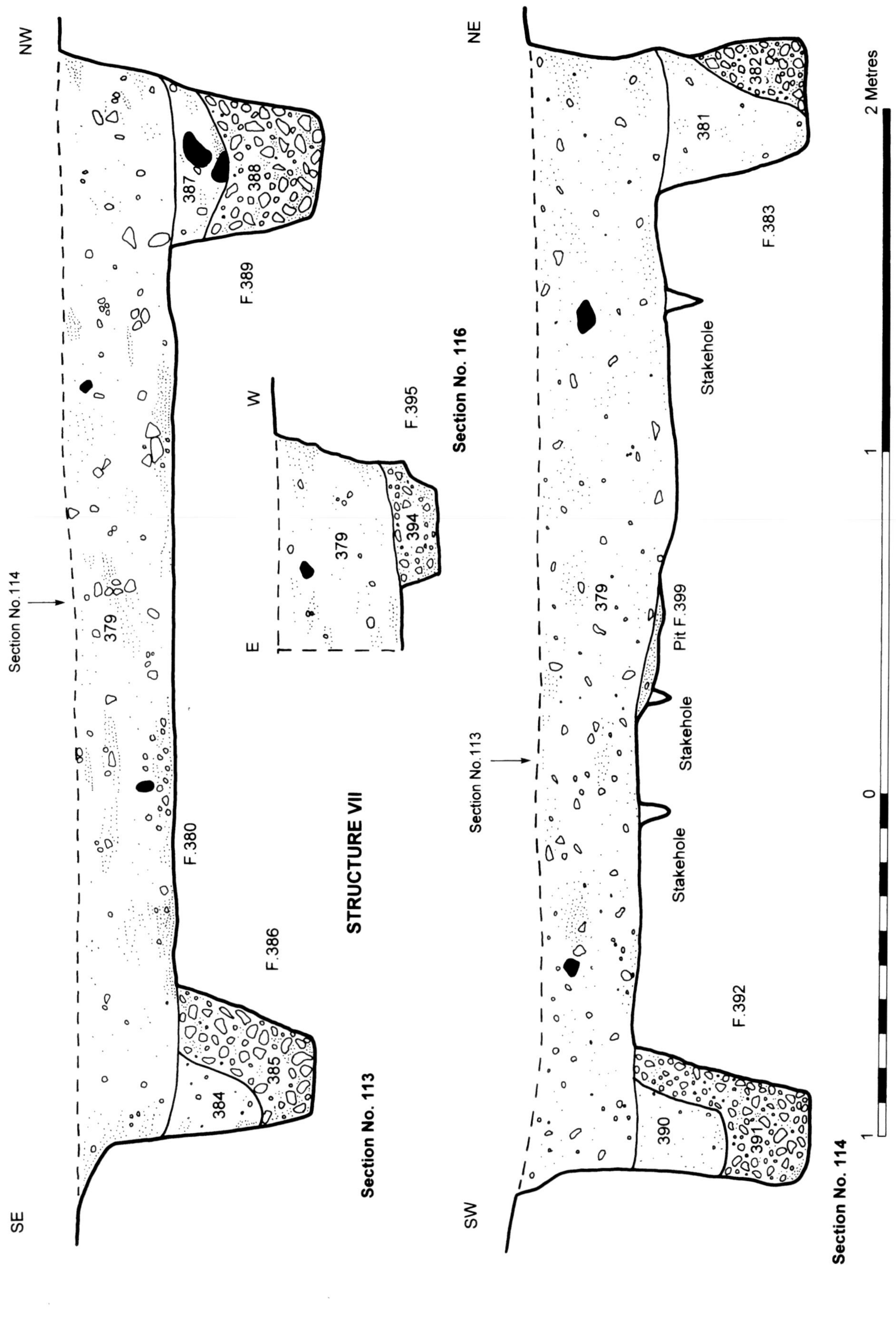

Fig 66. Church Whitfield: sunken-featured building, Structure VII.

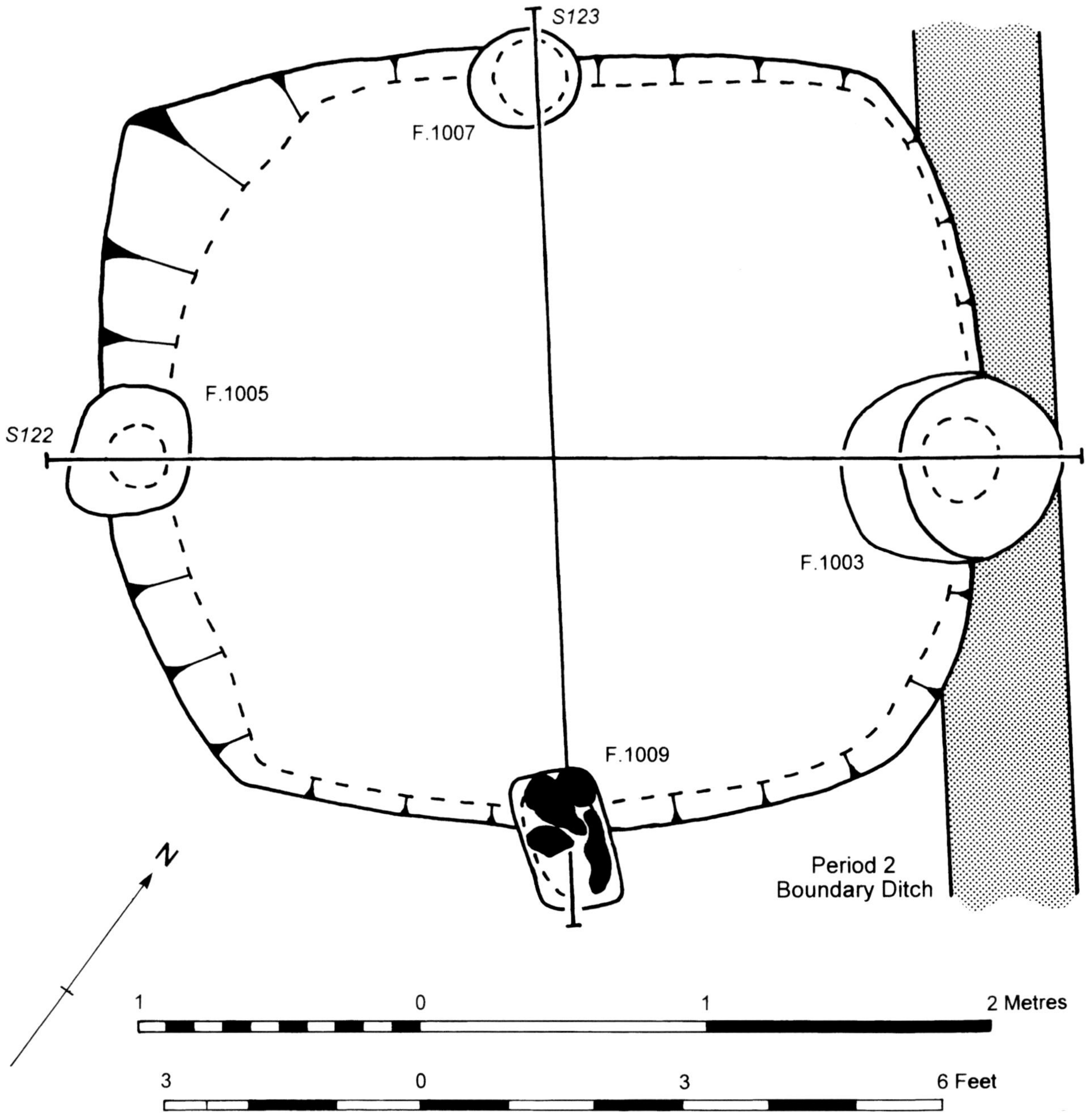

Fig 67. Church Whitfield: sunken-featured building, Structure VIII.

44). Small amounts of burnt daub, fragments of animal bone, oyster and limpet shell were also found, together with a quantity of prehistoric struck flints. Wet-sieving of a large bulk sample produced very little, apart from a few fragments of eggshell, probably from domestic fowl and goose.

Structure VIII

This was another four-post SFB, exposed and rapidly recorded after road construction had begun (Figs 46, 56, 60, 67 and 68; Table 22). Cutting into the Iron Age boundary ditch of Period 2, it lay just within Field 8, under the hedge adjacent to Archer's Court Road, some 15m north-west of wall-post Structure IV (Fig 56). The sunken area (F1001) was subrectangular in shape and measured 3.05m (north-east–south-west) by 2.74m (north-west–south-east). It was 0.18m deep with steep sides and a reasonably flat base (Fig 68, Sections 122 and123). A single post-hole was set in the middle of each of the four sides (F1003, F1005, F1007 and F1009).

Two of the post-holes were oval, one was subrectangular (F1005), while F1009 was rectangular. They were all cut 0.28m or more into the base of the structure (Table 22). F1009 contained several large flint packing stones. Post-holes F1003 and F1005, set on the long axis of the building, were slightly larger and deeper than the other two, implying that these held the principal posts. They both appeared to incorporate a wide, upper post-pit and a deeper post-hole. No trace of any post-pipe was visible within their fillings (Fig 68, Section 122, contexts 1002 and 1004; Section 123, contexts 1006 and 1008) and unlike Structure VII, there was no evidence that any of the posts had been set at an angle.

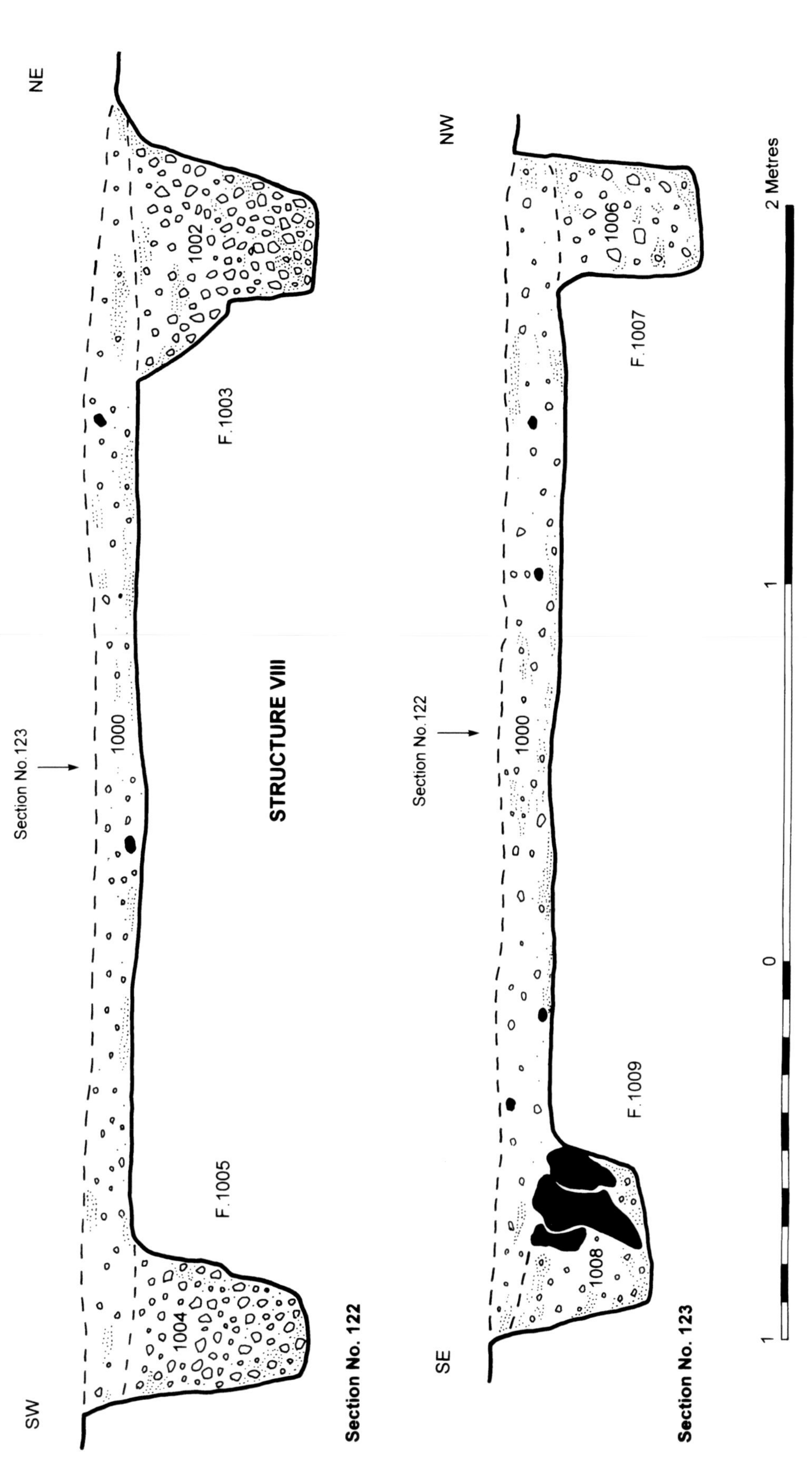

Fig 68. Church Whitfield: sunken-featured building, Structure VIII.

F No	Shape	Axis	Length (m)	Width (m)	Depth cut into floor (m)	Notes
F1003	oval	NE–SW	0.80	0.66	0.46	Ledge on SW side
F1005	sub-rect	NW–SE	0.46	0.44	0.46	Ledge on NW side
F1007	oval	N–S	0.38	0.31	0.38	-
F1009	rect	NW–SE	0.50	0.30	0.28	Flint packing stones

Table 22. Church Whitfield: post-hole dimensions, Structure VIII.

The filling of the sunken area consisted of an orange-brown silty clay with much small chalk and this produced forty-six sherds of Anglo-Saxon organic-tempered pottery (Fig 68, Sections 122 and 123; context 1000; Table 44). There were also a few residual Iron Age sherds and several fairly large fragments of Roman tile; small quantities of burnt daub were also recovered.

Wall-post buildings: Structures I and IV

Groups of heavily plough-damaged post-holes clearly represented the remains of two separate, surface-built structures utilising substantial earthfast timber uprights to support their walls (Structures I and IV). Both buildings were aligned north-east by south-west, along the axis of the ridge and stood some 55m apart. Structure I may be reasonably interpreted as a hall but the full extent of Structure IV remains problematical.

Structure I

Structure I was located on the north-western edge of Field 8, adjacent to Archer's Court Road (Figs 46 and 60; Pl 26). Although heavily damaged by the plough, twenty-five post-holes forming the incomplete outline of a large rectangular structure could be discerned (Fig 69; Pl 26). No trace of any associated stratified deposits or floors remained. The truncated post-holes which survived were generally circular or oval in shape and were cut to depths between 0.03 and 0.18m into the natural chalk (Fig 70; Table 23); several near the east corner had been completely destroyed.

Overall, the building measured (taking post-hole centres) 12.25m in length (north-east–south-west) by 4.00–4.14m in width (north-west–south-east), giving a floor area of around 50m². A broad gap in the post-hole spacings near the middle of each of the long walls probably indicates the position of two opposed doorways (Table 24). These were exceptionally wide, about 2.90m across. The only internal feature remaining was a shallow, centrally placed post-hole (F81) located between the two doorways. This may or may not be an original feature.

An absence of post-holes at the corners and a tendency for the individual side-wall post-holes not to form neatly matched opposing pairs set at right angles to the axis of the building are structural features noticeable in the overall layout (Fig 69). Such features have been reported in other Anglo-Saxon wall-post buildings. The lack of substantial corner posts is a frequent characteristic ('weak corners'; eg

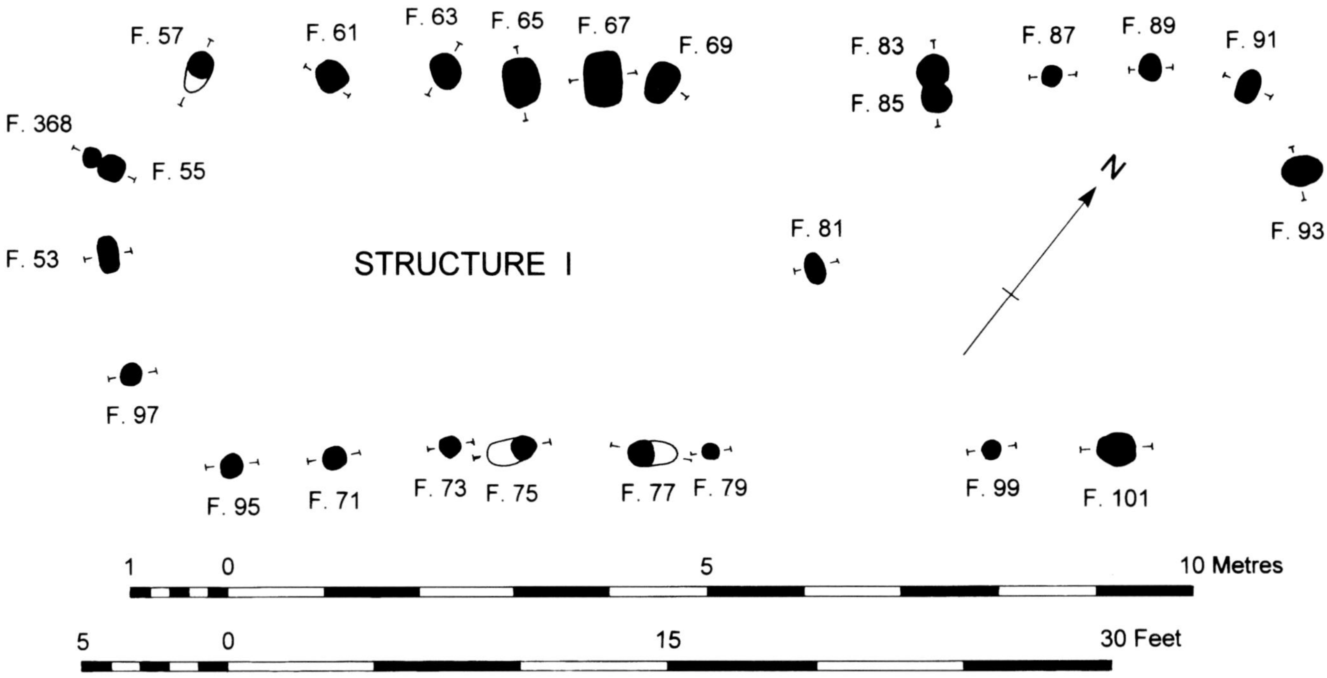

Fig 69. Church Whitfield: wall-post Structure I.

Blockley *et al* 1995, 345), whilst irregularity in post-hole spacing along side walls has been specifically noted and discussed by Philip Dixon (in Losco-Bradley and Kinsley 2002, 94).

F No	Shape	Axis	Length (m)	Width (m)	Depth (m)
F53	sub-oval	NW–SE	0.38	0.20	0.15
F55	sub-circ	-	diam. 0.26		0.08
F57	oval	N–S	0.43	0.25	0.17
F61	sub-circ	-	diam. 0.30		0.15
F63	oval	E–W	0.35	0.30	0.12
F65	sub-rect	NW–SE	0.44	0.32	0.10
F67	sub-rect	NW–SE	0.54	0.38	0.15
F69	ovoid	N–S	0.41	0.28	0.15
F71	circular	-	diam. 0.22		0.09
F73	sub-circ	-	diam. 0.21		0.06
F75	oval	NE–SW	0.54	0.27	0.10–0.15
F77	oval	NE–SW	0.49	0.25	0.11–0.17
F79	circular	-	diam. 0.15		0.05
F81	oval	NW–SE	0.32	0.18	0.05
F83	oval	N–S	0.34	0.30	0.14
F85	circular	-	diam. 0.30		0.13
F87	oval	NW–SE	0.21	0.18	0.06
F89	oval	NW–SE	0.27	0.20	0.09
F91	oval	N–S	0.36	0.23	0.09
F93	oval	NE–SW	0.43	0.28	0.09
F95	circular	-	diam. 0.23		0.13
F97	circular	-	diam. 0.21		0.05
F99	oval	NW–SE	0.17	0.16	0.04
F101	sub-oval	NE–SW	0.40	0.32	0.07
F368	oval	N–S	0.20	0.19	0.09

Table 23. Church Whitfield: post-hole dimensions, Structure I.

F No	Distance between post-hole centres (m)
F95–F71	1.07
F71–F73	1.23
F73–F75	0.75
F75–F77	1.25
F77–F79	0.70
F79–F99	2.91 (doorway)
F99–F101	1.27
F93–F91	1.05
F91–F89	1.01
F89–F87	1.02
F87–F83/85	1.19
F83/85–F69	2.86 (doorway)
F69–F67	0.61
F67–F65	0.82
F65–F.63	0.82
F63–F61	1.22
F.61–F57	1.32
F57–F55	1.40
F55–F53	0.90
F53–F97	1.22
F97–F95	1.42
F89–F101	4.00
F57–F95	4.14
F55–F93	12.25

Table 24: Church Whitfield: post-hole spacings, Structure I.

From the ground plan it would seem that Structure I had been laid out in a ratio of 3:1 (Fig 69). The presumed doorways lay immediately to the north-east of a centre-line drawn across the mid-point of the structure. In width, the entrances themselves represented about one quarter of the total length of the building. Two intercutting post-holes (F83 and F85) of roughly equal size and depth occurred on the north-eastern side of the doorway in the north-west wall. The more northerly (F83), lay on the line of the main wall. The other (F85) was situated immediately to the south-east, apparently just inside the building (Fig 69). Their uniform filling gives no clue as to whether these represent successive post-holes. On other Anglo-Saxon settlement sites, however, (eg Bishopstone, Sussex) single post-holes adjacent to a doorway have been interpreted as holding the post from which the actual door was hung (Bell 1977, 215). Whether this was the case in the present structure remains uncertain. There was no sign of a corresponding post-hole on the south-west side of the doorway and a single-leaf door with a span of nearly 3m is perhaps improbable. There were no traces of similar post-holes associated with the south-east entrance.

Elsewhere along the side walls, three elongated oval post-holes (F57, F75 and F77) each contained a deeper depression for the actual timber at one end (Figs 69 and 70). From these it may be suggested that circular posts around 0.25m in

Pl 26. Church Whitfield: Anglo-Saxon (Period 4) wall-post Structure I, looking south-west. Scales 1m.

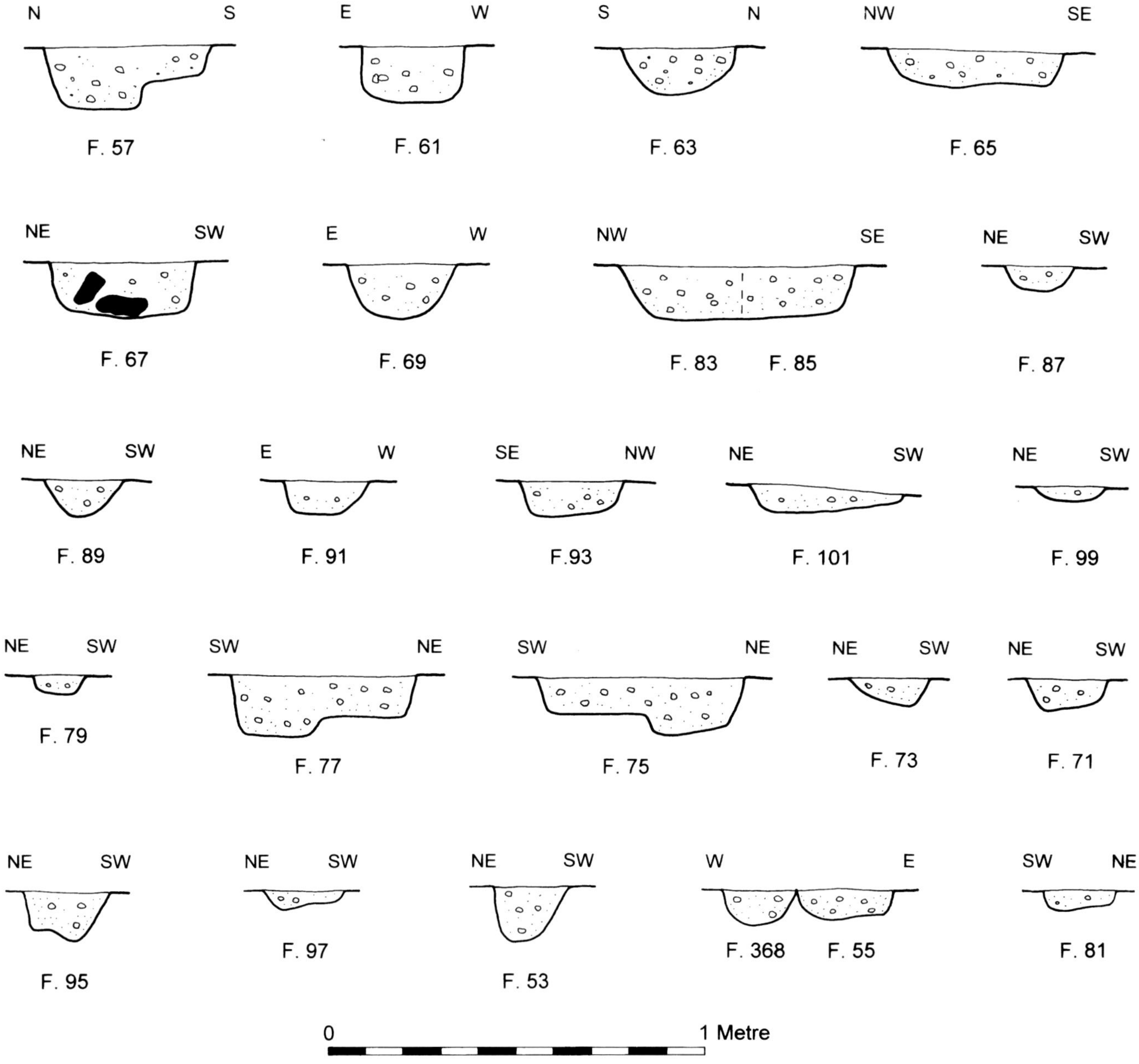

Fig 70. Church Whitfield: sections of post-holes, Structure I.

diameter had been employed for the uprights of the building. Probable flint packing stones occurred in three other post-holes (F65, F67 and F91). Two adjacent post-holes were recorded in the south-western end wall, near the west corner of the building (F55 and F368). The larger, F55, may have supported the main wall line. If so, the smaller F368 would fall just outside the building and is thus likely to represent a later repair or replacement of the original post.

The only datable finds recovered from any of the post-holes associated with Structure I were, a piece of Anglo-Saxon organic-tempered pottery from F67 (Table 44) and a sherd of residual second-century Roman sandy ware from F69.

Structure IV

Structure IV was located towards the south-western corner of Field 8 (Figs 46, 56, 60, 71 and 72; Tables 25 and 26) where a group of shallow post-holes formed the partial outline of another timber building. Again, plough-damage had been severe and the full extent of the structure remains uncertain. Any associated stratified deposits, floors and internal features had been destroyed but the surviving post-hole arrangement appears to incorporate two separate structural elements. Four outlying post-holes further to the south-west may hint that the original building was actually considerably larger than it might initially appear (see below; Fig 71). None of the post-holes associated with the structure produced any datable finds.

The main part of the surviving structure was represented by a setting of ten post-holes forming a rectangular building at least 6m long (north-east–south-west) and about 4.70m wide (north-west–south-east), taking the post-hole centres (Fig 71). The individual post-holes were all oval or subrectangular in shape and ranged in depth from just 0.05

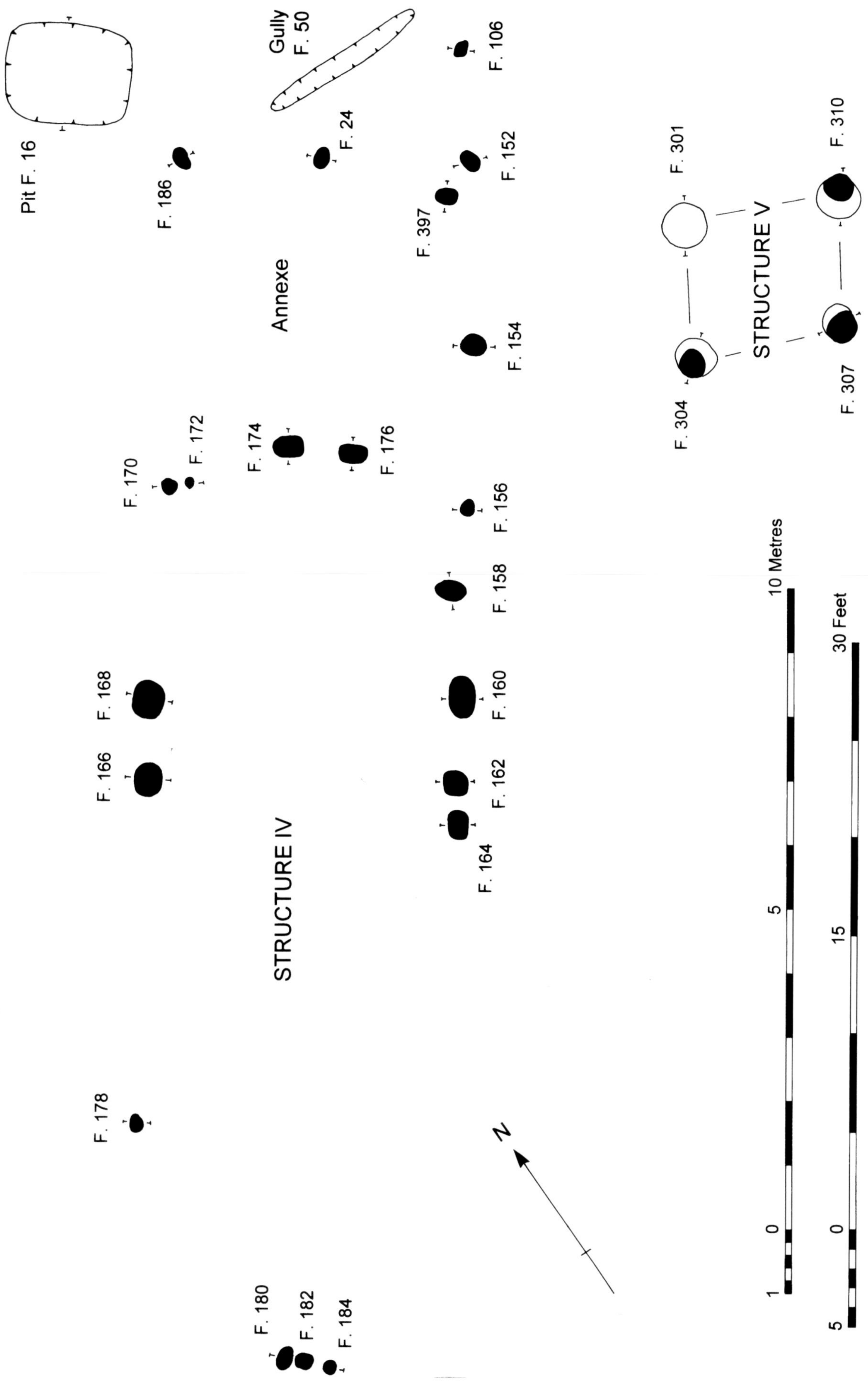

Fig 71. Church Whitfield: plan of wall-post Structure IV, four-post Structure V and pit F16.

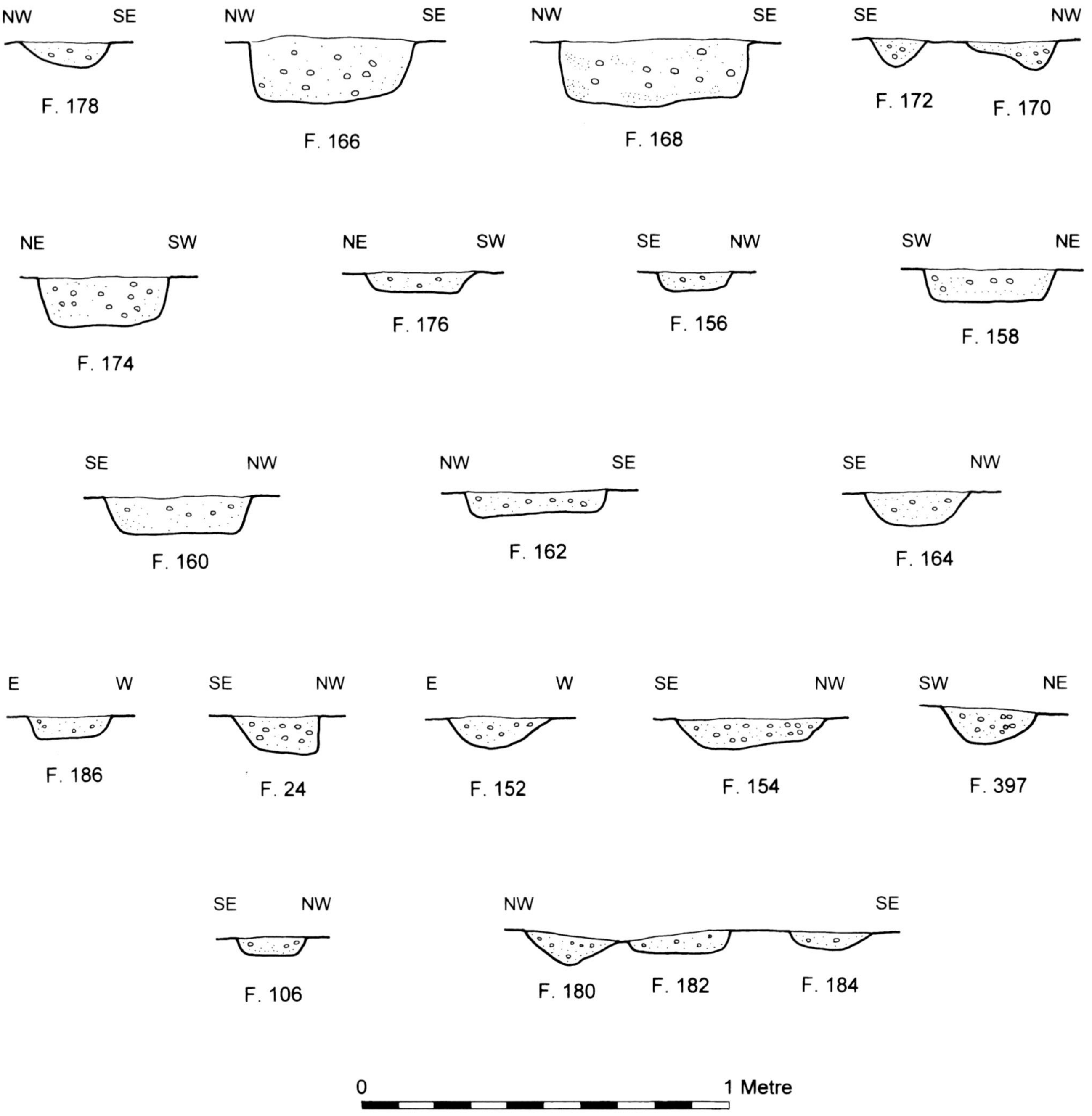

Fig 72. Church Whitfield: sections of post-holes, Structure IV.

to 0.19m into the chalk (Fig 72; Table 25). Some were of a substantial size, but none contained any packing stones. A smaller post-hole (F172) adjacent to post-hole, F170 in the north-west wall may represent the subsequent replacement of an original post.

Two post-holes (F174 and F176) appeared to mark the line of the north-east (end) wall but there were no associated corner posts and no corresponding post-holes to represent the south-west wall. This could perhaps suggest that the building was open on the south-west side. It is conceivable, however, that a line of three adjacent post-holes (F180, F182 and F184) discovered some 8.50m to the south-west of the main structure represent the missing end of the building (Fig 71). These fall more or less exactly where the south-west wall would have been placed if the structure was built in a ratio of 3:1, as with Structure I (see above). Additionally, an isolated post-hole further to the north (F178) falls on the projected line of the building's north-west wall. If these slight traces are accepted as evidence for the continuation of the building, a substantial structure with an overall length of about 14.20m and a floor area of over 60m^2 is indicated. Unfortunately, the surviving field evidence is insufficient to allow certainty on the point.

At the north-eastern end of the building rather more definite evidence for a continuation of the structure was recorded. Here, an additional group of four post-holes (Fig 71; F24, F152, F154 and F186) adjoining the main building appeared to represent some sort of extension or annexe. This was square in shape, around 4.50m across. A fifth post-hole (F397) set just inside the east corner could represent a later replacement of the original corner-post here.

F No	Shape	Axis	Length (m)	Width (m)	Depth (m)
Main building					
F156	oval	NE–SW	0.28	0.22	0.05
F158	oval	NW–SE	0.45	0.32	0.09
F160	oval	NE–SW	0.64	0.41	0.10
F162	oval	NE–SW	0.39	0.36	0.07
F164	sub–rect	NE–SW	0.45	0.31	0.09
F166	oval	NE–SW	0.54	0.44	0.18
F168	oval	NE–SW	0.60	0.51	0.19
F170	oval	N–S	0.26	0.25	0.08
F172	oval	NE–SW	0.20	0.15	0.08
F174	oval	NW–SE	0.44	0.35	0.13
F176	oval	NW–SE	0.45	0.30	0.05
F178	sub–oval	NE–SW	0.30	0.23	0.07
F180	oval	NE–SW	0.40	0.26	0.09
F182	oval	NW–SE	0.27	0.26	0.06
F184	oval	E–W	0.24	0.23	0.05
Extension					
F24	oval	NE–SW	0.35	0.24	0.10
F152	oval	N–S	0.35	0.26	0.09
F154	oval	NW–SE	0.41	0.36	0.08
F186	oval	N–S	0.39	0.23	0.06
F397	oval	NW–SE	0.35	0.26	0.10
Fence line					
F18	sub–rect	NE–SW	0.30	0.24	0.19
F20	oval	NE–SW	0.31	0.20	0.20
F106	oval	NE–SW	0.23	0.19	0.05

Table 25. Church Whitfield: post-hole dimensions, Structure IV (including extension and fence line).

Whether this north-eastern extension was contemporary with the original construction of the main building or represents a subsequent addition could not be determined. Nor is it clear if it was roofed or formed an open compound, perhaps for animals. Three more post-holes (Figs 60 and 71; F18, F20 and F106) roughly continuing the line of the main south-east wall of the main structure and its extension may represent the start of a fence line running out from the building.

Other possible Anglo-Saxon features (F215, F904 and F1010)

Three other pits may also be connected with the Anglo-Saxon settlement (Figs 46 and 60).

Pit F215 lay in Field 9 about 30m west of SFB Structure VI (Figs 46 and 60; Fig 64, Section 94). It was oval in shape and measured 1.22m (north-east–south-west) by 0.95m (north-west–south-east). Cut 0.19m into the chalk, it had

F152–F106	1.71
F152–F154	2.91
F154–F156	2.50
F156–F158	1.29
F158–F160	1.67
F160–F162	1.29
F162–F164	0.65
F168–F166	1.32
F166–F178	5.38
F168–F170	3.32
F176–F174	1.01
F160–F168	4.82
F170–F156	4.60
F174–F178	10.56
F174–F180	14.20

Table 26. Church Whitfield: post-hole spacings. Distance between centres in metres. Structure IV.

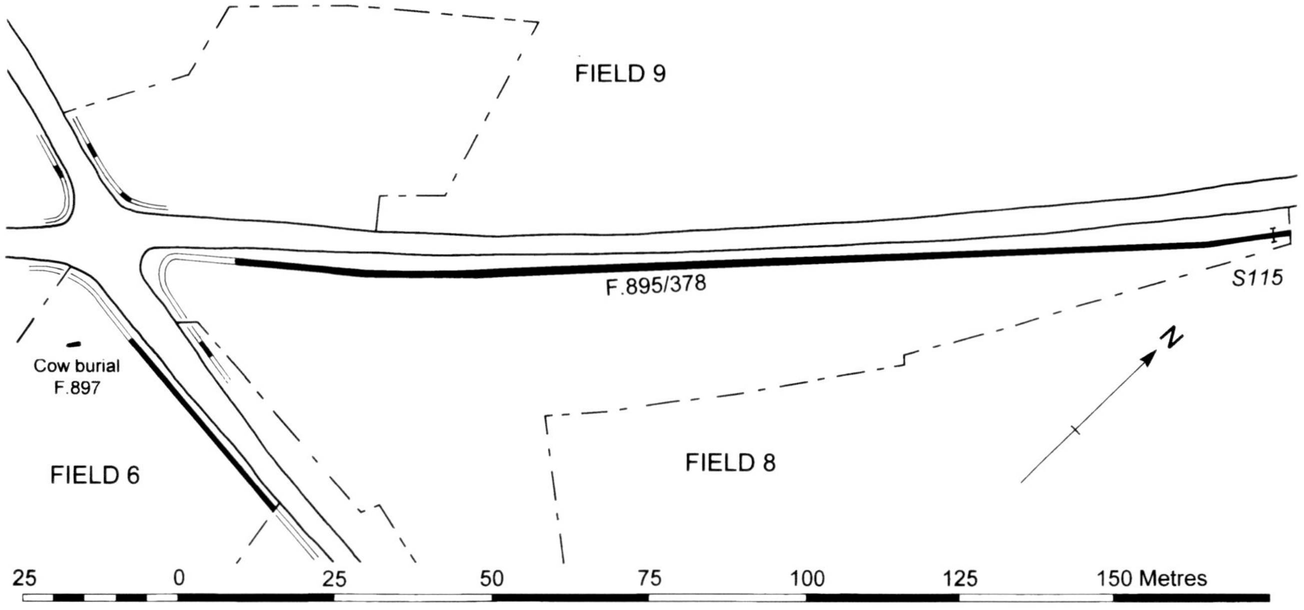

Fig 73. Church Whitfield: features assigned to Period 5.

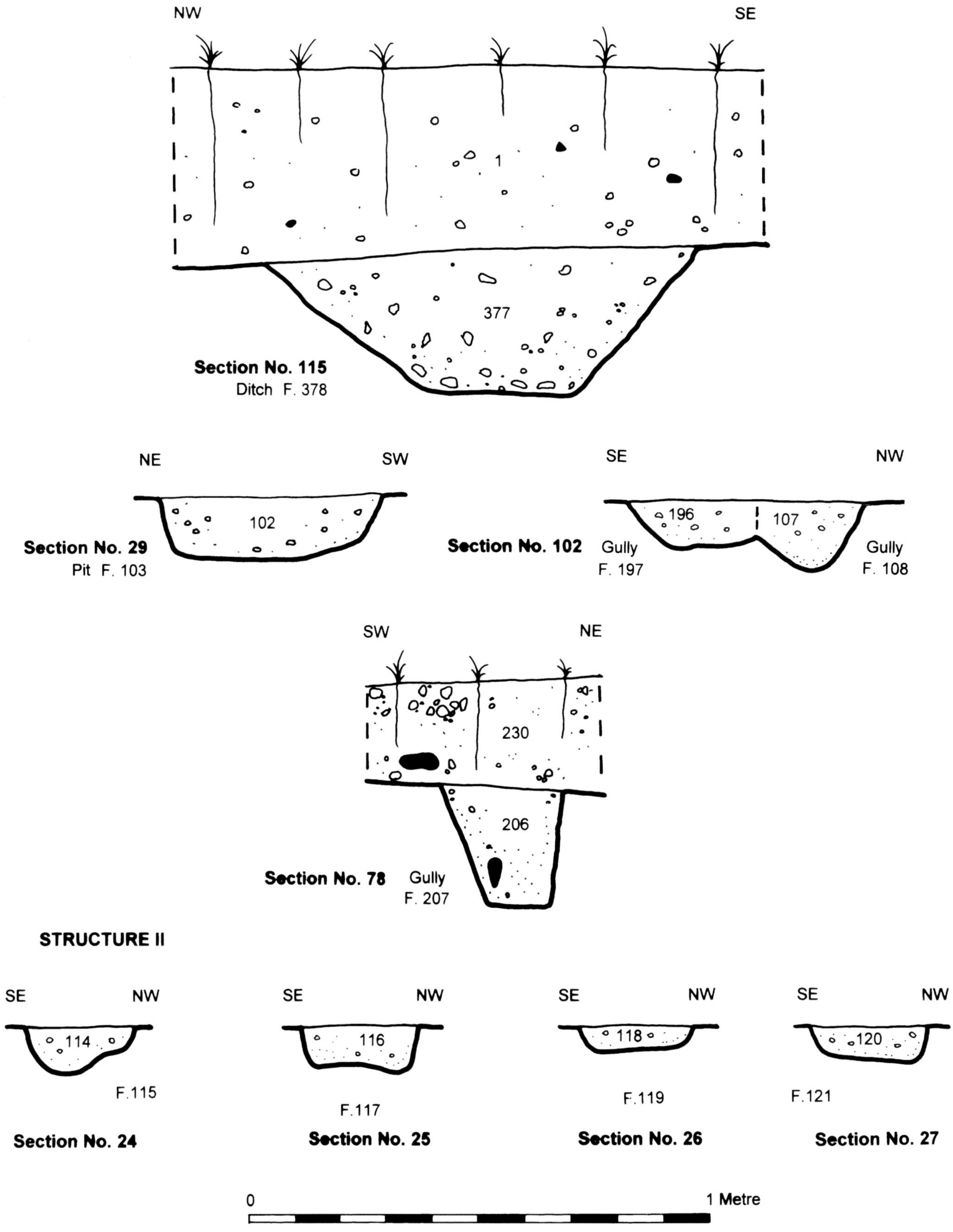

Fig 74. Church Whitfield: sections across miscellaneous features.

sloping sides and an undulating base. The filling produced three small sherds. Two of these are of Iron Age date but the third is a fragment of Anglo-Saxon organic-tempered ware (Table 44).

Pit F904 was a substantial feature revealed at the start of the roadworks but was buried before excavation could take place. It was discovered under the hedge bounding Field 8 (Figs 46 and 60) cut into by a post-medieval boundary ditch (F895/378) and the edge of Archer's Court Road. The recorded dimensions were 4m (north-east–south-west) by at least 1.50m (north-west–south-east). The soil and chalk filling produced two sherds from a single vessel of Anglo-Saxon organic-tempered ware (Table 44). The general size and shape of the feature, together the pottery recovered, make it highly likely that this represented another sunken-featured building, situated some 25m north-east of Structure I.

Pit F1010 was revealed in Field 6 during the realigning of Archer's Court Road, some 50m from the new by-pass cutting (see Fig 60). It could not be excavated but appeared to be a subrectangular pit, measuring 3.30m (south-west–north-east) by 2.30m (south-east–north-west). No dating evidence was recovered but from the shape it seems likely that this represented another Anglo-Saxon sunken-featured building, located some 90m south-west of the excavated Structure VII.

Period 5: medieval and later activity

Evidence for post-Anglo-Saxon activity was limited and it would seem that there had been no occupation on the site after the end of the seventh century (but *see* p 8). An isolated medieval cow burial was discovered in Field 6, whilst shallow roadside boundary ditches were located around the edges of all three fields investigated (Fig 71). Light scatters of medieval and post-medieval pottery were found in the ploughsoil across the site, together with several post-medieval coins, including one of Charles I (1634–36).

The cow burial was found in the north corner of Field 6 (Fig 73, F897) and presumably represents disposal of a farm animal. Two associated sherds of sandy medieval pottery might suggest that this event took place during the thirteenth or fourteenth century.

On the north-western side of Field 8, under the hedgerow adjacent to Archer's Court Road, a shallow, flat-bottomed ditch was revealed (Fig 73, F895/378) and sectioned at two points (Fig 74, Section 115). The soil filling (context 377) contained a number of sherds, all residual Iron Age pieces except one dated *c* AD 1650–1750. Several post-medieval brick fragments and a worn Roman coin of Faustina I (AD 138–141, *see* p 133) were also recovered.

More evidence for ditches bounding the existing lanes was revealed as the hedgerows and banks were grubbed out during the roadworks. Traces of a second small ditch were located in Field 8, running alongside Pineham Road and a corresponding one was observed on the south-western side of this road in Field 6. Short lengths of ditch were also seen bounding Field 9. None could be excavated but it may be reasonably assumed that they were all contemporary. With little doubt, they were originally accompanied by a low bank supporting a planted hedge. At least around Fields 6 and 8, these planted hedges grew and matured, so that by 1995 they were quite substantial (Pls 19 and 26).

The creation of these boundaries clearly indicates an intention to fix and formalise the line of the local routeways, probably long-established, in relation to the adjacent fields. The date at which this occurred remains uncertain. That it was well after the Anglo-Saxon settlement had been abandoned seems certain enough and the early map evidence confirms that the roads occupied their present lines by the start of the nineteenth century. A medieval, or more probably early post-medieval, date is thus implied.

The finds

The finds assemblage from the excavations included important groups of prehistoric flints, Iron Age pottery and animal bone together with a number of small finds and coins. The material has been processed and catalogued according to standard Canterbury Archaeological Trust procedures and the archive is held by Dover Museum.

The flint assemblage

Tania Wilson

Introduction

Five hundred and fifty-three flint artefacts were retrieved from Church Whitfield and these pieces are summarised by type in Table 27. With the exception of pit F103 of Bronze Age date, which yielded no flint artefacts, the site consisted in the main of features dating to the Iron Age and Anglo-Saxon periods. The majority of the flint assemblage (83 per cent) was recovered as residual material from the Iron Age features. In addition to the struck artefacts, two naturally produced pieces, a perforated pebble (FN 1127t; not illustrated) and a rounded flint ball (FN 1199j; not illustrated) were also found, both were retrieved from the upper fill of the recut of the late Iron Age enclosure ditch.

Methodology

All the flint artefacts were recorded and catalogued. Each piece was measured and weighed with dimensions recorded following Saville (1980, 16; 1981). In addition, the type of artefact, completeness, condition and raw material were recorded. Attention was paid to various technological attributes, particularly the nature of the striking platforms and the occurrence of hinge terminations. Cores were divided into Class A (single platform); Class B (two platforms); Class C (three or more platforms), struck nodules/lumps and fragments. The term chip is used to describe complete flakes of 15mm or less in length.

Identification	Quantity
Blades	4
Chips	3
Chunks	11
Cores and struck lumps	26
Flakes	478
Hammerstones and hammerstone frags	3
Retouched pieces	28

Table 27. Church Whitfield: flint artefacts, types and quantities.

	0–9 (mm)	10–19 (mm)	20–29 (mm)	30–39 (mm)	40–49 (mm)	50–59 (mm)	60–69 (mm)	>70 (mm)
Length	–	4	13	25	26	15	8	9
Breadth	1	6	20	25	27	13	5	3

Table 28. Church Whitfield: length and breadth measurements for complete flakes and chips (figures in per cent).

Raw material and condition

A small quantity of the artefacts have only slight cortication, though the majority have a thick white patina and hence it is difficult to determine the types of raw material which were being used. Where it could be determined, it appears that three main types tended to be selected: a black semi-translucent flint with a buff cortex, a pale brown-grey semi-translucent flint with a buff cortex, and glauconitic (Bullhead) flint.

Almost half the pieces within the assemblage are incomplete or have evidence of post-depositional damage, which is probably the result of redeposition and farming practices. Only 1 per cent of the struck flints had been burnt. Additionally, a large proportion is encrusted with a hard calcium carbonate deposit, which in some instances obscures areas of retouch.

The assemblage

Four hundred and seventy-eight waste flakes were collected from the site, weighing just over 9kg; 68 per cent are complete. Smaller quantities of other knapping debris are also represented. The dimensions of the complete flakes and chips are summarised in Table 28. Only four blades were recovered, two of which are complete.

Twenty-six cores and struck nodules were recovered. The quantities of the different core types and their weights are shown in Table 29. The maximum measurements range from 44mm to 159mm, with an average of 73mm. As the dimensions suggest, most cores are not reduced beyond the point of usefulness and several still bear large areas of cortex. Some examples, including a single platform core (Fig 75, FN 768b) may have been abandoned due to excessive stepping. One particularly large example (Fig 75, FN 1144) is worthy of note; its maximum dimension measures 159mm and it weighs some 1922g. There appears to be no reason why it was not reduced further, and its uniform appearance implies that it could have been shaped, perhaps for a specific use. A small area of crushing and some incipient cones of percussion on the platform may suggest that this piece was used as an anvil, though extensive calcium carbonate deposits make it difficult to be certain of this.

The majority of the cores have either single striking platforms or are globular in form. Some of the struck nodules have as little as one flake detached, though there is no evidence to suggest that these were abandoned because they were unsuitable. In addition to nodules selected for use as cores, there are also a number of examples that have natural, heavily patinated scars present, demonstrating the selection of previously shattered lumps.

Two hammerstones were also collected, with an average weight of 352.5g. One (Fig 75, FN 758) is crushed over three-quarters of its surface, and the second has limited crushing at one end of an otherwise unmodified small nodule. Additionally, one flake with crushing on its dorsal surface (suggesting that it was detached from a third hammerstone) was collected.

Twenty-eight retouched pieces were retrieved, and these are summarised in Table 30. As the table shows, a wide range of implement types are represented. In total, the retouched pieces form around 5 per cent of the assemblage from this site.

The most common type of retouched implement is the scraper, and both end-retouched and end-and-side retouched forms are present. End-retouched scrapers are the most common (77 per cent), and of the end-and-side retouched forms, those with retouch present along both sides appear to be preferred. The dimensions of the complete scrapers are shown in Table 31. Their average length is 57mm, the average breadth is 50mm and the thickness is 15mm; in general, therefore, they tend to be almost as wide as they are long, made on fairly slender flakes. The scrapers vary from well fashioned examples (eg Fig 76, FN 909), through those formed on primary flakes (eg Fig 76, FN 1153) to pieces with relatively minimal retouch (eg Fig 76, FN 1126b).

Three flakes have been reduced by further flaking. One particular example (Fig 76, FN 873) is disc-like in shape and has had flakes detached from around three-quarters of its circumference on both the dorsal and the ventral surfaces.

Two possible blunted-back knives were collected, both retouched along the left-hand side of fairly large flakes, and one example (Fig 77, FN 761) also has retouch thinning the bulbar end of the flake.

Type	Class A	Class B	Class C	Fragment	Struck nodule /lump
Quantity	10	2	9	1	4
Total weight (g)	2693	313	3572	77	1818
Average Weight (g)	269	157	397	77	455

Table 29. Church Whitfield: flint cores, quantities and average weight (g) by class.

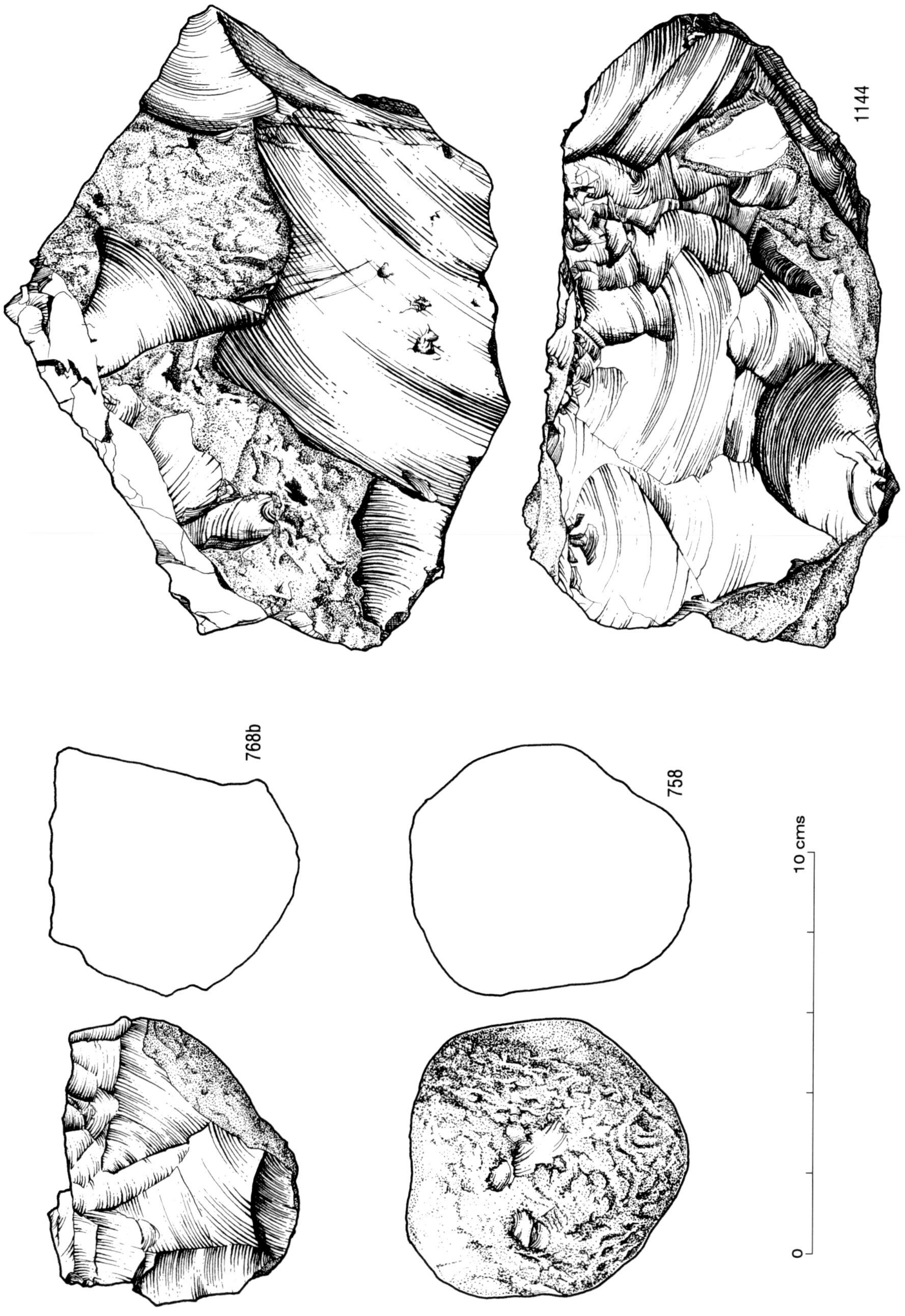

Fig 75. Church Whitfield: struck flints from the site. Scale (assumed) 2:3.

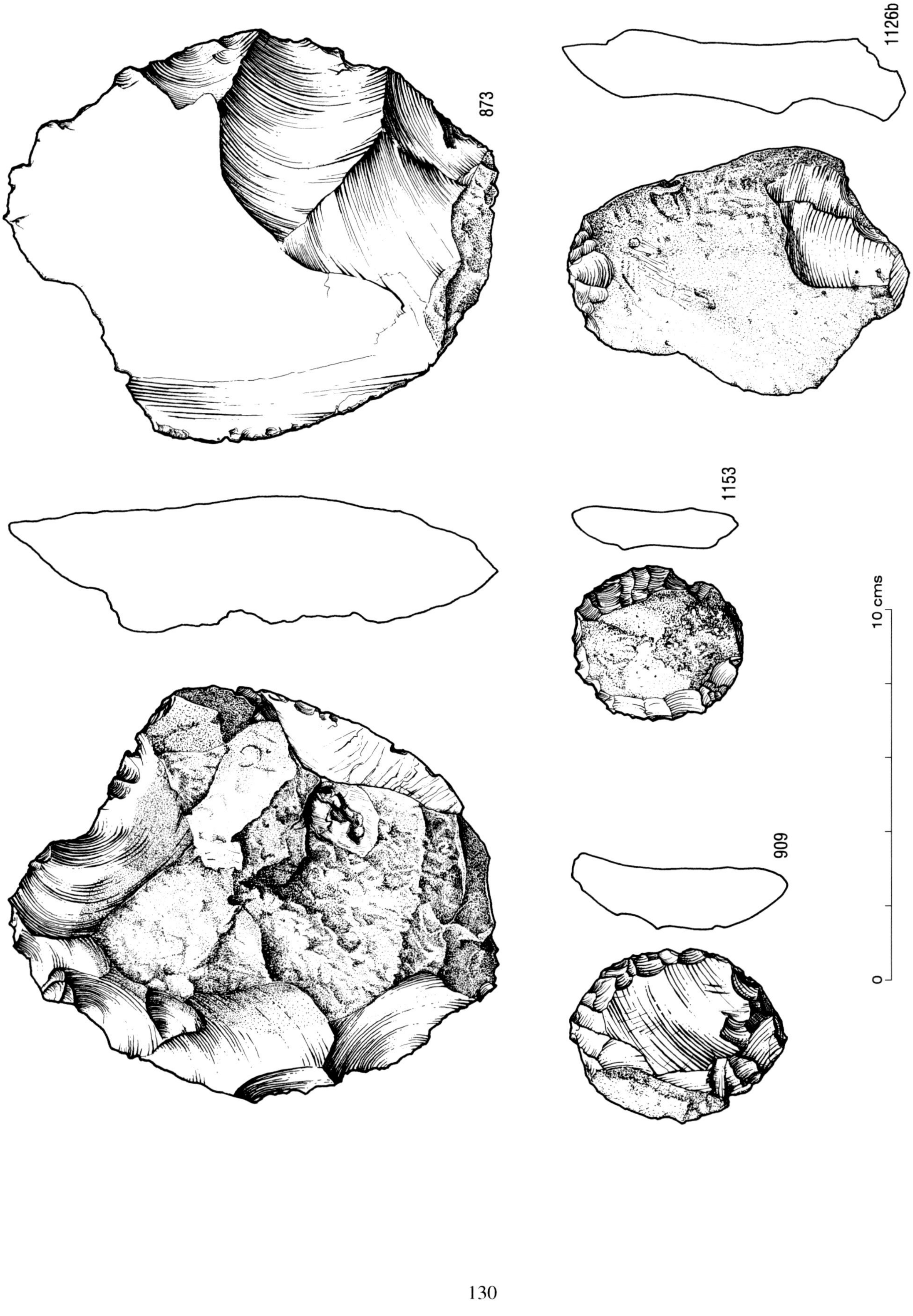

Fig 76. Church Whitfield: struck flints from the site. Scale (assumed) 2:3.

Type	Quantity
Flaked flake	3
Retouched flake	4
Knife	2
Notch	2
Plane	1
Point	2
Scraper	13
Waisted core tool	1

Table 30. Church Whitfield: quantities of retouched flint forms.

	0–9 (mm)	10–19 (mm)	20–29 (mm)	30–39 (mm)	40–49 (mm)	50–59 (mm)	60–69 (mm)	>70 (mm)
Length				9	9	46	27	9
Breadth				18	37	27	18	
Thickness		91	9					

Table 31. Church Whitfield: sizes of complete flint scrapers (figures in per cent).

Two notched flakes were also recovered, one with a notch at the distal end, and the other notched on the left-hand side.

Two pieces have been classified as points; both are made on average sized flakes and have only limited areas of retouch. Following this style, the miscellaneous retouched flakes also tend to have only limited areas of retouch.

Two further pieces are of particular note. The first (Fig 77, FN 535b) has been classified as a plane; it has a flat 'base' formed by the scar from a natural fracture and is wedge-shaped with abrupt retouch along the two longer sides. The second is a waisted core tool (Fig 77, FN 1208b). A piece of naturally shattered, tabular, glauconitic flint was selected to produce this piece, which has flaking along two sides forming the 'waist'; additional flaking has produced a slightly concave area at one end.

Finally, one blade was recovered which has slight chipping along both sides; this chipping may be worn down serration or the result of damage through use.

Technology

There is evidence for flake and blade production taking place, with hard hammer percussion being used throughout. However, the production of blades appears to be on a much smaller scale and, whilst several blades were recovered, only one core with blade removals was collected. In addition blade-like flakes are fairly well represented.

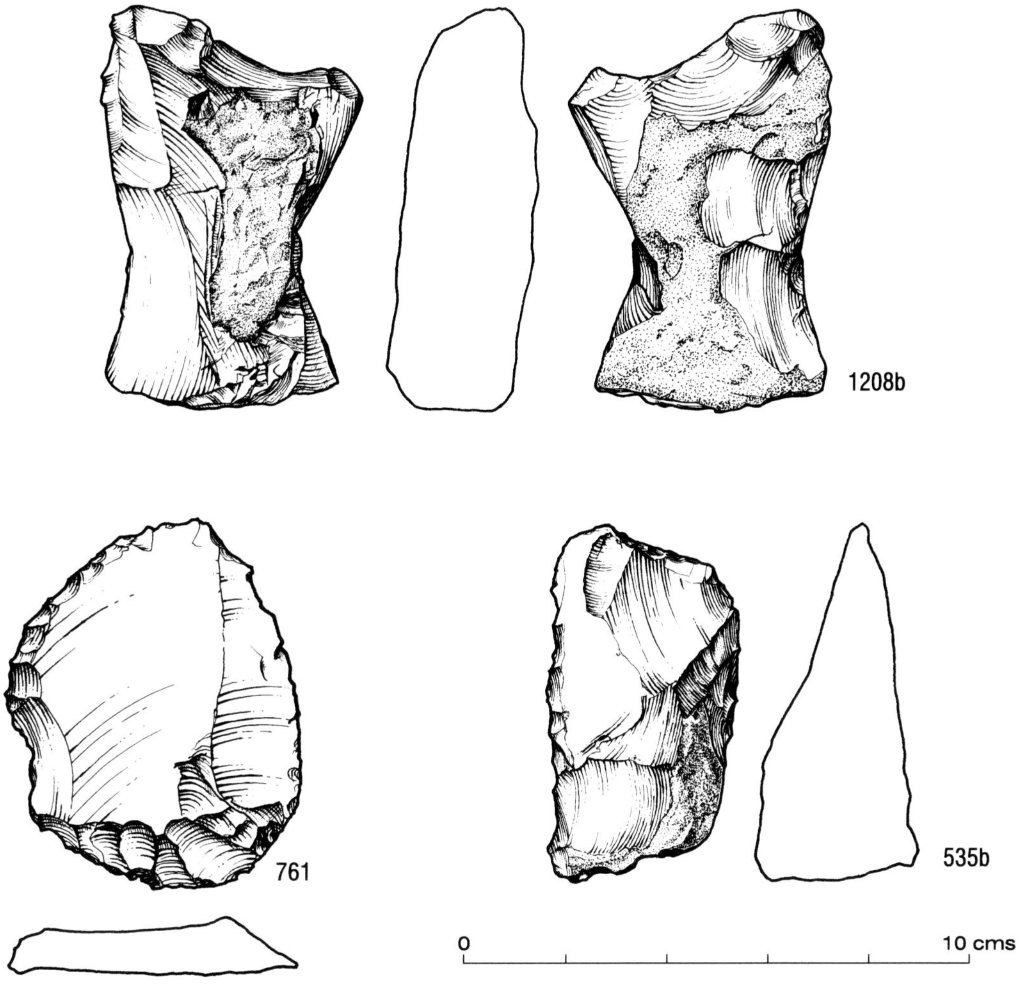

Fig 77. Church Whitfield: struck flints from the site. Scale (assumed) 2:3.

It appears that the cores are mainly divided into those with single platforms and those with multiple platforms; a small number of randomly struck nodules/lumps were recovered. As already noted, generally the cores are not worked beyond the point of usefulness; several have areas of cortex remaining and, in the case of the single platform examples, they are quite sparsely flaked. All these factors tend to imply the lack of an economical approach to flintworking which probably reflects the abundant availability of raw material locally.

Given this apparent lack of economy, there is still evidence to suggest that pre-determined knapping strategies were employed. There are some, albeit sparse, examples of pieces with platform abrasion and dihedral or faceted striking platforms, and pieces with evidence of core trimming and rejuvenation; this implies that care was taken to achieve a desired product. Furthermore, specialised cores such as the flat examples and a Levallois-type core are represented. Levallois-type cores are thought to have been used to create blanks for the production of transverse arrowheads (Gardiner 1987, 27).

Scrapers dominate the group but there is also a wide diversity of other implement types. In general, the scrapers are formed on blanks which are almost as wide as they are long, though there does not appear to be common blank type for the other retouched forms and some examples have simply taken advantage of natural, fortuitously shaped fragments. Due to the amount of patination, it is not possible to determine if specific types of raw material were selected for certain implement types.

Chronology

The Church Whitfield assemblage is charactersied by the waisted core tool, the 'plane', the knives, the scrapers and, to a lesser extent, the notched and serrated pieces. In general these types and the range of retouched forms reflect assemblages recovered from other sites dated to the early Neolithic period.

General discussion of the flint assemblage

It appears that the assemblage represents activity during the early to middle Neolithic period and hence few, if any, of the flints can be considered to be contemporary with the archaeological features encountered. This point tends to be supported by the high incidence of breakage and post-depositional damage.

It is clear from the quantities of cores and other debitage that knapping must have been taking place in the vicinity of the site. However, the quantity and diversity of the retouched pieces suggests that the area was something more than simply a flint-working site.

In stark contrast to sites such as Bury Hill and Offham where the retouched pieces form 1.3 per cent and 0.3 per cent of the assemblages respectively (Tucker 1986, 39), or indeed Area 9 at Monkton (Wilson 2008) which had retouched pieces forming only 0.7 per cent, the retouched pieces at Church Whitfield represent some 5 per cent. This brings them more into line with sites such as Hurst Fen in Suffolk where implements formed between 5 per cent and 6 per cent of the assemblage (Clark 1960, 214), and Broome Heath, Norfolk where the retouched assemblage formed 5 per cent (Wainwright 1972, 66).

Based upon these determinations it may be suggested that the Church Whitfield assemblage provides evidence of Neolithic domestic activities taking place within the immediate vicinity - activities that may represent a settlement. The exact location of the settlement site is unclear as there are no features of this date surviving, but it is wholly possible, given the nature of Neolithic sites, that any existing features were removed during the later activities. It seems certain, however, that the settlement was nearby, as studies have shown that there is usually relatively limited displacement of flintwork despite processes such as annual ploughing (Holgate 1988, 105).

Iron Age and Roman coins

Iron Age

David Holman

A late Iron Age potin coin (not illustrated) was discovered by the White Cliffs Metal Detector Club in the southern corner of Field 9 during October 1994. Despite an extensive search of the area at that time, this was the only significant archaeological discovery made. The coin lay in the ploughsoil at a point that can now be seen to fall within the western quarter of the Period 3 ditched enclosure (Fig 56).

The coin is datable to the mid second century BC and is thus broadly contemporary with pottery excavated from the late Iron Age enclosure ditch. It is a good example of a potin coin commonly known as the 'Thurrock' type, after a large hoard found at Corringham in Essex during 1987. The coin can be classified as Van Arsdell (1989) type 1408, although the reverse is more akin to his type 1410. The Whitfield coin is of unusual appearance owing to the exceptionally clear casting sprue image visible on the reverse, which may suggest a misaligned mould. Such coins were cast in strips and the sprue normally runs along the body of the bull on the reverse, but this is not the case with the present example. A full description of the coin with photographs has been submitted to the Celtic Coin Index held at Oxford, reference CCI 95.0936.

For many years these potin coins were thought to be early Gaulish imports owing to their great rarity in Britain, their similarity to certain Central Gaulish types and, with the better examples, their likeness to the bronze coins of Massilia (Marseilles) from which the designs were ultimately copied. Increasing numbers of these coins were found by metal-detectorists during the 1980s which led to the suspicion that they could be British, and metallurgical analysis has shown that this is indeed the case.

For the past twenty years, the present writer has been recording Iron Age coins found in Kent, mainly by detectorists, and to date in excess of 600 potin coins of the Thurrock type have been noted (although a few could conceivably be Gaulish in origin as it is sometimes virtually impossible to tell visually). Their principal distribution is in east Kent and it is now generally accepted that they represent the first potin coinage of the Cantiaci tribe (Holman 2005; Haselgrove 2006). Van Arsdell (1989) was incorrect in attributing them to the Trinovantes of Essex on the sole basis of the Thurrock hoard. The present writer has proposed the term 'Kentish Primary Series' rather than 'Thurrock' type for these potins (Holman 2000) so as to more accurately describe their origin; this terminology has since been adopted by other writers (eg Haselgrove 2006).

Such potin coins were apparently produced in vast quantities to judge from their surviving numbers; they comprise some 25 per cent of the total number of Iron Age coins recorded by the writer. How long they were being produced is unknown but they had been superseded by the 'Flat Linear series classified by Allen (1971) some time before 100 BC, even if some remained in circulation for many years after this.

Details of coin
Diameter: 17.4–17.6mm
Weight: 3.6g
Die axis: 270°
Description of obverse: Head of Apollo left, with neck protector (cf Van Arsdell 1989, VA 1408).
Description of reverse: Bull charging right, exergual line below, central boss (cf Van Arsdell 1989, VA 1410).
Casting sprue across image.

Roman
Ian Anderson

A heavily worn Roman coin (not illustrated) was recovered from the filling of post-medieval boundary ditch, F895/F378 (Period 5) in Field 8, where it cut through the late Iron Age enclosure ditch (Period 3).

Identification: Faustina I, *sestertius*, AD 138–41, Reverse very worn.

Although the minting of this coin can be dated to a three year bracket by the accession of Faustina's husband, the Emperor Antoninus Pius in AD 138, and her death in AD 141, its considerable wear suggests that it was in circulation for a long time. The contents of hoards show that some imperial bronze coins continued to circulate as late as the AD 270s. The Coombe Hill hoard in East Sussex, deposited *c* AD 270–73, contained Sestertii of Hadrian and Marcus Aurelius (Burnett and Bland 1986, 147–55), and one of three hoards at Oliver's Orchard, Colchester also deposited *c* AD 270–73, contained an *as* of Domitian and an illegible *as* and *dupondius* of the first to second century AD (Burnett and Bland 1986, 65–117). The Gallic emperor Postumus (AD 259–68) had some of his *sestertii* overstruck on earlier issues, indicating their availability. From this, the piece under discussion could have remained in circulation possibly as late as the third quarter of the third century AD.

Small finds
Joanne Gray and Ian Riddler

Only a limited collection of small finds was recovered from the Church Whitfield site. The illustrated fsih hooks, beads and grinding stone from Anglo Saxon contexts (Fig 78) are discussed here, followed by a selection of other small objects, mostly derived from Anglo-Saxon features and the late Iron Age enclosure. A complete listing is held with the site archive.

The relative lack of objects of early Anglo-Saxon date from the site stands in apparent contrast to the rich assemblages gleaned from Mucking, Pennyland or West Stow, or from the east Kent site at Manston Road, Ramsgate (Hamerow 1993, 60–73; Williams 1993, 102–27; West 1985, 122–8; Hutcheson and Andrews 2009). Other sites of this date, including Bishopstone, Old Down Farm, Willington and Witton have produced smaller finds assemblages, but even these are generally larger and more varied than the Church Whitfield sample (Bell 1977, 235–7; Davies 1980, 174–7; Wheeler 1978, 210–11; Wade 1983, 58–61). However, a few other settlements such as Prospect Park, Harmondsworth and Catterick also produced little in the way of small finds (Andrews and Crockett 1996, 39–40; Wilson *et al* 1996, 27).

Fish hooks
Ian Riddler

From the filling of SFB Structure III, four small fragments of iron (FN 1108) include three curved sections and one straight shaft (Fig 78). Two of the curved fragments taper towards their ends and can be viewed as fragments of fish hooks. They are relatively small and do not show any signs of barbs at their tapered ends; they belong to Rulewicz's Group 1, type A or C (Rulewicz 1994, 101–21).

Fishing hooks have seldom been recovered from an early Anglo-Saxon settlement. The Church Whitfield examples, viewed alongside the limited evidence for fish and molluscan remains, serve to emphasise the dependency on the resources of the sea argued for the settlement at Bishopstone, which is broadly applicable to early Anglo-Saxon coastal settlements (Arnold 1988, 18 and fig 2.1). New evidence from Ramsgate concerning the identification of early Anglo-Saxon fishing weights that had been used at sea is also relevant in this respect (Riddler 2001).

Beads
Ian Riddler

Two fragmentary glass beads (FN 1109) were retrieved from soil samples taken from the lower filling (context 140) of SFB Structure III (Fig 78). One example is a globular, monochrome

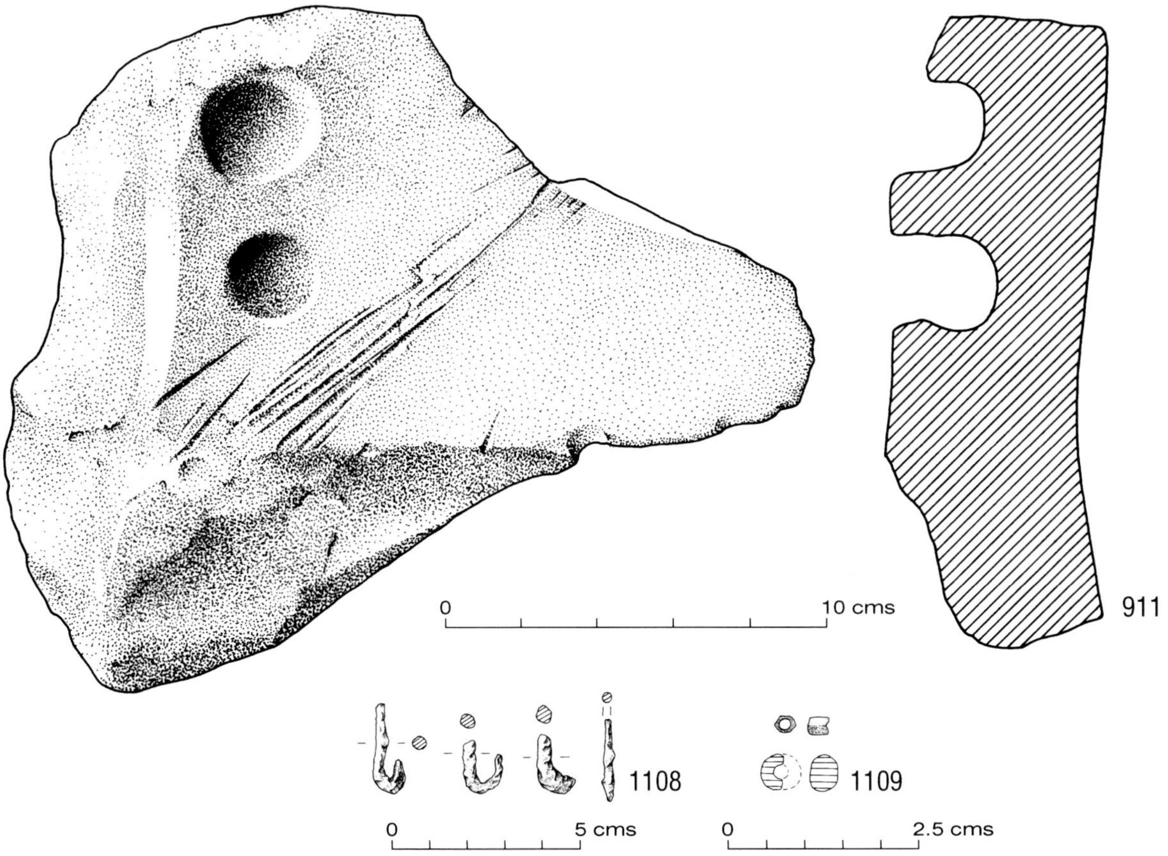

Fig 78. Church Whitfield: small finds: honestone, scale 1:2; iron hooked fragments, scale (assumed) 1:2; glass beads, scale 1:1.

bead of opaque yellow glass and the other is hexagonal in section, made of dark blue glass. Yellow monochrome beads were popular at the nearby Buckland cemetery and particularly in Period 3 dating to AD 550/60–580/600 (Brugmann 2012, 323). They were also encountered at Mill Hill, Deal in graves dating to *c* AD 500–570 (Parfitt and Brugmann 1997, table 11), which tends to suggest that they could occur throughout the sixth and early seventh centuries in east Kent. Similar beads have come from Manston Road, Ramsgate and Upton, Northamptonshire within contexts of late sixth- to seventh-century date (Hutcheson and Andrews 2009, 220–1; Jackson *et al* 1969, 212 and fig 6.5; Riddler and Trzaska-Nartowski 2012, 90–1). Glass beads occur in small quantities within other settlements, including Dover, Abbots Worthy, Botolphs, Mucking, Prospect Park, Steyning, Waterbeach, West Stow and Witton, where they appear to have been lost as single finds (Philp 2003, 114–5; Fasham and Whinney 1991, 50–1; Gardiner 1990, 265–6; Hamerow 1993, 60; Andrews and Crockett 1996, 39; Gardiner 1993, 50; Lethbridge 1927, fig 4.1–3; Evison and Cooper 1985, 71–5; Wade 1983, fig 61.22–5). The only complete necklace to have come from an early Anglo-Saxon settlement context was discovered in Canterbury, within the Cathedral precincts (Canterbury Archaeological Trust archive: Guido and Bayley forthcoming).

The opaque dark blue bead, in contrast, is hexagonal in section with a length of just over 2mm and a width of 2.5mm. This allows it to be defined as a short bead (Crummy 1983, 32), and it is likely to be of late Roman date (Guido 1978, 96–7; Brugmann 2004, 28). It has been noted that Roman vessel glass is generally more common than contemporary glass in early Anglo-Saxon contexts, but the situation is reversed in terms of beads (Evison and Cooper 1985, 71–2).

A third bead, recovered from the filling of a stake-hole (F715) cut into the floor of Structure III was unfortunately lost before any detailed analysis had been undertaken. Available records indicate that it was a monochrome annular bead of opaque yellow glass, with a diameter of about 3mm.

Grinding stone
Ian Riddler

A grinding stone (FN 911) found on the floor of SFB Structure III (see Fig 61) was fashioned from a re-used section of Roman architectural stonework (Fig 78). It is made from a fine-grained, reddish-brown calcareous siltstone and is broadly triangular in shape with two circular holes towards one corner, which lie in front of a smooth, worn and dished surface. This surface has been cut by a series of sharpening marks, which extend also to one of the edges of the stone. The stone weighs just over 1.8kg.

Hones and whetstones are comparatively frequent finds on Anglo-Saxon settlement sites; they are less common in grave contexts (Evison 1987, 111). This example is a large grinding stone comparable to a 'large, flat building stone re-used for sharpening' from Linford, Essex (Evison 1975, 74, 84–5 and fig 3). Another close parallel for the Whitfield object lies with a piece of fine-grained sandstone from Pennyland, interpreted as a sharpening block or anvil (Williams 1993, 126 and fig 65.108). This is of similar dimensions, with sharpening channels on one side. All three stones are large implements, 175–200mm in length, all of fine-grained sandstone with smoothed faces and all appear to be re-used architectural stones of Roman origin. They all have broad upper surfaces, which show traces of sharpening marks, particularly noticeable on the present example. Such stones would presumably have been set on a surface and used for sharpening large tools, smaller more portable hones and whetstones being used for smaller implements (MacGregor 1982, 79). The Whitfield stone can be compared with several blocks of sandstone from Usk which had been re-used as grinding stones during the Roman period as well as a medieval example from Monkton (Manning *et al* 1995, 263 and fig 81; Riddler 2008, 333).

Copper alloy objects
Joanne Gray

There are three copper alloy objects: a strip of sheet metal, a shaped sheet fragment and a looped fitting.

FN 13. Copper alloy strip discovered in the ploughsoil (Field 9, context 230). This area was machined and searched by metal detectorists. The strip is quite crudely cut and thought to be some sort of binding, or fastening. It weighs 6g and measures 191 x 12 x 1mm. There is a punched hole at one end and possibly a hook fastening that is broken at the other. It is most likely to date to the post-medieval period.

FN 1110. Shaped sheet fragment. This could have been part of an object, perhaps a mount, but due to its incompleteness it is not possible to date. It weighs <1g and measures 15 x 7 x 0.5mm. The fragment was found in the lower filling of SFB Structure III (context 140) which contained Anglo-Saxon pottery and residual Iron Age and Roman pottery.

FN 1434. Looped fitting, weighing 29g with a length of 51mm; the width of the loop is 46mm. The fitting is incomplete and the loop has been flattened giving it a subcircular appearance. It is unstratified, but likely to be medieval in date.

Iron objects
Joanne Gray

There are two iron objects; a spike and a box hinge fitting.

FN 151. Spike with a length of 103mm (weight 9g). It has a slightly decorative looped head, with a width of 14mm. It was found in the filling of SFB Structure III (context 21). The object is probably late medieval in date and so is apparently intrusive in this context.

FN 20. Box hinge fitting fragment; flat on one side and ridged on the other. Lozenge-shaped at one end, broken at the other, it appears to date to the later post-medieval period. At the shaped end there is also a broken iron nail or stud. Dimensions: 102 x 11–15 x 6mm. Weight: 18g. The object was discovered in the upper filling of the third recut of the Period 3 enclosure ditch F372 and is probably intrusive in that context.

Fired clay objects
Joanne Gray

There are three shaped fragments of fired clay. Two came from the upper fill of the north-east arm of the Period 3 enclosure ditch (context 136; FN 409) and one larger fragment from the fill (context 234; FN 848) of the third recut of the enclosure ditch (F248), also on the north-east side (Table 17).

FN 409. Two fragments show evidence of being shaped. The largest piece weighs 26g and measures 36 x 30 x 24mm, whilst the smaller fragment weighs 9g and measures 38 x 21 x 11mm. The larger piece has a curved side and evidence of a flat surface; there are also traces of burning. Both fragments probably derive from a loomweight.

FN 848. Also probably part of a loomweight. It weighs 88g and its measurements are 61 x 58 x 39.5mm. The fragment is too small to be able to assign to a particular type and period but it is presumably of late Iron Age date.

Fragment of shale
Joanne Gray

FN 534. Fragment of shale discovered in the lower filling (context 311) of the third recut of the Period 3 enclosure ditch (F372). The fragment has a laminated appearance with no finished edges, weighs 10g and is 46mm long, 30mm wide and 15mm thick. It was associated with late Iron Age pottery and some residual earlier Iron Age material. Brownish-black in colour, this fragment may have come from the shale beds of Kimmeridge in Dorset where shale was worked during the early Iron Age (Lawson 1975).

This fragment may have been part of a finished object or raw material to be reworked. Parallels suggest that shale was both transported in a rough state and as a finished product. An unworked shale fragment from the Kimmeridge beds was found at Dover in the Bronze Age boat (Bown *et al* 2004), whilst work at Burham in the Medway valley has shown that shale, probably imported from Kimmeridge, was being extensively worked there during the late Bronze Age (Milward 2009). Excavations at Danebury hillfort in Hampshire have also provided evidence of an unworked shale slab (Cunliffe 1991) and at Swine Sty in Derbyshire a number of rectangular blocks, 30–40mm wide, were thought to be blanks for small rings (Beswick 1994).

Fragments of worked stone
Joanne Gray

FN 191. Chalk fragment, measuring 59 x 46 x 14–23mm and weighing 42g, from the filling of SFB Structure III (context 21). There are traces of three parallel narrow grooves, measuring 24–28mm long by 3–4mm wide and 2–3mm deep, on one surface. Similar grooves, noted on thirty-three chalk fragments from the 'chalk plaque pit' at Amesbury

Period	Context No	Feature	Find No	No of frags	Weight (g)	Description	Length (mm)	Width (mm)	Thickness (mm)	Notes
2	15	Pit F16	189	2	418	Grey, buff calcareous glauconitic? Sandstone	78–85	46-57	33–35	
2	15	Pit F16	846	3	390	Orange brown-grey mottled red-brown calcareous sandstone	39–67	32.5–66	30–37	
2	25	Pit F26	1363	1	2,000	Millstone Grit	190	135	c.90	Quern fragment, Saddle type
3	3	Enclosure ditch re-cut F372	845	4	285	Orange brown-grey mottled red-brown calcareous sandstone	55-70	38-56	23.5–42.5	
3	216	Enclosure ditch re-cut F248	847	13	470	Grey brown calcareous sandstone	12.5–76	9.5-64	7–40	
3	254	Enclosure ditch re-cut F247	1365	2	225	Grey green glauconitic/cherty sandstone	66–86	51–74	18–24	
3	255	Enclosure ditch re-cut F252	849	1	895	Orange brown-grey mottled red-brown calcareous sandstone	120	80	c.78	
3	255	Enclosure ditch re-cut F.252	912	1	378	? Worked. Red orange brown calcareous sandstone	94	70	52	Worked?
3	255	Enclosure ditch re-cut F252	1209	1	52	Ferrogenous fine grained sandstone?	30	29	27	Roughly shaped rectangle
3	258	Enclosure ditch re-cut F247	913	1	55	Grey, glauconitic cherty? Limestone	55	43	23	
3	258	Enclosure ditch re-cut F247	1366	6	202	Derbyshire Millstone Grit	16-66	11-58.5	10–49	Largest fragment. Worked
3	260	Enclosure ditch re-cut F252	1210	1	67	Oolitic Limestone	55	48	20	Worn smooth surface; 20mm wide
3	375	Enclosure ditch re-cut F248	1104	1	58	Calcareous sandstone	53	34	23.5	One smooth surface
4	139	Filling of Structure III	192	2	31	Grey buff calcareous glauconitic sandstone	28–34	22–30	15–21	
4	140	On base of Structure III	911	1	1824	Fine-grained, reddish-brown calcareous siltstone	212	33–180	32–57	Re-used Roman fragment

Table 32. Church Whitfield: details of stone fragments from the excavations.

(Vatcher 1969), were thought to be probably made by animals (Harding 1988). Associated with twenty-one Anglo-Saxon and some residual Iron Age and Roman pottery.

FN 1018. Fragment of quern made from Millstone Grit, with one smooth surface. The piece is very worn and discoloured, measures 69mm long, 34mm wide and 34mm thick and weighs 96g. Found in the fill (context 258) of the third recut of the Period 3 enclosure ditch (F247), it was associated with a quantity of late Iron Age pottery. Millstone Grit is common to the Peak District of northern Britain and querns produced out of this stone are usually Roman in date. Querns of Millstone Grit are known from a number local Romano-British sites in east Kent (eg Dickson's Corner, Worth; Jones 2000, 139). The present fragment is quite possibly intrusive, associated with the small quantity of other Roman items discovered on the site and nearby (*see* p 8).

Another fourteen fragments of stone were recovered from the site from a variety of contexts. Due to their fragmentary condition it was not possible to identify the stone to particular quern types, nor to date them. Stone identification was carried out by Joan Blows, see Table 32.

Calcined flint
Keith Parfitt

Significant quantities of unworked burnt and calcined flint (112.5kg) were found, mostly in the Iron Age features of Periods 2 and 3. This material had been dumped, often with other rubbish, in the various fillings of pits and ditches. Substantial amounts came from pit F26 and pit groups B, C and D (all of Period 2). Such heated flints ('pot-boilers') are regularly found on Iron Age settlement sites in large numbers and it is generally assumed that they were used for drying-out slightly damp or unripe ears of harvested cereal, prior to threshing (Cunliffe 1991, 374–5). Other evidence, in the form of storage pits, a four-post structure and charred grain itself, implies that cereal crops were being stored and processed on the site (*see* p 172).

The pottery (Figs 79–92; Tables 33–44)

Beaker pottery
Alex Gibson

Three small sherds representing two or three Beaker vessels were recorded as residual pieces in the Period 3 enclosure ditch (not illustrated); one was plain and two were decorated with filled lozenge or chevron motifs executed with blurred toothed comb impressions. This motif is generally late in the Beaker stylistic sequences though in the absence of vessel forms and decorative schemes, it is impossible to be more specific regarding the typological positioning of these sherds. Such motifs are found on a Primary South British Beaker from Brendley and on late North British vessels from Dover and Folkestone (Clarke 1970, nos 387, 397 and 401). Finds from Monkton-Minster (Gibson

2008) also exhibit such filled motifs on late Northern and Final Southern Beakers. Filled chevrons are, however, also found on a European Beaker from Lower Fant (Clarke 1970, no 408), so the motif is not exclusively late.

Early Iron Age pottery (Figs 79–83; Tables 33–39)
Peter Couldrey

This report covers 890 sherds of pottery, weighing 15.8kg, dating from the fifth to mid fourth centuries BC. Two pits assigned to Period 2 (F16 and F26; Table 33), containing apparently undisturbed groups, produced 219 sherds, weighing 8.2kg. Another eighty-five sherds came from the Period 2 boundary ditch but most of the remaining sherds were scattered widely across the site, often occurring as a residual element in later features.

When studying the material, similar sherds from each context were grouped together and assumed to be from the same vessel. For each sherd, or group of sherds, the fabric, weight, position on the body of the pot, and the number of non-fitting sherds was recorded. In addition, for rims and bases, the diameter and percentage of the diameter represented by the surviving sherds were noted. These details are held in the site archive.

Fabrics

A preliminary assessment of the fabrics was undertaken by Nigel Macpherson-Grant. They fall into nine main groups, which have been identified on the basis of the main inclusions visible and variations in the clay matrix.

Fabric 1. Flint, moderate to common up to 2mm and sparse up to 4mm, with occasional moderate to common organic inclusions generally up to 3mm.

Fabric 2. Flint, moderate to common up to 2mm and with moderate quartz up to 1mm, moderate to common iron oxide up to 1mm, and moderate to common organic inclusions up to 4mm. The increased quantity of quartz gives this group a sandier feel than fabric 1.

Fabric 10. Flint, common up to 1mm and moderate to sparse to 3mm in size, and iron oxide, sparse to moderate up to 0.3mm in size.

Fabric 27. Flint, common up to 1mm and moderate to sparse to 3mm, with iron oxide moderate up to 1mm and grog moderate up to 2mm.

Fabric 30. Flint, moderate to common up to 2mm and organic inclusions represented by voids, common up to 5mm and occasionally up to 8mm.

Fabric 32. Organic inclusions represented by voids up to 4mm long, in a sandy matrix.

Fabric 34. Flint, moderate to common up to 2mm and sparse to moderate grog inclusions up to 2mm.

Fabric 35. Flint, moderate up to 1mm, with sparse to moderate organic inclusions up to 3mm.

Fabric 37. Grog, moderate inclusions up to 3mm in a sandy matrix.

Fabric 40. Flint, common up to 1mm and moderate up to 2mm, with common lumps of chalk up to 3mm.

All the flint-tempered fabrics contain both calcined and naturally occurring, unmodified flint fragments, though the latter form a small minority.

The distribution of fabrics in pits F16 and F26 is shown in Table 33.

Forms, affinities and chronology

Most of the rims and decorated sherds are illustrated in Figs 79–83. Apart from the few fragments of carinated shoulders, most of the forms are represented by one example and, for this reason, are discussed without establishing a typological scheme. This section begins by considering the chronology of the two pit groups, which produced the majority of recognisable forms, using typological parallels and the radiocarbon date. Finally, pottery from other contexts is considered.

Pit F16

Within this pit there were four contexts (contexts 15, 125 131 and 132) which produced a total of 184 sherds of pottery. Five cross-joins were found within the pit, all between the adjacent contexts 15 and 125.

Vessel number 1 (Fig 79, 1 and 1A), a painted jar with slightly out-turned rim, is similar to examples from Mont Troté (Rozoy 1986, pl 13, MT 32.3 and pl 53, 123.5), one of which, MT 123.5, has a painted design of black chevrons on the shoulder and neck. Rozoy places this form in his period 4, assigned to La Tène Ib (*c* 450–400 BC). Other examples of this general form are not uncommon (eg Charpy and Roualet 1987, 40, catalogue no 14a) and are dated to the fifth century BC. The cross (Croix de Saint-André) pattern is found either as part of a larger painted design (Rozoy 1986, pl 44, MT107.1), or as grooves on a later vessel (Rozoy 1986, pl 82, RO20.3). Similarly, this style of painted decoration, formed by the juxtaposition of pairs of chevrons, is generally assigned to the fifth century (Charpy and Roualet 1987, p.30, type 3a; p.50.21; p.61.55, pl V). Closer to home, painted designs based on individual crosses within panels, are found on smaller vessels from Barham Downs (Macpherson-Grant 1980, fig 4.8), Highstead (Couldrey 2007, fig 89, 368) and Ebbsfleet (Macpherson-Grant 1992, fig 6.7).

The fine, slightly everted rim, with linear grooved decoration, (Fig 79, 2 and 2A), is similar to examples found in northern France from the fifth to the fourth centuries BC. They occur on fine carinated jars and goblets: for example, from Avion Terril du 7 (Hurtrelle *et al* 1990, 50, fig 2.1) and Mont Troté (Rozoy 1986, pl 41, MT 102.5), dated from 450 to 400 BC. A slightly wider flaring rim, with multiple grooves producing the same pattern is known from Monchy-le-Preux (Jaques and Rossignol 1996, fig 3.8) and dated to the fifth century BC; while from Avion La République, fosse 27 (Hurtrelle *et al* 1990, 121, fig 19.19 and 22) a broadly similar example is dated *c* 400–350 BC. However, this style of decoration is simple and is not a precise chronological indicator.

In France, 'situlate' jars with carinated shoulders, similar to No 9, are commonly assigned to La Tène I: see examples from Marne: La Veuve-Recy (Charpy and Roualet 1987, 38, catalogue no 13a and pl II), Chouilly, 'Les Jogasses, tombe 1' (Charpy and Roualet 1987, 51, 24) and Cernon, 'La Côte des Prés', (Charpy and Roualet 1987, 57, no 45), all broadly dated to the fifth century BC. These have lightly grooved linear decoration, though with slightly more elaborate designs than our No 9. Plain horizontal grooved decoration does occur on early La Tène forms in the region, as at Bucy-le-Long (Aisne; Lobjois 1974, 79, 17. 010.02). Its appearance on such jars is particularly common at Kemmelberg, Belgium (Van Doorselaer *et al* 1987, figs 25–27, nos 120–131), while its appearance on an incomplete jar with pedestal base from Avion La République, fosse 27, has been placed in the first half of the fourth century BC (Hurtrelle *et al* 1990, 121, fig 19, 20).

The pedestal base, No 3, is also well known from early La Tène contexts, associated with carinated bowls (Rozoy 1986, pl 99, R 57.5), jars (Rozoy 1986, pl 54, MT123.8) or goblets with simple concave walls, which are often decorated with linear incised designs (Rozoy 1986, pl 54, MT 123.8; pl 66, MT 139.2). This example, although worn, evidently had a red finished surface. High pedestal bases continued in use later, but were generally associated with larger vessels.

The small fragment of rim and shoulder, No 13, shows traces of two vertical grooves rising up the body and finishing just beneath the shoulder. While the overall pattern is unclear, it is possible that they formed part of a vertical combed design, analogous to that found below the shoulders of vessels in La Tène I contexts at Duisans (Pas-de-Calais; Hurtrelle *et al* 1990, 27, fig 5, 19), dated to 500–450 BC, Bailleul-sire-Berthoult (Pas-de-Calais; Hurtrelle *et al* 1990, 39, fig 5,11 and 15) and Fontaine-Notre-Dame (Nord; Hurtrelle *et al* 1990, 56, fig 5, 23; 59, fig 7, 1) both dated to 450–400 BC. Similar decoration has also been recovered at Kemmelberg (van Doorselaer *et al* 1987, eg fig 29, nos 138–141) and Mont Troté (Rozoy 1986, MT 26.2).

The remaining rim fragments (Fig 79, 5, 6 and 7) and carinated shoulders (Fig 79, 8; Fig 81, 12) are not closely datable. They can be paralleled in early La Tène contexts, but also occur earlier. They are assumed to be contemporary with the other pottery in this pit.

In addition to these relatively fine wares, coarser vessels were produced. The jar (Fig 82, 16) has an exterior surface coated with heavy rustication, producing a wall up to 16mm thick. The shoulder (shown here as belonging to the same vessel) is rusticated below but wiped smooth above. This tradition of rustication has been recognised throughout east Kent (Macpherson-Grant 1992, fig 7) and appears to have been introduced by 600 BC or slightly later. Its arrival coincided with a general trend towards the use of rougher surfaces as found on the bowl (Fig 81, 10). This has roughly wiped surfaces with evidence of slurry being applied on parts of the interior. This trend continued throughout the fifth and fourth centuries BC both in Kent (Macpherson-Grant 1992) and on the Continent (Leman-Delerive 1989).

From the parallels listed above, the pottery from pit F16 may be dated to the fifth or early fourth centuries BC on stylistic grounds.

Note on radiocarbon date

A single radiocarbon date of 2220±50 BP (cal BP 2340–2115) was obtained from burnt grain in context 125 of pit F16 (Table 64). This calibrated at 2 sigma to 390–165 BC which while it just overlaps with the fifth- to early fourth-century dates proposed above, would also support a later, even middle Iron Age date.

Undoubtedly, there is an element of risk in employing typological comparisons to establish a chronology. The general problems of establishing chronologies for this period have been discussed by Willis (2002). Nevertheless it is worth recognising the nature of the evidence upon which these particular typological links are constructed. The dates suggested here have employed comparisons with a scheme proposed for material from north-east France (Hurtrelle *et al* 1990) which itself cross-refers to a chronological scheme developed for Champagne (Hatt and Roualet 1977). There are still very few independent dates for this period in east Kent or north-east France.

Furthermore, within east Kent at least, the longevity of these forms and styles of decoration has always posed a problem. Few sites in east Kent have produced middle Iron Age pottery. We have ceramics assigned to the second century BC (*see* p 148), but the chronology and nature of the transition between these assemblages remains unknown. Certainly at Church Whitfield there is little overlap between the two and a chronological gap is apparent. A larger number of independent dates would help to clarify this chronology.

Pit F26

Pit F26 contained just seventy-seven sherds, with fewer distinctive forms than pit F16. There were two possible instances of sherds from the same pots recovered from both pits (Fig 81, nos 13 and 14); but none of these joined and they cannot be used to claim simultaneous filling. Of the recognisable vessels, five share traits with those from pit F16: a high carinated shoulder on a jar (No 20), a bowl (No 21), a high rounded shoulder probably on a jar (No 17), and a carinated shoulder (No 19). This pit also produced three sherds with red-finished surfaces (not illustrated). None of these vessels are closely datable on their own, but they could all be broadly contemporary with those from pit F16, falling within the period *c* 475–350 BC.

There is no obvious distinction between the fabrics used in these two pits (Table 33). Fabrics 1, 2 and 30 were the most common, with twenty-seven maintaining a small presence. The new fabrics 10, 32 and 37 are each represented by just one sherd and, as mentioned above, it is probable that fabrics 32 and 37 are intrusive. When considering the degree of wear and average sherd size, however, there is evidence to suggest that some of the pottery discarded in pit F16 had been in use shortly before deposition, while that from pit F26 was more worn and might have been trampled in a midden for some time before being incorporated in the backfill of the pit.

Other contexts belonging to Period 2

In addition to the two pits discussed above, seven other contexts (from pit F14, pit group A and pit group D) contained sherds in similar flint-tempered fabrics, and none which are demonstrably later (Table 34). These features produced very few distinctive forms, however, with only one shoulder, seven bases and three rims. One jar with smooth surface above the shoulder and light rustication below is a common form occurring between about 600–350 BC. The others are not closely datable.

In addition, most of the pottery from pit group B, the layer sealing it (context 112) and the boundary ditch (F205 and F10/F209), could be regarded as early (Table 34). The small size and quantity of sherds in Fabrics 9 (described belwo as a late Iron Age fabric), 17, 34 and 35 may indicate an intrusive element, though the early introduction of grog at this time cannot be ruled out.

Ceramic evidence for earlier use of the site

Having proposed dates for the Period 2 features, it is worth considering whether there is any evidence for earlier settlement – apart from the Period 1 evidence – from elsewhere on the site. Two traits which are commonly associated with late Bronze Age and early Iron Age pottery were found in material on the site: finger-tip impressed decoration on rims and flat bases with abundant flint inclusions adhering beneath them. There was just one rim sherd with finger-tip impressions, recovered from the third recut of the late Iron Age (Period 3) enclosure ditch; it had a worn surface and weighed just 5g. The use of finger-tip impressions was common between about 850 and 500 BC and evidently continued into the fifth century. Its almost total absence here could be chronologically significant.

The second trait, abundant flint grits adhering beneath a base, was found on seven vessels (Table 35). Several sites dated to the fifth or fourth century BC have now produced such bases. In some cases they have provided the only evidence for an apparently earlier occupation (Macpherson-Grant 1992). In the light of this growing evidence, it is perhaps more plausible to suggest that their use continued longer than previously thought and extended into the late fifth or even fourth century BC. While during the late Bronze Age and early Iron Age this treatment is found on bases of both large storage jars and fine delicate bowls, during the fifth to fourth century BC it tends to be confined to coarser jars or bowls. Thus, there is no certain evidence of occupation at Church Whitfield from the first half of the first millennium BC.

Manufacture, use and deposition of pottery during Period 2

As is usual when considering the manufacture of pottery of this date, no certain evidence was found for its production or the preparation of raw materials on the site. However, the fill of pit F26 contained deposits of soil with burnt flints (contexts 25 and 129) and raw flint (context 25). These could have been related to pottery manufacture. Certainly, although no detailed examination of the local clays was undertaken, the components of the clay matrix of the pottery fabrics (quartz, iron oxides, glauconite and occasional siltstone) can all be found in Clay-with-Flints deposits (Smart *et al* 1966, 203–4). Pockets of Clay-with-Flints in the immediate area of the site (Fig 56) are likely to have provided a convenient source of raw material for these pots. They may also have provided the flint inclusions. A small percentage of the flints within the pottery was unaltered and could have derived from the Clay-with-Flints deposits, but the majority were calcined and could have originated in either the Clay-with-Flints or the chalk.

Thus, it appears that all the Period 2 pottery could have been made locally. Even the high quality red-finished pottery displays a wide variety of inclusions, suggesting that it was not produced with a strictly controlled fabric (Table 36), though all were all-flint tempered. A similar picture emerged from Middleton's broader study of red-finished pottery in east Kent where, in the majority of cases, locally available materials appear to have been used (Middleton 1995). The skills required for its production

Fabric	1	2	10	27	30	32	37	Total
Pit F16								
Context 15	23 (1166)	27 (694)		2 (127)	25 (933)			77 (2920)
Context 125	37 (2865)	18 (361)		2 (265)	1 (909)			58 (4400)
Context 131		1 (11)						1 (11)
Context 132		5 (6)		1 (4)				6 (10)
Total	60 (4031)	51 (1072)		5 (396)	26 (1842)			142 (7341)
Pit F26								
Context 25	11 (140)	37 (347)	1 (11)	4 (18)	16 (249)	1 (3)	1 (2)	71 (770)
Context 129	2 (10)	2 (73)						4 (83)
Context 130	1 (5)	1 (13)						2 (18)
Total	14 (155)	40 (433)	1 (11)	4 (18)	16 (249)	1 (3)	1 (2)	77 (871)

Table 33. Church Whitfield: distribution of sherds by fabric and context in Period 2 pits, F16 and F26. The figures show the number of sherds and, in parentheses, their weight (g).

Context	Feature	Fabric 1	2	9	10	17	30	34	35	Total	Average weight per sherd (g)
204	Boundary ditch F205, NW arm	27 (227)	9 (90)	1 (2)		1 (10)	3 (9)			41 (338)	8.2
9	Boundary ditch F10/209, SW arm	9 (51)	21 (426)					3 (13)		33 (490)	14.8
13	Pit F14	1 (5)	1 (2)							2 (7)	3.5
329	Pit F330, pit group A	5 (63)							1 (9)	6 (72)	12.0
334	Pit F335, pit group A						1 (35)			1 (35)	35.0
109	Layer sealing pit group A	5 (15)	5 (26)				1 (8)			11 (49)	4.5
38	Pit F37, pit group B	15 (106)	10 (548)					1 (6)		26 (660)	25.4
42	Pit F41, pit group B	1 (30)	4 (82)							5 (112)	22.4
343, 344	Pit F345, pit group B				1 (10)					1 (10)	10.0
350	Pit F355, pit group B	7 (104)	6 (129)				1 (46)			14 (279)	19.9
112	Layer sealing pit group B	29 (477)	3 (214)				2 (14)		1 (2)	35 (707)	20.2
48	Pit F49, pit group D		3 (14)				1 (8)			4 (22)	5.5
107	Pit F108, Pit Group D	1 (7)	1 (2)							2 (9)	4.5

Table 34. Church Whitfield: distribution of sherds in other features assigned to Period 2.

could have been available locally and need not have been dependent on specialist potters, though this does not rule out the possibility.

No direct evidence for the use of the pottery was recovered. The remains were too fragmentary and no internal deposits were identified. Furthermore, very few profiles survive to provide us with a clear idea of the full range of pottery vessels in use during Period 2. The range covers fine thin-walled beakers (Fig 79, 2), tall jars or vases (Fig 78, 1; Fig 79, 9), two possible bowls (Fig 81, 13; Fig 83, 21) and rims and shoulders from indeterminate closed forms (Fig 79, 4–8). The coarsewares are predominately jars (eg Fig 81, 14–15; Fig 82, 16) and a bowl (Fig 81, 10). A broad indication of the variety of vessels can be gained by examining the wall thickness and surface treatment of the surviving sherds. The overall picture (Table 37) shows that wall thickness varies from 2 to 18mm, with the majority centred on 7–9mm. In this respect the pottery from pit F16 is clearly distinguished from that from other Period 2 features, demonstrating a range of vessels with thinner walls (51 per cent falling between 5 and 7mm) than those from other features: F14, F26, F205 and context 112, sealing pit group B, with 59–61 per cent of sherds in the range 7–9mm; and F10/F209 with 62 per cent in the range 8–10mm.

The surface treatment can also serve to identify fine and coarse wares (Tables 38 and 39). This has been classified below, following the same criteria applied to the ceramics from Highstead and Dolland's Moor, (Couldrey 2007; Couldrey forthcoming), ordering the types from relatively fine to coarse.

The range of surface treatment within each of the Period 2 features provides an indication of the relative 'fineness' of the pottery. The range extends from red-coated (ST1) sherds to rusticated (ST8) and roughly combed (ST9) sherds. Certainly the overall range of vessels is comparable to that found at other sites of this period and the presence of painted pottery need not be seen as indicative of a high status settlement. Once again, the fill of pit F16 can be seen to be finer than the others.

There was no clear evidence for the deliberate deposition of pottery in any of the pits and the finer quality of the pottery from pit F16 may be due, at least in part, to survival. It has already been suggested on the basis of sherd size (Table 33), that at least some of the pottery recovered from F16, including some of the finer vessels, may have been buried shortly after going out of use. Once they were in the fill of the pit they would not have been disturbed further, whereas those vessels discarded on a midden may have been subjected to trampling and other disturbances, which may have been more destructive of the finer, thinner-walled vessels than those with thicker walls. Such an interpretation could account for the different patterns of sherd size and surface treatment recovered.

Continuity with Period 3

A report on the later pottery by Dr Isobel Thompson appears below and covers the material from the Period 3 enclosure ditch and other features. Nevertheless, it is worth considering whether there is any evidence for continuity, or the extent of the gap, between Periods 2 and 3, especially in view of the broad range of the radiocarbon dates obtained (Table 64).

	Fabric 1	2	30	Total
Enclosure ditch F233 – lower fill	2			2
Enclosure ditch re-cut F248	1	1	1	3
Context 109, seals pit complex A		1		1
Structure VI (F203)	1			1
Total	4	2	1	7

Table 35. Church Whitfield: distribution and number of base sherds with abundant flint grits adhering beneath them.

Fabric	1	2	27	30	Totals
Pit F16	3	12	2		17
Pit F26	2			1	3
Enclosure ditch, SW arm, F10/209, Context 9		1			1
Totals	5	13	2	1	21

Table 36. Church Whitfield: distribution of red-finished sherds.

Wall thickness (mm)	3	4	5	6	7	8	9	10	11	12	13	14	15	16	17	18
Pit F14					50	50										
Pit F16	1.8	6.4	17	19	15	8.3	10	7.3	5.5	4.6	3.7	0.9	0.9			
Pit FF26			2.1	6.2	10	27	22	11	10	6.2	4.1			1.0		
Boundary ditch F10/209			2.2	2.2	11	18	24	20	20	2.2						
Boundary ditch F205		1.9	3.7	7.4	20	22	19	11	5.6	3.7				1.9	1.9	1.9
Context 112 (layer sealing pit group B)				2.4	17	31	14	12	12	4.8	2.4	2.4	2.4			

Table 37. Church Whitfield: distribution of wall thickness shown as a percentage occurrence.

In east Kent, several sites have been found which show signs of occupation between *c* 475–350 BC and again during the late Iron Age, but very few sites appear to have been occupied between *c* 350–150 BC (Macpherson-Grant 1991). Here it has been demonstrated that during the fifth to fourth century there were strong links with ceramic developments in north-eastern France. After about 350 BC the early La Tène forms vanished, a development recognised over a wide area, from north-east France to Belgium (Cahen-Delhaye 1995) and into the southern Netherlands (van Heeringen 1989). They were replaced by forms which apparently do not share such distinctive traits and are therefore more difficult to recognise – which may, in part, account for the relatively few sites attributed to this period. In northern France the following traits have been included among those that are characteristic of the period: rims with rounded tops, rims exhibiting some thickening and rounding, the presence of foot-ring bases, tall S-profiled vessels and the almost complete absence of carinated forms and their decoration (Hurtrelle *et al* 1990, 214–5).

The few forms identified as belonging to this period in northern France are absent at Church Whitfield. Certainly, much of the pottery from the fill of the Period 3 enclosure ditch comprises curvilinear forms, such as vessels with everted rims and foot-ring bases (eg Fig 84, 33–38; Fig 85, 39–40 and Fig 86, 76–77), but these are difficult to match with those identified by Hurtrelle (1990). Perhaps the earliest link is provided by the S-profiled jar or vase, decorated with a single curvilinear groove (Fig 85, 39) and which would almost certainly have had a tall pedestal base. In northern France broadly similar forms are assigned to La Tène Moyenne, *c* 225–150 BC (Degenne and Duval 1983, 83, fig 12, 9; Lardy 1983, pl 13, V349).

Nevertheless, in spite of the new forms, there is a degree of continuity of tradition: many of the fine foot-ring vessels and coarser forms are still made in the same flint-tempered fabrics that are found in Period 2. Furthermore, small sherds of apparently Period 2 pottery were discovered throughout the fills of the enclosure ditch alongside a wider range of later fabrics.

Thus, there is no certain evidence of continuity between Periods 2 and 3. Indeed, the ceramic evidence suggests that there could be a gap of about 150–200 years between them. During this period the site was abandoned, or witnessed activities which left no discernible archaeological trace. If a midden had existed during Period 2, providing a source of small worn sherds for the fills of the Period 2 features, it is possible that it still existed to some degree in Period 3 and provided much of the material that filled the Period 3 features.

ST1	Coloured by painting
ST2	Highly burnished
ST3	Burnished or very smooth
ST4	Smooth
ST5	Wiped smooth
ST6	Wiped or roughly slurried
ST7	Heavily wiped or lightly rusticated
ST8	Rusticated
ST9	Roughly combed
ST10	Scored or heavily wiped groove

Table 38. Church Whitfield: surface treatment (ST) codes.

Illustrated vessels from Period 2 features (Figs 79–83)
Nigel Macpherson-Grant

Pit F16

1–1A Eleven fairly small and medium-sized sherds, two conjoining, from a tall-necked probably tripartite fineware jar with sharply angled neck-shoulder junction. Simple slightly everted rim; diam: 180mm. Interior with medium quality fairly glossy burnish on neck but patchy, light and irregular below; exterior with similar even but fairly matt burnish. Neck and upper body panels polychrome decorated with: on neck – a continuous series of diamond motifs, self-coloured with, broad frames in red-finish and outlined with white paint; on shoulder – an

Surface treatment	ST1	ST2	ST3	ST4	ST5	ST6	ST7	ST8	ST9	ST10	Total no of sherds
Pit F14						50	50				2
Pit F16	28		29	11	8	3	15	6			100
Pit F26	4		19	49	11	4	6	7			70
Boundary ditch F10/209	4			24	12	60					25
Boundary ditch F205			5	30	41	19	5				37
Context 112 (seal of pit group B)			4	26	44	11	4		11		27

Table 39. Church Whitfield: distribution of surface treatment (ST) shown as a percentage of unworn sherds.

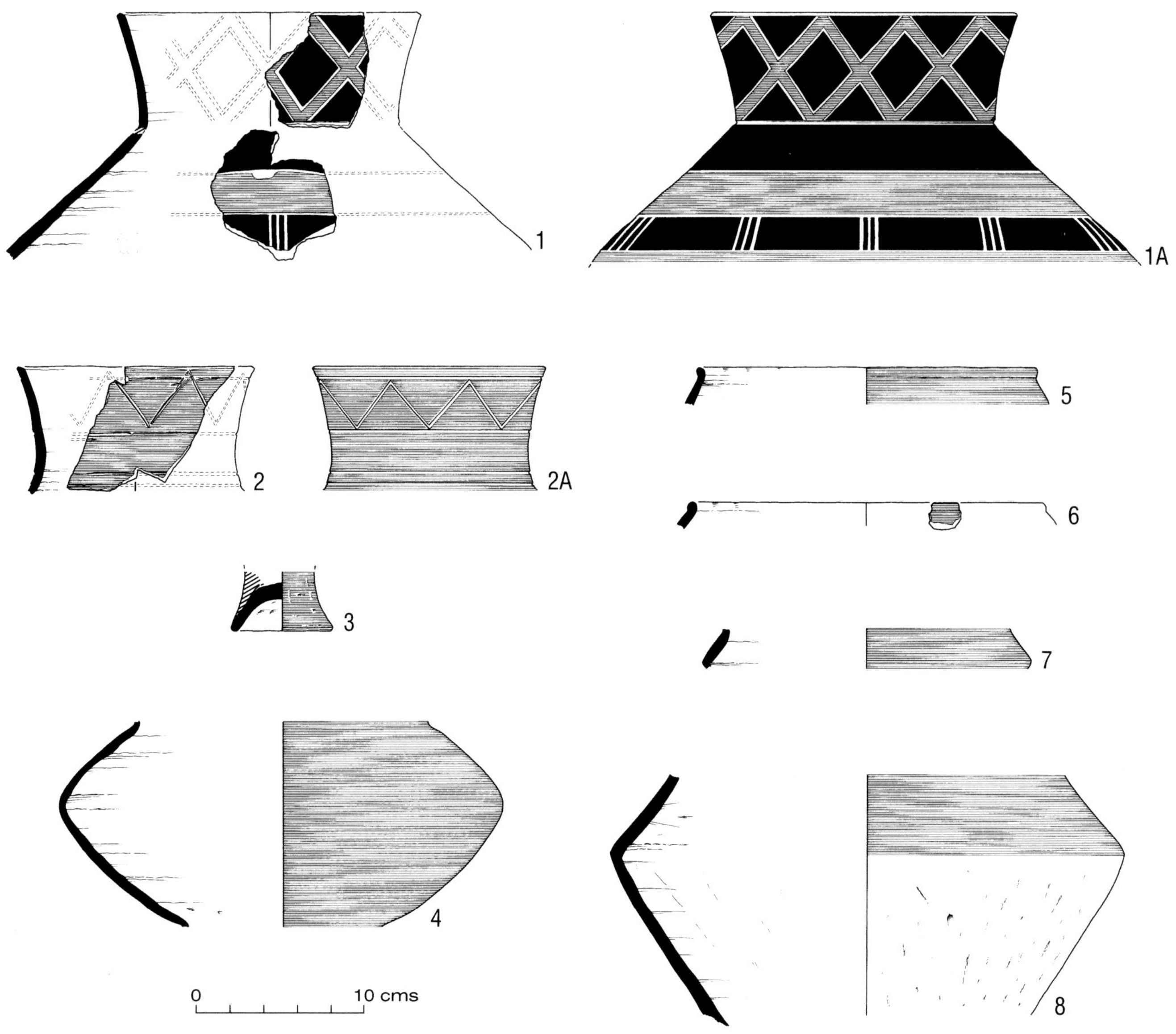

Fig 79. Church Whitfield: early Iron Age pottery from the site (Nos 1–8). Scale 1:4.

alternating sequence of probably three plain self-coloured and dull maroon red-finished horizontal bands bordered with white paint. The third panel has faint traces of three grouped white-painted vertical lines, probably one of a series spaced around the body (see Reconstruction 1A). Grey core with patchy brown-orange and dark grey partially oxidised surfaces. Variable condition, most sherds fairly fresh (some minor edge-wear), two with heavily unifacial damage. Fabric 2. Bulk of sherds from context 15, others from context 125.

2–2A Eight small and medium-sized sherds, seven conjoining, from a tall-necked fineware jar. Simple flaring rim with slight internal bevel; diam: 140mm. Crudely executed incised and red-finished decoration: with two horizontal neck panels bordered by horizontal lines, the upper panel filled with incised chevrons – the whole then overlain by a fairly bright maroon-red finish. Light grey core and patchy light brown and dark grey partially oxidised surfaces. Those from context 15 are smaller and more abraded, but all sherds have suffered varying degrees of use or post-loss damage to red finish. Fabric 2. Sherds evenly distributed between contexts 15 and 125

3 Six conjoining base sherds from fineware jar/bowl. Fairly neat separately moulded deep pedestal base luted on to main body. Diam: 80mm. Light irregular smoothing inside pedestal; smooth even vertical burnish externally with traces of dull maroon-brown red-finish over. Unusually, traces of red-finish within pedestal. Grey core, oxidised buff inside pedestal, partially oxidised patchy buff and grey exterior. Moderate edge-wear, worn red-finish probably due to use-wear. Fabric 2. Context 125.

4 Larger sherd from context 125, bulk smaller from context 15). Fourteen small to large shoulder and body sherds from a fineware bowl; accentuated shoulder. Diam: 265mm. Roughly smoothed interior with firm but irregular horizontal burnish over: good quality regular burnish external with traces of apparently all-over rich maroon-red red-finish. Dark grey core, essentially reduced dark grey surfaces with some drab brown patches. Hard fired product. Fabric 1.

5 Single small sherd from fineware bowl/jar with simple rounded and slightly everted rim, diam: 200mm. Rather irregular but firm internal burnish; even external burnish overlain with dull maroon-red red finish. Black core with pale brown margins below brown patchy drab grey and brown-buff partially oxidised surfaces. Fairly fresh. Fabric 2. Context 125.

6 Five small rim and shoulder sherds form a fineware bowl/jar with simple short upright and rounded rim, diam: 210mm. Interior with traces of light burnish; fairly even moderate

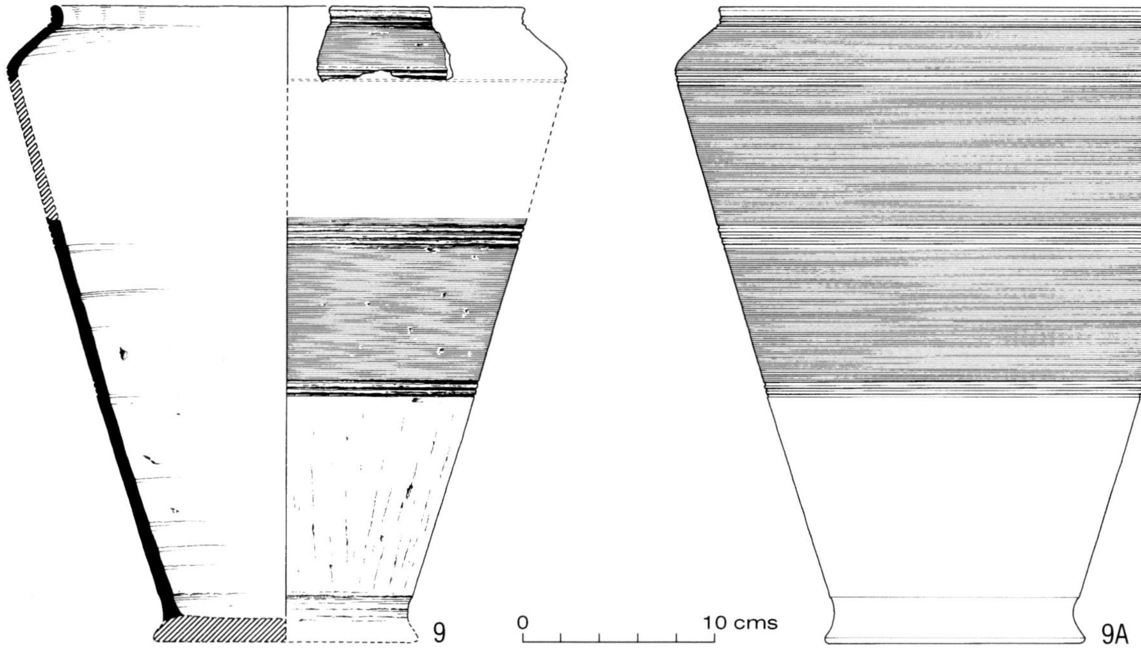

Fig 80. Church Whitfield: early Iron Age pottery from the site (No 9). Scale 1:4.

external burnish with traces of bright maroon-red red-finish over. One sherd with unifacial wear, most with fairly heavy edge-wear. Fabric 2. Context 132 .

7 Two small shoulder sherds from fineware bowl; angled shoulder with diam: 190mm. Irregular light burnish internally, even externally with traces of dull pink-red red-finish over. Grey core, grey interior, partially oxidised drab light chocolate-brown exterior, thick pale brown margins below surface. Moderate edge-wear. Fabric 30. Context 15.

8 Nine small to large shoulder and body sherds from a fineware jar. Angular shoulder. Diam: 300mm. Interior treatment: rather 'wet' irregular tooled horizontal burnish down to and immediately below shoulder angle: lower body with fairly even vertical smoothing overlain by sparse tooling. Exterior finish: fairly even moderate horizontal burnish above and immediately below shoulder, lower body with even moderate vertical tooled burnish. Upper body with patchy rich maroon-red red-finish; patchiness appears to be due to irregular multi-directional rubbing of the surface with a lump of ?wettened iron-oxide. Grey core, dark grey reduced interior, orange, rich brown and grey partially oxidised exterior. Sherds with some edge-wear. Fabric 2. Four sherds from context 125, the rest from context 15.

9–9A Thirteen medium and large sized sherds, six (lower body) conjoining, from sub-fineware situlate jar; base and upper body sherds missing but profile and main decoration reconstructable (9A). Simple short slightly everted internally round rim: diam: 260mm. Sharply-angled shoulder. Wiped internally, overlain by irregular light but firm burnish. Exterior divided horizontally into four panels each separated/bordered by groups of three or four close-set deeply incised horizontal lines, defining the neck, shoulder and lower edge decorated zone. Shoulder and both decorated body panels with rough but firm burnish; lower-body panel with similar but vertical burnish. Base junction lightly wiped horizontally. Upper three panels decorated with maroon-red red-finish. Dark grey core; predominantly reduced dark grey surfaces with brown patches. Essentially fresh, some post-loss contextual damage to red-finish; well-made, hard-fired product. Fabric 7. The bulk from contexts 15 and 125.

10 Forty-three mostly small, some moderate and large, sherds from a coarseware jar; reconstructable profile. Simple rim, diam.: 260mm; rounded shoulder, diam: 140mm. Rough multi-directional wiping internally but insufficient to seal coil pinches; exterior with rough, almost 'rusticated', mostly horizontal wiping and vertical immediately up from base. Black core with variable margins beneath overall partial oxidisation, dirty orange-brown and drab dark grey. Most sherds fairly fresh though rather brittle, one or two with fairly heavy edge-wear. Fabric 1. Contexts 15, 125, 132 with bulk of sherds from 15 and 125.

11 Single medium-sized sherd from coarseware jar base; diam: 130mm. Interior with good almost sub-fineware light burnished finish; exterior neatly wiped smooth, base underside with level light burnish. Brown-grey core, oxidised light brown interior (oxidisation extending deeply into base pad), grey reduced exterior with drab light brown patches. Fresh but one edge with slight edge-wear. Fabric 2. Context 15.

12 Three body sherds from a fineware bowl with trace of angled shoulder. Diam: 240mm. Rough irregular horizontal burnish internally, marginally smoother external burnish but (towards base) insufficient to seal primary smoothing. Grey core and brown margin beneath external surface, drab grey essentially reduced core with drab brown patches. Slightly worn, some edge-wear. Fabric 2. Context 15.

13 Two rim and shoulder sherds from a closed-form sub-fineware bowl. Diam: 200mm. Simple rim, rounded shoulder. Trace of possible incised/combed vertical decoration below shoulder, possibly grouped, as one of a series spaced round the body. Interior wiped horizontally, lower body portion with light irregular horizontal burnish; exterior wet smoothed horizontally overall with light irregular burnish on upper body only. Grey core with brown margin below exterior surface; dark grey essentially reduced surfaces with drab dark brown patches. Fairly fresh. Fabric 2. One sherd each from pit F16 (context 125) and pit F26 (context 130).

14 Two rim sherds from a coarseware storage jar, thickened and internally-bevelled rim with marked inner lip. Diam: 300mm. Light even burnish overall. Grey core and interior, exterior grey with drab orange-brown patches. Worn with external

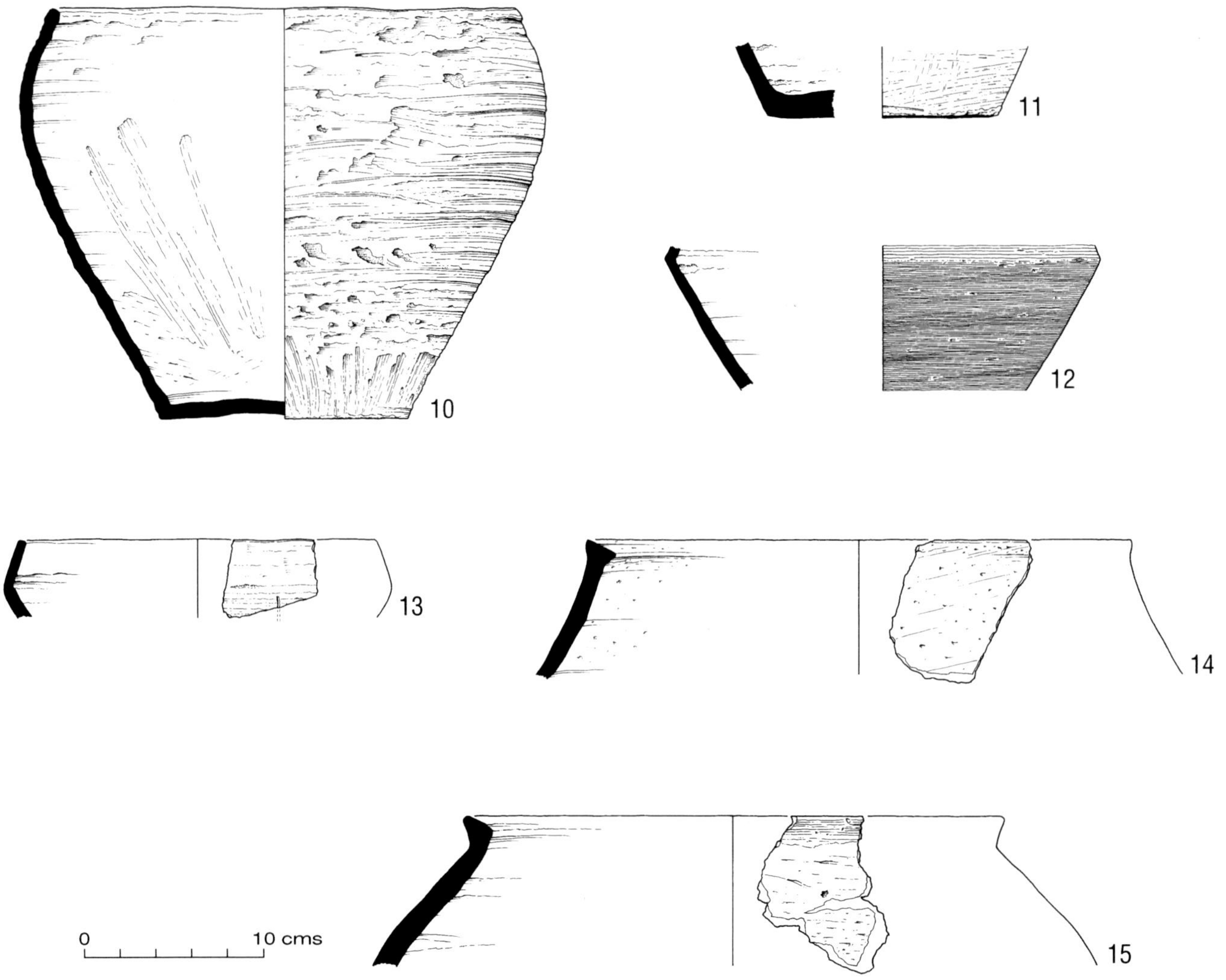

Fig 81. Church Whitfield: early Iron Age pottery from the site (Nos 10–15). Scale 1:4.

surface spalling and interior with leached and pitted surface. Fabric 40 . One sherd each from pit F16 (context 15) and pit F26 (context 25).

15 Two moderate sized conjoining sherds from a coarseware storage jar with thickened everted triangular-sectioned internally bevelled rim. Diam: 300mm. Minimal rough horizontal internal smoothing, roughly wiped externally with patchy light burnish over and on rim top. Dark grey core, partially oxidised drab brown-grey surfaces. Fairly fresh. Fabric 1. Context 15.

16 Five moderate very large shoulder, body and base sherds from a large fairly thick-walled coarseware storage jar. Diam: 220mm at shoulder, 140mm at base. Rough horizontal smoothing internally immediately under shoulder overhang but wiped fairly evenly below – even down to base; exterior with heavy coarse rustication. The latter has been smeared on vertically leaving faint traces of vertical lines separating broad 'panels' of rustication; this suggests that a loose 'ball' of clay was held in slightly cupped fingers and palm, pressed close to the pot wall and smeared upwards against it, the thumb and/or little finger occasionally leaving faint traces as the clay was applied. Base finished with a broad horizontal band of knife-trimming. Exterior above shoulder smoothed horizontally. The fabric has a markedly laminar structure. Grey core, drab brown-orange oxidised surfaces. Some unifacial wear exacerbated by fabric structure. Fabric 1. Contexts 15 and 125.

Pit F26

17 Single moderate-sized rim sherd from closed-form bowl/jar with simple rolled and undercut rim. Diam: 260mm. Smoothed horizontally overall, irregularly internally, more evenly on rim top and exterior. Grey core, partially oxidised overall drab buff-brown and pale grey. Fairly fresh with some slight edge-wear. Fabric 1. Context 25.

18 Single small rim sherd from fineware bowl; simple rim with slight external bevel. Diam: intermediate but fairly large. Light rather coarse internal burnish, medium external burnish – again rather coarse. Reduced, dark brown core, dark grey surfaces. Fairly fresh. Fabric 2. Context 25.

19 Single small coarseware jar/bowl shoulder sherd; diam: 240mm. Fairly even horizontal smoothing internally with exterior roughly smoothed below shoulder and trace of light burnish above. Black core, partially oxidised drab grey-brown overall with thin pink margin beneath internal surface. Worn. Fabric 1. Context 129.

20 Single moderate-sized rim and shoulder sherd from coarseware jar. Diam: 180mm. Simple thickened slightly out-turned rim.

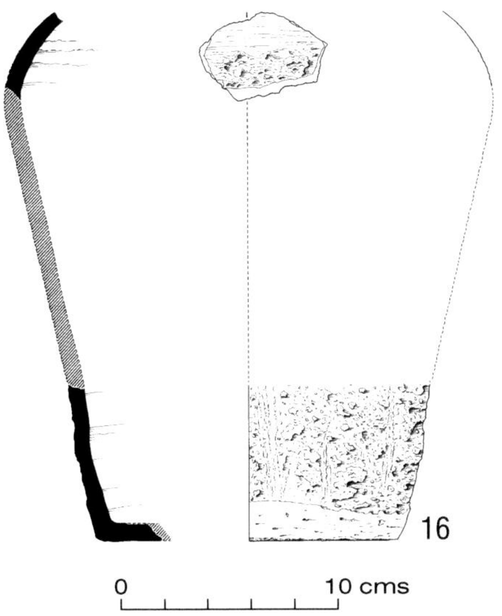

Fig 82. Church Whitfield: early Iron Age pottery from the site (No 16). Scale 1:4.

Angular shoulder. Roughly smoothed interior with some detectable vertical finger pulls, horizontally-wiped lower body, smoothed upper body with trace of light burnish above shoulder and on rim. Reduced dark grey throughout, drab dark brown patch externally. Fairly fresh. Fabric 1. Context 25.

21 Three small rim and shoulder sherds, two conjoining, from a fineware bowl, with simple internally-bevelled rim shoulder; rim diam: 220mm. Light rather irregular burnish internally, even medium-burnished exterior. Reduced throughout, with light grey core and darker surfaces. Fresh. Fabric 2. Context 25.

22 Two moderate-sized sherds from a fineware jar or beaker base, diam: 100mm. Fairly even internal smoothing, good even but matt external burnish. Reduced dark grey, thin vermillion margin beneath outer surface, later with dark brown-pink patches. Fairly fresh. Fabric 30. Context 25.

Late Iron Age pottery (Figs 84–91; Tables 40–43)
Isobel Thompson

The assemblage considered here comes from the Period 3 ditched enclosure. The size of the area enclosed, and the domestic nature of the pottery, suggests that the site was that of a single homestead of late Iron Age date. Few contemporary features, however, survived in the enclosure's interior, or outside it. No chronological overlap was present on the site with earlier, fifth- to fourth-century BC features (Period 2, see above) or later (Anglo-Saxon: Period 4) features. The pottery assemblage was of some interest, and for this reason all available portions of the ditch were completely excavated, representing about three-quarters of the entire ditch.

The enclosure ditch

At least 18kg of late Iron Age pottery was retrieved from the enclosure ditch (Table 40). Only very small amounts were recovered from other features which appear to be contemporary with it (Table 43), while two scraps of apparently late fabrics (Fabrics 9 and 17) were intrusive in earlier contexts (Table 34). The late Iron Age pottery from the site can be considered as a single assemblage. Unlike the very large pit group found at Hawkinge Airfield, some 11km to the south-west (Thompson 2001), it is not from a single context, but as several vessels were scattered through the ditch layers there is no clear chronological division between the various fills. Neither forms nor fabrics indicate any definable chronological progression in these fills. The higher layers have the most pottery in them, as the ditch was kept less clean and began to fill with debris. The condition of the sherds, broken up but without much wear, also indicates casual discarding of rubbish. In contrast to the Hawkinge pit, there are no complete vessel profiles here. This, and the general distribution within the four arms of the ditch, shows that the assemblage does not represent a termination deposit or other single chronological event.

Fabrics

Thirty indigenous hand-made late Iron Age fabrics were identified in the assemblage by Nigel Macpherson-Grant. Some of these have been combined and here they fall into three main groups: flint-tempered, the standard Iron Age tempering agent of crushed flint, with the addition of a variety of other substances; fabrics tempered with neither flint nor grog but with other substances, notably sand and chalk; and

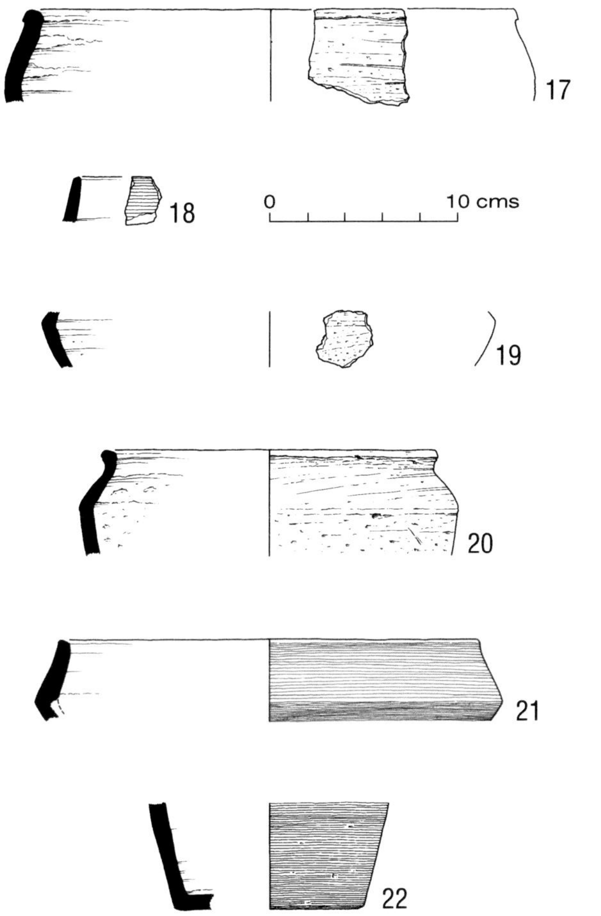

Fig 83. Church Whitfield: early Iron Age pottery from the site (Nos 17–22). Scale 1:4.

'Belgic' fabrics, which mostly contain grog temper. In the tables the 'Belgic' fabrics are nos 11, 12 and 14–17, and are shown separately after the others. They amount to less than 1kg out of the total 18kg of pottery recovered.

The fabric descriptions are given below. Those that appeared during Period 2 (Fabric Nos 1, 2, 10, 27, and 30) are described in Peter Couldrey's report above. The distribution of fabric by weight is presented in Table 40.

Fabric	Primary contexts	Main fill	First re-cut	Third re-cut	Mixed contexts	Total (g)
1	594	612	1687	3569	470	6932
2	304	310	867	2005	341	3827
4			34	8		42
5				270		270
6					250	250
7		13	7	150		170
8		15	34	158		207
9	2	7	81	86		176
10		59	226	1079		1364
13		5		227	378	610
19				42		42
20		5				5
21		6	28	23		57
22			16			16
23	5	14	33			47
24		27	16	10	21	79
25			5			5
26	9	18	146	260		433
27	81	15		195		291
29		40		41		81
30	33	31	147	307		518
31	19			28		47
33		7	7	12		26
34	11	22	26	55	230	344
35	252	32	86	383	110	863
36			27	254		281
39		14		97		111
42			15			15
Total	1310	1252	3488	9259	1800	17109
11	8	11	151	273	125	568
12			9	53		62
14			55			55
15				10		10
16	17	7	45	82	94	245
17			10	14		24
Total	25	18	270	432	219	964

Table 40. Church Whitfield: sherd weights (g) by fabric from the Period 3 enclosure ditch.

Flint-tempered fabrics

Fabric 5. Large flint grits, and possibly some sand.
Fabric 6. Shell with some flint.
Fabric 8. Flint-tempered sandy ware.
Fabric 9. Sand and flint with chalk/grog.
Fabric 29. Coarse sandy ware with sparse-moderate flint.
Fabric 36. Coarse flint-tempered with some grog.
Fabric 39. Sparse flint with organic inclusions.

Other 'non-Belgic' tempering

Fabric 4. Shelly.
Fabric 7. Sandy.
Fabric 13. Chalk.
Fabric 21. Sandy.
Fabric 26. Sand and chalk: profuse black sand with sparse-moderate quartz and moderate-profuse inclusions of black sand in calcareous/marl aggregate. A distinctive fabric with voids particularly noticeable on the interior surfaces.
Fabric 31. Iron oxide
Fabric 33. Organic inclusions

'Belgic' fabrics

Fabric 11. Grog-tempered.
Fabric 12. Standard grog-tempered.
Fabric 14. Thick and soft grog-tempered.
Fabric 15. 'Belgic' very fine sandy.
Fabric 16. Grog and flint.
Fabric 17. Grog and flint, but generally coarser than fabric 16. This contains some fine sand as well as grog and possibly some sparse flint.

Forms and decoration in non-'Belgic' fabrics

Table 41 shows that the characteristic forms in late Iron Age, non-'Belgic', fabrics are also to be found at Bigberry (Thompson 1983) and Hawkinge (Thompson 2001). The Bigberry assemblage, however, is not particularly like that from Hawkinge. Whitfield has links with both. Bigberry characterises east Kent late Iron Age ceramics, while Hawkinge is highly distinctive and has links with east Sussex and possibly further afield along the south coast. Some of the forms, like the everted-rim foot-ring bowls (eg Fig 84, 23 and 24), are ubiquitous, but others call for more comment.

The curvilinear decoration on the small pedestalled urn (Fig 85, 39) is reminiscent of the Margate and Birchington vessels, which have been dated *c* 150 BC at latest (Macpherson-Grant 1991, 44). The decoration on this pot is simpler, and may be later. It also may have links with the late Iron Age in Sussex, where such decoration is both common and varied in style (Luke Barber, pers comm; cf Elsdon 1975, figs 11–12, for some of this variety). There it lasted well into the first century AD, but was also used considerably earlier.

The 'saucepan' forms also show this link with south coast ceramic traditions. Only two or three such vessels appear to be present at Church Whitfield (eg Fig 87, 78), and they are rare (but not unknown) elsewhere in east Kent. In the Hawkinge pit group they are one of a range of characteristic forms, with many complete profiles and in more than one fabric. Indeed one example from Hawkinge, with shallow tooled decoration is very likely a Sussex product. None of the Church Whitfield examples appears to have been manufactured in Sussex, but the influence on style is evident.

The range of forms in these non-'Belgic' fabrics is quite distinct from those in recognisably 'Belgic' fabrics, apart perhaps from the flaring rim which was to become common on east Kent grog-tempered vessels. Some of the plainer rim forms, including closed jar forms with inturned rim (eg Fig 87, 73–74), occur in both late Iron Age and 'Belgic' fabrics, but are too simple to be characteristic.

Forms in 'Belgic' fabrics

The range of forms in these fabrics is small. All are of standard 'Belgic' forms (Table 42), the only ones identifiable in the mass of scraps. None are helpful for dating. Like the late Iron Age forms, most of them have parallels at Bigberry (Thompson 1983) and in the Hawkinge pit (Thompson 2001). Other sherds include a corrugated jar form (Fig 85, 47; Fabric 11), similar to one from Bigberry (Thompson 1983, fig 12, no 91), which was also grog-tempered; and a flat jar base (not illustrated) with overlapping horizontal/vertical tooling similar to an example from Bigberry (Thompson 1983, fig 11, no 67), and others with similar surface treatment at Hawkinge, all also grog-tempered.

Late Iron Age pottery in other features

Three features appear to be contemporary with the Period 3 enclosure itself: gully F207, pit F219 and probably pit F318. Only very small amounts of pottery were recovered from these features, and no recognisable forms were represented (Table 43).

A few sherds are intrusive in the much earlier, early Iron Age, contexts. One sherd, from pit F345, in pit group B, is in a fine flint fabric reminiscent of the even finer fabric characteristic of the Hawkinge assemblage, and has shallow-tooled curvilinear decoration. More substantial amounts of late Iron Age pottery came from the fills of two of the Anglo-Saxon SFBs (the majority from Structure VI, which was cut into the top of the enclosure ditch). Three rims and a base are represented only by scraps; another base is an almost complete foot-ring (Fig 91, 116). A sherd (Fig 91, 119), from Structure VI, has dotted and curvilinear decoration similar to Sussex motifs (Elsdon 1975, 59). A few more sherds were residual in a post-medieval field boundary ditch.

Conclusions and dating

The Church Whitfield late Iron Age pottery is valuable as a large assemblage, in a range of fabrics, from a well-defined context. In itself it provides a mass of data about the use of so many, apparently contemporary, fabrics at a crucial period when flint-tempering was beginning to give way to the very different grog-tempered 'Belgic' ceramic tradition.

Fabric	Description	Contexts	Parallels
1	Pedestalled urn with curvilinear decoration (one only)	234/255	Decoration is like Margate and Birchington (Macpherson-Grant 1990-91, 44) but simpler; cf also East Sussex
1, 2, 4, 19, 21, 26, 27, 29, 31	Everted-rim footring bowl	many	Standard form
1, 2, 13	Wide-mouthed bowl	234, 258/260, 311 etc.	Standard form; cf Bigberry fig nos 8, 11 (flint); Hawkinge rim 69
13, 26	Jar with deep offset shoulder	200, 258/260	cf Hawkinge rim 68 (fabric 26)
10, 35	Flat-topped storage jar rim	3, 223, 234	cf Bigberry fig no 6 (flint); fig. nos 87, 93 (flint)
1, 2	Jar with short offset shoulder	3, 234	As Bigberry fig 12, no 79 (flint)
13, 24	Deep 'saucepan'	3/258/260, 254/255, 256	cf Hawkinge, several in similar fabrics
1, 2, 8, 9	Jar with slightly everted rim	250, 254 etc	Bigberry fig 10, nos 14, 38; fig 11, no 60, etc (flint)
1, 7, 36	Everted storage jar rim	258 etc	Similar in flint at Bigberry and Hawkinge
21	Omphalos base, small	250	Hawkinge nos 62-3, in fabric 26
1, 2, 10	Jar/bowl with thick bead rim and deep offset	234, 260, 311	Hawkinge rim 46
5	Deep upright jar with bead rim	3	cf Hawkinge 'saucepan' forms
6	Small round jar, with combing	260	cf Hawkinge rim 55 (sandy)
1, 35	Large closed jar, inturned/bead rim	3, 255, 311	Not a Bigberry form; some similar at Hawkinge but smaller
35	Jar with flaring rim	216	More like a grog-tempered form

Table 41. Church Whitfield: pottery forms in Iron Age (non-'Belgic') fabrics from the Period 3 enclosure ditch.

Form	Fabric	Contexts	Parallels
A1(or F?)	12	260	Standard grog-tempered pedestal form
B2-1	12	258	Ripple-necked jar rim, narrow type; standard; cf Bigberry fig 10, nos 40-41 (grog); others at Hawkinge
C1-2	16	254/255	Bead-rimmed jar
?C2-3	16	894	Coarse jar with everted rim; cf Bigberry fig 10, no 9, and Hawkinge rim 28, both in grog
C6-1	11	258, 200/249/254/255	Standard grog-tempered form; the flaring rim is typical in east Kent; sherds of another in cf Bigberry fig 10, no 10, in grog
D2-4	11	255	Bowl form with rippled shoulder
?E1-2/4	15	311	Carinated cup sherds

Table 42. Church Whitfield: pottery forms in 'Belgic' fabrics from the Period 3 enclosure ditch.

Fabric	206 Gully F207	222 Pit F219	218 Pit F219	317 Pit F318	Total (g)
1		5			5
8		14			14
19			20		20
12				29	29
16	3				3

Table 43. Church Whitfield: sherd weights (g) by fabric from features contemporary with the Period 3 enclosure.

At more or less the same time other distinctive fabrics were appearing in this part of Kent, near the border with Sussex, the south coast, and a different set of ceramic traditions. Church Whitfield, with its links to the Hawkinge pit group, is one of the sites that will provide the basis for close study of this mix of traditions. The Whitfield enclosure ditch pottery is also perhaps a more 'normal' assemblage than the Hawkinge pit group, with its complete profiles in finely made fabrics. It must be assumed that few new sites comparable to Hawkinge are likely to be found, whereas other Church Whitfield-type sites may be.

The date assigned to the deposition of the Hawkinge pit group is *c* 80–30 BC. Church Whitfield is somewhat earlier. This conclusion is based partly on the proportions of fabrics present, although given the unusual nature of the Hawkinge pit group (which contained more than twice as much pottery by weight as the entire Whitfield assemblage), this may be misleading. The Hawkinge pit group includes a great deal more grog-tempered fabrics, by weight, than any of the other fabrics, and there is also a large amount of sandy chalk tempered fabrics, such as 26 and 13. Flint-tempered and coarse sandy fabrics are well represented but in smaller proportions than these others. Flint tempering is used for several foot-ring bowls in a very fine fabric that is not represented at Church Whitfield.

The vessels from Church Whitfield in 'Belgic' fabrics have links both with Bigberry and with the earliest forms at Canterbury. The flint-tempered vessels belong to prehistoric ceramic traditions in Kent and Sussex from the third to the first centuries BC and the 'sandy' fabrics, including fabric 26, are in forms dated from *c* 100–80 BC and later, with links as far west as Danebury. The small quantities of later fabrics mean that the pit group may not be as early as 80 BC, and so a fairly broad period had to be assigned to it. Apart from the fabrics, other traits in the Church Whitfield assemblage support a date earlier than Hawkinge. The curvilinear decorated pedestalled urn (Fig 85, 39) has links with middle Iron Age decorated vessels which date no later than *c* 150 BC, although its simpler motif may imply that it is not as early as these. The parallels with Bigberry, and the forms in general, all indicate a date earlier than 80 BC. The small proportion and narrow range of forms in 'Belgic' fabrics are, then, a reflection of their early appearance.

Bigberry's radiocarbon dates (Clark and Thompson 1989) centre on the later second century BC. Despite the lack of precision in radiocarbon dating of the period, these are consistent with the dates assigned to Church Whitfield, Period 3 (*c* 150–50 BC). Also, the potin coin found within the area of the enclosure dates to *c* 150–100 BC. It is thus extremely useful to find that the dating reached on typological grounds is the same as that provided by other evidence.

Illustrated vessels (Figs 84–91)

In the descriptions which follow 'Hawkinge' refers to the report on the late Iron Age pottery from that site (Thompson 2001) and 'Bigberry' refers to Hugh Thompson's report (Thompson 1983). Sherds from many of the vessels were distributed throughout the fills of the ditch. Here they are ordered according to their earliest occurrence, with details of the contexts from which all their sherds derived. When known, vessels in 'Belgic' fabrics have been classified according to their forms as defined in Thompson 1982.

The enclosure ditch: primary and lower fill (contexts 123, 124, 137, 138, 217, 224, 225, 232, 245, 257, 261, 262, 312 and 371)

23 Contexts 261, 258 and 260. A wide-mouthed bowl; cf Hawkinge rim 69 (small). Diam: 190mm. Grey core, surfaces with voids. Fabric 13. Weight 90g.

24 Contexts 261, 255, 262 and 265. A foot-ring base, rather crudely shaped and fairly heavy. Dense dark brown-grey, roughly tooled dark brown-grey surfaces, turning to a darker grey higher up the body. The illustration shows where the base has been repaired with resin. Diam: 840–870mm. Fabric 2. Weight 320g.

25 Contexts 261 and 260. The entire circuit of a flat jar base, with walls thin and broken up. Grey, red below grey-brown inside worn to red inside the base; interior partly sooted; underside pale brown-grey, smooth; outside darker grey, roughly wiped downwards leaving striations. Irregular diam: 750–780mm. Fabric 34. Weight 230g.

26 Context 312. A thick flat storage jar base, diam: irregular but between 140 and 200mm. Crumbling, grey-brown, grey upper surface and darker underside, roughly smoothed. Fabric 1. Weight 165g.

27 Context 123. A foot-ring with diam. of 80mm. Thick, dark-grey-brown, darker grey underside with tooling marks, brown-grey dark outside, and coarser (worn) untooled inside, no burnish. Fabric 2. Weight 50g.

28 Context 123. A foot-ring; one piece, diam: 70mm, battered and much of edge lost. Grey-brown core, pale brown thick layer beneath brown inside and dark grey outside, tooled smooth outside and under base. Fabric 27. Weight 81g.

The enclosure ditch: middle and upper fill (contexts 122, 136, 223, 240, 241, 250, 251, 256 and 374)

29 Context 256. Presumably the rim of an everted-rim foot-ring bowl or similar, as at Bigberry. Diam: *c* 170mm, quite neatly made, thick. Finely-grained grey core, darker grey-brown surfaces, smooth, and tooled to a dark finish outside and over the rim. Fabric 29. Weight 40g.

30 Context 256. Possibly a 'saucepan' form, similar in general form and fabric to Hawkinge. Rim diam: 170mm, base *c* 60–80mm. Grey all through; similar to Rim No 28. Fabric 24. Weight 14g.

31 Context 256. An upright form, diam: irregular but *c* 140mm. Dark grey, somewhat less dark inside; outside was probably roughened. Fabric 2. Weight 27g.

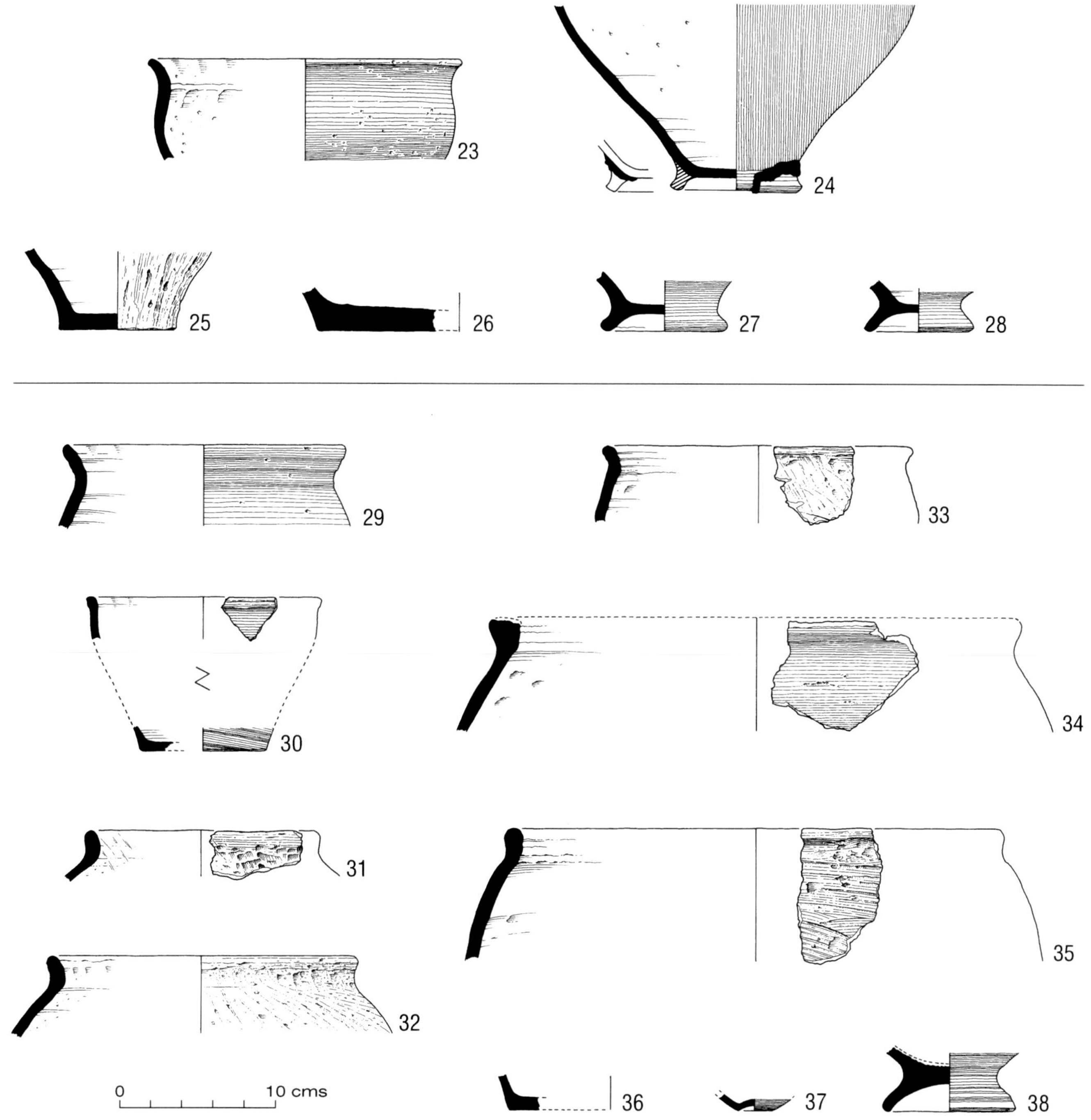

Fig 84. Church Whitfield: late Iron Age pottery from the site (Nos 23–38). Scale 1:4.

32 Context 256. A rim with diam. of *c* 250mm. Neatly made and well finished over rim; dark grey, brown inside surface, dark grey outside less well finished. Fabric 1. Weight 54g.

33 Context 256. A bowl form with everted rim, as Bigberry fig 10, 11; fig 11, 75–6, diam: 170mm. Very dark grey, inside surface less rough than outside. Fabric 2. Weight 28g.

34 Context 223 and 234. A flat-topped storage jar rim, as Bigberry fig 10, no 6; fig 12, no 93, also flint-gritted. Fairly dark grey all over, worn to some red on rim, tooled grey surfaces, coarse but originally well finished. Diam: >320mm. Fabric 35. Weight 110g.

35 Context 250. A jar with small slightly everted rim, diam: 260mm. Form similar to Bigberry fig 11, no 58, etc. Black with dark grey surfaces, well tooled inside, wiped and not as well finished outside. Fabric 1. Weight 60g.

36 Context 256. A flat jar base. Grey-brown, upper side of base grey-brown, underneath and outside dark grey, interior wall sooted. Irregular diam: 90–120mm. Fabric 35. Weight 32g.

37 Context 250. An omphalos base, presumably from a small rounded form as at Hawkinge (nos 62–3). Diam: *c* 250mm; brown-grey with grey surfaces, worn and battered. Fabric 21. Weight 4g.

38 Context 122. A foot-ring, diam: 84mm large, large, bulky and irregularly shaped. Thick dark grey, upper surface missing, other surfaces heavily tooled dark grey and brown, compacted to a shiny finished but cracked. Fabric 1. Weight 170g.

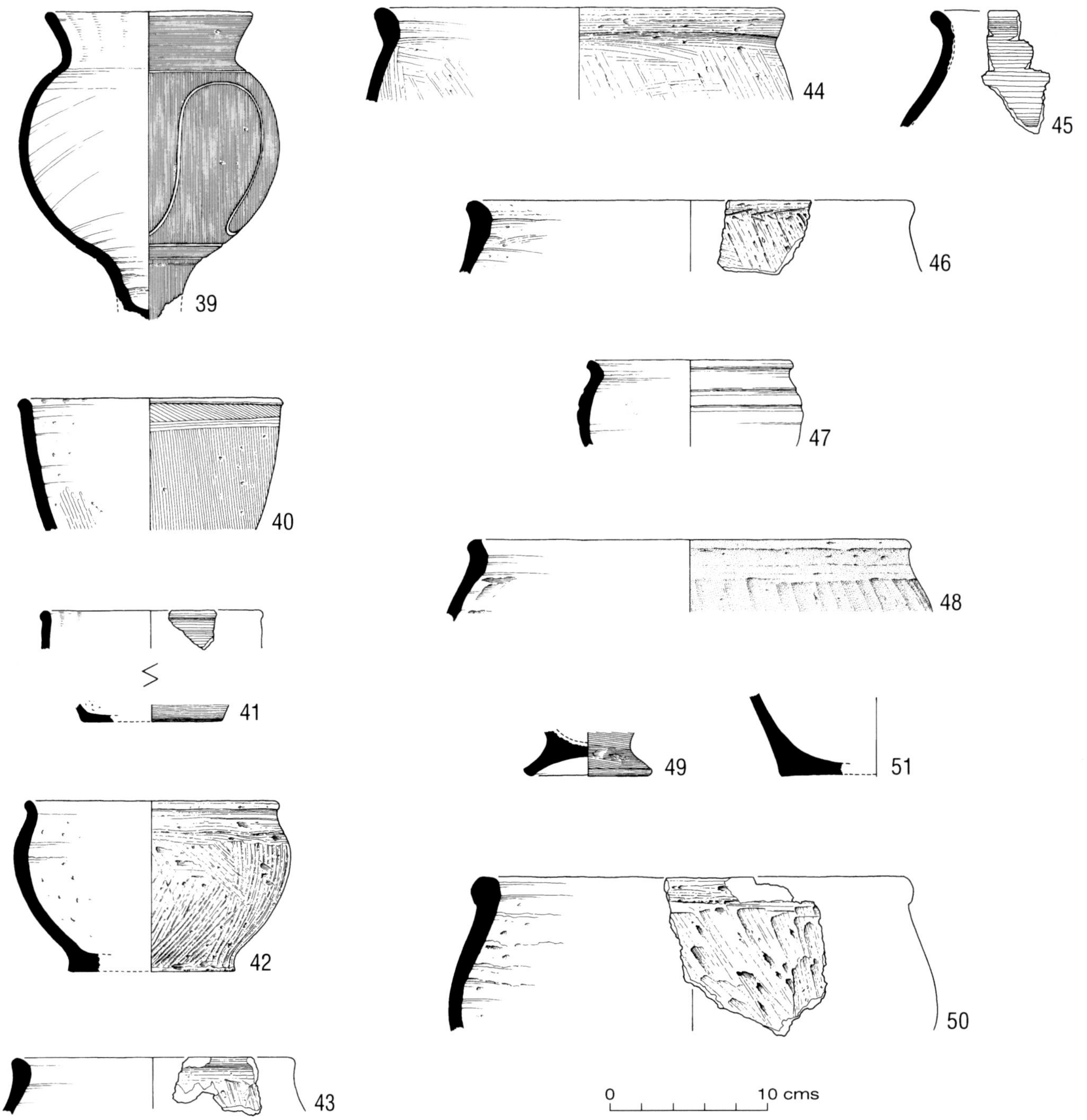

Fig 85. Church Whitfield: late Iron Age pottery from the site (Nos 39–51). Scale 1:4.

The enclosure ditch: first recut, F252 (contexts 249, 255, 260 and 263)

39 Contexts 255 and 234. A small pedestal urn with curvilinear decoration on the body, between grooves at shoulder and above the pedestal. The profile is almost complete, but the vessel is very fragile, much is missing and only about a quarter of the rim circuit is present (diam: 120mm). Grey-brown core, some red below patchy dark grey-brown surfaces, outside now worn and flaking but has a good deal of surviving burnish making a dark grey finish. The decoration is shallow tooling, not incised. As such it is reminiscent of, but simpler than, the curvilinear decoration on the vessels from Margate and Birchington (Macpherson-Grant 1991, 44), which are mid to late Iron Age; cf also the varied decoration on late Iron Age vessels in East Sussex (Elsdon 1975, figs 11–12). Fabric 1. Weight 340g.

40 Contexts 260, 3 and 258. A saucepan form, diam: 170mm. Dark grey, smooth inside, vertical tooling outside. A neat plain vessel, cf Hawkinge rims 5, 51, 57, 96, and Dover Spine Main (Macpherson-Grant 1997; 2002). Fabric 13. Weight 216g.

41 Context 255 and 254. A probable saucepan form. Dark grey, smooth outside and under base; rim diam: *c* 100mm, base diam: not quite 90mm. Fabric 24. Weight 21g.

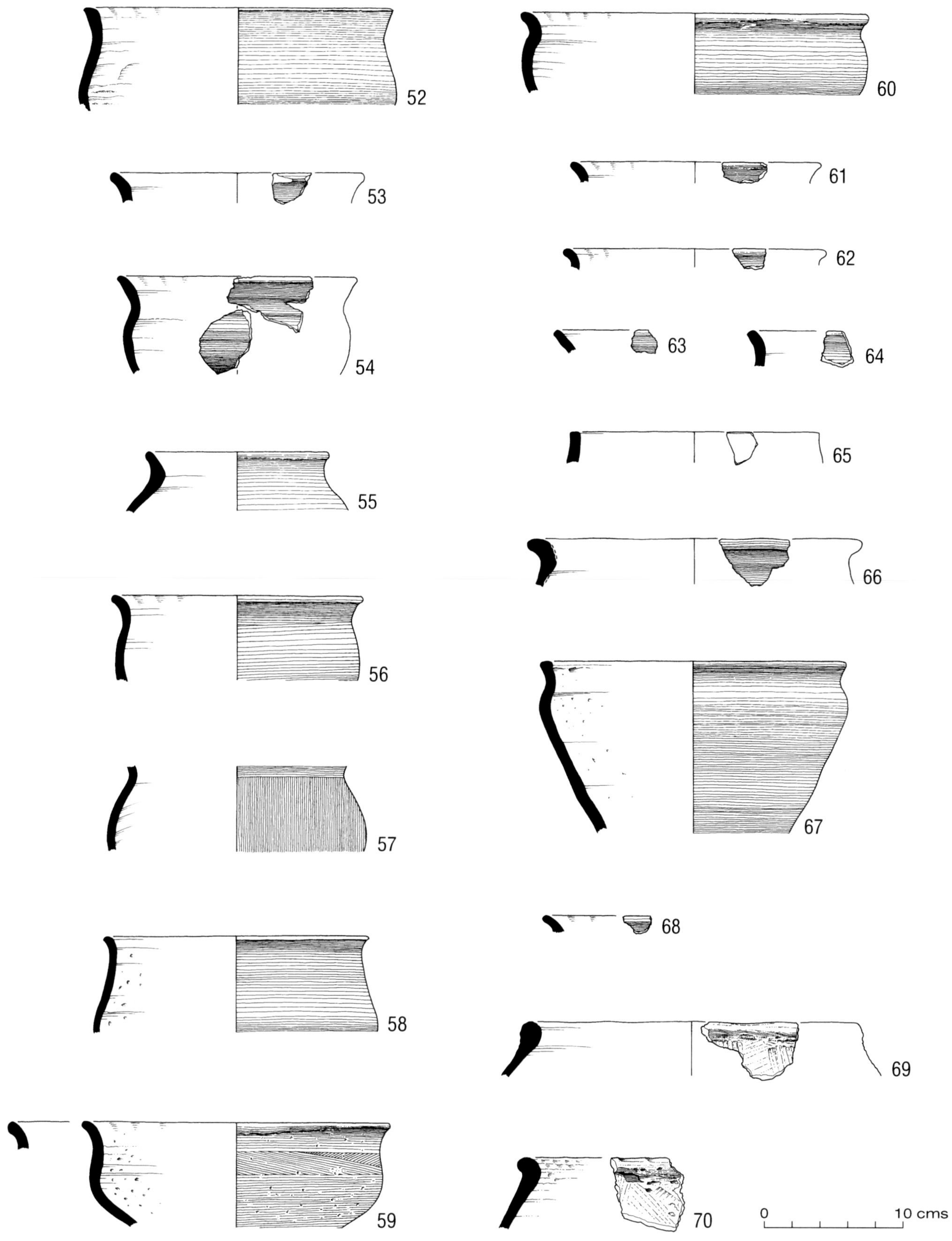

Fig 86. Church Whitfield: late Iron Age pottery from the site (Nos 52–70). Scale 1:4.

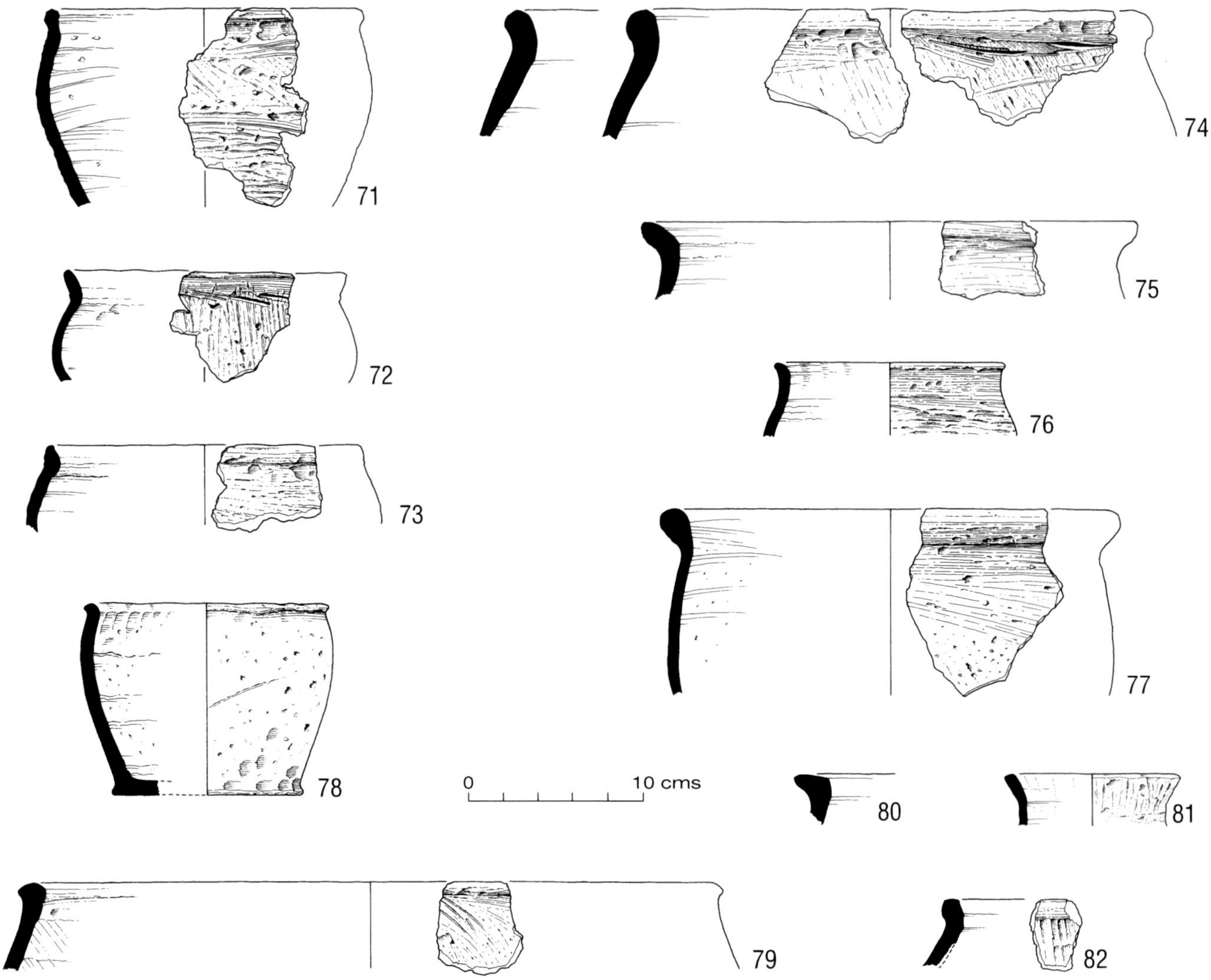

Fig 87. Church Whitfield: late Iron Age pottery from the site (Nos 71–82). Scale 1:4.

42 Contexts 260 and 254. A small closed round form with short upright rim, cf Hawkinge rim 55 (in greensand, but also combed). Dark grey-brown inside tooled dark grey worn to brown, outside partly dark grey-black, lower half red-brown, rough faint vertical combing. Rim *c*110mm, base 60–70mm. Fabric 6. Weight 250g.

43 Context 255. Upright form, three joining sherds and two others, diam: 120mm or a fraction more. Grey, smooth grey inside with dark grey over rim, dark grey outside, almost vertical shallow incised lines. Fabric 2. Weight 26g.

44 Context 260. A thick upright rim, as Bigberry fig 10, nos 9, 88, diam: 270–280mm, dark grey, smooth inside, sooted outside. Fabric 1.

45 Contexts 260 and 258. An upright rim above curving shoulder; cf Hawkinge rim 68 in a similar fabric, diam: *c* 180mm. Soft brown-grey, brown below grey surfaces, tooled, inside largely worn off. Fabric 13. Weight 72g.

46 Context 255. A bead rim, cf Bigberry fig 12, no 82. Diam: 320mm or a little more. Dark grey, smooth dark grey inside, red-brown outside wiped and dragged. Fabric 1. Weight 69g.

47 Context 255. Form D2–4, wide bowl with rippled neck, diam: 130mm. Dark grey-brown with smooth inside and tooled dark grey outside, not the best finish and careless shaping, irregular grooves, although inside curves evenly. Tooling extends over rim. Fabric 11. Weight 43g.

48 Context 260. A jar with slightly everted rim, as Bigberry fig 11, no 64 and fig 12, no 84 (both in grog), diam: irregular but *c* 230mm. Grey-brown, lumpy inside, smoothed over outside but irregular shaping. Fabric 8. Weight 44g.

49 Context 255. An irregular foot-ring, diam: 80mm. Grey-brown, tooled all over surfaces, rough outside where it is darker grey-brown. Fabric 26. Weight 87g (255).

50 Context 260. A large jar with bead rim, cf Hawkinge rim 46, diam: irregular and at least 320mm. Dark grey, rougher inside, some wiping outside. Fabric 10. Weight 150g.

51 Context 255. A flat jar base, crumbling; diam: just under 100mm. Grey, horizontal wiping inside, fairly smooth; rusticated outside, wiped downwards with drag marks. Fabric 1. Weight 360g.

The enclosure ditch: third recut, F246, F247, F248 and F372 (contexts 3, 200, 216, 234, 239, 254, 258, 311 and 375)

52 Contexts 234 and 258. A wide bowl, as Bigberry fig 10, nos 8, 11 (flint-gritted), diam: *c* 220mm. Brown and grey core, heavily tooled and burnished surfaces, slightly better finished on outside; compacted to shiny finish on inside. Fabric 2. Weight 70g.

53 Context 311. A scrap of an everted rim, diam: 110mm. Dense fabric, dark grey with brown surfaces, smooth. Fabric 30. Weight 5g.

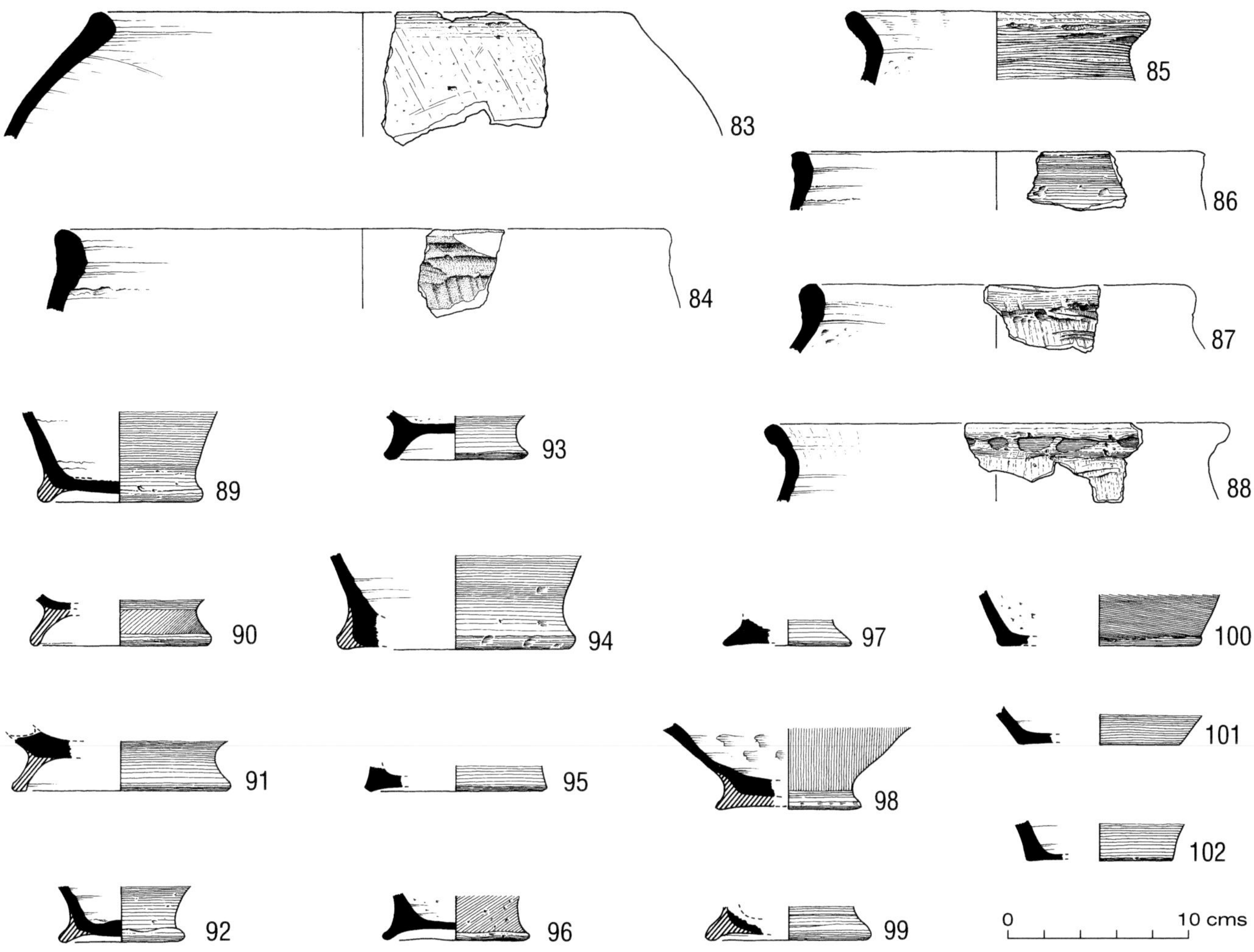

Fig 88. Church Whitfield: late Iron Age pottery from the site (Nos 83–102). Scale 1:4.

54 Context 3. A probable everted rim foot-ring bowl, diam: 150mm. Brown-grey, dark grey surfaces, smooth, burnished outside. Fabric 2. Weight 30g.

55 Context 258. An everted rim, as Bigberry fig 10, no 14, fig 11, no 61, etc (also in flint), diam: up to *c* 160mm. Grey with dark grey-brown inside, smooth but no burnish; outside dark grey, tooled and some burnish, rather more irregular shaping. Fabric 2. Weight 25g.

56 Context 311. Brittle grey core, dark grey surfaces, quite a thick vessel, tooled outside with some brown patches. Fabric 1. Weight 30g.

57 Context 234. A rim of thin, fine fabric but apparently not quite the best as at Hawkinge, although now worn and battered. Diameter unknown. Grey-brown, outside finely tooled. Fabric 9. Weight 25g.

58 Context 200. A rim, as Hawkinge rim 68, and in same fabric. Grey-brown, rather darker surfaces, smooth, and smoother on outside. Fabric 26. Weight 55g.

59 Context 234. A wide bowl, diam: *c* 220mm. Grey-brown throughout, once tooled, smooth but burnished only in patches. Fabric 13. Weight 80g.

60 Context 234. An upright bowl, cf Bigberry fig 10, no 19, etc, and Hawkinge rim 42, diam: 230mm. Dark grey, inside well tooled, outside brown, with dark grey patches, well tooled; horizontal tooling down to girth. Fabric 1. Weight 78g.

61 Context 234. An everted rim, diam: 170mm. Brown, dark grey tooled surfaces, crumbling and flaking. Fabric 2. Weight 57g.

62 Context 234. A scrap from an everted rim, diam: 160mm. Grey, darker grey outside, smooth, no burnish. Fabric 26. Weight 70g.

63 Context 3. A scrap from a rim of unknown diam:. Dark grey, smooth surfaces, burnish outside. Fabric 30. Weight 3g.

64 Context 234. A scrap of an everted rim, diam: unknown. Grey with slightly darker smooth inside. Fabric 26. Weight 7g.

65 Context 234. A scrap of an upright rim, diam: *c* 130mm. Grey, tooled smooth outside. Fabric 13. Weight 29g.

66 Context 258. A storage jar, similar to forms found in flint at Bigberry and Hawkinge. Darkish grey, worn inside rim, otherwise tooled fairly smooth. Fabric 1. Weight 28g.

67 Context 234. A rim, as Bigberry fig 12, no 79 (flint), with an irregular diam: *c* 160mm. Dark grey, mostly brown smooth inside, tooled dark grey inside rim, robust tooling all over dark grey/brown outside; irregular shaping. Fabric 2. Weight 239g.

68 Context 311. A scrap of an everted rim, diam: 120mm. Grey-brown with dark grey tooled outside. Fabric 1. Weight 3g.

69 Context 254. A rim similar to several from Hawkinge, diam: irregular, *c* 270mm. Very dark grey; inside brown; smooth inside, lumpy outside. Fabric 1. Weight 45g.

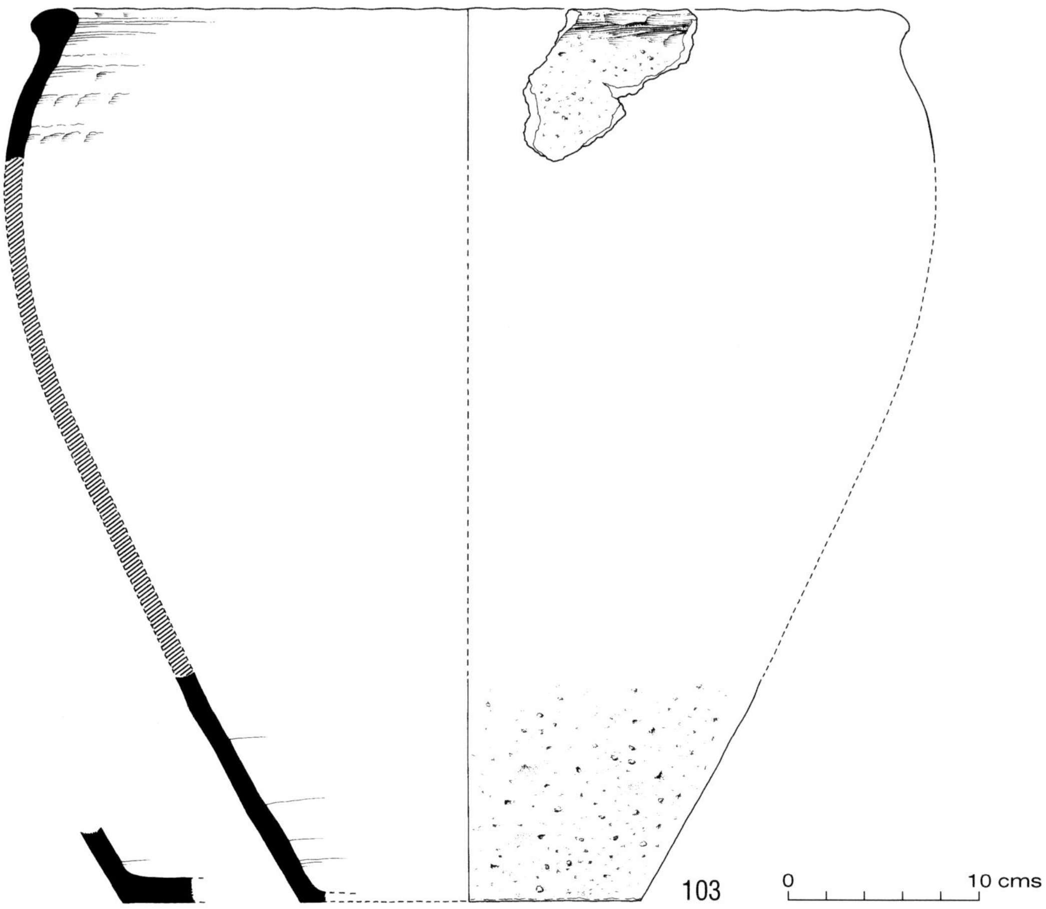

Fig 89. Church Whitfield: late Iron Age pottery from the site (No 103). Scale 1:4.

70 Context 254. Similar to rim 42, irregular diam: *c* 200mm. Dark grey, friable, slightly less dark outside, rim formed with some sort of tool which slipped leaving a gouge mark on rim and running down the neck. Fabric 1. Weight 43g.

71 Contexts 3 and 234. A rim similar to Bigberry fig 12, no 79, and from Hawkinge, diam: *c* 240mm.; base 80mm. Roughly shaped, dark grey, slightly less dark outside and brown patches near base. Fabric 1. Weight 170g.

72 Context 3.A rim similar to Bigberry fig 10, nos 19, etc; 81 (in a sandy fabric); Hawkinge rims 43–5, similar form but finer fabric, diam: 130mm. Grey-brown, some red-brown at rim, grey inside, dark grey outside; irregular shaping, outside rusticated on lower half; shallow vertical tooled/incised decoration on neck, done with a tool. Fabric 2. Weight 100g.

73 Context 3. A jar with lid-seated rim, diam: 160mm. Very dark grey, knife-shaped and dragged outside, tooled inside. Fabric 1. Weight 30g.

74 Context 311. A heavy rim, diam: *c* 290mm, on thin walls. It is crumbling and partly crushed. Red-brown unstable fabric, underfired; dark grey surfaces, very worn inside, fairly smooth; outside rim roughly shaped, tooled below; lumpy. Fabric 36. Weight 230g.

75 Context 3 and 311. A large everted rim, diam: 280mm. Grey, darker grey surfaces, soot on inside surface of one rim sherd. Fabric 1. Weight 87g.

76 Context 254. A rim, as Bigberry fig 10, nos 14, 38, fig 11, no 60 (flint), diam: just over 120mm. Brown, dark grey surfaces, smoothed surfaces, horizontal wipe and drag marks below neck outside. Fabric 2. Weight 25g.

77 Context 234. A rim, as Hawkinge rim 46, diam: 260mm. Thin bodied, thick rim, quite neatly made, grey with dark grey surfaces, smooth inside, wiped outside with drag marks; neck smoothed out. Fabric 1. Weight 137g.

78 Context 3. A bead-rim jar, similar to 'saucepan' forms at Hawkinge in Fabric 26, diam: 130mm. The base is irregular but a little smaller. Dark grey, smoothed but irregular inside; outside mostly red-brown with dark grey patches, fairly smooth. Fabric 5. Weight 270g.

79 Context 3. An inturned bead rim, similar to scraps in flint fabrics at Hawkinge. One sherd, diam: *c* 280mm; dark grey, patchy grey-brown surfaces, roughly finished. Fabric 1. Weight 34g.

80 Context 311. A flattened rim as Bigberry fig 11, no 63; Hawkinge rim 18, in grog. One sherd, crumbling. Diam: irregular, *c* 220mm. Grey, dark grey surfaces. Fabric 1. Weight 27g.

81 Context 3. A small everted sherd, diam: *c* 100mm. Grey, brown-red surfaces, redder outside, irregular shaping; smooth. Fabric 2. Weight 9g.

82 Context 254. A slightly everted rim, of unknown diameter. Dark grey-brown, slightly browner inside and dark grey outside. Fabric 8. Weight 18g.

83 Context 311. A large solid plain closed rim, as several in flint fabrics at Hawkinge, but larger, diam: *c.* 240mm. Grey-brown, fairly smooth grey-brown surfaces, sooted outside on body except over most of rim. Fabric 35. Weight 126g.

84 Context 234. A slightly everted rim, diam: *c* 220mm. Grey-red with dark grey inside, grey outside rim and red-brown below, wipe marks. Fabric 9. Weight 38g.

85 Context 234. An everted rim jar, diam: irregular, *c* 160mm. Dark grey, more or less smooth inside, shallow combing all over outside, horizontal on neck, more or less vertical on body. Fabric 1. Weight 174g.

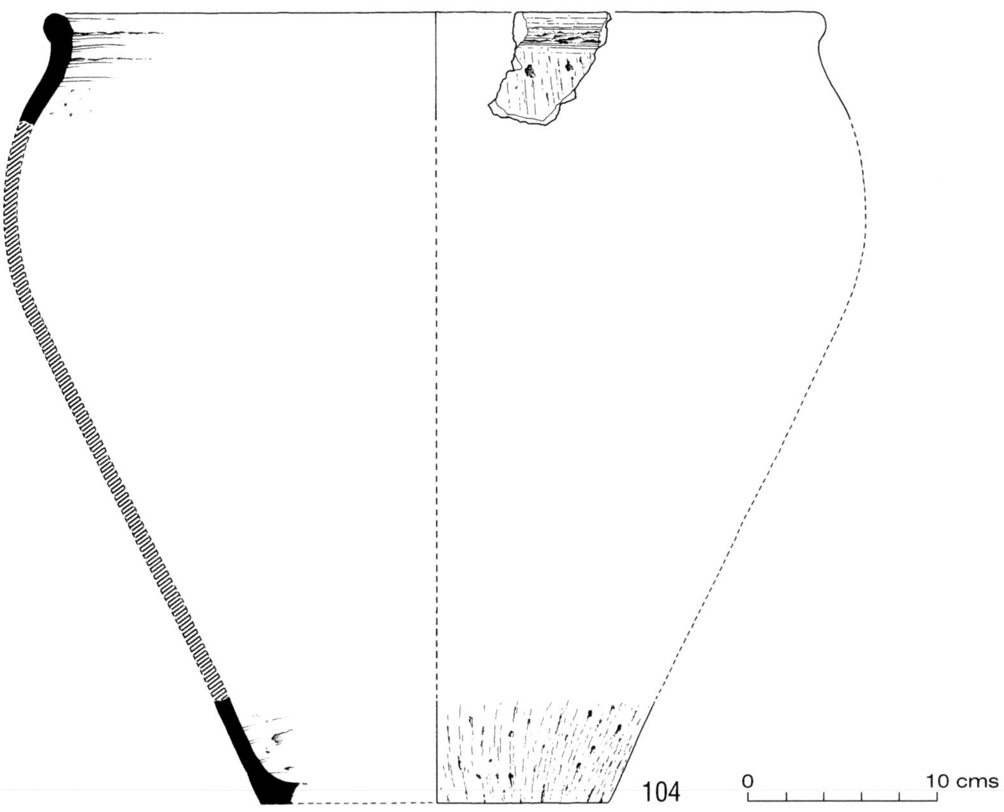

Fig 90. Church Whitfield: late Iron Age pottery from the site (No 104). Scale 1:4.

86 Context 3. A bead rim, diam: 140mm. Dark brown, dark grey surfaces, tooled, darker and smoother outside and on rim. Fabric 36. Weight 24g.

87 Context 234. A rim of diam: 230mm. Dark grey, lumpy surfaces, slightly better finished on inside. Fabric 39. Weight 51g.

88 Context 216. A flaring rim, diam: 250mm. The wall is quite thin, grey with dark grey surfaces, smooth inside, rusticated outside. Fabric 35. Weight 50g.

89 Context 3. A jar with slight bead at base, diam: 95mm. Thick and coarse; grey-brown with grey surfaces, fairly dark, smooth but not burnished. Fabric 27. Weight 160g.

90 Context 234. A foot-ring, diam: 100mm. but slightly irregular. Grey-brown, well finished and burnished surfaces including underside. Body sherd less dark, possibly only the foot being dark grey-brown. Fabric 29. Weight 20g.

91 Context 258. A pedestal, angular in form, diam: 110mm. Quite neat; grey-brown, not dark, heavily tooled surfaces, very dark grey underneath, patchy dark brown-grey outside, smooth and shiny; slightly worn foot. Fabric 2. Weight 60g.

92 Context 258. A foot-ring, diam: 70mm. Grey-brown, darkish grey surfaces, smoothed mostly underneath. Fabric 2. Weight 32g.

93 Context 234. A foot-ring, diam: 90mm. Dark grey, very smooth surfaces, neatly finished. Fabric 2. Weight 35g.

94 Context 200. A large foot-ring, diam: *c* 120mm. Grey with patchy grey inside, smoothed but still gritty, outside and underside dark grey tooled. Fabric 19. Weight 42g.

95 Context 234. A foot-ring scrap, diam: just over 80mm. Darkish grey-brown, smoothed surfaces. Fabric 2. Weight 10g.

96 Context 3. A foot-ring, diam: *c* 80mm. Grey-brown, inside well tooled and compacted, underside only compacted in part, patchy dark grey-strong brown surface outside and underneath. Fabric 26. Weight 38g.

97 Context 200. A foot-ring, diam: *c* 50mm, or slightly larger. Softish grey-brown, grey underside, brown outside. Fabric 21. Weight 13g.

98 Context 234. A foot-ring bowl, diam: 150–160mm. Stubby foot, thick, quite irregular shaping, very dark grey with heavily tooled and burnished surfaces, some brown inside. Fabric 2. Weight 170g.

99 Context 258. A foot-ring, diam: 90mm. Brown-grey, tooled and compacted surfaces, irregular. Strong patchy colours, mostly brown outside and dark grey underneath. Fabric 2. Weight 16g.

100 Context 3. A thin flat base; diam: 120mm. Grey-brown, dark grey tooled and burnished outside; not tooled inside. Fabric 26. Weight 25g.

101 Context 258. A flat base, diam: 110mm. Grey with some pink below grey surfaces, tooled smooth outside and underneath; shiny. Fabric 26. Weight 18g.

102 Context 234. A small sherd from flat base, diam: just over 80mm. Grey, smooth grey surfaces. Fabric 27. Weight 15g.

103 Contexts 3 and 234. A flat-topped rim and plain base from a storage jar, as Bigberry fig 12, no 87 (flint), and Hawkinge rims 90, 91 (sandy). Grey-brown, inside grey-brown, outside red at rim shading to dark grey on body, surfaces compacted with tooling and smooth apart from the flint grits. Quite hard. Rim diam: at least 320mm. and base *c* 180mm. Fabric 10. Weight 400g.

104 Context 3. Rim with diam: of 300mm; grey-brown, grey-brown inside with pale brown smooth inside to rim; outside red-brown except rim bead, which is sooty; drag marks. Two base sherds, possibly from the same vessel; diam: 170mm, outside more grey but with red-brown patches. Fabric 1. Weight 40g + 64g.

105 Context 258. A flat-base jar, diam: 100mm. Black with dark grey surfaces, tooled to compacted finish on both surfaces, dark brown on much of outside lower half. Fabric 1. Weight 140g.

106 Context 234. A flat base, diam: 100–110mm. Fairly pale grey, tooled smooth outside. Fabric 13. Weight 12g.

107 Context 258. A thick flat jar base, large, diam: 130mm. Dark

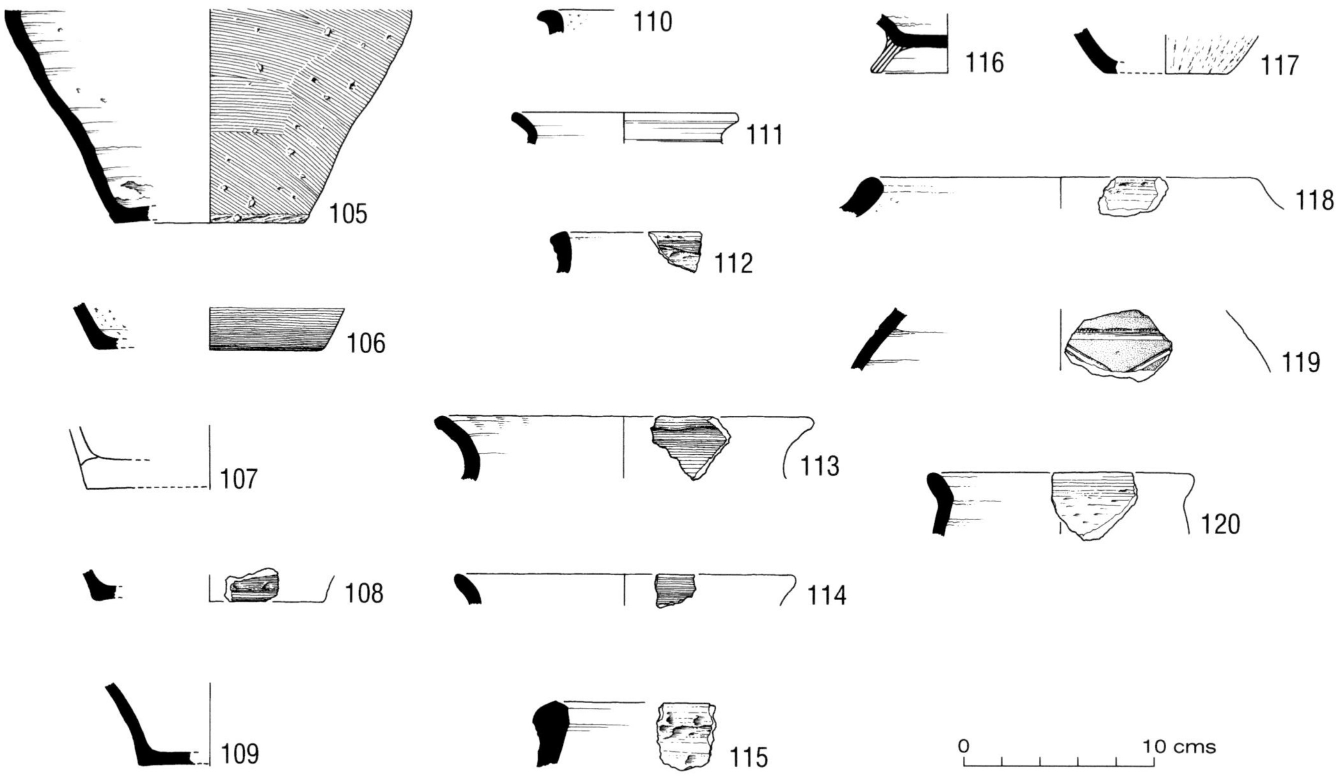

Fig 91. Church Whitfield: late Iron Age pottery from the site (Nos 105–120). Scale 1:4.

grey, thin wall, slightly lumpy surfaces; smooth underside. Fabric 35. Weight 44g.

108 Context 258. A scrap, diam: *c* 100mm. Very dark grey, more or less smoothed. Fabric 2. Weight 6g.

109 Context 234. A thin flat jar base, diam: 80mm. Grey-brown, grey surfaces, more or less smooth inside and roughened outside. Fabric 1. Weight 95g.

110 Context 3. A scrap of an everted rim, of unknown diameter. Grey with dark grey surfaces. Fabric 11. Weight 3g.

111 Context 3. An everted rim, diam: 110mm, and two larger curved body sherds, joining into what may be the lower part of a pedestal urn. Very good fabric but soft and fragile. Dark grey fine core, very smooth red-brown outside, dark grey inside, tooled. Fabric 16. Weight 33g.

112 Context 239. One scrap from a rim, diam: *c* 130mm; brown-grey, brown-red smooth inside, patchy dark grey-brown outside, roughly modelled. Fabric 2. Weight 5g.

Other features, apparently contemporary with the enclosure ditch

Upper fill of Pit 219 (context 218)

113 One sherd from an everted rim, diam: 120mm, not large; fairly crudely shaped, grey-brown, tooled and burnished dark grey inside and less dark outside. Fabric 19. Weight 20g.

Fill of Anglo-Saxon SFB, Structure VI, context 202/231

114 A scrap from a rim, diam: *c* 140mm; brown core, dark grey surfaces, tooled smooth outside. Fabric 27. Weight 5g.

115 One small sherd, thick rim, grey, smooth inside, patchy dark grey outside, roughly shaped. Diam: *c* 180mm. Fabric 2. Weight 17g.

116 A foot-ring, as Hawkinge bases 12 and 13. Six joining sherds, much of circuit, plus three extra scraps. Diam: 81mm. Grey-brown, dark grey inside base, grey on inside walls; tooled inside base but not much above; outside smoother grey, fairly dark; darker and not so well finished under base. Fabric 2. Weight 103g.

117 One sherd from flat base, diam: 60mm, very dark grey, rough surfaces. Fabric 1. Weight 9g.

118 One scrap from a rim, diam: *c* 120mm – irregular; dark grey, brown-grey inside, dark grey outside, worn; rough. Fabric 10. Weight 17g.

119 A sherd with row of rouletted dots, and faint curvilinear grooves; cf Bigberry fig 10, no 7 (flint). Buff-grey, pink below grey-brown surfaces, worn edges. Fabric 28. Weight 25g.

Fill of post-medieval gully, F895/F378, context 894

120 One sherd from an everted rim, diam: irregular but *c* 130mm. Fairly thick, grey-brown, slightly worn grey-brown inside, dark grey rather roughened outside. Similar to Bigberry fig 10, no 9 and Hawkinge rim 28, both in grog temper. 'Belgic' fabric 16. Weight 16g.

Anglo-Saxon pottery (Fig 92; Table 44)
Mark Davey

The four Anglo-Saxon SFBs (Structures III, VI, VII and VIII) and one of the wall-post buildings (Structure I) produced a combined total of 109 sherds (878g, see Table 44). The pottery from the SFBs proved to be almost exclusively of the same type, dating, most probably, from the sixth to seventh century AD and consisting of simple hand-made jars or cooking pots (Fig 92).

Fabrics

Pottery fabric codes are those devised by Canterbury Archaeological Trust (Macpherson-Grant 1995). All but two of the 109 sherds from the building assemblages are of early to mid Saxon organic-tempered ware (Fabric EMS4). This tradition, also known as grass-, chaff- or vegetable-tempered ware, is widespread across southern England, and in the south-east of the country is considered to be typical of the sixth and seventh centuries. The general characteristics of this fabric include the burnt-out remains of organic material added to the clay prior to firing, these remains taking the form of voids, burnt fragments or smudges. Sherds often have a burnt-out 'corky' appearance. The organic content can vary from profuse, giving the sherd a laminated appearance, through to moderate or sparse.

The organic-tempered material from Church Whitfield was divided into two broad groups, namely sparse-tempered and profuse-tempered, the main criteria for this division being degree of lamination, the siltiness of the fabric and the amount of organic-temper present. As a result of this division, sixty-eight sherds (63 per cent by sherd count), could be described as sparse-tempered and forty sherds (37 per cent) abundant. The actual fabric is a soft, sand-free very fine silty matrix with a few inclusions of red iron oxide. The sherds display minimal evidence for burnishing and the overall impression is that the assemblage is primarily reduced, (ie grey or black in colour), with sixty-five sherds, (60 per cent by sherd count), of the assemblage being totally reduced and only ten sherds, (9 per cent), having an oxidised (orange) exterior; of the remaining sherds, seven, (7 per cent), had either a partially oxidised or mottled exterior, and twenty-six sherds, (24 per cent), had a chocolate-brown exterior. This colour variation is to be expected from pottery fired in either a clamp or bonfire kiln. Surface treatment is restricted solely to the profuse-tempered sherds with irregular and superficial wiping to the sherd exteriors.

The only other Anglo-Saxon pottery type, which might overlap in date with the organic-tempered ware, is a single, quite fresh body sherd of early – mid Saxon coarse sandy ware, (EMS1A), from the upper filling of SFB Structure III (context 21). This sherd is reduced, and has a sandy matrix with rounded quartz, and equates broadly with the fabric from Canterbury, although it is not necessarily a Canterbury product. Its date is likely to fall within the period *c* AD 450–650. Unlike the organic-tempered wares, this piece is less likely to have been produced in the immediate vicinity. In addition, a probably late Saxon, non-local profuse shell-filled sherd came from the filling of SFB Structure VI, but this is likely to be intrusive (see below).

Vessel forms

The main vessel uses would have been for storage, cooking and food consumption, the sherds recovered suggesting a range of hand-made, simply shaped, locally produced domestic wares such as jars and cooking pots with 'flattened rounded' bases and everted or simple rims (Fig 92). Several sherds have varying degrees of external sooting, indicating their use as cooking pots, with some evidence of internal sooting. Sherds with no evidence of sooting indicate storage jars; there is no evidence for dishes or bowls. Using wall thickness as an indicator of vessel type, only one organic-tempered sherd was over the 5–10mm range; this sherd probably represents a storage jar or water carrier. With the exception of No 1 none of the material is decorated, the latter having an angular profile with pinch-moulding on the upper body panel; this is an unusual regional trait, although it is sufficiently bold to suggest deliberate, if poorly-executed, decoration.

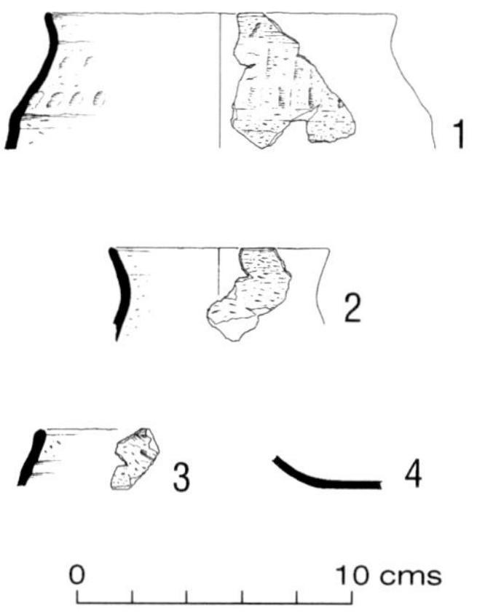

Fig 92. Church Whitfield: Anglo-Saxon pottery from the site. (Nos 1–4). Scale 1:4.

	Fabric		
	Organic ware EMS4	Sandy ware EMS1A	Shelly ware LS4
Structure I	1		
Structure III	46	1	
Structure VI	13		1
Structure VII	1		
Structure VIII	46		
Pit F215	1		
Pit F904	2		
Enclosure ditch (intrusive)	1		
Totals	111	1	1

Table 44. Church Whitfield: distribution of Anglo-Saxon pottery.

Source

Organic-tempered ware is generally considered to have been produced from locally available materials very close to its place of use. The production characteristics of the present assemblage such as firing, sherd hardness, surface treatment, wall thickness and a limited range of forms results in an assemblage within a narrow range of parameters; this being the case, it is quite probable that the Church Whitfield organic-tempered wares, as at Mucking, were produced by each household for their own use (Hamerow 1993, 56).

Context

With regard to assemblages from the buildings, Structure III produced the largest (forty-seven sherds or 43 per cent by sherd count), Structure VIII the second largest (forty-six sherds, 42 per cent), Structure VI the third (fourteen sherds, 13 per cent) and both Structures I and VII the least (one sherd from each, 1 per cent). In addition, odd Anglo-Saxon sherds came from the filling of pit F215; unexcavated feature F904 (probably another SFB) and the upper filling (context 258) of the late Iron Age enclosure ditch (Table 44).

Examination of the layers found within each SFB indicates that Structure III has evidence for three stages of backfilling, with the sherds from the upper fill (context 21) being quite fresh and probably representing backfill/natural exposure, suggesting abandonment; similarly, the sherds from the middle fill (context 139) are fairly fresh, the similarity of the sherds indicating that both layers were probably formed within a relatively short time span of each other. In contrast, the sherds from the lower fill (context 140) are heavily weathered, indicating a primary fill/occupation deposit, the degree of sherd wear being due to normal domestic activity.

Structure VI has one main fill (context 202/231). The sherds contained in it are mostly fresh, indicating a primary/occupation deposit. The single fill of Structure VII (context 379) contains quite a fresh sherd, again indicating a primary fill/natural backfill.

Structure VIII contains a single fill (context 1000) which again is contemporary and represents a primary deposit. The weathering on a few of the sherds could be post-loss, whilst the smaller sherds may represent longer-term evidence for occupation. The fact that the sherds from this layer are, on the whole, bigger and fresher, may suggest either contemporary breakage and loss, or that the building and fill were used for the disposal of contemporary breakages.

Only five Anglo-Saxon sherds were recovered from post-holes within structures; one from the filling of F67 (context 66) in hall Structure I, three very small, worn and abraded sherds from F143 (context 141) in SFB Structure III and one fresh sherd from F238 (context 237) of Structure VI.

Dating and discussion of the Anglo-Saxon pottery

Regional

The general dating evidence for organic-tempered wares sees the tradition possibly beginning in the sixth century, although it does occur at, for example, Mucking from the fifth century, before peaking in the seventh. It slowly dies out, being replaced by mineral-tempered fabrics sometime in the eighth century, evidence from London indicating a late ninth- to early eleventh-century date for its demise (Vince 1991, 48).

Local

The Marlowe excavations in Canterbury (Blockley *et al* 1995) have provided the main local dating evidence for organic-tempered and many other Anglo-Saxon wares; thus, at Canterbury, EMS4 is dated to between *c* AD 550–750, before being replaced by the later organic-tempered fabric MLS1, the excavations suggesting that this is generally later in the range than earlier (Macpherson-Grant 1995, 834). The Marlowe I and IV sequences show organic-tempered pottery reaching a peak during the mid to later seventh century, with the Marlowe I sequence being consistent with that throughout southern England. The ceramic evidence from Church Whitfield indicates a period of occupation during the later sixth and seventh centuries AD. The fact that the EMS4 sherds from Whitfield are sand-free suggests that they do not belong to the later part of the *c* AD 550–725 date range.

Other evidence has come from Minster, Sheppey (Pratt 1999), whilst a few sherds of EMS4 have been recovered from Minnis Bay, Chestfield and Great Mongeham (Parfitt and Brugmann 1997, 9). Organic-tempered ware is also recorded at Dover (Parfitt 1995d; Philp 2003, 90–114). The main significance attached to the Church Whitfield site is that at the time of excavation the assemblage was one of only a very few fairly large domestic Anglo-Saxon pottery assemblages from rural east Kent to have been recorded, Eurotunnel sites at Folkestone and the sites from Sheppey (in archives held at the Canterbury Archaeological Trust), being the others. The Sheppey sites are particularly interesting, as they have produced sherds of EMS4 with Ipswich Ware, suggesting that EMS4 must overlap in some parts of Kent with the currency of Ipswich Ware, *c* AD 720–850.

Other pottery from Anglo-Saxon structures

Apart from the prehistoric material, a small quantity of Roman pottery (nineteen sherds, 196g), was recovered from the Anglo-Saxon structures. This ranges in date from 'Belgic' through to late Roman. There are also two sherds of post-Roman pottery (8g). These comprise one sherd of ?late Saxon non-local profuse shell-filled, *c* AD 850–950 and a sherd of medieval Tyler Hill (Canterbury) sandy ware (M1) dating to the thirteenth/fourteenth century. The probably intrusive shell-filled Saxon sherd came from SFB Structure VI (context 202) and is very worn. Evidence from Canterbury suggests a date of *c* AD 875 into the tenth century. Although the sherd is most probably not from North France/Flanders, similar wares occur at Folkestone, whilst at Dover such wares continue into the early medieval period, this early medieval fabric tending to be oxidised and less profusely shell-tempered (John Cotter, pers comm).

The bone

Human bone

Trevor Anderson†

Deliberate deposition of human bones occurred in two cases; an articulated skeleton in a rather cramped and shallow grave (see above, F146) and a disarticulated cranium in the base of late Iron Age enclosure ditch of Period 3 (context 371). In addition, fragments (142g) of human bone were found in four other deposits assigned to Periods 2 and 3 (Table 45).

The articulated skeleton, F146

The human skeleton found in grave F146 (Fig 53) was extended and supine, without any grave goods. The size and shape of the grave is similar to those discovered at Mill Hill, Deal, which have been dated to the late Iron Age period (Parfitt 1995a). Iron Age inhumations, with the exception of those associated with the 'Arras culture' in Yorkshire (Stead 1991), have rarely been recognised in Britain. In the south-east of England, almost all the 350 burials dating to this period are cremations (Mays and Anderson 1995), although the number of inhumation finds is starting to increase (eg Tothill Street, Minster in Thanet; Bailey 2010)

The skeleton is represented by incomplete long bones and fragmented crania. The hands, feet, ribs and spine have not survived, or, at best, are represented by eroded fragments. The large, robust bones indicate that the remains are male. The only complete long bone, the right femur, provides a stature estimation of 1.801m (5ft 11ins; Trotter and Gleser 1958). The degree of sutural closure suggests that he was *c* 30–40 years old.

The disarticulated cranium from the Period 3 enclosure ditch

The disarticulated cranium found in the base of the Period 3 enclosure ditch (*see* p 105; Figs 56 and 58) was incomplete and had also suffered some *post-mortem* damage (Pl 23), although all but one of the maxillary teeth were available for study. The skull is clearly male; the lack of dental attrition and sharpness of the sutures suggest a young adult, *c* 25–30 years. There was no evidence of bone pathology. Apart from minor deposits of calculus on the right second molar, the dentition was free from disease. Both third molars, the 'wisdom teeth', were congenitally absent.

The cranium had been placed in the bottom of the enclosure ditch with other objects. The lack of cervical vertebrae argues that it does not represent the deposition of a recently beheaded individual. Also, the absence of the mandible indicates that the remains were buried in the ditch as a dry skull, rather than a fleshed individual. Consequently, it does not seem to represent a severed head which had formerly been displayed above ground level. The recovery of a child's hand bone from the soil within the skull might suggest that the cranium was originally buried.

Disarticulated bones are regularly found outside formal cemetery areas on Iron Age settlement sites (Whimster 1981, 182–3). This was certainly the case at Church Whitfield (Table 45). The fact that the present example was incomplete when discovered suggests that it could have been damaged during exhumation or was crushed (accidentally or deliberately?), when the ditch was infilled.

Animal bone

Robin Bendrey

Hand excavation recovered 4,986 fragments of bone weighing 34,324.5g. The majority of the animal bone derived from the late Iron Age (Period 3), in particular the enclosure ditch (Tables 46 and 47). Smaller assemblages were also derived from Periods 1, 2 and 4. Several bulk samples also produced animal bone (Table 61).

Feature	Context	Period	Weight (g)	Notes
Pit F16	15	2	34	Small fragments including the metphysis of a left femur
Pit F16	125	2	6	Fragment of a cranial vault from a sub-adult
Grave F146	147	3	-	Partially decayed skeleton of a *c* 30–40 year old male
Enclosure ditch F4/233	371	3	-	Disarticulated skull of a *c* 25–30 year old male
Enclosure ditch F4/233	371	3	-	Child's hand bone in soil within skull (see above, 371)
Enclosure ditch re-cut F372	3	3	56	Mid-shaft of a left femur, circumference 75.5mm
Enclosure ditch re-cut F246	239	3	46	Incomplete adult frontal bone

Table 45. Church Whitfield: contexts containing fragments of human bone.

	No of fragments (NISP)						Weight (g)						Mean fragment weight (g)					
Period	1	2	3	4	PS	Total	1	2	3	4	PS	Total	1	2	3	4	PS	Total
Cattle		83	473	20	1	577		3270	15349	397	26	19042		39.4	32.5	19.9	26.0	33.0
Sheep/goat †		63	137	15	3	218		261	678	72	18	1029		4.1	4.9	4.8	6.0	4.5
(sheep)		9	15	2		26		55	97	15		167		6.1	6.5	7.5		6.4
(goat)			4			4			20			20			5.0			5.0
Horse		57	114	1		172		1668	4033	18		5719		29.3	35.4	18		33.3
Pig		7	42	16		65		90	418	114		622		12.9	10.0	7.1		9.6
Dog			140	1		141			338	2		340			2.4	2.0		2.4
Red deer	23		1			24	65		14			79	2.8		14.0			3.3
Roe deer				4		4				33.5		33.5			–	8.4		8.4
Cattle–sized		374	2189	84		2647		870	5639	381		6890		2.3	2.6	4.5		2.6
Sheep–sized		61	286	36		383		54.5	222	56		332.5		0.9	0.8	1.6		0.9
Indeterminate		213	496	46		755		62.5	156	26		244.5		0.3	0.3	0.6		0.3
Total	23	867	3897	225	4	5016	65	6331	26964	1114.5	44	34518.5	2.8	7.3	6.9	4.9	11.0	6.9

Table 46. Church Whitfield: distribution of animal bone by site period. PS: ploughsoil from field 9. †: sheep/goat includes specimens identified at species level.

Period	1	2	2	2	2	2	2	2	3	3	3	4	4		
Feature/ Structure	Pit F103	Boundary ditch F10/209 & 205	Pit groups A	B	C	D	Pit F16	Pit F26	Enclosure ditch	Pit F219	Gully F108	SFB Structure III	SFB Structure IV	Ploughsoil Field 9	Total
Cattle		16	5	6 (5)		2	11 (10)	43 (41)	472 (462)	1		10	10	1	577
Sheep		3		5 (4)			4	51 (36)	132 (128)	1		11	4	3	214
Horse		2		16 (11)				39 (1)	113 (105)	1			1		172
Pig		3						4	41	1		16			65
Goat									4						4
Dog									140 (17)			1			141
Red deer	23								1						24
Roe deer												4			4
Cattle–sized		122	12	93	5	12	51	79	2185	3	1	38	46		2647
Sheep–sized		19		2			5	35	283	3		32	4		383
Indeterminate		57					29	127	494	2		35	11		755
Total	23	222	17	122	5	14	100	378	3865	12	1	147	76	4	4986

Table 47. Church Whitfield: distribution of animal bone by feature (NISP). (x): number in brackets is NISP adjusted for articulations (one group of articulating bones equals a count of 1).

The animal bones were identified with the aid of a comparative osteological reference collection, and a number of publications (Bailon 1999; Baxter 1998, 6–11; Eisenmann 1986, 75–6; Eisenmann and Bekouche 1986; Gleed-Owen 1998; Hillson 1986; Lawrence and Brown 1973); and recorded using the diagnostic zones of Dobney and Reilly (1988). Fragments not identified to species were awarded an animal-size category, or were labelled indeterminate. The criteria of Boessneck (1969) and Payne (1985) have been used to differentiate between the bones of sheep and goat (Table 46). Bones identified to sheep/goat are considered within the taxon sheep in the report and Tables 46–61. Cattle, pig and sheep mandibular toothwear data have been recorded following Grant (1982).

Measurements have been taken following von den Driesch (1976), except where indicated. The assemblage is quantified by number of fragments (NISP), minimum number of elements (MNE) and bone weight. MNE is counted as the most frequently occurring zone (Dobney and Reilly 1988) from left and right elements.

Condition of the bone

The animal bone is generally poorly preserved. The material is characterised by surface erosion and root etching, and the bone is often brittle and friable. Surface damage to the bones has reduced the quantity and quality of data available from the assemblage. Direct evidence of butchery, in the form of chop and cut marks, is very limited, largely due to the poor preservation of the material (Table 53). The poor state of preservation is shown by the high proportion (by number) of unidentified fragments, and by their low mean fragment weight (Table 46), and by the high numbers of loose teeth (Tables 49, 50 and 52).

Taxonomic identifications

The following taxa were identified in the hand-recovered bone assemblage: cattle, *Bos* sp domestic; sheep, *Ovis* sp domestic; horse, *Equus caballus* sp domestic; pig, *Sus* sp domestic; goat, *Capra* sp domestic; dog, *Canis* sp domestic; red deer, *Cervus elaphus* L; and roe deer, *Capreolus capreolus* L.

Taxa identified from the bulk samples (Table 61) include: mole, *Talpa europaea* L; field vole, *Microtus agrestis* (L); wood mouse, *Apodemus sylvaticus* (L); common toad, *Bufo bufo* L; and common frog, *Rana temporaria* L. Other bones were identified to: *Apodemus* sp, which may be from yellow-necked mouse, *Apodemus flavicollis* (Melchior) or wood mouse, *A sylvaticus* (L); mouse/vole, *Myomorpha*; toad, *Bufo* spp; frog, *Rana* spp; and frog/toad, *Anura*.

Species and skeletal part representation

Period 1: late Neolithic – Bronze Age

The animal bone from Period 1 (Table 46) consists of a quantity of very fragmented red deer antler from an isolated pit (F103), which may all derive from a single specimen. A radiocarbon date obtained from this material indicates that it is of early Bronze Age date (*see* p 87).

Period 2: early Iron Age

Animal bone from Period 2 came from a range of features including: the boundary ditch, two single pits and four pit groups (Table 49). Cattle are the most common taxon by NISP, followed by sheep (Tables 46 and 54); however, the greater representation of sheep teeth (elements that survive well) by MNE may indicate that sheep were more common (Table 48). Horse is largely represented by articulations, and pig is of only minor importance (Table 47). Table 49 shows the distribution of identified bones from this period.

Cattle is the most commonly identified taxon from the Period 2 boundary ditch, probably reflecting disposal practices and conditions of preservation (Table 49).

Pit group B produced limited bone from pits, F34 and F38, with more material deriving from context 112, a loam

	Cattle			Sheep			Horse			Pig		
Period	2	3	4	2	3	4	2	3	4	2	3	4
Element												
horn core		2		2	1							
mandible	2	13		2	9			6			4	1
dI	–/–	–/–	–/–	–/–	–/–	–/–	–/–	–/–	–/–	–/–	2/–	–/–
I	–/–	2/–	–/–	1/–	–/–	–/–	–/–	2/–	–/–	–/–	3/–	–/–
C	–/–	–/–	–/–	–/–	–/–	–/–	–/–	–/–	–/–	1/–	2/–	1/–
dP2	–/–	–/–	–/–	–/–	–/–	–/–	–/–	–/–	–/–	–/–	–/–	–/–
P2	–/–	–/–	–/–	–/–	–/–	–/–	–/–	–/–	–/–	–/–	–/1	1/–
dP3	–/–	–/–	–/–	–/–	–/–	–/–	–/–	–/–	–/–	–/–	–/–	–/–
P3	–/1	4/1	–/–	–/1	–/1	–/–	–/–	–/–	–/–	–/–	–/1	–/–
dP4	–/–	1/–	–/–	–/–	2/–	–/–	–/–	–/–	–/–	–/–	–/–	–/–
P4	–/1	2/1	1/–	2/2	–/2	1/–	–/–	–/–	–/–	1/–	–/5	–/–
M1	–/–	–/4	–/–	2/1	4/4	–/–	–/–	–/–	–/–	–/–	–/4	–/–
M1/2	1/–	7/–	2/–	–/–	9/–	–/–	–/–	3/–	–/–	1/–	–/–	–/–
M2	1/–	–/4	–/–	2/1	4/5	–/–	–/–	1/–	–/–	–/–	1/5	–/–
M3	1/–	5/1	–/–	1/–	4/2	1/–	–/–	–/–	–/–	–/–	–/2	–/–
cervical vertebra	5	5	1	1				6	1			
thoracic vertebra		2		1								
lumbar vertebra	5	1						1				
sacrum												
rib	2		1									
scapula	2	41	1	2	1			5			4	1
humerus	5	21		2	8	1		2			3	1
radius	5	20	1	4	6	1		2				
ulna	3	9			2	1		1		1	2	
metacarpal	2	16	1	2	2		2	5				5
pelvis	3	11			1	1	1	3		1	1	
femur	6	7	1	2	3			1		1	1	
tibia	6	11	1	6	15	1		3				
astragalus		5					1	2				
calcaneum		7	1				1	2				
metatarsal	4	20	1		9	1	2	8				3
1st phalanx		6				1	4	5			1	1
2nd phalanx		1	1				3					1
3rd phalanx							2					

Notes: Horse incisors are the total of upper and lower incisors divided by two. Counts for pig metapodials and phalanges include lateral specimens.

Table 48. Church Whitifeld: representation of hand-recovered bones and mandibular teeth of cattle, sheep, horse and pig (MNE). Counting of teeth, for example 5/1, signifies loose teeth/teeth in mandibles.

layer sealing the fills of all the pits. Context 112 produced fifteen horse fragments; most probably from the same animal, possibly representing a buried skull. These include six loose upper cheek teeth (left and right teeth from the same animal), five further fragments of horse teeth, three skull fragments and a pelvis (Table 49). A horse occipital fragment was also identified from pit F38.

Cattle bones outnumber those of sheep from pit F16 (Table 49). All the identified bone derived from the final filling (context 15), which included an articulating cattle radius and ulna (an articulating humerus, radius and ulna were recorded during excavation, but there was no humerus in the bags for this context).

Three contexts from pit F26 produced bone, the majority from the upper two-thirds of the pit (context 25). In context 25 sheep bones are the most numerous with forty-seven fragments. Twenty-three were loose teeth, most of which came from articulating toothrows: these derive from five upper toothrows (four right and one left) and two lower toothrows (one left and one right). Thirty-five cattle fragments were present, including a range of cranial and post-cranial elements, and three articulating lumbar vertebrae. All thirty-nine horse bones derived from four articulating lower legs, all from the same animal (Table 49; Fig 49). Cut marks are recorded on the proximal metatarsal, two tarsals, 1st phalanx and 2nd phalanx of the right hind leg, on the calcaneum and astragalus of the left hind leg and the metacarpal of the left fore leg. The cut marks on the tarsals and metapodials probably derive from the disarticulation of the limb extremities from the carcase, and the presence of cut marks on the phalanges is suggestive of skinning. Pig bones include two ulna fragments, one pelvis and one femur.

The presence of whole skeletons, skulls and articulating limbs in Iron Age pits is often interpreted as acts of deliberate deposition (*see* p 171; Bendrey *et al* 2010; Morris 2011; Grant 1984b). The evidence from the Period 2 pits could suggest deliberate depositions, or they could represent primary butchery waste with the heads and lower limbs of horses and sheep discarded at an early stage of processing.

	Boundary ditch				Pit groups					Single pits					
					A	B			D	F16		F26			
Element	Cattle	Horse	Sheep	Pig	Cattle	Cattle	Horse	Sheep	Cattle	Cattle	Sheep	Cattle	Horse	Sheep	Pig
cranium						–	4				1	4		11	
mandible	3					1					2	2		2	
loose teeth	3	2		3		2	11	2				2		24	
hyoid						1									
atlas												1			
axis										1		1		1	
cervical												3			
thoracic														1	
lumbar										2		4			
sacrum															
rib												2			
scapula						1			1			1		2	
humerus					1	1			1			5		2	
radius	1		1		1			1		1		3		3	
ulna										1		2			2
pelvis	2						1			1		3			1
femur	2				1			1		2		5		1	1
tibia	2		2		1			1		3	1	3		2	
astragalus													1		
calcaneum													1		
carpal/tarsal													10		
metacarpal	2												5	2	
metatarsal	1				1							2	6		
1st phalanx													4		
2nd phalanx													3		
3rd phalanx													2		
sesamoid															
Total	16	2	3	3	5	6	16	5	2	11	4	43	39	51	4

Table 49. Church Whitfield: bones identified to species from Period 2 features (NISP).

Period 3: late Iron Age

The bulk of the Period 3 animal bone derived from the enclosure ditch, and a small quantity came from a pit within the enclosure (F219) and from a gully (F108; Table 47).

Cattle bones are the most common recovered from the enclosure ditch, followed by sheep, horse and pig (Table 47). Four fragments of horn core from the same context represent goat. A single red deer calcaneum is also present. A large number of the dog bones (124 fragments) represent a single skeleton from context 271.

Analysis of the skeletal element representation indicates an assemblage greatly affected by taphonomic attrition: the sheep bone assemblage (Fig 94) is dominated by the more robust skeletal elements, such as the tibia, metatarsal and mandible; and mandibles and teeth are well represented in the pig assemblage (Fig 96). The latter pattern is largely influenced by the pigs being culled before adulthood, and so many of the post-cranial elements are unfused, of low density, and therefore unlikely to survive harsh conditions of preservation. The bone assemblages of the smaller animals (sheep and pig) have suffered to a greater extent by taphonomic attrition than the larger animals (cattle and horse). This can be seen in a comparison of the MNE data between the large and small species (Table 48): teeth are better represented in the sheep and pig remains, especially loose sheep teeth, compared to the cattle and horse bones where post-cranial elements are generally better represented. This implies the bones of the small species have undergone a greater degree of fragmentation and destruction. Davis (1997, 4–6) suggests that high teeth-to-bone ratio, especially of sheep and pig-sized animals, partly due to post-mortem loss of bone by gnawing from dogs, appears to characterise rural settlements.

Others factors that would account for this disparity between large and small taxa include the fact that the larger bones of horse and cattle would better survive processes such as post-depositional chemical action, and possibly disposal practices – the larger bones of cattle being cleared from living/working areas within the enclosure and deposited into the ditch, and the smaller bones of sheep being less efficiently cleaned away (due to their small size) and so affected to a greater extent by such factors as weathering.

The dominance of cattle by NISP from this period is largely an artefact of poor preservation and recovery bias. Consideration of the assemblage by MNE goes some way to removing this bias (Table 48). Although cattle post-cranial elements show higher values than the sheep bones they are probably over-represented due to disposal practices and, as stated above, the conditions of preservation and recovery. Consideration of teeth counts, elements less prone to taphonomic destruction than bones, would suggest that there were originally more sheep slaughtered than cattle. In the same respect, as suggested by teeth counts, pigs were more important than horses.

	Cattle	Sheep	Horse	Pig	Dog	Goat	Red deer
cranium	22	4	14	3	7	4	
mandible	58	17	17	15	5		
loose teeth	77	56	18	9	14		
hyoid	1						
atlas			3		1		
axis	4		1		2		
cervical	3		2		5		
thoracic	2				17		
lumbar	1		1		6		
rib					17		
scapula	63	1	6	4	1		
humerus	35	9	2	4	4		
radius	35	8	3		2		
ulna	17	2	2	2	3		
pelvis	25	1	4	1	2		
femur	17	3	3	2	2		
tibia	29	19	4	1	5		
fibula					2		
astragalus	5		2		2		
calcaneum	10		2		1		1
carpal/tarsal	1		3		3		
metacarpal	23	2	7		4		
metatarsal	37	11	14		6		
metapodial	1		1		8		
1st phalanx	6		5		13		
2nd phalanx	1				4		
3rd phalanx				1	1		
Total	473	133	114	42	137	4	1

Table 50. Church Whitfield: bones identified to species from Period 3 contexts (NISP).

Table 51 gives the distribution of the animal bone within the enclosure ditch. The quantities of bone from the different arms of the ditch and from the different fills and recuts varies, but is probably largely linked to the extent of excavation and the removal of the earlier fills by recuts. The proportions of cattle, sheep, horse and pig in the different fills and recuts of the ditch are reasonably consistent through the duration the ditch was open, except for the contents of the upper fill, but this assemblage may be biased by its small size (Fig 99).

Pit F219 (Table 47), within the enclosure, produced bone from two contexts, which includes a cattle ulna, a pig femur, a sheep tooth and a horse tooth.

Gully F108, outside the enclosure, produced a single unidentified cattle-sized fragment.

Period 4: early Anglo-Saxon

Sunken-featured buildings Structures III and VI both produced identifiable animal bone from their fills. The small quantity of bone limits analysis (Table 52). Ranking the taxa in order of importance as represented by NISP gives the order: cattle, pig and sheep. The same order is shown by bone weight. Single bones of horse and dog were also recovered, and four fragments of roe deer.

Pig is the most common taxon from Structure III but is absent from Structure IV. Structure III also produced the only records of roe deer from the site, including two fragments of antler (Table 52), one of which was still attached to the frontal bone.

Other

The ploughsoil from Field 9 (context 230) produced three sheep fragments and one cattle. The medieval cattle skeleton from F897 was not available for study.

Age and sex data

Ageing data is limited (Tables 55–59). Table 55 lists all mandibles with one or more molars that could be placed into the age categories of Halstead (1985) for cattle, Payne (1973) for sheep, and Hambleton (1999) for pigs.

The cattle mandibles indicate animals kept for meat (age stages C and D) and kept into adulthood for secondary products, such as milk, traction and breeding (age stages G and H; Table 55). Table 56 tabulates all toothwear, including loose teeth, and shows that permanent fourth premolars (P_4) outnumber deciduous fourth premolars (dP_4) by four to one for cattle in Period 3. This suggests that there were a higher proportion of adult animals than is represented by the mandibles. There is a suggestion in the cattle post-cranial fusion data (vertebra, distal radius and distal femur) that there is a slightly younger age group represented in Period 2 than Period 3 (Table

	North-west arm				South-west arm		South-east arm			North-east arm		
	lower fill	middle fill	first re-cut	third re-cut	middle fill	upper fill	lower fill	upper fill	third re-cut	lower fill	upper fill	third re-cut
Cattle	11	71	85	151			1	6	94	14	11	28
Sheep	3	15	15	45			1	1	32	3	6	11
Horse	6	14	29	28	1	3		3	16	1	4	8
Pig	1	7	7	9				3	9			5
Goat									4			
Dog		5	1	130					2		1	1
Red deer									1			
Cattle–sized	31	364	500	746			2	24	357	26	33	102
Sheep–sized	4	21	15	203			1	3	16	2	4	14
Indeterminate	8	51	44	190		1		8	116	4	22	50
Total	64	548	696	1502	1	4	5	48	647	50	81	219

Table 51. Church Whitfield: details of animal bone from Period 3 enclosure ditch (NISP).

	Structure III					Structure VI		
	Cattle	Sheep	Pig	Roe deer	Dog	Cattle	Sheep	Horse
antler				2				
mandible			2					
loose teeth		4	2	1		4	1	
vertebra						1		1
rib						1		
scapula	1		1					
humerus			1				1	
radius		3				2		
ulna		1						
pelvis		1						
femur						1		
tibia	2	1			1	1	1	
calcaneum	1							
metacarpal	2		5					
metatarsal	1	1	3	1				
1st phalanx	1		1				1	
2nd phalanx	1		1					
3rd phalanx	1							
Total	10	11	16	4	1	10	4	1

Table 52. Church Whitfield: bones identified to species from Period 4 structures (NISP).

58), though such a result could also be an artefact of preservation.

The sheep mandibles also show two peaks in the age data (Table 55), suggesting that meat production and secondary products, such as wool, were of importance.

The pigs were slaughtered before adulthood, for meat (Table 55).

Evidence suggesting that animals may have been bred on or near site is in the form of neonatal bones, one each of cattle and sheep, from Period 3. These very young bones will be under-represented, in relation to the adult remains, due to the conditions of preservation.

The epiphyseal fusion data for horse, from Period 3, shows all elements to be fused (Table 58). The vertebrae are the latest fusing elements, at about five years of age (Silver 1969, 285). All the post-cranial elements from Period 2 are from the lower leg bones from one individual in pit F26. These are all fused, suggesting an animal older than 20 months of age (Silver 1969, 286). Analysis of the ages of the loose teeth shows all animals to be mature, with some very elderly specimens (Table 59). The articulating cheek teeth from Pit group B had M^1 in full wear, M^2 just coming into wear and P^2 unworn, indicating an age of about 2½ years (Silver 1969, 293). This is the only immature specimen from the site.

Sexual data are basically limited to the information from pig canines (Mayer and Brisbin 1988). Four male lower canines were recovered: one each from Periods 2 and 4, and two from Period 3. A single female lower canine came from Period 3.

Metrical data

Table 60 gives a summary of the most common measurements taken from the bones, and includes, where possible, the same measurements from different periods.

The cattle measurements are consistent with data from other Iron Age sites, for example Owslebury (Maltby 1987a, table CowMet. 1), but are insufficient to fully explore the size of the animals. Withers heights have been calculated from the greatest lengths of one radius from Period 2, using the factor of Matolcsi (von den Driesch and Boessneck 1974, 336–8), and two metacarpals and a metatarsal from Period 3, using the factors of Fock (*ibid*). The Period 2 specimen gave a height of 1.045m, and the three bones from Period 3 gave a mean of 1.073m and a range of 1.041–1.099m. This is consistent with a shoulder height range of 1.00–1.13m from Iron Age Gussage All Saints (Harcourt 1979).

Only very limited metrical data were available from the sheep bones, the most common of which is summarised in Table 60. A single estimated withers height of 0.557m was calculated, following Teichert (von den Driesch and Boessneck 1974), from a Period 2 metacarpal.

The mean withers' height, using the factors of Kiesewalter (von den Driesch and Boessneck 1974) of the animal from Period 2 is 1.226m, or just over 12 hands. A metatarsal from Period 3 gave a withers' height of 1.316m, or just under 13 hands. Maltby (1981, 192) states that there is evidence for horses ranging from 10 to 14 hands on Iron Age sites. The mean withers height of an Iron Age horse skeleton from nearby Mill Hill is 1.250m, or slightly more than 12 hands (Legge 1995, 148). Legge (1995, fig 51)

Period	Description	Taxon	Carnivore gnawing	Burnt	Cut mark	Chop mark
2	Pit F16	Cattle	1			
		Cattle-sized		4		
	Pit F26	Cattle	1	1		
		Sheep		1		
		Horse			8	
		Cattle-sized		2		
		Sheep-sized		5		
3	Enclosure ditch	Cattle	15	3	2	1
		Sheep	4	1		
		Horse	1	1		
		Pig	1			
		Cattle-sized	3	23	2	
		Sheep-sized	1			
4	Structure III	Cattle	1			
		Pig		1		
		Cattle-sized	1			
Total			29	42	12	1

Table 53. Church Whitfield: summary of features producing common classes of taphonomic data (NISP).

	Period 2		Period 3		Period 4	
	NISP	%	NISP	%	NISP	%
Cattle	79	51.6	463	62.6	20	38.5
Sheep	50	32.7	129	17.4	15	28.8
Horse	14	9.2	106	14.3	1	1.9
Pig	10	6.5	42	5.7	16	30.8
Total	153	100.0	740	100.0	52	100.0

Table 54. Church Whitfield: proportion of the main taxa (NISP, adjusted for articulations).

Age stage	A	B	C	D	E	F	G	H	I
Cattle	0–1 month	1–8 months	8–18 months	18–30 months	30–36 months	young adult	adult	old adult	senile
Period 2				1			1		
Period 3			1					2	
Sheep	0–2 months	2–6 months	6–12 months	12–24 months	24–36 months	36–48 months	48–72 months	72–96 months	96–120 months
Period 2				1			1		
Period 3			1	1			1	3	
Pig	0–2 months	2–7 months	7–14 months	14–21 months	21–27 months	27–36 months	adult	old adult	senile
Period 3			2	1		2			

Table 55. Church Whitfield: aged cattle, sheep and pig mandibles. Suggested ages after Halstead (1985), Payne (1973) and Hambleton (1999).

plots the measurements from the metacarpal of the Mill Hill animal against measurements from Iron Age horses from other sites. The metacarpal from Church Whitfield Period 2 (with a greatest length of 198.5mm) is very similar in size to the Mill Hill specimen, and both lie in the range of measurements from the later phases from Danebury, compared to the earlier phases which are larger (Grant 1984a; Legge 1995, fig 51).

A small metrical data set is available from the pig material, almost entirely consisting of measurements from teeth (Table 60). The sample is too small to examine the presence of any bimodality in the measurements which may infer the presence of wild boar (Payne and Bull 1988), but the size of the material does suggest that all the pigs were domestic animals.

Shoulder height estimations for the dog skeleton from the enclosure ditch are only possible from metapodial measurements, using the factors calculated by Clark (1995, 22). Four complete metacarpals returned a mean reconstructed shoulder height of 417mm, and a range of 412–423mm. This is towards the lower end of the shoulder height range, of 290–580mm calculated for Iron Age dogs by Harcourt (1974, table 9). Dogs of different sizes may have been used for different purposes, such as sheep dogs, guard dogs and pets (Grant *et al* 1991, 478). It is possible that, especially in a small rural community, a dog fulfilled a variety of roles. Legge (1995, 148–9) suggests that a dog from Iron Age Mill Hill, Deal, with a mean shoulder height of 385mm, was probably a household pet rather than a working dog. (This is based on limb bone lengths plotted by Harcourt (1974) which have a suggestion of bimodality, divisible into lap dogs and working dogs, and the greatest length of the Mill Hill humerus falls into the lap dog range.) The greatest length of the humerus, or any of the major limb bones, was not available from the Church Whitfield animal, but assuming consistent results between the metapodials and the long bones then the size would probably have been at the lower end of the working animal size range. Assigning a specific function according to size limits is unreliable (Harcourt 1974, 171), but the Church Whitfield animal may have been a small working dog.

Pathology and non-metrical variation

Trauma to a left cattle scapula, from Period 3, is witnessed by a break which has partially healed, with misaligned halves and exostoses. A left cattle unfused metacarpal, also from Period 3, exhibits some porous bone around the distal end of the diaphysis.

The congenital condition of the reduction or absence of the hypoconulid of the lower third cattle molar (M_3) is recorded in one out of seven M_3s from Period 3. One M_3 from Period 2 has a normal hypoconulid. The absence of the hypoconulid on the M_3 also caused a recognisable condition in the upper third molar (M^3), in which the posterior column is unworn, or significantly less worn than the anterior column. An unworn posterior column is recorded in three out of eight M^3s from Period 3.

Two sheep pathologies are oral. A right sheep P_4, from Period 2, has caries in the occlusal surface. A sheep mandible, from Period 3, exhibits alveolar recession and *ante mortem* tooth loss.

Evidence of pathology from the horse material is restricted to the bones of the lower legs. From Period 2 (pit F26) an articulating distal metacarpal, first phalanx and sesamoid exhibit considerable bone growth around the articular area and the articular surfaces are unaffected. The production of these osteophytes is associated with inflammatory periarticular soft tissue changes, possibly due to an injury.

Two proximal metatarsals from the Period 3 enclosure ditch are from the same animal. In both these specimens the anterior wall of the diaphysis is relatively thick and the posterior is relatively thin. This may reflect remodelling of bone due to how the weight of the animal is acting through the legs in relation to their confirmation. The left metatarsal has fused with both splint bones and two tarsals, with exostoses around the affected area but not affecting the articular surface. This is a case of bone spavin. Bone spavin is degenerative joint disease of the hock joint, and affects the distal intertarsal and the tarsometatarsal joints (Devereux and Morrison 1992, 72), which causes exostoses limiting the movement of the joint (Baker and Brothwell 1980, 117). A number of possible, probably interrelated, causes include: hereditary factors which affect conformation, severe concussion (due to faulty conformation, faulty shoeing, heavy work or working on hard surfaces) and rotation of the lower limb from the hock downwards (*ibid*, 118). Poor conformation of the animal may cause bone spavin: Adams (1987, 18–21) states that medial deviation of the hock joints (cow hocks) and excessive angulation of the hock joints (sickle hocks) are thought to predispose to bone spavin. Although spavin is multi-causal, the principal cause

			C	V	E	½	U	a	b	c	d	e	f	g	h	j	k	l	m	n
Taxon	Tooth	Period																		
Cattle	dP4	3								1										
	P4	2												1						
	P4	3											2	2						
	P4	4											1							
	M1	3							1				1				1	1		
	M2	2														1				
	M2	3			1									1			2			
	M1/2	2											1							
	M1/2	3															5			
	M1/2	4															1	1		
	M3	2		1										1						
	M3	3								1				2		3				
Sheep	dP4	3													2					
	P4	2				1														
	P4	3														1		1		
	P4	4												1						
	M1	2												2	1					
	M1	3							1			1		3			1		2	
	M2	2									1		1	1						
	M2	3								1	2		2	1	3					
	M1/2	3								1			1	5	1	1				
	M3	2			1									1						
	M3	3								1				5						
	M3	4										1								
Pig	P4	2						1												
	P4	3					2	2					1							
	M1	3									1	1	1		1					
	M2	3						2	1	1				1	1					
	M1/2	2									1									
	M3	3								1		1								

Table 56. Church Whitfield: wear stages of all cattle, sheep and pig teeth, following Grant (1982).

may be heavy traction on hard surfaces (Luff and Brothwell 1993, 109). The right metatarsal has bone growth around the proximal end, and also some pitting to the articular surface. Baker and Brothwell (1980, 118) state that in many cases the articular surfaces are relatively unaffected by spavin. While this is certainly true for the other (left) specimen, the present specimen has some damage/pitting of the proximal articular surface, and it is not fused to the tarsals. Baker and Brothwell (1980, 119) refer to a couple of examples of spavin on equine cannon bones from Dragonby where there is slight pitting of the exposed articular surfaces possibly suggestive of infective arthritis.

The two pathological metatarsals may be explained by the animal experiencing a problem or pain in one leg and subsequently favouring the other, and the greater stress on that leg causing a different problem. The changes to these metatarsals would seem to suggest that the animal had undergone various stresses to the lower limbs, possibly associated with poor conformation. Such pathologies not only occur in work beasts but also in old animals. They are recorded, for example, from Iron Age deposits at Gussage all Saints (Harcourt 1979) and Owslebury (Maltby 1987a), at which sites there is a dominance of old animals.

The final example of pathology on the horse bones is a small rough, pitted area of bone growth on the medial side of the proximal diaphysis of a tibia from Period 3.

Two dog mandibles have abnormal fourth premolars (P_4), possibly of congenital origin. A dog mandible has a P_4 with conical form and almost circular cross-section, instead of the usual more blade-like form. Hillson (1986, 274) states that canid non-carnassial premolar teeth may be reduced in form. The left mandible from the dog skeleton (context 271) seems to have retained the deciduous fourth premolar (dP_4), ie it was not replaced by the permanent fourth premolar (P_4), or replaced with a tooth of similar form to the dP_4. In an animal, milk teeth may be retained and stay functional if permanent teeth fail to develop (Baker and Brothwell 1980, 137–8). The right mandible from the same animal has the M_2 alveolus, and no M_3. The M_2 and M_3 are absent from the left mandible, nor are the alveoli present; however there is some bone loss in this region and the alveoli may have healed over. Clark (2000, 165) lists a number of non-metric characteristics, the presence of which 'precludes a specimen from being 'prehistoric' '.

No absence of mandibular M_3 has yet been recorded in British material of prehistoric date. This condition is almost certainly brought about by diminution of jaw length where osteological reduction proceeds faster than tooth reduction and so there can be too little space for the eruption of M_3.

There appears to be sufficient space behind the M_2 alveolus in the right mandible to have included the M_3,

Taxon	Tooth	Period	C	V	E	½	U	a	b	c	d	e	f	g	h	j	k	l	m	n
Cattle	M1/2	2											1							
	M2	2														1				
	M3	2		1										1						
	P4	2												1						
	dP4	3								1										
	M1	3							1				1				1	1		
	M1/2	3															5			
	M2	3			1									1			2			
	M3	3								1				2		3				
	P4	3											2	2						
	M1/2	4															1	1		
	P4	4											1							
Sheep	M1	2												2	1					
	M2	2									1		1	1						
	M3	2			1									1						
	P4	2				1														
	dP4	3													2					
	M1	3							1			1		3			1		2	
	M1/2	3								1			1	5	1	1				
	M2	3								1	2		2	1	3					
	M3	3								1				5						
	P4	3														1		1		
	M3	4										1								
	P4	4												1						
Pig	M1/2	2									1									
	P4	2						1												
	M1	3									1	1	1		1					
	M2	3						2	1	1				1	1					
	M3	3								1		1								
	P4	3					2	2					1							

Table 57. Church Whitfield: wear stages of all cattle, sheep and pig teeth, following Grant (1982). By period.

	Cattle						Sheep						Horse		Pig					
Period	2		3		4		2		3		4		3		2		3		4	
	F	U	F	U	F	U	F	U	F	U	F	U	F	U	F	U	F	U	F	U
vertebra	2	6	2	4		1		1					3							
scapula	1		22				1						4				1			
humerus P		2		1																
humerus D	4		12				1						2							
radius P	5		23		2		1						2							
radius D	1	2	3	1									1							
ulna P		1	1							1						1				
pelvis	1		7										1							
femur P		1	5															1		
femur D	1	3	1	1									1			1				
tibia P	1*	2	3	1				1												
tibia D	1		12				3				1		3							
metacarpal P			7	1			1						3						2	1
metatarsal D	2		7	1									2						1	1

Table 58. Church Whitfield: epiphyseal fusion data for cattle, sheep, horse and pig. P: proximal, D: distal, F: fused, U: unfused, *: fusing.

which may suggest that this tooth has been lost before death and the alveolus healed over. The presence of 'lap dogs' in the later Iron Age in Britain has been suggested to be an import from the Roman Empire (Cram 2000, 171). The absence of the M_3 from the late Iron Age mandible from Church Whitfield might be seen in a similar light, if it is a true absence and was not lost *ante mortem*.

Bulk samples

Four samples came from pit F16 (Period 2; Table 62). The mole bones are more recent in appearance than the other bone, and appear to come from a single skeleton, and are therefore probably intrusive. Toad bones can probably be attributed to common toad, *Bufo bufo* L.; and frog to common frog, *Rana temporaria* L. These may be pit-fall victims.

Period	Description	Tooth	Mesio-distal diameter (mm)	Crown height (mm)	Estimated age (years)
2	Boundary ditch fill	P2	-	4.7	20+
		P3/4	27.1	30.5	11–15
3	Enclosure ditch	P2	34.6	32.7	10–11
		P3/4	27.5	43.6	9–11¼
		M1/2	27.9	69E	5½–8
		M1/2	25.0	57.8	7–9½
		M1/2	25.1	76.2	4–6½
		M1/2	25.4	67.8	5½–8
		M2 †	21.9	34.6	13–14
		M3 †	15.6	30.6	13–14
		M3	-	64.2	7–8
		M1/2	18.8	17.9	18+
		M1/2	21.9	36.0	9¾–14
		M1/2	25.1	37.6	9¾–14
		M2	22.8	27.3	14–15

Table 59. Church Whitfield: ages of loose horse teeth, by crown height measurement, following Levine (1982). †: articulating teeth, E: estimated.

		Period	Mean	Min.	Max.	n	sd	CV
Cattle	M3 length (L)	3	33.3	31.1	35.5	5	1.73	5.18
	M3 breadth (B)	3	13.3	11.7	14.2	5	1.11	8.34
	scapula (GLP)	2	58.0	58.0	58.0	1		
	scapula (GLP)	3	61.4	57.1	64.7	6	2.79	4.55
	scapula (SLC)	2	48.9	48.9	48.9	1		
	scapula (SLC)	3	45.0	35.3	50.7	22	4.08	9.06
	radius (Bp)	3	70.1	64.2	73.4	5	3.72	5.31
	metacarpal (Bp)	3	53.2	52.4	54.2	4		
	metacarpal (Bp)	4	49.8	49.8	49.8	1		
	tibia (Bd)	3	53.5	51.1	57.8	8	2.31	4.32
	astragalus (Bd)	3	37.1	33.7	38.5	4		
	metatarsal (Bp)	3	42.3	40.0	44.5	7	1.49	3.52
Sheep	M3 length (L)	2	18.7	18.7	18.7	1		
	M3 length (L)	3	20.4	20.0	21.1	4		
	M3 breadth (B)	2	7.1	7.1	7.1	1		
	M3 breadth (B)	3	7.7	7.4	8.0	5	0.23	2.97
	tibia (Bd)	2	22.2	21.6	23.1	3		
Pig	M1 (L)	3	15.7	14.9	16.9	4		
	M1 (WA)	3	9.4	9.1	9.6	4		
	M1 (WP)	3	10.1	9.7	10.9	4		
	M2 (L)	3	20.7	19.1	23.2	4		
	M2 (WA)	3	12.4	11.9	12.9	6	0.44	3.51
	M2 (WP)	3	13.4	13.1	13.9	4		
	M3 (L)	3	31.5	29.7	33.3	2		
	M3 (WA)	3	14.2	13.3	15.0	2		
	M3 (WA)	4	15.9	15.9	15.9	1		

Table 60. Church Whitfield: summary of common measurements (mm). (Pig measurements taken following Payne and Bull 1988.)

Bulk samples were taken from two of the Anglo-Saxon SFBs (Table 62). The presence of roe deer in Structure III concurs with the hand-recovered assemblage, which only produced roe deer bone. At least one of the pig bones from Structure III is neonatal, suggesting breeding may have been practised on or near the site during the Anglo-Saxon period.

Field vole and wood mouse are identified from Structure III. The habitat of the field vole is mainly rough, ungrazed grassland (Evans 1977, 189), whereas that of the wood mouse is extremely varied: it occurs wherever there is cover in the form of trees, shrubs, or rocks, and also in hedgerows, fields and gardens (Flowerdew 1977b, 210–2). The species identified are consistent with a rural settlement, such as that seen at the Roman settlement at Monkton (Bendrey 2008c) where field vole and wood mouse were the most common, rather than an urban one like medieval Townwall Street, Dover (Bendrey 2006), which produced mostly house mouse and black rat, both commensal species.

Discussion

Neolithic – Bronze Age

Red deer is the only taxon recorded from Period 1. The small quantity of antler is too fragmented and poorly preserved to provide further information beyond identification to species.

Iron Age

There is an increase of cattle and horse, and a decrease in sheep and pig, between Periods 2 and 3 (Table 54). Rather than indicating a change in emphasis of animal husbandry between the early Iron Age and the late Iron Age, however, this probably represents the different feature types sampled (pits providing most of the assemblage from Period 2, and ditches the bulk from Period 3). Maltby (1987b, 11; 1981, 165–6) describes similar variation between feature type in Iron Age deposits from Winnal Down and Easton Lane, due to differential preservation and disposal practices, with more cattle and horse bones in the ditches, and sheep/goat and pig making a greater contribution in the pits. This was also seen in Iron Age deposits from Dolland's Moor, on the Channel Tunnel terminal site (Bendrey 2002).

Cattle dominate the assemblages by NISP and by bone weight (Table 46). Sheep are the second most common by NISP. Horse is represented largely by articulations in Period 2, but becomes more important in the Period 3. Pigs only make a relatively minor contribution in both assemblages. The bones of sheep and pigs are under-represented, and cattle and horse over-represented, due to conditions of preservation and recovery, and disposal practices. Post-cranial pig bones especially, due to the immaturity of the animals, have suffered much destruction (Fig 96). Considering teeth MNE counts, therefore, probably gives a better picture of species abundance: with sheep most common, followed by cattle, pig and horse. Cattle, however, with greater body size, would probably have provided the most meat to the diet.

Dog bones are all from the enclosure ditch, the great majority deriving from a single skeleton. Goat is represented by four fragments of horn core. Hunting is witnessed by the presence of a single red deer bone.

Feature	Pit F16				Structure III	Structure VII
Context	125	131, 134	132	128, 31-133	140	379
Pig					4	
Sheep/goat					2	
Roe deer					1	
Mole	17				1	
Field vole					1	
Wood mouse					1	
Apodemus sp			1			
Mouse/vole	2			4	2	2
Common toad	18					
Toad	9					
Common frog	1		1			
Frog	10		1			
Frog/toad	35			2		
Indeterminate	67	8	4	19	345	34
Total	159	8	7	25	357	36

Table 61: Church Whitfield: distribution of animal bone from bulk samples (NISP). †: see taxonomic descriptions p 160.

The most useful Iron Age bone assemblages from Kent, for comparative purposes, are from Dolland's Moor (Bendrey 2002) and Farningham Hill (Locker 1984). Dolland's Moor produced the same order of importance of the common taxa: sheep, cattle, pig and horse. At the late Iron Age enclosure on Farningham Hill cattle and sheep were the most common, with sheep being more common in the pits and cattle in the ditches. Pig make a minor contribution and horse even less. This contrasts with the Church Whitfield assemblage where horse was more prominent.

The large sample from Period 3 allows detailed analysis of skeletal element representation, which suggests that animals were being slaughtered and processed on site. In general, smaller and less dense bones are under-represented, suggesting bias due to preservation and recovery. The patterns of sheep and pig bones (Figs 94 and 96) are very similar to those from Dolland's Moor (Bendrey 2002), where similar processes are probably present.

The cattle bones include all parts of the skeleton, with the scapula very well represented (Fig 93). The Period 3 deposits and the total assemblage from Farningham Hill (Locker 1984, tables I and J) show similar NISP patterns (Fig 97), although comparison of the skeletal element representation of cattle and sheep between the two sites is impaired by different counting procedures. Locker (1984) gives counts of the number of fragments (without loose epiphyses) of ox (including ox sized) and ovicaprid (including ovicaprid sized). At Church Whitfield the numbers of fragments for all the selected elements were totalled and their relative percentage contribution (% NISP) calculated. Nonetheless, there are some strong similarities between the samples. The scapula, for example, is the most common element in the Church Whitfield cattle assemblage and the second best represented at Farningham Hill (and was in fact the best represented cattle bone from the pits). Similarities are also visible in the sheep assemblages from Church Whitfield and Farningham Hill (Fig 98), which suggest that similar practices, involving butchery and disposal, were undertaken at both sites.

At Church Whitfield the majority of cattle and sheep were kept into adulthood, probably primarily for traction and wool respectively, with a smaller number of animals culled for meat. A small number of neonatal bones from Period 3 suggest that animals were being bred on or near site. Dolland's Moor shows a similar picture with young cattle and sheep culled for meat and adult animals being kept for secondary products (Bendrey 2002). The cattle and sheep at Farningham Hill were mainly kept into maturity (Locker 1984).

Most horse bones from Iron Age sites are from mature animals (Maltby 1981, 184). This indicates that meat production was not the main purpose with horses, their prime importance being for transport (*ibid*). Harcourt (1979, 158) argues that the lack of neonatal remains of horse from Gussage All Saints infers that horses were not being bred, but rather that wild animals were caught and trained (see Bendrey *et al* 2009 for a critique of this). Mature animals predominate in the horse assemblage from Church Whitfield, and there is no evidence for neonates (but there is little evidence of neonates from any species, due to the conditions of preservation). The occurrence of arthropathies affecting the lower limbs may imply the heavy use of horses on hard surfaces (concussive damage) or as traction/draught animals; equally they may be age related changes affecting elderly animals. Harcourt (1979, 158–8) attributes the presence of osteoarthrosis of the proximal metatarsal in five specimens from Gussage all Saints to draught use of the animals. Maltby (1987a) argues that as many of the horses from Owslebury were mature it would be expected to find age related pathologies.

Maltby (1981, 184) states that horsemeat made an important contribution to the diet in at least some parts of England during the Iron Age (but see above). The high percentage contribution of horse in Period 3 (Fig 95; Table 54) is comparable to samples from Easton Lane and Winnal Down, Hampshire, where horse contributed an important part to the diet (Maltby 1987b, table 19). Comparison of the mean fragment weight of similar sized species can inform on

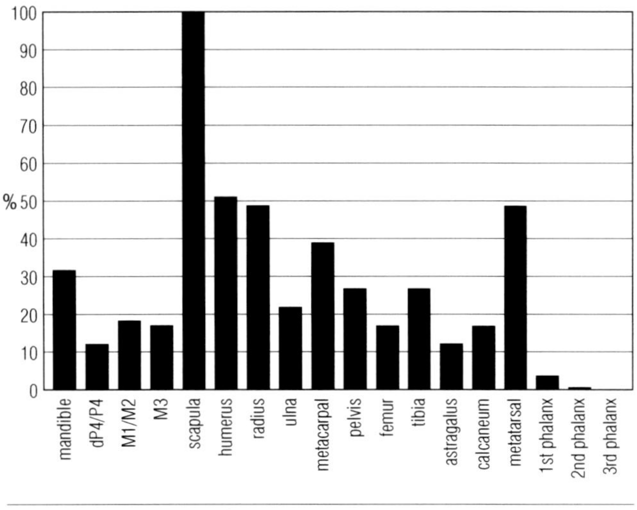

Fig 93. Church Whitfield:Cattle (Period 3): MNI by anatomical element (frequency expressed as a percentage of the most common element).

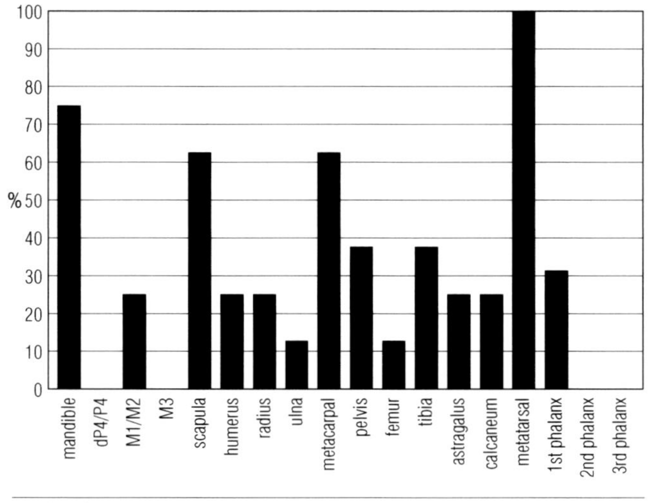

Fig 95. Church Whitfield: Horse (Period 3): MNI by anatomical element (frequency expressed as a percentage of the most common element).

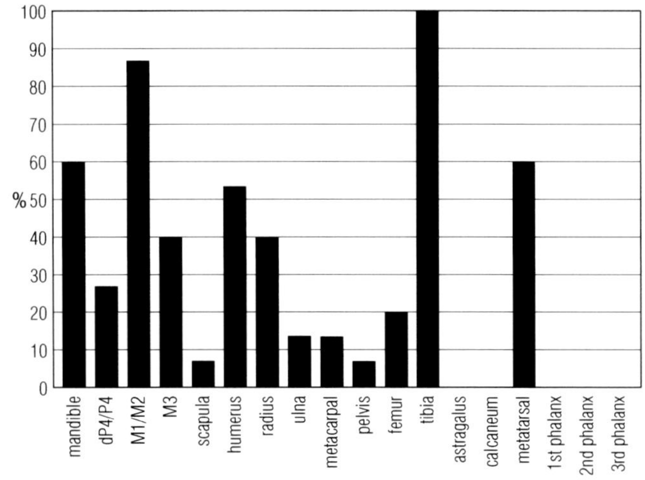

Fig 94. Church Whitfield: Sheep (Period 3): MNI by anatomical element (frequency expressed as a percentage of the most common element).

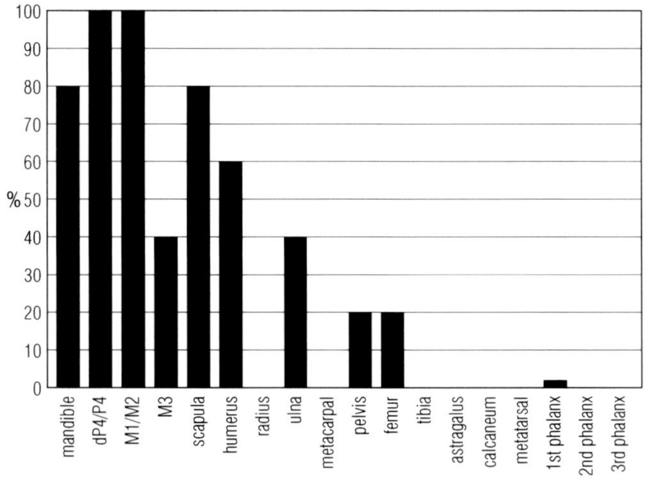

Fig 96. Church Whitfield: Pig (Period 3): MNI by anatomical element (frequency expressed as a percentage of the most common element).

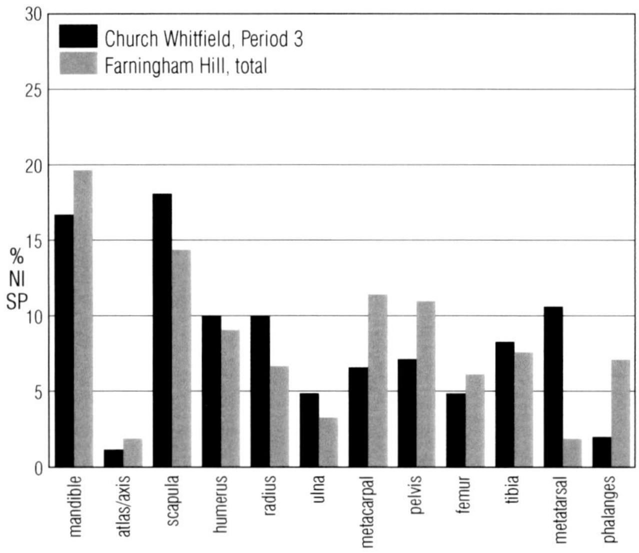

Fig 97. Church Whitfield: comparison of the representation of cattle bones by NISP between Church Whitfield (Period 3) and Farningham Hill (pits and ditches).

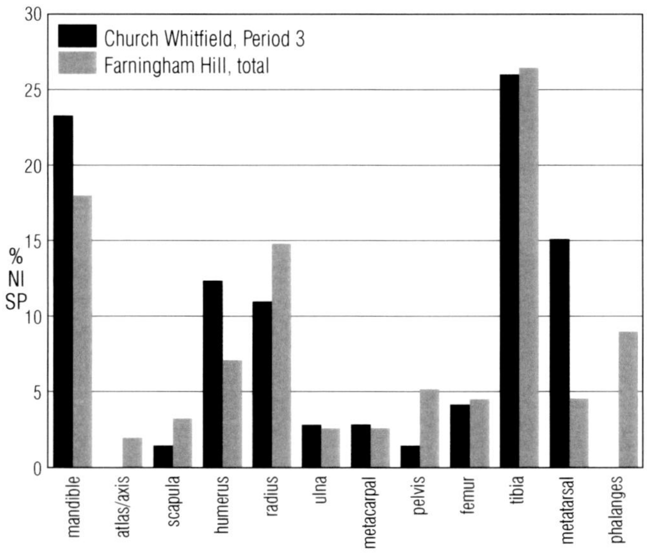

Fig 98. Church Whitfield: comparison of the representation of sheep bones by NISP between Church Whitfield (Period 3) and Farningham Hill (pits and ditches).

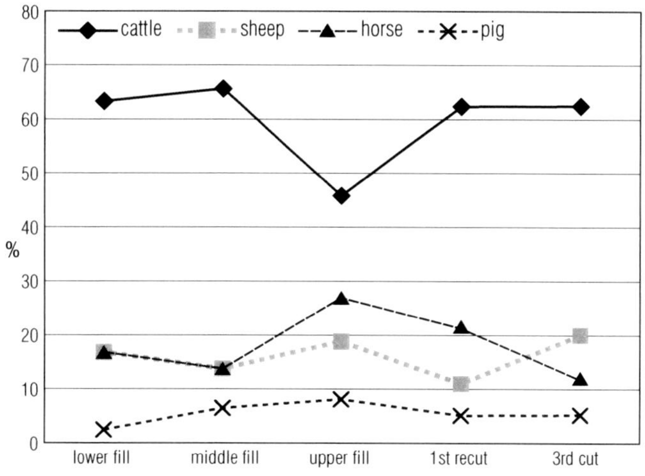

Fig 99. Church Whitfield: percentage representation, by NISP, of cattle, sheep, horse and pig within the fills of the Period 3 enclosure ditch (data in Table 38).

the butchery and use of the animals. Horse bone fragments from archaeological sites are generally considerably larger than cattle (eg Bendrey 2006), suggesting that they are not butchered to the same degree. The values for cattle and horse from Period 3 are more similar, suggesting a similar taphonomic history for the two taxa (such a comparison is not valid for Period 2 as the bulk of the horse bones are articulating deposits).

Articulating skeletons, partial articulations and complete skulls from Iron Age sites are often interpreted as deliberately placed deposits (Grant 1984b) and a number of Iron Age pits from Dolland's Moor produced skulls and articulations suggestive of deliberate deposition (Bendrey 2002). Other explanations include natural deaths and butchery waste (Grant 1984b, 222).

Several collections of animal bones from Church Whitfield may be interpreted as deliberately placed deposits, though their significance is unclear.

The horse remains from Pit group B (Period 2) are too fragmented to be certain whether a complete skull was originally deposited. Similarly, the sheep upper toothrows and skull fragments from pit F26 (Period 2) may represent skulls. These remains could represent the deliberate deposition of horse and sheep skulls, or they could represent primary butchery (heads and feet are removed at an early stage of the butchery process). The articulating lower limbs of a horse were recovered from pit F26. The good quality of preservation and the lack of fragmentation, compared to the rest of the assemblage, may indicate that they were deliberately deposited. The positioning of the cut marks on these bones suggests that they derived from the disarticulation of the lower limbs from the carcase, and also the skinning of the animal.

Deliberate deposition is also suggested by the collection of finds recorded by the excavator at the east corner of the enclosure ditch (context 371) that included a human skull in association with a cattle humerus and a phallus-shaped flint.

A dog skeleton was also buried in the enclosure ditch. Although small, this animal was probably large enough to have been a working dog, such as a sheep dog.

Anglo-Saxon

The assemblage from Period 4 is very limited (Table 52). Cattle are the most important animal, by number and weight, followed by pig and then sheep. A neonatal pig bone suggests that breeding was occurring on site. Hunting is represented by the bones of roe deer.

The importance of pig in the Anglo-Saxon assemblage is paralleled in a number of, but not all, Anglo-Saxon assemblages from Kent: it was the most important at Long Pepper Field, West (Bendrey 2002) and at Keston (Harman 1973), and is the second most numerous animal after cattle at Linacre Garden (Driver 1990). The Church Whitfield sample is very small but, with these other Anglo-Saxon bone assemblages from Kent, suggests that pigs may have been of more importance than in other periods, though its significance is uncertain (Bendrey 2002). It may, for instance, represent a strategy using the rapid reproduction capacity of pigs to provide a quick source of meat for newly established settlements (eg Crabtree 1989), or a dietary preference (King 1978, 226).

Conclusions

Similarities between the patterns of skeletal representation from the late Iron Age enclosure ditch (Period 3) and other Iron Age sites in Kent (Bendrey 2002; Locker 1984) indicate that similar processes are being undertaken at these small rural settlements: namely that the animals were being culled, processed and consumed on site. This is shown by the presence of most elements of the common animals, and those that are under-represented can be explained by preservational and recovery bias, as they are generally smaller or of low density.

These conditions of preservation and recovery have greatly affected the assemblage in favour of the larger species, cattle and horse, and against the smaller, sheep and pig. Consideration of the tooth counts, by MNE, goes some way to rectifying this bias, and suggests that originally sheep were the most common, followed by cattle, pig and horse. The same order of importance was probably also present in the early Iron Age deposits (Period 2). Sheep may have been the most common, but cattle would probably have supplied the most meat to the diet due to their greater carcase weight. The age data indicate that both were kept for meat and for secondary products.

Several deposits could suggest deliberate deposition, but may equally reflect butchery discard. Of particular interest are the four butchered articulating lower limbs of horse from Period 2: cut marks on tarsals and metapodials indicate disarticulation from the rest of the animal, and cut marks on phalanges suggest that the animal was skinned.

The Anglo-Saxon sample, though very small, is interesting as pig is the second most common animal. The importance of pig, above sheep, is also seen at a number of other Anglo-Saxon sites in Kent, but its significance is not fully understood.

Environmental evidence

Charred plant remains

Gill Campbell

Four samples were taken from the Period 2 pit F16 and processed using standard methods of recovery for charred plant remains with a mesh of 0.5mm used for the flot. These samples were assessed in 1996 by scanning each flot under a microscope at magnifications up to x20. The material sorted from residues was also examined. All the flots produced large assemblages of charred plant remains. In addition, one of the residues contained a considerable number of large legumes, some of which could be identified as *Pisum sativum* L (pea). Two samples (from contexts 125 and 132) were selected for full analysis.

Methods

As the assemblages from both samples were large, sub-sampling of the flots was necessary. This was achieved using a riffle box. Fifty per cent of the sample from context 125 and 25 per cent of that from context 132 was analysed. Identifications were made using magnifications up to x40 and with the aid the English Heritage reference collection at the Centre for Archaeology, Fort Cumberland. The results are presented in Table 62. Nomenclature follows Clapham *et al* (1989) for wild plants, Miller (1987) for wheat, and Zohary and Hopf (1994) for the other cultivated plants. Barley grain from context 125 was submitted for radiocarbon dating (Beta 142011; Table 64).

Results

In both samples *Hordeum* sp (barley) grain was the most abundant. All the grain appeared to derive from a hulled form. The presence of six-row rachis fragments and the number of twisted lateral grains indicated that hulled six-row barley, rather than hulled two-row barley was present. The barley grain from context 125 was dated by radiocarbon to 2220±50 BP (Table 64).

The samples also produced small amounts of emmer wheat (*Triticum dicoccum*) and spelt wheat (*Triticum spelta*). Oat grain was also recovered. Some florets showed that both common cultivated oat (*Avena sativa*) and wild oats were present. Both samples also produced large legumes. Some specimens, where parts of the testa and hilum had survived, were identified as *Pisum sativum* (pea). The better examples were submitted to Ann Butler at the Institute of Archaeology, UCL. She was able to confirm the identification and selected one specimen, which retained the clearest rim of testa around the hilum, for electron microscopy. The micromorphology of the testa was compatible with the cultigen *P sativum* ssp *sativum* while the cell anatomy suggested a charring temperature above 310° centigrade (Pl 27).

Both samples also contained a small number of weed seeds. Most of these were large seeded weeds, often found associated with clean grain. Some small weed seeds such as small legumes and grasses were also present.

Discussion

Both samples consisted largely of charred cereal grain, mainly hulled six-row barley, with small amounts of emmer wheat, spelt wheat, oat and peas. The samples probably represent stored barley grain, which was accidentally burnt while being parched to harden the grain before removal of the hulls. The other cultivated species present probably grew as volunteers in the barley crop.

The presence of emmer in roughly equal quantities to spelt wheat is of interest. Both wheats are found across Kent in the Iron Age, for example at Wilmington (Hillman 1982), Shelford Farm Estate (Carruthers and Allison 2010), White Horse Stone, Eyhorne Street and Saltwood Tunnel (Giorgi *et al* 2006). This shows that both emmer and spelt were grown throughout this period in contrast to evidence from the Hampshire chalklands, where emmer wheat ceased to be cultivated at the beginning of the Iron Age (Campbell 2000, 46).

The record of pea is also worth noting. Peas are found in small quantities in Kent from the late Bronze Age onwards (Giorgi *et al* 2006; Curruthers and Allison 2010) and together with horse beans (*Vicia faba* var *minor*) were abundant in a late Bronze Age pit at Holborough Quarry (Pelling 2008). It seems likely that both peas and beans were grown in Iron Age Kent, although as Jones (1996) states, species may persist as contaminants of local crops years after their cultivation ceased.

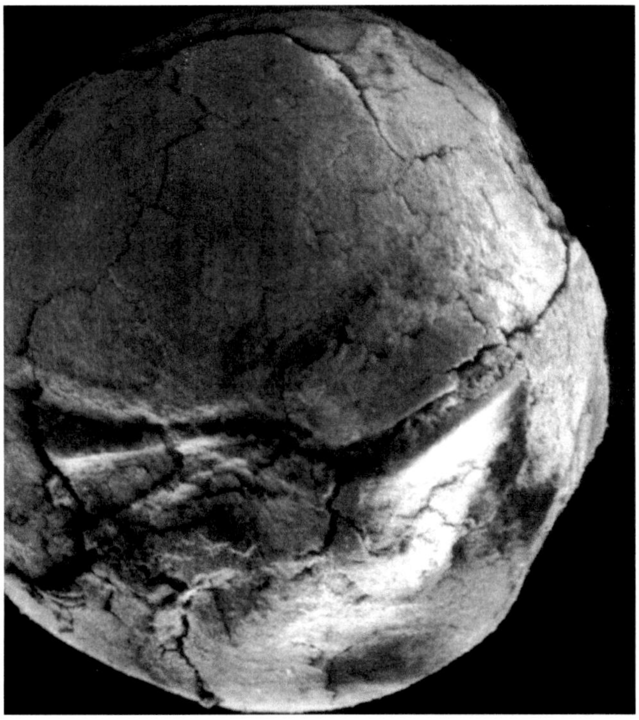

Pl 27. Church Whitfield: SEM microphotograph of *Pisum sativum* (pea). The micromorphology of the testa was compatible with the cultigen *P sativum* ssp *sativum* while the cell anatomy suggested a charring temperature above 310° centigrade (comment and picture by Ann Butler).

Taxon (element if not a seed)	Common name	Context 125	Context 132
Raphanus raphanistrum L (seed case)	wild radish	1	
Brassica cf nigra (L) Koch	black mustard	3	6
Brassica/Sinapis sp	cabbage, mustard, charlock etc.		10
Silene sp	Campion	1	
Caryophyllaceae/ Chenopodiaceae indet		1	
Pisum sativum L	pea	1	6
Vicia/Lathyrus sp	vetch/tare	3	9
Vicia/Pisum sp	vetch/ tare/ pea	3	5
Leguminosae (small) indet		2	
Fallopia convolvulus A Love	black bindweed	3	
Rumex acetosella agg	sheep's sorrel	1	
Rumex sp(p)	dock	27	16
Polygonaceae indet		1	
Galeopis sp	hemp-nettle	1	
Plantago media/lanceolata	plantain		2
Galium cf *aparine* L	cleavers	1	
Tripleurospermum sp	Mayweed		1
Poa annua type	annual meadow grass	11	3
Bromus hordeacus type	brome	67	14
Bromus sp	brome	27	1
Hordeum cf *murinum* L	wall barley	1	
Avena sativa L(floret)	common cultivated oat	1	
Avena sativa/strigosa (floret)	cultivated oat	6	1
A fatua/sterilis	wild oat	17	1
Avena sp	oat	75	72
Avena type (twisted awn)	oat	70	
cf *Avena* sp	oat		4
Gramineae (large) indet	grass	42	40
Gramineae (small) indet	grass	10	18
Gramineae indet. (floret base)	grass	36	2
Triticum dicoccum type (grain)	emmer wheat	40	28
T dicoccum Schubl (Schrank) (glume base)	emmer wheat	6	
T dicoccum Schubl (Schrank) (spikelet fork)	emmer wheat	7	
T cf *dicoccum* Schubl (Schrank) (spikelet fork)	emmer wheat	1	
T spelta type (grain)	spelt wheat	31	20
T spelta L (glume base)	spelt wheat	7	1
T spelta L (spikelet fork)	spelt wheat	5	3
T cf *spelta* L (glume base)	spelt wheat	1	
T dicoccum/spelta (grain)	emmer or spelt wheat	77	108
T dicoccum/spelta (glume base)	emmer or spelt wheat	10	8
T dicoccum/spelta (spikelet fork)	emmer or spelt wheat	12	
Triticum sp (hulled grain)	hulled wheat	4	
Triticum sp (grain)	wheat	39	36
Triticum sp (tail grain)	wheat		1
Triticum sp (glume base)	wheat	10	2
Triticum sp (spikelet fork)	wheat	5	
Triticum/Secale sp (grain)	wheat or rye	2	
Triticum/Secale sp (awn)	wheat or rye	1	
Hordeum vulgare L (rachis)	six-row barley	27	1
Hordeum sp (hulled, straight grain)	hulled barley	531	648
Hordeum sp (hulled, twisted grain)	hulled barley	961	656
Hordeum sp (hulled grain)	hulled barley	374	792
Hordeum sp (grain)	barley	15	21
Hordeum sp (sprouted grain)	barley	1	
Hordeum sp (awn)	barley	1	
Hordeum sp (floret)	barley	2	
Hordeum sp (rachis)	barley	7	
Secale/Hordeum sp (rachis)	rye or barley	32	1
Cereales indet (grain)	cereal	++++	49
Cereales indet (chaff)	cereal	++++	2
Cereal size (embryo)		7	37
Gramineae size (embryo)		168	
Gramineae size (culm node)		1	
IGNOTA		7	9
Total number of items identified		2803	2635

Table 62. Church Whitfield: details of charred plant remains from Pit F16.

Pulses tend to be under-represented in the archaeobotanical record as their processing does not involve exposure to fire, but they are often recovered in small numbers in assemblages of charred cereal grain, where they are thought to represent contaminants of the main cereal crop. Furthermore, the presence of cultivated legumes as contaminants is often taken as evidence for a crop rotation involving the use of legumes to maintain the fertility of the soil. This may have been the case in Kent, perhaps suggesting an intensive rather than extensive cropping regime here during the Iron Age (van der Veen and O'Connor 1998). High population pressure may be reflected or limited access to land regarded as suitable for cultivation, but more research is clearly required.

Land snails

Mark Robinson

Church Whitfield lies on the chalk of the North Downs, resulting in the good preservation of mollusc shells. One column sample was analysed from the fills of the Period 3 enclosure ditch (north-east arm, F233; column from Section 86; Fig 58).

Methods

The sample was analysed following the methods outlined in the report on the Eastling barrow material (*see* p 69) The results are shown in Table 63 which gives the minimum number of individuals represented. *Cecilioides acicula* was excluded because it is a species which burrows deeply. Nomenclature follows Kerney (1999).

A molluscan diagram has been plotted, largely following the groups used by Evans (1972, 194–203). *Punctum pygmaeum* and *Nesovitrea hammonis* have not been separated out because they were uncommon, being left respectively in the other shade-loving species and the Zonitidae. Unidentified specimens of *Vallonia* were attributed as best as possible to *V costata* and *V excentrica* types, the remainder then being divided according to the ratio between the two. Unidentified *Venigo* sp have been included with *V pygmaea*.

Feature	Enclosure ditch F233				Enclosure ditch F248	
Context	217	217	217	245	216	216
Depth (cm)	50–60	40–50	30–40	64–68	20–30	10–20
Vertigo pygmaea (Drap)			1			
Pupilla muscorum (L)	7	6	9	11	7	12
Vallonio costata (Müll)	4	1	4	5	8	12
V excentrica Sterki	7	4	7	8	10	24
Vallonia sp	24	18	20	48	37	44
Puntum pygmaeum (Drap)						1
Vitrina sp						3
Vitrea sp						1
Nesovitrea hammonis (Ström)			1			
Aegopinella nitidula (Drap)		2	2		2	3
Limax or *Deroceras* sp						1
Helicella itala (L)	16	12	12	18	25	22
Monacha cartusiana (Müll)	5	1		1	2	3
M cantiana (Mont)			1			
Trichia hispida gp	12	12	3	3	13	20
Arianta arbustorum (L)						1
Cepaea sp			1		1	1
Total	75	56	61	94	105	148

Table 63. Church Whitfield: details of land snails from the Period 3 enclosure ditch (F233 and F248).

Period and Context	Material	Beta ref no	Date BP	Calibrated date (1 sigma)	Calibrated date (2 sigma)
Period 1					
Pit F103, 102	antler	142012	3380±50	1735–1620 BC	1765–1530 BC
Period 2					
Pit F16, 125	burnt grain	142011	2220±50	375–195 BC	390–165 BC
Period 3					
Placed deposit, 371	animal bone	142009	2120±40	190–80 BC	350–310 BC or 210–45 BC
Potsherd, 256	carbon residue	141267	2080±50	170 BC–40 BC	200 BC–AD 30
Dog burial, 271	animal bone	142010	2050±40	100 BC–5 BC	170 BC–AD 45
Grave F.146, 147	human bone	141266	2230±60	385–195 BC	400–155 BC

Table 64. Church Whitfield: radiocarbon dates from the site.

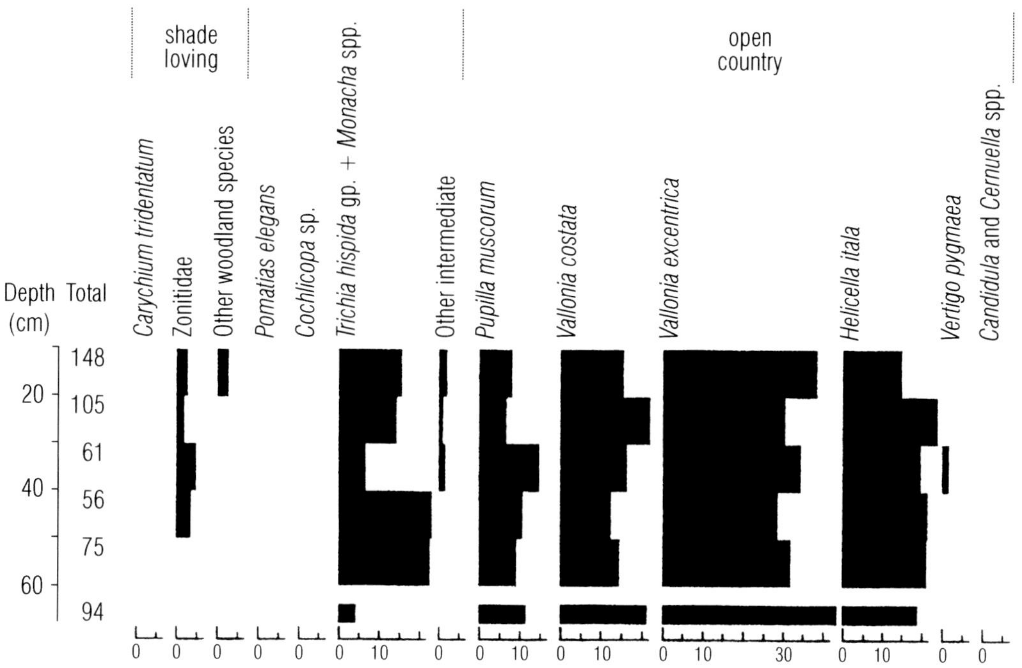

Fig 100. Church Whitfield: molluscs from Iron Age ditch Column 1 S.86.

Interpretation

The ditch had been cut about 0.65m into the chalk bedrock. It had been recut once and context 216 represented the fill of the recut (F248). The fills of both phases of the ditch were colluvial in origin, containing many fragments of chalk and there was no evidence of a completely stable phase with soil formation, although sedimentation of the recut was probably less rapid.

The assemblages throughout Column 1 were dominated by snails of dry, open habitats. *Vallonia excentrica* was most numerous in all the samples, but *Pupilla muscorum*, *Vallonia costata*, *Helicella itala* and *Trichia hispida* gp were also well represented (Fig 100). The assemblages would be appropriate to both short turfed grassland and Iron Age cultivation soils. The complete absence of *Carychium tridentatum* and the poor representation of the other shade loving groups (Zonitidae and other woodland species) suggested an absence of any woodland, hedge or scrub in the immediate vicinity and that there was no more than low growing herbaceous vegetation in the ditch itself. *H itala*, which was relatively abundant, is more characteristic nowadays of stable grassland habitats but it does seem to have been able to survive under conditions of prehistoric cultivation (Evans 1972, 180–2). The general uniformity of the molluscan assemblages, including those from the primary fill of the enclosure ditch, was possibly a reflection of the majority of the shells entering the ditch with colluvial sediments, rather than the shells representing the fauna of the ditch itself. It is possible that these sediments had been derived from cultivation adjacent to the enclosure. There was no evidence for changing conditions following the recut of the ditch.

One species present throughout the sequence, *Monacha cartusiana*, is very much a species of south-east England, particularly east Kent (Kerney 1999, 188). Another species, *Monacha cantiana*, is now known to be present in Kent by the Iron Age, although it is a later colonist elsewhere in the British Isles (Kerney 1999, 189).

Radiocarbon dating

Keith Parfitt

Six organic samples were selected for radiocarbon dating. Four were taken from late Iron Age contexts associated with the Period 3 farmstead (Table 64). These were chosen in the hope that they might provide dates to establish when grog-tempered pottery was first introduced into east Kent. The results, however, are not particularly consistent or very precise, due to the now well known technical problems associated with calibrating dates that fall within the Iron Age period. Similarly, a sample of burnt grain from early Iron Age pit F16 appears too young in comparison with the stylistic dating of the associated pottery (*see* p 138). More usefully, a piece of deer antler submitted from the otherwise undated pit F103 established that it was of early Bronze Age date.

The Iron Age and Anglo-Saxon settlements

Previous discoveries and cropmarks in the immediate area (*see* p 5; Figs 2 and 3, 1–3) make it clear that excavations at the Church Whitfield crossroads have revealed only part of a more extensive multi-period archaeological complex.

The settlement sequence examined, although of some considerable interest in its own right, must thus be considered incomplete. Most of the remains exposed relate to either the Iron Age or Anglo-Saxon periods. Residual prehistoric struck flints and three small sherds of Beaker pottery, however, attest to some earlier activity in the area, during the Neolithic and early Bronze Age (Period 1). Only one early Bronze Age feature has been identified through radiocarbon dating (Fig 46; pit F103; Table 64).

No late Bronze Age features were located but activity nearby is indicated by a socketed bronze axe found on the Roman road in 1937 (Amos 1937; see above), together with a small quantity of pottery recovered during evaluation work on the line of the new by-pass to the south, at Pineham (Parfitt 1995b; Fig 3; Table 1). Despite the close proximity of an important Roman road, remains of the Romano-British period from the excavations were confined to a few stray finds, including a second-century coin.

The Iron Age settlements, Periods 2 and 3

Two separate periods of Iron Age occupation were represented on the excavated site (Periods 2 and 3). These were perhaps separated in time by around two centuries and the earlier, Period 2, settlement appears to have had no particular influence on the siting of the subsequent farmstead in Period 3. Contrasting with Wessex, Sussex and to a lesser degree, west Kent, east Kent in the Iron Age was not a region dominated by hillforts (Cunliffe 1982, 44; Champion 2007, 118–19) and it would seem that most, if not all, the population lived in scattered villages, hamlets or farmsteads such as those examined at Church Whitfield.

Situated high on chalk downland, the excavated settlements at Whitfield lie some 3km from the River Dour, the nearest source of fresh running water. In the absence of any evidence for deep wells, dew ponds and other means of rainwater collection must have been employed to provide for the site. The same would be true for the succeeding Anglo-Saxon settlement.

Period 2

The earliest Iron Age occupation, broadly dated to *c* 550–350 BC, is represented by a number of widely scattered features (Fig 47). Two large storage pits (F16 and F26) and perhaps a four-post structure (Structure V), apparently enclosed by an extensive but insubstantial rectilinear boundary ditch, probably represent elements of a ditched farmstead, spread over a considerable area that continued beyond the limits of the excavation. An isolated ditch found in Field 9, well to the north-west of the main area, may be related. Animal bone, charred grain and peas recovered indicate that the economy of this site was based on mixed farming. Odd human bones found in the filling of pit F16 (Table 45) suggest that its deceased inhabitants were sometimes excarnated.

Four groups of shallow chalk quarry pits do not seem to be directly related to the enclosed settlement and probably belong to a phase when the focus of occupation lay somewhere beyond the excavated area. Early Iron Age pottery collected from an adjacent field, on the eastern side of the Roman road (Fig 3, 1) suggests further habitation in that area.

Period 3

At the end of Period 2, in the mid fourth century BC, an apparent phase of abandonment occurred which lasted until a new rectangular ditched farmstead enclosure was established around 150 BC (Period 3), a little to the south-west of the preceding settlement. The rarity of Iron Age settlement sites falling within the period *c* 300 to 150 BC has been noted across Kent and other parts of south-east England (*see* p 141; Macpherson-Grant 1991; Champion 2007, 119). The explanation still requires much more research but whatever the reason, the trend seems to be repeated at Church Whitfield.

The new farmstead, rather smaller in area than its predecessor, apparently lay in an open landscape without woodland and was perhaps occupied for around a century. Heavy plough erosion had unfortunately destroyed many of the associated features inside the enclosure. Nevertheless, a single storage pit was located, together with a pair of post-holes that might conceivably relate to a centrally placed round-house. Several small gullies located outside the main ditch suggest that the enclosure was adjoined by ancillary animal compounds and ditched fields (Fig 55).

During the occupation of the site domestic rubbish had been dumped into the enclosure ditch. The substantial pottery assemblage recovered is of particular interest. The bulk consists of late Iron Age flint-tempered wares but also present is a small quantity (less than 5 per cent by weight) of grog-tempered ware, of typical 'Belgic' (Aylesford-Swarling) type. The farmstead seems to have been occupied at a time when this new style grog-tempered pottery was just starting to be produced. Eventually, vessels in the new fabric replaced virtually all earlier forms across most of south-east Britain but on the present site, pottery tempered with grog was still very much in the minority (*see* p 146; Table 40). Only two grog-tempered sherds were recorded from the lower filling of the enclosure ditch, and perhaps significantly, one of these occurred with the special placed deposit discovered at the east corner (context 371, see above). Comparable assemblages of transitional late Iron Age pottery are becoming better known; material from local sites at Green Lane, Whitfield (Parfitt 2002b; Fig 3, 12) and Capel-le-Ferne (Macpherson-Grant 2002) have now been published, together with finds from Highstead in north-east Kent (Couldrey and Thompson 2007). On the evidence of the pottery overall, occupation at Church Whitfield seems to have come to an end somewhere between *c* 75 and 50 BC and unlike many other late Iron Age settlements excavated in Kent, the present one did not continue to be occupied into the Roman period.

Although surrounded by a ditch with a single entrance and situated on a ridge-top, the small Period 3 farmstead, like its predecessor, was not strongly defended. The surrounding ditch as originally excavated is unlikely to have been more than about 1.50m deep and the later re-cuts were even shallower. The ditch was most probably accompanied by an internal bank. During the excavations, the spoil from a length of ditch was used to recreate such a bank. From this it may be suggested that the original would have stood to only around 1m in height. To have been in any way effective as a barrier to keep livestock in and wild animals and intruders out, this bank would fairly certainly have required a surmounting palisade or hedge.

Comparison with other Iron Age ditched farmstead sites in southern Britain (Fig 101) shows that Church Whitfield is one of the smallest, with an area of under 0.13 hectares. The area enclosed was probably just sufficient to contain the dwelling of a single family group. Their social status must remain uncertain but finewares amongst the pottery assemblage and the previous discovery of a Celtic coin perhaps indicates they were above subsistence level. Equally, however, the overall size of the area enclosed, the small scale of the associated earthworks and the absence of a very substantial round-house, taken with the general lack of quality small finds, suggests that the farmstead did not belong to a family of especially high standing.

Caesar records that in the mid first century BC the population of southern Britain was exceptionally large and that the ground was thickly studded with homesteads closely resembling those of the Gauls (*De Bello Gallico* V, 12). Occupied until about the time Caesar was writing, it seems likely that the present enclosure represents exactly this type of homestead. Indeed, lying within sight of the Channel coast at Deal, the purported site of Caesar's landing, our settlement at Church Whitfield might conceivably have been one of those to which Caesar was specifically referring.

Some physical remains of the site's inhabitants were discovered. A single inhumation grave (F146) containing an adult male was located just outside the main enclosure and may have formed part of a small associated cemetery otherwise destroyed. In contrast, a human skull placed on the bottom of the ditch at the eastern corner of the enclosure, would seem to represent a deliberate deposition for some ritual purpose (Pl 23). Other skull fragments and part of a human leg bone also found in the filling of the enclosing ditch could derive from similar deposits, but more probably they represent scattered residues from the excarnation of bodies, a rite which also seems to have occurred on the site during Period 2 (see above; Table 45). Similar finds of human bones in non-funerary contexts, particularly skulls, have been made at many other Iron Age settlements in southern Britain (Whimster 1981, 182–3; Cunliffe 1991, 505–6).

Like its predecessor in the early Iron Age, the economy of the Period 3 farmstead was probably based on a mixed farming economy of crop cultivation and animal husbandry. The large collection of animal bone from the enclosure ditch indicates that sheep, cattle, pigs and horses were kept and butchered on the site. The dog skeleton probably represents a small working animal. The general lack of extensive grain storage facilities, in the form of four-post structures and pits such as those found in Period 2, suggests that, if cereal cultivation featured extensively in the farmstead's economy, the bulk of the grain was stored elsewhere.

By *c* 50 BC the Period 3 farmstead site seems to have been given up. Rather than the area being completely abandoned, however, it seems likely that the focus of settlement had shifted to a new site somewhere nearby. No evidence for such a later settlement was recorded in the excavation but rectilinear ditched enclosures noted as cropmarks at the north-eastern end of Field 8 and seemingly cut across by the Roman road (Fig 2) could represent part of a subsequent farmstead.

The Anglo-Saxon settlement, Period 4

Renewed occupation within the excavated area occurred during the post-Roman period when an Anglo-Saxon settlement was established, probably sometime during the sixth century AD. The preceding late Iron Age site seems to have had no influence on the layout of this, suggesting that virtually all traces of it had gone. Probably representing an extended farmstead or hamlet, the overall extent of the new settlement remains uncertain. It consisted of at least six, perhaps eight, structures comprising several sunken-featured buildings (SFBs, more traditionally termed *grubenhaüser*) and two larger, wall-post buildings. The excavated structures covered an area measuring at least 110m (north-east–south-west) by 60m (north-west–south-east) (Fig 60) but other buildings probably existed beyond (*see* p 109). A number of pit-like features visible on air photographs, north of the excavations in Field 8, may include more SFBs.

Kent has long been known for its large numbers of early Anglo-Saxon cemetery sites (Richardson 2005), but associated settlement evidence has, until very recently, continued to be elusive outside the major centres at Canterbury and Dover (Hawkes 1982). The number of rural buildings being discovered is now increasing. Most of the remains located consist of single sunken-featured buildings, which are often likely to be elements of larger sites that mostly lay outside the area being investigated. At the time of excavation, Church Whitfield, together with another site found about the same time at Manston Road, Ramsgate, represented the two most extensively excavated Anglo-Saxon rural settlements in east Kent. The main buildings revealed on the Ramsgate site consisted of five SFBs, producing sixth- to seventh-century pottery, decorated bone comb fragments and other material. More buildings probably lay beyond the excavation limits (Hutcheson and Andrews 2009). An important new complex of Anglo-Saxon buildings currently being investigated at Lyminge near Folkestone (see www.lymingearchaeology.org) promises to further advance our knowledge very significantly.

The Church Whitfield site is located some 19km south of Ramsgate and 16km east of Lyminge, but is just 4.5km inland from the early Anglo-Saxon coastal settlement at Dover, established within the walls of the old Roman Shore Fort, probably by the end of the fifth century (Philp

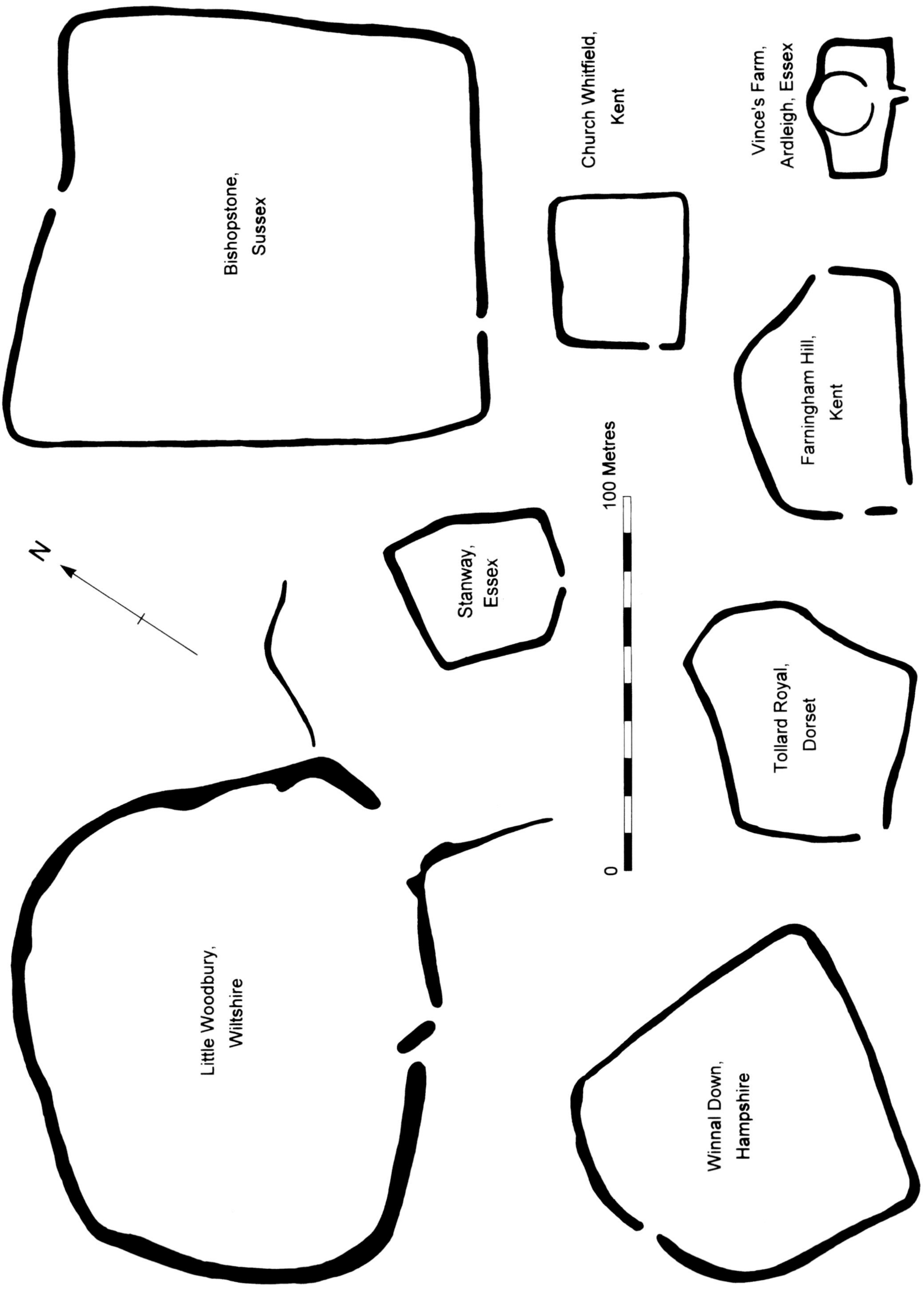

Fig 101. Church Whitfield: comparative plans of some Iron Age farmstead enclosures.

2003, 123). The close proximity of a major Roman road leading up onto the downs directly from the former *Portus Dubris* could well have been one of the factors influencing the choice of the present settlement's location (and see below).

Dating evidence for Church Whitfield is essentially confined to the small assemblage of pottery, comprising little more than 100 sherds, largely contained within SFB Structures III and VIII (Table 44). It would appear that the settlement was quite short-lived, being abandoned by the start of the eighth century. It perhaps came into being during the reign of King Ethelbert I (AD 560–616), when the Anglo-Saxon kingdom of Kent reached the height of its wealth and power (Witney 1982, 88). Since the full extent of the settlement has not been revealed it is possible that areas of earlier and later habitation exist in adjacent, unexcavated areas, with the site perhaps eventually being replaced by new ones established next to the parish church and at Pineham.

As with the preceding Iron Age settlements (see above), the site was probably based on a mixed economy of crop cultivation and animal husbandry. Animal bones recovered from the SFB fills suggest that cattle, pigs and sheep were kept and butchered on the site. Eggshell fragments imply that poultry was kept, whilst hunting is suggested by the presence of roe deer. Shellfish remains, fish bones and fish hooks imply that the resources of the sea and/or river were also being utilised, at least on an occasional basis.

The Anglo-Saxon buildings

The sunken-featured buildings recorded represent a familiar Anglo-Saxon building-type, although broadly comparable structures are also known from a few Romano-British contexts in Kent (Parfitt 1990, 16; Hicks 2008) and beyond, eg King Harry Lane at St Albans (Stead and Rigby 1989, 7) and nearby Gorhambury (Neal *et al* 1990, 75).

Of the four Whitfield SFBs excavated, Structures VII and VIII were of the same, slightly less common design, with a large post set in the middle of each of the four sides of the sunken area (Pl 25). This form is not frequently found amongst the known range of English SFB types but there are single parallels recorded from West Stow, Suffolk (SFB 8; West 1985, 18), Heybridge, Essex (GH 5; Drury and Wickenden 1982, 6), Puddlehill, Dunstable, Bedfordshire (Hut 5; Mathews 1962) and Sutton Courtenay, (House VI; Leeds 1923; 1927). An interesting detail was that two opposing posts in Structure VII were set leaning inwards at a slight angle. This must reflect something of the form of the superstructure of the building.

The precise arrangement of the flooring within SFBs continues to be debated nationally (Hamerow 2011, 146). The collective evidence from Church Whitfield seems to show that it was the base of the sunken area that served as the building's floor, rather than this being a cellared area covered by suspended wooden flooring, as has been suggested elsewhere (Tipper 2004). Specifically, Structures III and VII had stake-holes and other features cut into the sunken area, clearly implying that this was their floor level (Figs 61 and 65; Pls 6 and 7). In Structure VII there was an extensive worn area caused by regular activity on this level. The evidence in favour of sunken floors at Church Whitfield is consistent with the findings at a number of other sites, eg Catholme (Losco-Bradley and Kinsley 2002, 89), but remains at variance with Stanley West's original interpretation of the structures at West Stow (West 1985, 116–21).

Despite their poorly preserved post-holes and very limited dating evidence, it seems reasonably certain that the two wall-post buildings recorded at Church Whitfield (Structures I and IV) are also of Anglo-Saxon date. The overall layout of the better preserved Structure I leaves no doubt that it represents a substantial hall building of a type well-known from a number of other Anglo-Saxon settlement sites in England (Fig 69; Pl 26). There is perhaps just sufficient remaining of Structure IV to suggest that this was another (Fig 71). Whether these two structures were contemporary or successive replacements of the same building remains unknown; nor is it clear if any other large buildings await discovery in unexcavated parts of the site.

The identification of at least Structure I as an example of an Anglo-Saxon hall is of particular interest and importance as it represents one of the first such buildings to be recorded in rural east Kent. The outline of a superficially similar, hall-like building was revealed at the Manston Road settlement but the amount of Bronze Age pottery associated led the excavators to the conclusion that it must be prehistoric (Hutcheson and Andrews 2009, 203–5). Elsewhere, work on the Wainscott by-pass near Strood, has revealed most of the outline of a large, bow-sided building perhaps of eighth- or ninth-century date (Clark *et al* 2009, 76–7). An incomplete structure examined at the South Darenth Roman villa complex in west Kent (Philp 1984, 81–2) could be either Anglo-Saxon or late Roman in date. Large timber buildings, probably belonging to the seventh century, have been recorded within the old Roman city of Canterbury (Blockley *et al* 1995, 345–6) and one or two of a similar date have been discovered more locally at Dover (Philp 2003, 29–38). Overall, however, timber hall buildings remain extremely rare across Kent.

The ground plan of Structure I at Church Whitfield indicates that the building was of substantial proportions and considerably larger than many comparable hall buildings known on other Anglo-Saxon settlements (James *et al* 1984). The outline suggests that it had been laid out in a ratio of 3:1, following a three-square-module (James *et al* 1984, 186–8, fig 6). Structure IV might have been similarly proportioned and if so, would have been the larger of the two buildings, with the square annexe at its north-east end adding to the overall length (Fig 71).

Martin Welch noted that the inferred 3:1 ratio would be more typical of buildings dating to the ninth century (Welch 2007, 205). If such a middle Saxon date for the Church Whitfield buildings is accepted, it implies that they are later than the excavated SFBs, which in turn must mean that there are two separate phases of Anglo-Saxon habitation on the site. Without any useful stratigraphic relationships available, there is nothing to disprove this suggestion but the available dating evidence does not really seem sufficient to give any further support to the idea. On balance, all the Anglo-Saxon structures presently seem best viewed as a single, more or less contemporary group, with one or more halls associated with ancillary SFBs. The four excavated SFBs all lay closer to Structure IV and may have been deliberately grouped around it, although they need not all be exactly the same date. Further to the north-east, Structure I, appears somewhat isolated (Fig 60) but another possible SFB was observed nearby (F904) and it seems likely that other buildings existed beyond the limits of the excavation.

The Anglo-Saxon settlement and the local road system

The Iron Age and Anglo-Saxon settlements discovered during the excavations were situated adjacent to a present-day crossroads (Figs 4 and 46). Crossroad locations are often considered to be historically significant points in the landscape and the lanes which intersected at the investigated site are likely to be of some antiquity. Early map evidence certainly confirms that these roads were in place by the start of the nineteenth century (*see* p 3). The local road system is, thus, potentially of some significance to our understanding of the evolution of the site and the new by-pass works provided a rare opportunity to archaeologically consider its development.

It remains very difficult to establish a precise date when these local routes first came into being. The ancient road system of the area has not survived untouched, however, for there is the clear cropmark of another, long abandoned, trackway crossing Archer's Court Road at right angles, to connect with the Roman road, some 375m north-east of the crossroads.

Archer's Court Road itself, running south-west to north-east between present day Whitfield and Sutton Downs, is effectively a ridgeway following the dip-slope of the North Downs on a single alignment from a point above the Dour valley for some 6km towards Deal (Fig 3). The fact that the only entrance into the late Iron Age (Period 3) ditched enclosure fell on its line initially appeared significant but the absence of a corresponding entrance opposite seems to preclude any notion that the farmstead originally stood astride a through-routeway. The angle of the same enclosure to the line of the Pineham to Church Whitfield road and the fact that it cuts across the southern corner of the enclosure ditch would seem to indicate that there was no close relationship between this trackway and the late Iron Age farmstead (Fig 55). The overall impression gained therefore is that both routeways came into being sometime after the late Iron Age site had been abandoned. A Roman origin, however, would seem to be precluded by the fact that the main Richborough to Dover road (Margary 1967, Route 100) lies only a short distance to the east of the crossroads (Fig 4).

The overall conclusion reached is that the local roads crossing the excavated site are probably of post-Roman date, originating sometime in either the Anglo-Saxon or medieval period. This raises questions as to whether the Anglo-Saxon settlement was specifically established at a pre-existing crossroads, or whether these local routes developed as tracks connecting with the newly founded site. Either way, there seems to be no evidence in the layout of the settlement which would preclude a direct connection between this habitation site and the crossroads; in all probability it is a significant association.

Bibliography

Adams, O R 1987, *Lameness in Horses*, Lea and Febiger, Philadelphia

Allen, D F 1971, 'British Potin Coins; a Review' in D Jesson and D Hill (eds), *The Iron Age and its Hillforts*, Southampton

Allen W 1965, *The African Husbandman*, Lit Verl, Berlin

Amorosi, T 1989, *A Postcranial Guide to Domestic Neo-Natal and Juvenile Mammals*, British Archaeological Reports (International Series) 533, Oxford

Amos, E G J 1937, 'Dover Report for 1937', *Archaeologia Cantiana* xlix, 287

Amour-Chelu, M 1998, 'The animal bone' in F Pryor, *Etton, excavations at a Neolithic causewayed enclosure near Maxey, Cambridgeshire, 1982–7*. English Heritage, London, 273–88

Ampe, C, Bourgeois, J, Crombe, P, Fockedey, L, Langohr, R, Meganck, M, Semey, J, Van Stryndonck, M and Verlaeckt, K 1996, 'The circular view: aerial photography and the discovery of Bronze Age funerary monuments in East and West Flanders (Belgium)', *Germania*, 74:1, 45–94

Anderson, T 1994, 'A Bronze Age burial from St Margaret's at Cliffe', *Archaeologia Cantiana* cxiv, 357–61

Andrews, P and Crockett, A 1996, *Three Excavations along the Thames and its Tributaries, 1994*, Wessex Archaeology Report 10, Salisbury

Annable, F K and Simpson, D D A 1964, *Guide Catalogue of the Neolithic and Bronze Age Collections in Devizes Museum*, Wiltshire Archaeological & Natural History Society, Devizes

Arnold, C J 1988, *An Archaeology of the Early Anglo-Saxon Kingdoms*, London

Ashbee, P and Dunning, G C 1960, 'The round barrows of East Kent', *Archaeologia Cantiana* lxxiv, 48–57

Bailey, A 2010, 'Funerary remains from Tothill Street, Minster', *Canterbury's Archaeology 2008–2009*, 69–70

Bailon, S 1999, *Differenciation Ostéologique des Anoures (amphibia, anura) de France*, CNRS Fiches d'Ostéologie Animale pour l'Archéologie, Série C, No 1

Baker, J and Brothwell, D R 1980, *Animal diseases in archaeology*, Academic Press, London

Barclay, A and Halpin, C 1997, *Excavations at Barrow Hills, Radley, Oxfordshire. Vol. 1: The Neolithic and Bronze Age monument complex*, Thames Valley Landscape Series, Oxford Archaeological Unit, Oxford16

Barrett J C 1990, 'The monumentality of death: the character of early Bronze Age mortuary mounds in southern Britain', *World Archaeology* 22:2, 179–89

Baxter, I 1998, 'Species identification of equids from Western European archaeological deposits: methodologies, techniques and problems' in S Anderson and K Boyle (eds), *Current and Recent Research in Osteoarchaeology*, Oxbow Books, Oxford, 3–17

Bell, M 1977, 'Excavations at Bishopstone, East Sussex [Rookery Hill]', *Sussex Archaeological Collections*115, 192–242

Bendrey, R 2002, 'The animal bones from excavations at the Channel Tunnel Terminal at Cheriton, Folkestone', unpublished report for the Canterbury Archaeological Trust

Bendrey, R 2006, 'Mammal Bones' in K Parfitt *et al*, 321–53

Bendrey, R 2007, 'The development of new methodologies for studying the horse: case studies from prehistoric southern England', unpublished PhD thesis, University of Southampton

Bendrey, R 2008a, 'An early domestic horse find from Chalk Hill, Ramsgate?', *Canterbury's Archaeology 2006–2007*, 44

Bendrey, R 2008b, 'Diseased, broken and squashed in a hole: the deposition of a horse at Downlands, Walmer', *Canterbury's Archaeology 2006–2007*, 44

Bendrey, R 2008c, 'The Animal Bone' in P Bennett *et al*, 233–62

Bendrey, R 2010a, 'The horse' in T O'Connor and N Sykes (eds), *Extinctions and Invasions: A Social History of British Fauna*, Windgather Press, 10–16

Bendrey, R 2010b, 'The animal bone' in C Jarman, *Excavations at Downlands, Walmer, Kent*, Canterbury Archaeological Trust Occasional Paper 7. Canterbury Archaeological Trust, Canterbury, 67–71

Bendrey, R 2012, 'From wild horses to domestic horses: a European perspective', *World Archaeology* 44, 135–57

Bendrey, R, Taylor, G M, Bouwman, A S and Cassidy, J P 2008, 'Suspected bacterial disease in two archaeological horse skeletons from southern England: palaeopathological and biomolecular studies', *Journal of Archaeological Science* 35 (6), 1581–90

Bendrey, R, Hayes T E and Palmer M R 2009, 'Patterns of Iron Age horse supply: an analysis of strontium isotope ratios in teeth', *Archaeometry* 51, 140–50

Bendrey, R, Leach,S and Clark, K 2010, 'New light on an old rite: reanalysis of an Iron Age burial group from Blewburton Hill, Oxfordshire' in J Morris and J M Maltby (eds), *Integrating Social and Environmental Archaeologies; Reconsidering Deposition*, British Archaeological Reports (International Series) S2077, Archaeopress, Oxford, 33–44

Bendrey, R, Cassidy, J P, Bokovenko, N, Lepetz, S and Zaitseva, G 2011, 'A possible case of 'poll-evil' in an early Scythian horse skull from Arzhan 1, Tuva Republic, Central Asia', *International Journal of Osteoarchaeology*, 21 (1), 111–18

Bendrey R, Thorpe N, Outram, A and van Wijngaarden-Bakker, L H in press, 'The origins of domestic horses in north-west Europe: new direct dates on the horses of Newgrange, Ireland', *Proceedings of the Prehistoric Society* 79.

Bennell, M 2002, 'Iron Age Material: Capel-le-Ferne' in Researches and Discoveries in Kent, *Archaeologia Cantiana* cxxii, 402–12

Bennett, P 1978, 'A Roman building near Sandwich', *Archaeologia Cantiana* xciv, 191–4

Bennett, P, Couldrey, P and Macpherson-Grant, N 2007, *Highstead near Chislet, Kent, Excavations 1975–1977*, The Archaeology of Canterbury, New Series, IV, Canterbury

Bennett, P, Clark, P, Hicks, A, Rady, J and Riddler, I 2008, *At the Great Crossroads. Prehistoric, Roman and medieval discoveries on the Isle of Thanet 1994–95*, Canterbury Archaeological Trust Occasional Paper No 4, Canterbury

Bersu, G 1940, 'Excavations at Little Woodbury, Wiltshire, Part 1: The Settlement revealed by excavation', *Proceedings of the Prehistoric Society* xl, 206–13

Beswick, P 1994, 'Shale ring' in J Barrett, 'Excavation of a Bronze Age unenclosed cemetery, cairns and field boundaries at Eaglestone Flat, Curbar, Derbyshire, 1984, 1989–90', *Proceedings of the Prehistoric Society* 60, 287–370, (333–4)

Blockley, K, Blockley, M, Blockley, P, Frere, S S and. Stow, S 1995, *Excavations in the Marlowe Car Park and Surrounding Areas*, The Archaeology of Canterbury V, Whitstable

Boessneck, J 1969, 'Osteological Differences between Sheep (*Ovis aries* Linné) and Goat (*Capra hircus* Linné)' in D Brothwell and E Higgs (eds), *Science in Archaeology*, Thames and Hudson, London, 331–58

Bown, P, Bristow, C and de Silva, N 2004, 'The Shale' in P Clark (ed), 216

Bradley, R 1993, *Altering the Earth: The Origins of Monuments in Britain and Continental Europe*, Society of Antiquaries of Scotland Monograph Series: 8, Edinburgh

Bradley, R 2007, *The Prehistory of Britain and Ireland*, Cambridge, Cambridge University Press

Brent, C 1866, 'Bronze Age urn from Westbere', *Journal of the British Archaeological Association* xxii, 241–2

Bristow, P H W 1998, *Attitudes to Disposal of the Dead in Southern Britain 3500 BC - AD 43*, British Archaeological Reports (British Series) 274, Oxford

Bronk Ramsey, C, Higham, T H F, Owen, D C, Pike, A W G and Hedges, R E M 2002, 'Radiocarbon dates from the Oxford AMS system: Archaeometry datelist 31', *Archaeometry* 44, 1–149

Brothwell, D R and Powers, R 1966, 'The prehistoric skeletons from West Overton' (144–7) in I F Smith and A A Simpson, 'Excavations of a round barrow on Overton Hill, North Wiltshire', *Proceedings of the Prehistoric Society* xxxii, 122–55

Brothwell, D R and Powers, R 1967, 'Appendix I, Human skeletal material', 359–63 in P M Christie, 'A barrow cemetery of the second millenium BC in Wiltshire England', *Proceedings of the Prehistoric Society* xxxiii, 336–66

Brück, J 2000, 'Settlement, landscape and social identity: the early-middle Bronze Age transition in Wessex, Sussex and the Thames Valley', *Oxford Journal of Archaeology* 19:3, 273–300

Brugmann, B 2004, *Glass Beads from Early Anglo-Saxon Graves*, Oxbow, Oxford

Brugmann, B 2012, 'Buckland Cemetery Chronology' in K Parfitt and T Anderson, 323–66

Bull, R 2012, 'The Prehistoric Landscape at Whitehill Road, Longfield and New Barn, Kent (Archaeological Zones 1 and 2)', CTRL Integrated Site Report Series, Oxford Wessex Archaeology Joint Venture: London

Buikstra, J E and Goldstein, L 1973, *The Perrins Ledge Cemetery*, Illinois State Museum

Burnett, A M and Bland, R F (eds) 1986, *Coin Hoards from Roman Britain Volume VI*, British Museum Occasional Paper No 58, British Museum Publications, London

Butler, C 2002, 'Detailed assessment of the surface flintwork' in K Parfitt 2002a, 6–8

Butterworth, C A and Lobb, S J 1992, *Excavations in the Burghfield aea, Berkshire: developments in the Bronze Age and Saxon Landscapes*, Wessex Archaeology Report 1, Salisbury

Cahen-Delhaye, A 1995, 'Les relations extérieurs des populations celtiques en Belgique du Ve au IIIe Siècle' in *L'Europe Celtique du Ve au IIIe Siècle avant J-C*, Memoire de la Société Archéologique Champenoise 9, 27–36

Callou, C 1997, *Diagnose différentielle des principaux éléments squelettiques du lapin (genre Oryctolagus) et du lièvre (genre Lepus), en Europe occidentale*, Fiches d'Ostéologie Animale pour l'Archéologie. Série B: Mammifères, No 8

Campbell, G 2000, 'Plant utilisation: the evidence from charred plant remains' in B Cunliffe, *The Danebury Environs Programme: The prehistory of a Wessex Landscape Volume 1: Introduction*, English Heritage and Oxford University Committee for Archaeology Monograph 48, Oxford, 45–59

Camps, F E (ed) 1968, *Gradwohl's Legal Medicine*, second edition, John Wright and Sons, Bristol

Carlson, D S G, Armelagos, G J, Van Gerven, D P 1974, 'Factors influencing the etiology of cribra orbitalia in prehistoric Nubia', *Journal of Human Evolution* 3, 405–10

Champion, T C 2004, 'Exotic materials in the Early Bronze Age of Southeastern England' in H Roche, E Grogan, J Bradley, J Coles and B Raftery (eds), *From megaliths to metals: essays in honour of George Eogan*, Oxbow, Oxford, 48–52

Champion, T 2007, 'Prehistoric Kent' in J H Williams (ed), 67–132

Champion, T, Gamble, C Shennan, S and Whittle A 1992, *Prehistoric Europe*, Academic Press, London

Charpy, J J and Roualet, P 1987, *La Céramique Peinte Gauloise en Champagne du VIe au Ier siècle avant Jésus-Christ*, Musée D'Epernay

Clapham, A R, Tutin, T G and Moore, D M 1989, *Flora of the British Isles*, first paperback edition, Cambridge

Clark, A J and Thompson, F H 1989, 'Revised radiocarbon dates for three hillforts in Kent and Surrey', *Antiquaries Journal* lxix, 2, 303–4

Clark, J G D 1960, 'Excavations at the Neolithic Site at Hurst Fen, Mildenhall, Suffolk (1954, 1957 and 1958)', *Proceedings of the Prehistoric Society* xxvi, 202–45

Clark, K M 1995, 'The later prehistoric and protohistoric dog: the emergence of canine diversity', *Archaeozoologia*, VII/2, 9–32

Clark, K M 2000, 'Dogged persistence: the phenomenon of canine skeletal uniformity in British prehistory' in S J Crockford (ed), *Dogs through Time: An Archaeological Perspective*, British Archaeological Reports (International Series) 889, 163–9

Clark, P (ed) 2004, *The Dover Bronze Age Boat*, English Heritage, London

Clark, P 2008, 'Transformation of meanings: some implications of the prehistoric discoveries', P Bennett *et al*, 88–100

Clark, P and Rady, J 2008, 'The Prehistoric Period' in P Bennett *et al*, 9–100

Clark, P, Rady, J and Sparey-Green, C 2009, *Wainscott Northern By-pass, Archaeological investigations 1992–1997* Canterbury Archaeological Trust Occasional Paper No 5, Canterbury

Clarke, D L 1970, *Beaker Pottery of Great Britain and Ireland*, Cambridge University Press, Cambridge

Clarke, D V, Cowie, T G and Foxon, A 1985, *Symbols of Power at the Time of Stonehenge*, HMSO and the National Museum of Antiquities of Scotland, Edinburgh

Clutton-Brock, J and Burleigh, R 1991, 'The skull of a Neolithic horse from Grime's Graves, Norfolk, England' in R H Meadows and H-P Uerpmann (eds), *Equids in the ancient world*, Volume II, Wiesbaden; Dr Ludwig Reichert Verlag, 242–9

Coles, J M and Harding, A F 1979, *The Bronze Age in Europe*, Methuen, London

Corbet, G B 1977, 'Common shrew *Sorex araneus*' in G B Corbet and H N Southern, 46–54

Corbet, G B and Southern, H N (ed) 1977, *The Handbook of British Mammals*, Blackwell Scientific Publications, Oxford

Corke, D 1977, 'Yellow-necked mouse *Apodemus flavicollis*' in G B Corbet and H N Southern, 217–19

Couldrey, P 2007, 'The late Bronze Age/early Iron Age pottery' in P Bennett *et al*, 101–70

Couldrey, P forthcoming, 'The later prehistoric ceramics from Dolland's Moor' in J Rady, *The Archaeology of the Channel Tunnel UK Terminal, Cheriton, near Folkestone, Kent and its environs*, Canterbury Archaeological Trust

Couldrey, P and Thompson, I 2007, 'The Late Iron Age Pottery' in P Bennett *et al*, 176

Crabtree, P 1989, 'Sheep, Horses, Swine, and Kine: A Zooarchaeological Perspective on the Anglo-Saxon Settlement of England', *Journal of Field Archaeology* 16, 205–13

Cram, L 2000, 'Varieties of dog in Roman Britain' in S J Crockford (ed), *Dogs through Time: an Archaeological Perspective*, British Archaeological Reports (International Series) 889, 171–80

Cross, R P 1991, 'A256 Whitfield to Eastry improvement road: report on the initial archaeological field survey', unpublished Canterbury Archaeological Trust archive report no 1991/14

Cross, R P 1994, 'A256 Whitfield to Eastry improvement road: report on the archaeological evaluations 1992–1993', unpublished Canterbury Archaeological Trust archive report no1994/22

Cross, R P and Redding, T 2000, 'Archaeological investigations at Maydensole, near Dover 1996–1999', *Kent Archaeological Society Newsletter* 46, 1–5

Crummy, N 1983, *The Roman Small Finds from Excavations in Colchester 1971–9*, Colchester Archaeological Reports 2, Colchester

Cruse, R J 1985, 'Excavations at Prings Quarry, Upper Halling', *Archaeologia Cantiana* cii, 129–33

Cruse, R J and Harrison, A C 1983, 'Excavation at Hill Road, Wouldham', *Archaeologia Cantiana* xcix, 81–108

Cunliffe, B 1975, *Iron Age Communities in Britain*, London

Cunliffe, B 1982, 'Social and economic development in Kent in the pre-Roman Iron Age' in P E Leach, 40–50

Cunliffe, B 1991, *Iron Age Communities in Britain*, 3rd edition, London

Curruthers, W and Allison, E 2010, 'Shelford Farm Estate, Broadoak, Canterbury, Kent: charred plant remains and other biological material from the palaeoenvironmental samples, (SQA13.EX02, SQAP.01, SQAPB.01, SWAP.01)', unpublished Canterbury Archaeological Trust archive report no 2010/37

Cybulski, J S 1977, 'Cribra orbitlia a possible sign of anemia in early historic native populations of the British Columbian coast', *American Journal of Physical Anthropology* 47, 31–40

Dacre, M and Ellison, A 1981, 'A Bronze Age urn cemetery at Kimpton, Hampshire', *Proceedings of the Prehistoric Society* 47, 147–204

Davies, S M 1980, 'Excavations at Old Down Farm, Andover. Part I: Saxon', *Proceedings of the Hampshire Field Club and Archaeological Society* 36, 161–80

Davis, S J M 1997, *Animal bones from the Roman site Redlands Farm, Stanwick, Northamptonshire, 1990*, Ancient Monuments Laboratory Report 106/97

Degenne, M and Duval, A 1983, 'La Nécropole de Breuil-Le-Sec (Oise)' in *Les Celtes dans le Nord du Bassin Parisien*, Revue Archéologique de Picardie 1, 74–95

Devereux, S and Morrison, L 1992, *The Veterinary Care of the Horse*, J A Allen, London

Dickinson, T M, Fern, C J R and Richardson, A F 2011, 'Early Anglo-Saxon Eastry: archaeological evidence for the beginnings of a district centre in the kingdom of Kent' in H Hamerow (ed), *Saxon Studies in Archaeology and History* 17, 1–86

Dobney, K and Reilly, K 1988, 'A method for recording archaeological animal bones: the use of diagnostic zones', *Circaea* 5.1, 79–96

Donaldson, P 1977, 'The excavation of a multiple round barrow at Barnack, Cambridgeshire 1974-1976', *Antiquaries Journal* 57, 197–231

Driver, J C 1990, 'Faunal Remains' in J C Driver, J Rady and M Sparks, *Excavations in the Cathedral Precincts, 2 Linacre Garden, 'Meister Omers' and St Gabriel's Chapel*, The Archaeology of Canterbury IV, Maidstone, 228–57

Drury, P J and Wickenden, N P 1982, 'An Anglo-Saxon settlement within the Romano-British small town at Heybridge, Essex', *Medieval Archaeology* 26, 1–31

Edmonds, M 1995, *Stone tools and society: working in stone in Neolithic and Bronze Age Britain*, Batsford, London

Eisenmann, V 1986, 'Comparative osteology of modern and fossil horses, half-asses, and asses' in R H Meadow and H-P Uerpmann, 67–116

Eisenmann, V and Bekouche, S 1986, 'Identification and discrimination of metapodials from Pleistocene and modern *Equus*, wild and domestic' in R H Meadow and H-P Uerpmann, 117–63

Ellison, A and Drewett, P 1971, 'Pits and post-holes in the British Early Iron Age; some alternative explanations', *Proceedings of the Prehistoric Society* xxxvii, 183–94

Elsdon, S 1975, *Stamp and roulette decorated pottery of the La Tène period in eastern England: a study in geometric designs*, British Archaeology Reports (British Series) 10, Oxford

Erith, F H and Longworth, I H 1960, 'A Bronze age Urnfield on Vince's Farm, Ardleigh, Essex', *Proceedings of the Prehistoric Society* xxvi, 178–92

Evans, D 1977, 'Field vole *Microtus agrestis*' in G B Corbet and H N Southern, 185–93

Evans, J G 1972, *Land snails in Archaeology*, Seminar Press, London

Everitt, A M 1986, *Continuity and Colonisation: the evolution of Kentish Settlement*, Leicester University Press, Leicester

Evison, V I 1975, 'Pagan Saxon Whetstones', *Antiquaries Journal* lv, 70–85

Evison, V I 1987, *Dover: Buckland Anglo-Saxon Cemetery*, HBMC Archaeological Report 3, London

Evison, V I and Cooper, V 1985, 'The Beads' in S West, 71–5

Fasham, P J 1985, *The Prehistoric Settlement at Winnall Down, Winchester*, Hampshire Field Club Monograph 2, Stroud

Fasham, P J and Whinney, R J B 1991, *Archaeology and the M3*, Hampshire Field Club Monograph 7, Stroud

Ferembach, D, Schwidetzky, I, Stloukal, M 1980, 'Recommendations for age and sex diagnoses of skletons', *Journal of Human Evolution* 9, 517–49

Field, D 1998, 'Round barrows and the harmonious landscape: placing early Bronze Age burial monuments in South-East England', *Oxford Journal of Archaeology* 17:3, 309–26

Flowerdew, J R 1977a, 'Bank vole *Clethrionomys glareolus*' in G B Corbet and H N Southern, 173–84

Flowerdew, J R 1977b, 'Wood mouse *Apodemus sylvaticus*' in G B Corbet and H N Southern, 206–17

Fokkens, H 2012, 'Access to origins: about the meaning of continuity and discontinuity in the use of barrow 'cemeteries'' in D Bérenger, J Bourgeois, M Talon and S Wirth (eds), *Gräberlandschaften der Bronzezeit, Internationales Kolloquium zur Bronzezeit, Herne, 15–18 Oktober 2008* Vol 51, Darmstadt: Verlag Philip von Zabern, 553–72

Fornaciari, G, Mallegni, F, Bertini, D, Nuti, V 1982, 'Cribra orbitalia and elemental bone iron in the Punics of Carthage', *Ossa* 8, 63–77

Fowler, P 1967, *Wessex*, Heinemann, London

Gardiner, J 1987, 'The Late Neolithic Flint Assemblage' in B Cunliffe, *Hengistbury Head, Dorset, Vol 1: the prehistoric and Roman settlement, 3500 BC–AD 500*, Oxford University Committee for Archaeology Monograph 13, Oxford, 24–38

Gardiner, M 1990, 'An Anglo-Saxon and Medieval Settlement at Botolphs, Bramber, West Sussex', *Archaeological Journal* 147, 216–75

Gardiner, M 1993, 'The Excavation of a Late Anglo-Saxon Settlement at Market Field, Steyning, 1988–9', *Sussex Archaeological Collections* 131, 21–67

Garwood, P 1997, 'The chronology of depositional contexts and monuments' (with contributions by A Barclay) in A Barclay and C Halpin, 275–93

Garwood, P 1999, 'Grooved Ware in Southern Britain, Chronology and Interpretation' in R Cleal and A MacSween, *Grooved Ware in Great Britain and Ireland*, Oxford, 145–76

Garwood, P 2007, 'Before the hills in order stood: chronology, time and history in the interpretation of early Bronze Age round barrows' in J Last (ed), *Beyond the Grave: new perspectives on round barrows*, Oxford, Oxbow Books, 30–52

Gaunt, J, Parfitt, K and Halliwell, G 1977, 'Surveys along the Dover by-pass', *Kent Archaeological Review* 48, 196–200

Gerloff, S 1975, *The early Bronze Age daggers in Great Britain and a reconsideration of the Wessex Culture*, Beck, Munich

Gibson, A M 1980, 'The Beaker Pottery from the Wynian Abbott Collection' in F Pryor, *Excavation at Fengate, Peterborough, England*, The Third Report, Northamptonshire Archaeological Society Monograph 1/Royal Ontario Museum Archaeology Monograph 6, 234–45

Gibson, A 1986, *Neolithic and Early Bronze Age Pottery*, Shire Publications, Aylesbury

Gibson, A 1993, *Neolithic and Bronze Age Pottery from Lord of the Manor Ramsgate, Kent*, report prepared for Thanet Archaeologicl Trust/ Canterbury Archaeological Trust

Gibson, A 1994, *The Neolothic and Bronze Age pottery from Castle Hill ring-ditches, Folkestone*, Report No 1, prepared for Canterbury Archaeological Trust

Gibson, A 1995, *The Neolithic pottery from Cross Roads and St Richards's Road, Deal, Kent*, Report No 21, prepared for Canterbury Archaeological Trust

Gibson, A M 1996, 'The Neolithic and Early Bronze Age Pottery from Monkton-Minster, Kent', Report No 39, prepared for Canterbury Archaeological Trust

Gibson, A M 1997, 'The Neolithic and Bronze Age Pottery from the Eastry By-pass Excavations, Kent', Report No 41, prepared for Canterbury Archaeological Trust

Gibson, A 1998, 'The Neolithic and Early Bronze Age Pottery' in 'The Prehistory of Holywell Coombe' in R C Preece and D R Bridgland, *Late Quaternary Environmental Change in North-west Europe*, Chapman and Hall, Cambridge, 295–9

Gibson, A 2008, 'The Prehistoric Pottery' in P Bennett *et al*, 46–65

Giorgi, J, Stafford, E and Gardiner, J (ed) 2006, *Palaeoenvironmental evidence from Section 1 of the Channel Tunnel Rail Link, Kent*, CTRL Specialist Report Series, London and Continental Railways.

Givens, D M and Marley, M S D 2008, 'Infectious causes of embryonic and fetal mortality', *Theriogenology* 70(3), 270–85

Gleed-Owen, C P 1998, 'Quaternary herpetofaunas of the British Isles: taxonomic descriptions, palaeoenvironmental reconstructions, and biostratigraphic implications', unpublished PhD thesis, University of Coventry

Glover, J 1982, *The Place Names of Kent*, Meresborough Books, Rainham

Grant, A 1982, 'The use of tooth wear as a guide to the age of domestic ungulates' in B Wilson *et al*, 91–108

Grant, A 1984a, 'The animal husbandry' in B Cunliffe, *Danebury: An Iron Age Hillfort in Hampshire*, Council for British Archaeology Research Report 52, London, 496–548

Grant, A 1984b, 'Survival or Sacrifice? A critical appraisal of animal bones in Britain in the Iron Age' in C Grigson and J Clutton-Brock (eds), *Animals and Archaeology: 4. Husbandry in Europe*, British Archaeological Reports (International Series) 227, 221–7

Grant, A with Rush, C and Serjeantson, D 1991, 'Animal husbandry' in B Cunliffe and C Poole, *Danebury: an Iron Age hillfort in Hampshire. Volume 5. The Excavations, 1979–88: the finds*, Council for British Archaeology Research Report 73, London, 447–86

Green, M 1992, *Animals in Celtic Life and Myth*, London

Greenfield, E 1960, 'A Neolithic pit and other finds from Wingham, East Kent', *Archaeologia Cantiana* lxxiv, 58–72

Grigson, C 1966, 'The animal remains from Fussell's Lodge long barrow', *Archaeologia* 100, 63–73

Grinsell, L V 1975, *Barrow, pyramid and tomb: Ancient burial customs in Egypt, the Mediterranean and the British Isles*,Thames and Hudson, London

Grinsell, L V 1992, 'The Bronze Age round barrows of Kent', *Proceedings of the Prehistoric Society* 58, 355–84
Guido, M 1978, *The Glass Beads of the Prehistoric and Roman Periods in Britain and Ireland,* Reports of the Research Committee of the Society of Antiquaries of London 35, London
Guido, M and Bayley, J forthcoming, 'The glass beads' in Excavations in the Cathedral Precincts, I: The '*Aula Nova*', Almonry Chapel and Lanfranc's Dormitory, The Archaeology of Canterbury III
Halliwell, G and Parfitt, K 1985, 'The prehistoric land surface in the Lydden Valley: an initial report', *Kent Archaeological Review* 82, 39–43
Halstead, P 1985, 'A study of mandibular teeth from Romano-British contexts at Maxey' in F Pryor, C French, D Crowther, D Gurney, G Simpson and M Taylor (eds), *Archaeology and Environment in the Lower Welland Valley Volume 1,* East Anglian Archaeology 27, Gressenhall, 219–4
Hambleton, E 1999, *Animal husbandry regimes in Iron Age Britain: a comparative study of faunal assemblages from British Iron Age sites,* British Archaeological Reports (British Series) 282, Oxford
Hamerow, H 1993, *Excavations at Mucking. Volume 2: the Anglo-Saxon Settlement,* English Heritage Archaeological Report 21, London
Hamerow, H 2011, 'Anglo-Saxon timber buildings and their social context' in H Hamerow, D Hinton and S Crawford (eds), *The Oxford Handbook of Anglo-Saxon Archaeology,* Oxford University Press, 128–55
Hammond, J 2010, 'In search of the people of La Manche: A comparative study of funerary practices on either side of the English Channel during the period 2500 BC – 1500 BC', unpublished PhD thesis, University of Kent, Canterbury
Hamson, R J 1977, *The Bell Beaker Cultures of Spain and Portugal,* Peabody Museum of Archaeology and Ethnology, Harvard University, Cambridge, Massachusetts
Harcourt, R A 1974, 'The dog in prehistoric and early historic Britain', *Journal of Archaeological Science* 1, 151–76
Harcourt, R A 1979, 'The animal bones' in G Wainwright, *Gussage All Saints: an Iron Age Settlement in Dorset,* HMSO, London, 150–60
Harding, P 1988, 'The chalk plaque pit, Amesbury', *Proceedings of the Prehistoric Society* 54, 320–27
Harding, P and Beswick, P 2005, 'Excavations at a Bronze Age barrow on Carsington Pasture by Time Team 2002', *Derbyshire Archaeological Journal* 125, 1–20
Harman, M 1973, 'The Mammalian Bones from the Saxon Hut at Keston' in B Philp, *Excavations in West Kent 1960–1970,* Second Research Report in the Kent Monograph Series, Dover, 160–1
Harrison, R J 1977, *The Bell Beaker Cultures of Spain and Portugal,* Peabody Museum of Archaeology and Ethnology Harvard University, Cambridge, Massachusetts
Harrison, R J 1980, T*he Beaker Folk: Copper Age Archaeology in Western Europe,* Thames & Hudson, London
Haselgrove, C 2006, 'Early potin coinage in Britain: an update' in P de Jersey (ed), '*Celtic Coinage: New Discoveries, New Discussion*', British Archaeological Reports (International Series) 1532, 17–27
Hasted, E 1800, *The History and Topographical Survey of the County of Kent* IX and X, Canterbury
Hatt, J J and Roualet, P 1977, 'La chronologie de La Tène en Champagne', *Revue Archéologique de l'Est* 18, 1–2, 7–36
Hawkes, C F C 1940, 'Bronze key-ring from an unusual burial at Pineham, Whitfield, Kent', *Antiquaries Journal* xx, 121–2
Hawkes, S C 1982, 'Anglo-Saxon Kent *c* 425–725' in P E Leach, 64–78
Healey, E and Jelley, D 1988, 'The Flint', pp 182–9 in B E Vyner, 'The Street House Wossit: the excavation of a late Neolithic and early Bronze Age palisaded ritual monument at Street House, Loftus, Cleveland', *Proceedings of the Prehistoric Society* 54, 173–202
Healy, F 1988, *The Anglo-Saxon cemetery at Spong Hill, North Elmham, Part VI: occupation during the seventh to second millennia BC,* East Anglian Archaeology 39, Gressenhall
Hearne, C M, Perkins, D R J and Andrews, P 1995, 'The Sandwich Bay Wastewater Treatment Scheme Archaeological Project 1992–1994', *Archaeologia Cantiana* cxv, 239–354
Hengen, P 1971, 'Cribra orbitalia: pathogenesis and probable etiology', *Homo* 22, 557–76
Hicks, A 2008, 'The Roman Settlement' in P Bennett *et al,* 101–56
Higham, T F G, Bronk Ramsey, C, Brock, F, Baker, D and Ditchfield, P 2007, 'Radiocarbon dates from the Oxford AMS system: Archaeometry datelist 32', *Archaeometry* 49, S1–S60
Hill, J D 1995, *Ritual and rubbish in the Iron Age of Wessex,* British Archaeological Reports (British Series) 242, Oxford
Hillman, G C 1982, *Late Iron Age glume wheats from Wilmington gravel pit, Kent,* Ancient Monument Laboratory Report 3611, London
Hillson, S 1986, *Teeth,* Cambridge University Press, Cambridge
Holck, P 1987, *Cremated Bones. A Medico-Anthropological Study of an Archaeological Material on Cremation Burials,* Anatomisk Institutt: Antropologiske Skrifter nr 1, Oslo
Holden, E W and Bradley, R J 1975, 'A late Neolithic site at Rackham', *Sussex Archaeological Collections* 113, 85–103
Holgate, R 1988, 'A review of Neolithic domestic activity in southern Britain' in J C Barrett and I A Kinnes (eds), *The Archaeology of Context in the Neolithic and Bronze Age,* University of Sheffield Department of Archaeology and Prehistory, 104–12
Holleyman, G and Yeates, C W 1960, 'Excavations in the Ditchling Road area north of Brighton', *Sussex Archaeological Collections* 98, 133–49
Holman, D 2000, 'Iron Age Coins in Kent', *Archaeologia Cantiana* cxx, 205–33
Holman, D 2005, 'Iron Age coinage and settlement in East Kent', *Britannia* xxxvi, 1–54
Houliston, M 1994, 'A256 Whitfield to Eastry improvement road: archaeological evaluations 1994', unpublished archive report, prepared September 1994
Hurtrelle, J, Monchy, E, Roger, F, Rossignol, P and Villes, A 1990, 'Les débuts du second âge du fer dans le nord de la France', *Les Dossiers de Gauheria* 1, Lens
Hutcheson, A and Andrews P 2009, 'A Late Bronze Age, Anglo-Saxon and Medieval Settlement Site at Manston Road, Ramsgate' in P Andrews, Egging Dinwiddy, K, Ellis, C, Hutcheston, A, Philpotts, A, Powell, B and Schuster, J (eds), *Kentish Sites and Sites of Kent: a miscellany of four archaeological excavations,* Wessex Archaeology Report 24, 199–248
Jackson, D A, Harding D W and Myres, J N L 1969, 'The Iron Age and Anglo-Saxon site at Upton, Northants', *Antiquaries Journal* xlix, 202–21
James, F 1899, 'Bronze Age burials at Aylesford' *Proceedings of the Society of Antiquaries of London,* second series 17, 373–7
James, S, Marshall, A and Millett, M 1984, 'An Early Medieval building tradition', *Archaeological Journal* 141, 182–215
Jaques, A and Rossignol, P 1996, 'La Céramique Laténienne en Artois: Premiers Résultats des Fouilles des Années 1990–1995', *Revue Archéologique de Picardie* 3, 23–39
Jones, H 2000, 'Quernstones' in K Parfitt (2000a), 138–9
Jones, M K 1996, 'Plant exploitation' in T Champion and J R Collis (eds), *The Iron Age in Britain and Ireland: Recent Trends,* Sheffield, 29–40
Kaagan, L M 2000, 'The horse in Late Pleistocene and Holocene Britain', unpublished PhD dissertation, University College London
Keith Lucas, B 1984, 'Kentish Turnpikes', *Archaeologia Cantiana* c, 345–69
Kelly, S E (ed) 1995, *Charters of St Augustine's Abbey and Minster-in-Thanet,* Anglo-Saxon Charters IV, Oxford University Press
Kent, S 1987, 'The influence of sedentism and aggregation on porotic hyperostosis and anaemia: a case study', *Man* 21, 605–36
Kerney, M P 1999, *Atlas of the land and freshwater molluscs of Britain and Ireland,* Harley Brooks, Colchester
King, A C 1978, 'A comparative survey of bone assemblages from Roman sites in Britain', *Bulletin of the Institute of Archaeology* 15, 207–32
King, A C 2005, 'Animal remains from temples in Roman Britain', *Britannia* 36, 329–70
Kinnes, I A, Gibson, A M, Ambers, J, Bowman, S, Leese, M and Boast, R 1991, 'Radiocarbon dating and British Beakers: The British Museum programme', *Scottish Archaeological Review* 8, 3, 5–68
Lanting, J N and van der Waals, J D 1972, 'British Beakers as seen from the Continent', *Helinium* 12, 20–46
Lardy, J-M 1983, 'La nécropole d'Epais-Rhus (Val d'Oise), approche chronostratigraphique partie protohistorique' in *Les Celtes dans le Bassin Parisien,* Revue Archeologique de Picardie, 127–58
Last, J 1998, 'Book of Life: biography and memory in a Bronze Age barrow', *Oxford Journal of Archaeology,* 17:1, 43–53
Lawrence, M J and Brown, R W 1973, *Mammals of Britain: Their Tracks, Trails and Signs,* Blandford Press, London
Lawson, A J 1975, 'Shale and jet objects from Silchester', *Archaeologia* 105, 241–75
Leach, P E (ed) 1982, *Archaeology in Kent to 1500,* Council for British Archaeology Research Report 48, London
Leeds, E T 1923, 'A Saxon village near Sutton Courtenay, Berkshire', *Archaeologia* 72, 147–92
Leeds, E T 1927, 'A Saxon village near Sutton Courtenay, Berkshire (second report)', *Archaeologia* 76, 59–79

Legge, A J 1995, 'A horse burial and other grave offerings' in K Parfitt 1995a, 146–52

Leman-Delerive, G 1989, *Les Habitats de L'Âge du Fer à Villeneuve d'Asq*, Revue du Nord Hors-Série, Collection Archéologie No 2

Lethbridge, T C 1927, 'An Anglo-Saxon hut on the Car Dyke, at Waterbeach', *Antiquaries Journal* vii, 141–6

Levine, M A 1982, 'The use of crown height measurements and eruption-wear sequences to age horse teeth' in B Wilson *et al*, 223–350

Livett, G M 1928, 'Whitfield alias Beuesfeld', *Archaeologia Cantiana* xl, 141–58

Lobjois, G 1974, 'Une nécropole se La Tène Ia, Bucy-le-Long (Aisne)', *Cahiers Archéologiques de Picardie*, supplément au Bulletin de la Société des Antiquaires de Picardie, 67–96

Locker, A 1984, 'The Animal Bone' in B J Philp, Microfiche 5

Loftus Brock, E P 1895, 'The Saxon Church at Whitfield, near Dover, Kent', *Archaeologia Cantiana* xxi, 301–5

Longworth, I H 1984, *Collared Urns of the Bronze Age in Great Britain and Ireland*, Cambridge University Press, Cambridge

Losco-Bradley, S and Kinsley, G 2002, *Catholme. An Anglo-Saxon Settlement on the Trent gravels in Staffordshire*, Nottingham

Luff, R and Brothwell, D 1993, 'Health and Welfare' in R Luff, *Animal bones from excavations in Colchester, 1971–85*, Colchester Archaeological Trust, 101–26

Lyman, R L 1994, *Vertebrate Taphonomy*, Cambridge University Press, Cambridge

Ma, X 2008, 'Pig husbandry strategies in an emergent complex society in central China', *Bulletin of the Indo-Pacific Prehistory Association* 24, 91–102

MacGregor, A 1982, *Anglo-Scandinavian Finds from Lloyds Bank, Pavement and other Sites*, The Archaeology of York 17/3, London

Macpherson-Grant, N 1977, *The excavation of a Neolithic/Bronze Age site at Lord of the Manor, Ramsgate*, Isle of Thanet Archaeological Unit Report 1, Broadstairs

Macpherson-Grant, N 1980, 'Archaeological work along the A2: 1966–1974', *Archaeologia Cantiana* xcvii, 133–83

Macpherson-Grant, N 1991, 'A re-appraisal of prehistoric pottery from Canterbury', *Canterbury's Archaeology 1990–91*, 38–48

Macpherson-Grant, N 1992, 'The Pottery' in D Perkins, 'Archaeological evaluations at Ebbsfleet in the Isle of Thanet', *Archaeologia Cantiana* cx, 269–311, 286–301

Macpherson-Grant, N 1995, 'Pottery from the Canterbury Archaeological Trust Sites' in K Blockley *et al*, 834–52

Macpherson-Grant, N 1997, 'The late Iron Age pottery from the Dover Spine Main, context 2', unpublished report for R P S Clouston project 2905

Macpherson-Grant, N 2002, 'The Pottery' in M Bennell, 402–11

Macpherson-Grant, N and Perkins, D R J 1977, *The Excavation of a Neolithic/Bronze Age site at the Lord of the Manor, Haine Road, Ramsgate*, Isle of Thanet Archaeological Unit Publication 1, Ramsgate

Macpherson-Grant, N and Perkins, D R J 1980, 'Lord of the Manor Site 2 and 3', *The Isle of Thanet Archaeological Unit: Interim reports 1977–1980* (privately printed, Thanet), 5–17

Macpherson-Grant, N, Savage, A, Cotter, J, Davey, M and Riddler, I 1995, 'Canterbury Ceramics 2. The Processing and Study of Excavated Pottery', unpublished Canterbury Archaeological Trust report

Mallye, J B, Cochard, D and Laroulandie V 2008, 'Accumulations osseuses en périphérie de terriers de petits carnivores: les stigmates de prédation et de fréquentation', *Annales de paléontologie* 94, 187–208

Maltby, J M 1981, 'Iron Age, Romano-British and Anglo-Saxon husbandry – a review of the faunal evidence' in M Jones and G W Dimbleby (eds), *The environment of man: the Iron Age to the Anglo-Saxon Period*, British Archaeological Reports (British Series) 87, 155–203

Maltby, J M 1987a, *The Animal Bones from the Excavations at Owslebury, Hants. An Iron Age and Early Romano-British Settlement*, Ancient Monuments Laboratory Report, 6/87

Maltby, J M 1987b, *The Animal Bones from the 1982–1983 Excavations at Easton Lane Interchange (W29), Hants*, Ancient Monuments Laboratory Report 7/87

Manning, W H, Price, J and Webster, J 1995, *Report on the Excavations at Usk 1965–76. The Roman Small Finds*, University of Wales Press, Cardiff

Margary, I D 1967, *Roman Roads in Britain*, revised edition, John Baker, London

Mathews, C L 1962, 'Saxon remains on Puddlehill, Dunstable', *Bedfordshire Archaeological Journal* I, 48–57

Mayer, J J and Brisbin, I L 1988, 'Sex identification of *Sus scrofa* based on canine morphology', *Journal of Mammalogy* 69 (2), 408–12

Mays, S and Anderson, T 1995, 'Archaeological research priorities for human remains from South-East England', *Archaeologia Cantiana* cxv, 355–88

McKinley, J 1989, 'Cremations expectations, methodologies and realities' in C A Roberts, F Lee, R Bintliff (eds), *Burial Archaeology Current Research Methods and Developments*, British Archaeological Reports (British Series) S211, 65–76

McKinley, J 1997, 'Bronze Age 'Barrows' and funerary rites and rituals of cremation', *Proceedings of the Prehistoric Society* 63, 129–45

McKinley, J 2005, 'The human bone' in P Harding and P Beswick, 7–8

Meadow R H and Uerpmann H-P (eds) 1986, *Equids in the Ancient World*, Wiesbaden

Mellor, D J and Stafford, K J 2004, 'Animal welfare implications of neonatal mortality and morbidity in farm animals', *The Veterinary Journal* 168(2), 118–33

Middleton, A P 1995, 'Prehistoric red-finished pottery from Kent' in I A Kinnes and G Varndell (eds), *'Unbaked Urns of Rudely Shape': Essays on British and Irish Pottery for Ian Longworth*, British Museum, 203–10

Miller, T 1987, 'Systematics and evolution' in F G H Lupton (ed), *Wheat breeding: its scientific basis*, London, 1–30

Millet, M and James, S 1983, 'Excavations at Cowdery's Down, Basingstoke, Hampshire 1978–81', *Archaeological Journal* 140, 151–279

Milward, J 2009, 'Broken bracelets and boundaries – the discovery of a late Bronze Age/early Iron Age settlement at Burham, Kent', *Kent Archaeological Society Newsletter* 81, 2–3

Minter, K S and Herbert, E F (eds) 1973, *Archaeological Discoveries in Broadstairs and St Peter's up to 1972*, Broadstairs

Mizoguchi, K 1993, 'Time in the reproduction of mortuary practices', *World Archaeology*, 25:2, 223–35

Molyneux, J 1986, *The Church of St Peter, Whitfield: A Short History*, Dover

Moody, G 2008, *The Isle of Thanet from Prehistory to the Norman Conquest*, Birmingham, Tempus

Morris, J 2011, *Investigating animal burials: ritual, mundane and beyond*, British Archaeological Reports (British Series) 535, Archaeopress, Oxford

Musty, J 1969, 'The excavation of two barrows, one of Saxon date, at Ford, Laverstoke, near Salisbury, Wiltshire', *Antiquaries Journal* 49, 98–117

Neal, D S, Wardle, A and Hunn, J 1990, *Excavation of the Iron Age, Roman and Medieval Settlement at Gorhambury, St Albans*, English Heritage Archaeological Report 14, London

Neal, E 1986, *The Natural History of Badgers*, Croom Helm, London and Sydney

Needham, S 1996, 'Chronology and periodisation in the British Bronze Age', *Acta Archaeologica* 67, 121–40

Needham, S 2006, 'Precious cups of the Early Bronze Age' in S Needham, K Parfitt, K and G Varndell (eds), *The Ringlemere Cup: Precious Cups and the Beginning of the Channel Bronze Age*, British Museum Research Publication 163, London, 53–67

Oakley, K P, Barker, H and Sieveking, G de G 1967, 'The skeleton of Halling man', *Archaeologia Cantiana* lxxxii, 218–20

O'Connor, T P 1985, 'On quantifying vertebrates: some sceptical observations', *Circaea* 3, 27–30

O'Connor, T P 2000, *The Archaeology of Animal Bones*, Sutton, Stroud Publishing

O'Kelly, M J, Cleary, R M and Lehane, D 1983, *Newgrange, Co. Meath, Ireland. The Late Neolithic, Beaker Period Settlement*, British Archaeological Reports (International Series) No 190, Oxford

Ortner, D J and Putschar, W G J 1985, *Identification of Pathological Conditions in Human Skeletal Remains*, Smithsonian Contribution to Anthropology 28, Smithsonian Institution Press, Washington

Parfitt, K 1974, 'A probable Iron Age site at Whitfield, near Dover', *Kent Archaeological Review* 38, 243

Parfitt, K 1975, 'Iron Age site at Whitfield, near Dover', *Kent Archaeological Review* 40, 289

Parfitt, K 1976, 'A Neolithic/Bronze Age site at St Margaret's-at-Cliffe', *Kent Archaeological Review* 46, 141–6

Parfitt, K 1979, 'The Sandwich by-pass, 1978: an interim report', *Kent Archaeological Review* 56, 133–4

Parfitt, K 1980, 'A probable Roman villa on the Sandwich by-pass', *Kent Archaeological Review* 60, 232–48

Parfitt, K 1981, 'The Ringwould water main', *Kent Archaeological Review* 65, 107–11

Parfitt, K 1986, 'Two barrows at Eythorne', *Kent Archaeological Review* 84, 77–8

Parfitt, K 1990, 'Excavations at Mill Hill, Deal 1982–1989; an interim report', *Kent Archaeological Review* 101, 9–18
Parfitt, K 1992, 'A possible Anglo-Saxon Cemetery at Sutton-by-Dover', *Kent Archaeological Review* 108, 192
Parfitt, K 1994, 'Buckland Anglo-Saxon Cemetery, Dover: an Interim Report', *Archaeologia Cantiana* civ, 454–6
Parfitt, K 1995a, *Iron Age Burials from Mill Hill, Deal*, British Museum Press, London
Parfitt, K 1995b, 'Whitfield-Eastry by-pass 1995: report on evaluation trenching, Project 1 (south of Pineham)', unpublished Canterbury Archaeological Trust report for Kent County Council, 1995/20
Parfitt, K 1995c, 'Whitfield Churchyard extension archaeological evaluation report', unpublished Dover Archaeological Group report for Kent County Council, December
Parfitt, K 1995d, 'Royal Victoria Hospital, Dover', *Canterbury's Archaeology 1993–1994*, 20–1
Parfitt, K 1995e, 'Whitfield Eastry by-pass 1995: report on evaluation trenching, Project 6 (north of Tilmanstone)', unpublished Canterbury Archaeological Trust report for Kent County Council, June
Parfitt, K 1999, 'Report on a watching brief conducted at the new Dover Ship's Stores Building, Honeywood Road, Whitfield, Dover', unpublished Canterbury Archaeological Trust report for Kent County Council, 1999/101
Parfitt, K 2000a, 'A Roman occupation site at Dickson's Corner, Worth', *Archaeologia Cantiana* cxx, 107–48
Parfitt, K 2000b, 'A Victorian photograph of Whitfield Church (Pre-Restoration)', *Archaeologia Cantiana* cxx, 381–5
Parfitt, K 2002a, 'Report on archaeological work along the Dover Eastern Docks Supply Water Main',unpublished Canterbury Archaeological Trust assessment report, 2003/137
Parfitt, K 2002b, 'A prehistoric site off Green Lane, Whitfield, near Dover', *Archaeologia Cantiana* cxx, 373–96
Parfitt, K 2003, 'A watching-brief at White Cliffs Business Park, Honeywood Parkway, Whitfield, February 2003' unpublished Canterbury Archaeological Trust report
Parfitt, K 2004, 'A round barrow near Haynes Farm, Eythorne', *Archaeologia Cantiana* cxxiv, 397–415
Parfitt, K 2010, 'Report on evaluation trenching in 2010 off Honeywood Parkway, White Cliffs Business Park, Dover', unpublished Canterbury Archaeological Trust report, 2010/15
Parfitt, K, Allen, T and Rady, J 1997, 'Whitfield-Eastry by-pass', *Canterbury's Archaeology 1995–1996*, 28–33
Parfitt, K and Anderson, T 2012, *Buckland Anglo-Saxon Cemetery. Excavations 1994*, The Archaeology of Canterbury, New Series, VI, Canterbury
Parfitt, K and Brugmann, B 1997, *The Anglo-Saxon Cemetery on Mill Hill, Deal, Kent*, Society for Medieval Archaeology Monograph 14, London
Parfitt, K and Corke, B 2005, "Eden Roc', Bay Hill, St Margaret's at Cliffe', *Canterbury's Archaeology 2004–2005*, 31–2
Parfitt, K, Corke, B and Cotter, J 2006, *Townwall Street, Dover, Excavations 1996*, The Archaeology of Canterbury, New Series, III, Canterbury
Parfitt, K and Corke, B 2010, 'Deal Waterworks, St Richard's Road', *Canterbury's Archaeology 2008–2009*, 42–3
Parfitt, K and Dickinson, T M 2007, 'The Anglo-Saxon cemetery at Old Park, near Dover, revisited' in Martin Henig and Tyler Jo Smith (eds) *Collectanea Antiqua: Essays in Memory of Sonia Chadwick Hawke*, British Archaeological Reports (International Series) 1673, Oxford
Parfitt, K and Halliwell, G 1996, 'More Palaeolithic Discoveries in east Kent', *Kent Archaeological Review* 123, 58–64
Parfitt, K and Halliwell, G 2010, 'A New Mesolithic Site at Westcliffe, St Margaret's, near Dover', *Kent Archaeological Review* 180, 233–9
Parfitt, K and Needham, S P 2007, 'Excavations at Ringlemere Farm, Woodnesborough 2006-2007', *Archaeologia Cantiana* cxxvi, 39–56
Parker, S 1988, 'The cremation deposit', pp 194–5 in B E Vyner, 'The Street House Wossit: the excavation of a Late Neolithic and Early Bronze Age palisaded ritual monument at Street House, Loftus, Cleveland', *Proceedings of the Prehistoric Society* 54, 173–202
Parker Pearson, M 1993, *Bronze Age Britain*, English Heritage, Batsford, London
Parrington, M 1978, *The excavation of an Iron Age Settlement, Bronze Age ring ditches and Roman features at Ashfville Trading Estate, Abingdon (Oxfordshire)*, Council for British Archaeology Research Report 28, London
Payne, G 1884, 'A Celtic interment at Sittingbourne, Kent', *Proceedings of the Society of Antiquaries of London*, second series 10, 29–30
Payne, S 1973, 'Kill-off patterns in sheep and goats: the mandibles from Asvan Kale', *Anatolian Studies* 23, 281–303
Payne, S 1985, 'Morphological distinctions between the mandibular teeth of young sheep, *Ovis*, and goats, *Capra', Journal of Archaeological Science* 12, 139–47
Payne, S and Bull, G 1988, 'Components of variation in measurements of pig bones and teeth, and the use of measurements to distinguish wild from domestic pig remains', *Archaeozoologia*, I/1.2, 27–66
Pearson, M P, Pollard, J, Richards, C, Thomas J, Tilley C and Welham, K 2008, 'The Stonehenge riverside project: exploring the Neolithic landscape of Stonehenge, *Documenta Praehistorica* xxxv, 153–6
Pelling, R 2008, 'Holborough Quarry, Snodland, Kent: the charred plant remains (Site Code HQS.EX04)', unpublished report for Canterbury Archaeological Trust
Perkins, D 1999, 'A Gateway Island' unpublished PhD thesis, Institute of Archaeology, University College, London
Perkins, D 2010, 'The distribution patterns of Bronze Age round barrows in north-east Kent', *Archaeologia Cantiana* cxxiv, 277–314
Perkins, D R J and Gibson, A M 1990, 'A Beaker burial from Manston near Ramsgate', *Archaeolgia Cantiana* cviii, 11–27
Perkins, D R J and Macpherson-Grant, N 1981, *The Isle of Thanet Archaeological Unit: interim excavation reports 1977–80*, Ramsgate
Philp, B J 1973, 'Site 1: a Neolithic site near Baston Manor, Hayes, Kent', *Excavations in West Kent 1960–1970*, Second Research Report in the Kent Monograph Series, Dover, 5–19
Philp, B J 1984, *Excavations in the Darent valley, Kent*, Fourth Research Report in the Kent Monograph Series, Dover
Philp, B J 2003, *The Discovery and Excavation of Anglo-Saxon Dover*, Ninth Research Report in the Kent Monograph Series, Dover
Philp, B and Keller, P 2002, *The Anglo-Saxon Cemetery at Eastry, near Dover*, Kent Archaeological Rescue Unit, Kent Special Subjects Series No 14, Dover
Philp, B J, Parfitt, K, Willson, J, Dutto, M and Williams, W 1991, *The Roman Villa Site at Keston, Kent: First Report (Excavations 1968–1978)*, Sixth Research Report in the Kent Monograph Series, Dover
Piningre, J-F 1990, *La nécropole de l'âge du bronze de Conchil-le-Temple (Pas-de-Calais). Catalogue de l'exposition Les enclos funéraires de l'âge du bronze dans le Nord/Pas-de-Calais*, Cahiers de Préhistoire du Nord: 8, Lille, 79–88
Pitt-Rivers, A H L F 1882, 'Excavations at Caesar's Camp, near Folkestone, Conducted in June and July 1878', *Archaeologia* 47, 429–65
Pollard, H M and Russell P M G 1969, 'Excavation of Round Barrow 248b, Upton Pyne, Exeter', *Proceedings of the Devon Archaeological Society* 27, 39–78
Pratt, S 1999, 'St George's School, Minster-in-Sheppey', *Canterbury's Archaeology 1996–97*, 21
Proudfoot, E V W 1963, 'Report on the excavation of a bell barrow in the parish of Edmondsham, Dorset, England, 1959', *Proceedings of the Prehistoric Society* 29, 395–425
Prummel, W 1987a, 'Atlas for identification of foetal skeletal elements of cattle, horse, sheep and pig. Part 1', *Archaeozoologia* 1 (1), 23–30
Prummel, W 1987b, 'Atlas for identification of foetal skeletal elements of cattle, horse, sheep and pig. Part 2', *Archaeozoologia* 1 (2), 11–42
Prummel, W 1989, 'Appendix to atlas for identification of foetal skeletal elements of cattle, horse, sheep and pig', *Archaeozoologia* 3 (1,2), 71–8
Rady, J 1997, 'Whitfield Eastry by-pass (A256): archaeological watching brief 1995–1996', unpublished Canterbury Archaeological Trust archive report
Rawlings, F J 1872, 'Note on Ringwould barrows', *Proceedings of the Society of Antiquaries of London*, second series 5, 380–1
RCHME 1989, 'The classification of cropmarks in Kent. A report for the Monuments Protection Programme', unpublished Royal Commission for Historic Monuments (England) internal report, July
Reu J D, Hammond, J, Toron, S and Bourgeois, J 2012, 'Spatial and chronological continuities of Bronze Age cemeteries in north-western Europe, Gräberlandschaften der Bronzezeit : paysages funéraires de l'âge du Bronze', *Bodenaltertumer Westfalens* 51, 265–82
Richardson, A 2005, *The Anglo-Saxon Cemeteries of Kent*, British Archaeological Reports (British Series) 391, Oxford
Riddler, I D 2001, 'Anglo-Saxon ceramic weights from Ramsgate Harbour Approach Road', *Canterbury's Archaeology 1998–1999*, 64–5
Riddler, I D 2008, 'The small finds' in P Bennett *et al*, 331–3
Riddler, I D and Trzaska-Nartowski, N I A 2012, '*Lundenwic* and the Middle Saxon Worked Bone Interlude', *Anglo-Saxon Studies in Archaeology and History* 18, 75–96

Rozoy, J G 1986, *Les Celtes en Champagne – Les Ardennes au second Age du Fer: le Mont Troté, Les Rouliers*, 2 Vols, Mémoires de le Société Archéologique Champenoise 4
Rulewicz, M 1994, *Rybolowstwo Gdanska na tle Osrodkow Miejskich Pomorza od IX do XIII Wieku*, Gdansk Wczesnosredniowieczny 10, Wroclaw
Russel, A D 1990, 'Two Beaker burials from Chilbolton, Hampshire', *Proceedings of the Prehistoric Society* 56, 153–72
Saville, A 1980, 'On the measurement of struck flakes and flake tools', *Lithic Studies Society Newsletter* 1, 16–20
Saville, A 1981, *Grimes Graves, Norfolk. Excavations 1971–72: Volume II. The Flint Assemblage*, HMSO, London
Schlafer, D H and Miller, R B 2007, 'Female genital system' in M G Maxie (ed), *Jubb, Kennedy, and Palmer's Pathology of Domestic Animals*, Vol 3, fifth edition, Elsevier, Edinburgh, 429–564
Schuster, J 2010, 'Cliffs End Farm, Ramsgate: Archaeological Assessment Report', Wessex Archaeology, Salisbury
Serjeantson, D 2011, *Review of animal remains from the Neolithic and Early Bronze Age of southern Britain*, Research Department Report Series 29-2011, English Heritage
Shephard-Thorn, E R 1988, *Geology of the Country around Ramsgate and Dover*, Memoir of the Geological Survey, London
Sheridan, J A 2012, 'A Rumsfeld reality check: what we know, what we don't know and what we don't know we don't know about the Chalcolithic in Britain and Ireland' in M J Allen, J Gardiner and J A Sheridan (eds), *Is there a British Chalcolithic? People, Place and Polity in the Later Third Millennium*, Oxbow/Prehistoric Society (Prehistoric Society Research Paper 4), Oxford, 40–55
Simpson, K 1964, *Forensic Medicine*, fifth edition, Edward Arnold Ltd, London
Silver, I 1969, 'The ageing of domestic animals' in D Brothwell and E S Higgs (eds), *Science and Archaeology*, Thames and Hudson, London, 250–68
Smart, J G O, Bisson, G and Worssam, B C 1966, *Geology of the County around Canterbury and Folkestone*, Memoire of the Geological Survey of England and Wales
Smith, M 1951, *The British Amphibians and Reptiles*, Collins, London
Stallibrass, S 1990, 'Canid Damage to Animal Bones: Two Current Lines of Research' in D E Robinson (ed), *Experimentation and Reconstruction in Environmental Archaeology*, Oxbow Books, Oxford, 151–65
Stead, I M 1991, *The Iron Age Cemeteries in East Yorkshire*, English Heritage Archaeological Report 22, London
Stead, I M and Rigby, V 1986, *Baldock: the Excavation of a Roman and pre-Roman Settlement, 1968–72*, Britannia Monograph 7, London
Stead, I M and Rigby, V 1989, *Verulamium: the King Harry Lane Site*, English Heritage Archaeological Report 12, London
Stoddart, D M 1977, 'Water vole *Arvicola terrestris*' in G B Corbet and H N Southern, 196–204
Stone, J F S 1938, 'An early Bronze Age grave in Fargo Plantation near Stonehenge', *Wiltshire Archaeological and Natural History Magazine* 48, 357–70
Sykes, N J and Curl, J 2010, 'The Rabbit' in T O'Connor T and N J Sykes (eds), *Extinctions and Invasions: A Social History of British Fauna*, Windgather, Oxford, 116–26
Taylor, A F and Woodward, P J 1985, 'A Bronze Age barrow cemetery and associated settlement at Roxton, Bedfordshire', *Archaeological Journal* 142, 73–149
Taylor, H 1933, 'A cyst of the Beaker period at Corston, near Bath', *Proceedings of the University of Bristol Spelaeological Society* 4, 126–37
Taylor, H and Taylor, J 1980, *Anglo-Saxon Architecture: Vol. II*, Cambridge University Press, Cambridge
Tester, P J and Caiger, J 1951, 'Research in south-east Kent 1949–50', *Archaeologia Cantiana* lxiv, 150–1
Thomas, J 1999, *Time, culture, and identity: an interpretative archaeology*, Routledge, London
Thomas, N 1966, 'Notes on some early Bronze Age objects in Devizes Museum', *Wiltshire Archaeological and Natural History Magazine* 61, 1–8
Thompson, F H 1983, 'Excavations at Bigberry, near Canterbury, 1978–80', *Antiquaries Journal* lxiii, 237–78
Thompson, I 1982, *Grog-tempered 'Belgic' Pottery of South-Eastern England*, British Archaeological Reports (British Series) 108, Oxford
Thompson, I 2001, 'Late Iron Age pottery from Hawkinge Airfield, Folkestone, Kent (site code HAF 98)', unpublished report for Archaeology South-East
Tipper, J 2004, *The Grubenhaus in Anglo-Saxon England: an analysis and interpretation of the evidence from a most distinctive building type*, Landscape Research Centre, Yedingham
Trotter, M and Gleser, G C 1958, 'A re-evaluation of estimation of stature based on measurements of stature taken during life and long bones after death', *American Journal of Physical Anthropology* 16, 79–123
Tucker, S 1986, 'The flint industry' in P Drewett, 'The Excavation of a Neolithic Oval Barrow at North Marden, West Sussex, 1982', *Proceedings of the Prehistoric Society* 52, 31–51
Van Arsdell, R 1989, *Celtic Coinage of Britain*, Spink, London
Van Doorselaer, A, Putman, R, Van der Gucht, K and Janssens, F 1987, *De Kemmelberg, een Keltische bergvesting*, Westvlaamse Archaeologica Monografieëen III, Kortrijk
Van der Veen, M and O'Connor, T 1998, 'The expansion of agricultural production in late Iron Age and Roman Britain' in J Bayley (ed), *Science in Archaeology: an agenda for the future*, London, 127–43
Van Heeringen, R M 1989, 'The Iron Age in the Western Netherlands V: Synthesis', *Berichten van de Rijksdienst voor het Oudheidkundig Bodemonderzoek* 44, 157–255 (241–339)
Vatcher, F de M 1960, 'The excavation of a group of barrows at Down Farm, Pewsey, Wilts', *Wiltshire Archaeological and Natural History Magazine* 57, 339–51
Vatcher, F de M 1969, 'Two incised chalk plaques near Stonehenge Bottom', *Antiquity* 43, 310–11
Vigne, J-D 1995, *Détermination ostéologique des principaux éléments du squelettte appendiculaire d'Arvicola, d'Eliomys, de Glis et de Rattus*, CNRS Fiches d'Ostéologie Animale pour l'Archéologie, Série B: Mammifères, No 8
Vince, A (ed) 1991, *Aspects of Saxo-Norman London: II, Finds and Environmental Evidence*, Lambeth and Middlesex Archaeological Society Paper 12, London
von den Driesch, A 1976, A *Guide to the Measurement of Animal Bones from Archaeological Sites*, Peabody Museum Bulletin 1, Harvard University Press
von den Driesch, A and Boessneck, J A 1974, 'Kritische Anmerkungen zur Wiederistholerberechnung aus Längenmassen vor- und frühgeschichtlicher Tierknocken', *Saugetierkundliche Mitteilungen* 22, 325–48
Von Endt, D W and Ortner, D J 1982, 'Amino acid analysis of bone form and a possible case of prehistoric iron deficiency anemia from the American south west', *American Journal of Physical Anthropology* 59, 377–85
Wade, K 1983, 'The early Anglo-Saxon period' in A J Lawson, *The Archaeology of Witton, near North Walsham, Norfolk*, East Anglian Archaeology 18, Gressenhall, 50–69
Wainwright, G J 1972, 'The excavation of a Neolithic settlement on Broome Heath, Ditchingham, Norfolk, England', *Proceedings of the Prehistoric Society* 38, 1–97
Wainwright, J G and Longworth, I H 1971, *Durrington Walls: Excavations 1955–68*, Reports of the Research Committee of the Society of Antiquaries of London 29, London
Walker, P L 1986, 'Porotic hyperostosis in a marine dependent Californian Indian population', *American Journal of Physical Anthropology* 69, 345–54
Welch, M 2007, 'Anglo-Saxon Kent' in J Williams (ed), 187–248
Welcker, H 1885, cited in H Nathan and N Haas (1966), ''Cribra orbitalia' A bone condition of the orbit of unknown nature', *Israel Journal of Medical Sciences* 2, 171–91
West, S E 1985, *West Stow: The Anglo-Saxon Village*, East Anglian Archaeology 24, Gressenhall
Wheeler, H 1978, 'Excavations at Willington, Derbyshire, 1970–1972', *Derbyshire Archaeological Journal* 99, 58–220
White, D A and Reed, R 1970, 'The excavation of a bowl barrow at Oakley Down, 1968', *Proceedings of the Dorset Natural History and Archaeological Society* 92, 159–67
Whimster, R 1981, *Burial Practices in Iron Age Britain*, British Archaeological Reports (British Series) 90, Oxford
Wijngaarden-Bakker, L H van 1974, 'The animal remains from the Beaker settlement at Newgrange, Co. Meath – first report', *Proceedings of the Royal Irish Academy* 74C, 313–85
Williams, J 1976, 'A Gallo-Belgic Stater found at Whitfield nr Dover', *Kent Archaeological Review* 46, 134–6

Williams, J H 2003, 'New Light on Roman Kent', *Journal of Roman Archaeology* 16, 219–36
Williams, J H (ed) 2007, *The Archaeology of Kent to AD 800*, Kent County Council, Maidstone
Williams, R J 1993, *Pennyland and Hartigans: two Iron Age and Saxon sites in Milton Keynes*, Buckinghamshire Archaeological Society Monograph Series 4, Aylesbury
Willis, S 2002, 'A date with the past: late Bronze Age and Iron Age pottery and chronology' in A Woodward and J D Hill (eds), *Prehistoric Britain: The Ceramic Basis*, Oxbow, Oxford, 4–21
Willson, J 1985, 'A possible Bronze Age barrow at Walmer', *Kent Archaeological Review* 82, 26–30
Willson, J 1986, 'A pagan burial from Whitfield', *Kent Archaeological Review* 83, 54–7
Willson, J 1990, 'Rescue excavations on the Anglo-Saxon cemetery at Eastry 1989', *Kent Archaeological Review* 100, 229–31
Willson, J 1993, 'A Bronze Age site on the Eastry By-pass (Site 3)', *Kent Archaeological Review* 112, 38–47
Wilson, B, Grigson S and Payne S (eds) 1982, *Ageing and Sexing Animal Bones from Archaeological Sites*, British Archaeological Reports (British Series) 109, Oxford
Wilson, P R, Cardwell, P, Cramp, R J, Evans, J, Taylor-Wilson, R H, Thompson, A and Wacher, J S 1996, 'Early Anglian Catterick and *Catraeth*', *Medieval Archaeology* 40, 1–61
Wilson, T 2008, 'The Lithic Assemblage' in P Bennett *et al*, 65–81
Witney, K P 1982, *The Kingdom of Kent*, Chichester
Woodruff, C H 1874, 'On Celtic tumuli in East Kent', *Archaeologia Cantiana* ix, 16–30
Woodruff, C H 1880, 'An account of discoveries made in Celtic tumuli near Dover, Kent', *Archaeologia* 45, 53–6
Woodward, A 2002, *British Barrows: A matter of life and death*, Tempus, Stroud
Zohary, D and Hopf, M 1994, *Domestication of Plants in the Old World*, Oxford

Index